TOUCHSTONE

Other Books by Edward N. Luttwak

THE GRAND STRATEGY OF THE SOVIET UNION

STRATEGY AND POLITICS
Collected Essays

THE GRAND STRATEGY OF THE ROMAN EMPIRE
From the First Century A.D. to the Third

THE ISRAELI ARMY
(with D. Horowitz)

THE POLITICAL USES OF SEA POWER

DICTIONARY OF MODERN WAR

COUP D'ETAT

THE PENTAGON AND

☆

The Question of Military Reform

THE ART OF WAR

✩

Edward N. Luttwak

A TOUCHSTONE BOOK
PUBLISHED BY INSTITUTE FOR CONTEMPORARY STUDIES
SIMON & SCHUSTER, INC.
NEW YORK

First Touchstone Edition, 1986
Published by Simon & Schuster, Inc.
Simon & Schuster Building
Rockefeller Center
1230 Avenue of the Americas
New York, New York 10020
TOUCHSTONE and colophon are registered trademarks of
Simon & Schuster, Inc.
Designed by Eve Kirch
Manufactured in the United States of America

10 9 8 7 6 5 4
10 9 8 7 6 5 4 3 2 Pbk.

Library of Congress Cataloging in Publication Data
Luttwak, Edward
  The Pentagon and the art of war.
  Bibliography: p.
  Includes index.
  1. United States—Armed Forces.   2. United States—Military policy.   I. Title
UA23.L86   1984   355'.0335'73   84-22120
ISBN: 0-671-52432-1
ISBN: 0-671-61770-2 Pbk.

— ACKNOWLEDGMENTS —

I am deeply grateful to the officers of all four services with whom I have worked over the years. From the four-stars to those quite junior at the time, many earned my deep respect; but especially in a book often critical of the institutions they serve, only one officer can be mentioned by name: Major General Don Morelli of the Army's Training and Doctrine Command, a brilliant and free-spirited officer prematurely retired in 1984 because of insidious, deadly illness. It was A. Lawrence Chickering, moral philosopher and close friend, who encouraged me to consolidate in this book my diverse studies of the American armed forces; as executive director of the Institute for Contemporary Studies, he secured a grant from the Smith Richardson Foundation which removed my best excuse for delay. In the attempt to clarify the prose of a text greatly technical and sometimes statistical, I asked Robert Asahina, my editor at Simon and Schuster, to truly edit the text; he did so with an elegant efficiency which I found inspiring.

To my daughter Yael

CONTENTS

CONTENTS

In bello nihil tam leve est quod non magnae
interdum rei momentum faciat.

—TITUS LIVIUS XXV, 28

THE PENTAGON AND
THE ART OF WAR

INTRODUCTION

Only those unhappy Americans who regard the military power of the United States as an evil to be diminished have good reason to be satisfied with the peacetime effectiveness of the defense establishment and the recent combat record of the armed forces. Vast sums of money and the true dedication of many have gone into the upkeep of American military power, only to yield persistent failure in the conduct of war and an unfavorable balance of strength for safeguarding the peace. Any fair-minded survey of the armed forces reveals high competence in a great many things, from the routine daring and fine expertise of pilots who land 20-ton jet fighters onto the rolling decks of aircraft carriers to the worldwide logistics that supply millions of diverse items to our forces scattered around the globe. There is no lack of individual talent, courage, or patriotism. Nevertheless, the armed forces have failed us.

Irrefutable facts overwhelm the patriotic impulse to overlook our failures in war—from Vietnam in its most varied and prolonged entirety; to the clumsy *Mayagüez* raid of 1975, in which forty-one died to save forty; to the Iran rescue attempt of 1980, which ended in bitter humiliation, with eight dead and none rescued; to the avoidable tragedy of Beirut, which took the lives of 241 Marines and other servicemen in October 1983; to the Grenada operation of the same month, in which the high heroism of the troops had to redeem gross failures of planning and command; to the Lebanon bombing raid of December 4, 1983, in which the Navy lost two costly aircraft, where others bombed day after day losing no aircraft at all. As against all this, only the most feeble military successes can be counted: the destruction of two jet fighters of

17

the third-rate Libyan air force in 1982 and perhaps the petty skirmishing of the Marines in Lebanon during 1983.

The other, continuing failure—in the peacetime effort to maintain a tolerable military balance—is a matter of degree. That a distinctly poorer and technically inferior Soviet Union has been able to exceed the United States in most categories of military strength is partly the result of the far greater economic sacrifice that the Kremlin has been able to impose on its peoples. Almost twice as rich, the United States has devoted far smaller resources to its defense, by deliberate political choice. But there has also been a failure of policy and military decision, exposed by the low yield of effective and strategically relevant military power from our defense expenditures.

Seemingly so very different in every way, the failures in war and the continuing failure of peacetime have the same source. Shaped by laws, regulations, and military priorities that date back to 1945–1948, the very structures of the armed forces and of the Defense Department are now badly outmoded; and we now know that the system is quite incapable of self-reform.

In the immediate aftermath of the Second World War, the aim of the legislators and military planners was to prepare the nation for another great worldwide conflict, another protracted nonnuclear war that would be just like the war just ended. It was taken for granted that victory would once again require the mobilization of ten or twelve million soldiers, sailors, airmen, and marines in several-million-man armies, thousands of warships, and tens of thousands of aircraft. Also taken for granted was the ability of American industry to rapidly mass-produce the necessary weapons, while millions of enlisted men and junior officers would quickly learn all necessary skills.

Some things, however, cannot be improvised so quickly. A rifleman can be turned out in fourteen weeks of basic training or less, but a general should have many years of experience; a car plant can produce military trucks by swift conversion, but it takes years to form an able team of tank designers. It was the aim of the military planners of 1945–1948 to create a peacetime defense establishment specifically designed for rapid expansion.

Accordingly, when the wartime forces were dissolved after the surrender of Japan in August 1945, as much of the "overhead" of military headquarters and civil administration as possible, and as many senior officers as possible, were retained in the permanent peacetime service. Just as most of the training camps, headquarters facilities, supply depots, and technical centers hurriedly established after Pearl Harbor were kept going after 1945, so were the officer slots. On June 30, 1945, when 12,123,455 men and women were on active duty, there were 17,057 officers at the rank of colonel/Navy captain and above, including 101 three-star generals and admirals. On May 31, 1983, when only 2,127,422 men and women were on active duty, there were 15,455 officers at the rank of colonel/Navy captain and above, including 118 three-star generals and admirals—actually 17 more than in 1945.* Very few of these officers can find normal command or staff duties in the small peacetime forces. So the vast majority are placed in layers of higher headquarters and a multitude of administrative, logistic, and equipment-acquisition commands, all of which have expanded over the years to keep officers busy in peacetime, in readiness for the day when all might be fully employed in the war-mobilized forces.

It is true that many weapons have become more complicated than they were in 1945, and it may be that the world itself has become more complicated, if only because of the advent of nuclear weapons. But it cannot seriously be argued that today's peacetime forces require almost as much leadership, command, and administration as the vast armed forces of the Second World War, which fought in both Europe and Asia on a dozen widely separated fronts, whose air and naval operations spanned the globe, and which had many duties that are now quite absent, from the military government of tens of millions of civilians in occupied areas to the upkeep of hospitals in India, airfields in Central Africa, and clandestine weather stations in Mongolia.

What has happened, of course, is that an overhead of greatly disproportionate size had found employment for itself in the systematic overcomplication of every aspect of peacetime defense and of whatever warfare we have had. Work that belongs together is subdivided among many different departments, commands, directorates, and offices, with much overlapping. Problems that should be seen and solved as a whole are fragmented among competing services and military branches, as well as diverse civilian Pentagon offices of conflicting jurisdiction. Even for quite petty matters, responsibility is shared among multiple layers of management, both civil and military.

When there is fighting to be done, grossly overelaborate planning gives rise to supervision by vastly overstaffed headquarters very remote from the scene of combat. There are usually several different headquar-

* See the tables in the Appendix.

ters involved, with no real center of higher decision, because there is no central defense staff. As their name suggests, the Joint Chiefs of Staff are merely a committee of the service chiefs, and the officers who serve on their "joint staff" are merely service representatives whose careers depend on how well they serve the particular interests of their particular services. The combat operations that are thus planned are naturally clumsy. Because the interests of each service must be accommodated, the ancient and supreme military principle of simplicity is constantly violated; because everything is done by committee, bureaucratic compromises displace the tactical ingenuity, operational art, and sharp choices that strategy always demands.

In the peacetime workings of the defense establishment, the combination of civilian and military overmanagement systematically rejects any simple, direct, and economical solution. The civilian off-the-shelf item is refused if a special military item can be produced instead—thus employing the hordes of development and procurement officers and their civilian staffs. A well-proved and still quite modern weapon is declared "obsolescent" if a slightly more advanced weapon can be developed by chronically underemployed research-and-development centers. And there is also a great readiness to invent new administrative tasks, new reporting requirements, and new ancillary functions far removed from any warlike purpose.

Because this large overhead consumes so much of the total manpower in uniform, the combat forces actually deployed are small. Because of the overcomplicated way that these forces are manned, equipped, and maintained, their cost is needlessly large.

Actually, the fundamental idea is still sound. We should indeed prepare to fight a long and large worldwide conflict, with many millions bearing arms and with no use of nuclear weapons at all. If we are capable of fighting only a short war, an enemy prepared to outlast us will win—unless we resort to nuclear weapons. So a capacity to mobilize is the best guarantee we can have of avoiding nuclear war (of our making, at any rate). It might seem, therefore, that the training, command, and acquisition overhead is fully justified, that we should praise the ingenuity that has found so many ways to keep so many busy, in readiness for the day when their knowledge and talents might be greatly needed. But if that were true, we should design our weapons, warships, aircraft, missiles, and lesser ordnance for mass production at short notice. What is now in service, by contrast, is clearly fit only for immediate use in a short war fought out of existing stocks. The very high unit costs of the overambitious armaments designed by an overelaborate defense establishment make it quite impossible to keep large reserve stocks. At the same time, their very intricate designs, exotic materials, and difficult manufacturing processes would prohibit mass production in wartime. Thus the present defense establishment does not prepare us for rapid mobilization to fight a protracted conflict—and it is needlessly overexpensive for a short war.

In the meantime, the education and career management of our officers, the methods of planning and command, and the entire structure of the forces and departments—all designed for the global war that was envisaged a long time ago—have proved to be quite ineffective in coping with the smaller combat that actually happens. A military structure geared to restage the D-Day landings and to conduct worldwide operations has shown itself unable to plan, command, and fight well on any smaller scale.

To be sure, the major task of the defense establishment, especially in the nuclear age, is not to fight but to dissuade war, by means of persuasive deterrence, both nuclear and nonnuclear. That, however, we would best do by maintaining effective fighting forces, both active and reserve, not by retaining an overlarge overhead that cannot truly mobilize very much, or very fast.

This book diagnoses the fundamental maladies of our defense establishment. In the concluding chapter, remedies, just as fundamental, are offered. There is, however, one species of reform that is denied to us by all-too-plain strategic realities: in the face of the true dimensions of Soviet military power, we cannot ensure both savings and our safety by simply cutting defense expenditures. First there must be serious and deep reform; only then will we have our choice between more military strength and less expenditure.

CHAPTER ONE

☆

The Anatomy of Military Failure

The peacetime defects of the military establishment and its failure in war are closely connected, and the causes of both are best revealed by a review of the painful record of Vietnam. A reluctance to look back upon defeat is quite natural but also most dangerous, for it leaves unexamined fatal defects of structure and system that still endure. Much of what went wrong for years in Vietnam belonged to the time and the place, but much resulted from military institutions that remain unreformed; and which failed again in the Iran raid, Beirut, and Grenada; and which continue to fail in converting manpower and money into effective military power.

☆

South Vietnam, Cambodia, and Laos were conquered only after there were no American forces left to defend them. But the clear mark of military failure remains affixed on the long, variegated, and futile struggle of American arms in Indochina. We may place as much blame as we desire on the higher civilian authorities—President Johnson, Secretary of Defense McNamara, and their underlings—whose fanciful and bookish policies of "graduated escalation" merely encouraged Hanoi's ruthless implacability. We must place severe blame on the deceivers and the deceived who stimulated the outcry for withdrawal and abandonment by claiming that the enemy had the just cause. Those among them who truly believed in Hanoi's benevolence can witness their illusion refuted in the open boats, full of misery, of Hanoi's refugees. Nor can a

23

good many members of Congress escape blame: some were prominent in deceiving; others joined the ranks of the deceived.

But for all the blame cast upon others, the failure of the entire military structure and command system—not just leaders now gone but institutions still unchanged—looms large and unforgivable. First came the excess and bureaucratic self-indulgence unleashed by the absence of strategic discipline and operational art in the conduct of the war. Then came the doubts of the decently patriotic, followed by their resentment at seeing young lives and much treasure lost in a war so ill fought, and finally their opposition. Even now the presumption of failure attends each use of force by the United States, undermining support for any active policy that might call for combat. The revolt of the media against the war was obviously decisive, but its success owed much to the same military defects. To be sure, many journalists who covered the war were captive to deep-rooted prejudice.[1] The dangerously respectable belief, so often proclaimed from pulpit and podium, that war can serve no good human purpose, that it must be not only brutal but also futile, was so widespread among reporters that they could only misreport. And alert editors at home were quick to correct any lapse into objectivity. Yet though the myths and outright falsehoods given such wide currency came from many sources, including Hanoi, it was our own military self-indulgence that provided the best raw material for the prejudiced manipulation of the American public.

Almost every branch and subbranch of the Army, Navy, Marine Corps, Air Force, and even the Coast Guard was allowed a role in Indochina, though most had no business fighting the guerrillas and terrorists who were the main enemy before 1968 and Tet, and many remained unsuited to or overrepresented in fighting the North Vietnamese regulars who largely took over thereafter. But under a system that exists precisely not to make choices, each service and almost every one of its branches and subbranches had to have its fair share of the extra war funds and extra war promotions. For the services, any participation in the war meant some expansion, and for their officers, a tour in Vietnam was certainly "career enhancing," even if it was only for six months and far from combat.*

Notwithstanding the strength of the North Vietnamese, which became considerable, it is almost embarrassing to survey the vast array of

---

* With a Vietnam "tour" in their record, Army officers could reach the rank of major in only six years.[2]

American forces ranged against them. The Army's Infantry branch was of course predominant; it fielded complete divisions, seven at peak. But the Army's Armor branch was also present with full-weight battle tanks, even though there was no front to pierce or enemy armor to outmaneuver. The Artillery—light, medium, and heavy—was notoriously abundant; no fewer than sixty-three battalions were fielded at the peak in 1968, even though the enemy steadfastly declined to gather in mass formations vulnerable to artillery fire. The newer Aviation cadre waxed great in Vietnam with hundreds and hundreds of helicopters in no fewer than 142 companies and Air Cavalry "troops." The horseless Cavalry had its fair share, with its distinctive squadrons and troops, both armored and airborne. And of course the Special Forces also had a role, in what should have been their very own war.[3]

The "brown shoe" aviators of the Navy, very much a separate branch and almost a separate service, had their aircraft carriers offshore throughout the war, even though there was no lack of airfields for the cheaper Air Force. The surface Navy, with its own distinct "black shoe" officer cadre, had a large role too, in part because aircraft carriers need a panoply of escorts, in part because the gun cruisers and even a battleship recovered from disuse were employed in firing their great guns against the shore—as if there were not already enough artillery on land. A new "riverine" navy of fast boats and armored barges came into existence in Vietnam, and the Navy's SEAL (Sea, Air, Land) commandos found much to do—but not alone, for the Navy's other elite, the Underwater Demolition Teams, were also present. The Marine Corps naturally came over the beach in its own preferred style, with two of its very large divisions, each with as many men as two Soviet divisions, and each with its own armor and artillery, as well as an "air wing" that amounted to a small air force all by itself.

The Air Force—still dominated in those days by its Strategic Air Command, again virtually a separate service—was present mainly with the fighters and fighter-bombers of the rival Tactical Air Command. But SAC's heavy B-52 bombers also made frequent appearances from their distant bases. The Airlift Command, though lowest in bureaucratic standing, could not be denied a large role in a land so remote and so lacking in roads; its many transport aircraft, heavy, medium, and light, were greatly used. Finally the "air commandos," who went into combat with large helicopters, very light aircraft, and converted transports bristling with guns, formed a separate "Special Operations" force; until then an obscure subbranch, they made a great career in Vietnam. With admirable restraint, the Air Force did not field its own elite ground troops to serve alongside the Army's Rangers and the Special Forces, the Navy's SEALs and UDTs, and the Marines' "force-recon" elite; the "air commandos" were merely pilots, gunners, and ground crews.

In a war where the enemy was almost always hidden or disguised, where the American forces were mostly confined within the borders of South Vietnam while the enemy was present in Laos and Cambodia as well, there was exceptional scope for Intelligence, security and secret operations. The Army's Intelligence branch was clearly more important than ever in a war where finding the target was all; but so, it seems, were the Intelligence branches of the other three services, along with the security agencies of each. Some things were too delicate to be left to the commandos of each service, and the most special of all the special forces was a joint-service affair with a mild and academic cover name, the "Studies and Observation Group." Its tasks included the deep infiltration of enemy territory for intelligence-gathering, aircrew rescue, sabotage, kidnapping, and assassination, as well as "black" propaganda by radio and planted rumor. A small and suitably discreet army of some 2,000 Americans and 8,000 local recruits was thus employed, with its own air squadrons, a flotilla of fast boats, and large cohorts of native auxiliaries. Uncharacteristically, the SOG never did grow into a bureaucracy with its own career cadre; its men were merely assigned from the different services. They therefore had no reason to pursue institutional aggrandizement—no careers could be made by its growth. That may have been the reason for its notable success amidst so much failure. Naturally such deviance was ill regarded: the SOG did not survive Vietnam, and neither did the new American expertise in the planning and conduct of commando operations.

With Army, Naval, Air, and Marine Intelligence in the field along with their several Vietnamese counterparts and the SOG, there was much Intelligence, but evidently not enough. The Defense Intelligence Agency was also present in force, as were the National Security Agency and, of course, the civilian CIA. Along with the combat forces and the secret units came the "support" branches of each service, the Engineers, Military Police, and Signals Corps among others; and behind the entire combat echelon stood a much larger body of service branches for repair and maintenance, for medical, ordnance, and quartermaster duties, for transportation and construction, finance and administration, and more.

As each service and virtually every branch took a "role-enhancing" slice of the war, a vastly complicated bureaucratic jungle was created, unmanaged by a coherent strategy. The chief military officer during the crucial years, Army General William C. Westmoreland, who was in charge of the "Military Assistance Command, Vietnam," from June 1964 till July 1968, had only a formal authority over all the forces that belonged to the other services. Their true control remained with their own staffs and chiefs in Washington—because the Vietnam command was "unified" rather than "specified." The difference between these two obscure bureaucratic categories—seemingly a minor administrative detail, a mere triviality in a war that we would all very much like to think was lost for inevitable and far greater reasons that would require no remedy today—is in fact most significant. Westmoreland's predecessor, Army General Paul D. Harkins, had caused much controversy by attempting to persuade the Joint Chiefs to make his command "specified," whereby his service would have full control, with the other services brought in as needed, but under Army authority.[4] It might seem that the plain realities of Vietnam would inescapably ensure the predominance of the Army; though not exclusively a guerrilla war even before 1968, it remained a ground war in which air and naval operations should have been secondary.

But the Joint Chiefs could not be distracted by such a minor matter as the actual character of the war. They were, and still are, a "unified" body, with all their staff positions shared under strict and elaborate rules worked out over the years by interservice bargaining. Inevitably, the sharp choices of strategy are thereby subordinated to the conveniences of bureaucratic harmony. The Joint Chiefs could only reproduce their own image, and the Vietnam command duly became a "unified," or more precisely a "subunified," command under the Pacific Command —itself unified, with all the services on a perfectly equal footing. This is not, of course, a system that has ever been tried successfully in war by this or any other nation. During the Korean war, administrative arrangements scarcely mattered so long as General Douglas MacArthur was in command; even after his departure the Army remained in control. In each case, clear choices could be made and priorities firmly set, as war unfailingly requires. But subjection to a dominant service was greatly irritating to the rest and caused much friction; corporate harmony was judged more important than the needs of war, and the obvious remedy was the unified system.

As soon as the Vietnam command was formed, each service was most anxious to ensure its "equitable representation and equal rank in the key staff positions,"[5] as a participant in the debate, an Air Force general, was later to write. His loyal concern with "equity" was understandable, for there was so much to share. The Saigon headquarters grew and grew, offering high-ranking posts to officers in huge numbers. By 1968, staff officers and their clerks and aides numbered 6,407 for the Army "element" alone; after that, the headquarters grew even more— even though the number of American troops was in decline—reaching 13,095 for the Army alone by 1971.[6] The Air Force had thousands more, and the Marine Corps and the rest of the Navy were not left out either. Nevertheless, the same Air Force general was later to complain that the staff was "heavily weighted in favor of ground officers,"[7] a result blamed on the machinations of the Army and Marine Corps, rather than accepted as the natural consequence of a ground war.

Foreign military men who visited the Saigon headquarters were much amazed by the hordes of senior officers from the Army, Navy, Marine Corps, and Air Force, all trying to have a hand in directing the war, while closely watching one another to protect the diverse interests of their different services. By 1968 there were 110 generals and admirals actually in Vietnam, 64 of them for the Army alone;[8] a small number were actually in command of forces in the field, but most were in Saigon, along with hundreds and hundreds of colonels.

Regardless of their personal inclinations, these men were forced to occupy much of their time with office politics, because the petty politics of interservice rivalry was in fact the only medium of decision. If many of these officers seemed overconcerned with matters of protocol and precedence,* if many spent much of their time in bars, at pools, and on tennis courts, it was all because of sheer frustration. All were eager to help win the war by well-made plans and clever schemes, but none was empowered to decide—everything had to be mediated, compromised, and "sold." Such procedures are perfectly appropriate in the management of a well-established and very secure business corporation—a municipal gas company for example; they suit even better an amicable golf club. Amidst the urgencies of war, they were tragically inappropriate. General Bruce Palmer, Jr., who served as Westmoreland's Army Deputy, has written: "With respect to operational planning, Westmoreland encouraged a sort of competition among his subordinate commanders, each vying for more forces or support, the commander with

---

* Much consternation, for example, was caused by a visiting VIP who was chief of his country's formidable infantry but a mere colonel, and thus a nonentity by Saigon standards.

the most convincing case getting the most resources." In other words, Westmoreland had no plan, and did not command; he merely "managed" the war.[9]

Actually, there was no vivid atmosphere of war surrounding the command. Most officers were prisoners in the bureaucratic labyrinth, their contact with the fighting very remote. For the Army, it was the small units that saw most of the combat, and they were already amply staffed and commanded at brigade level. Nevertheless, divisional headquarters units were also large, with almost five hundred men each, a good many of them officers; above them were the corps-level headquarters with hundreds more.* And each of the other services also had its own layers and layers of overofficered headquarters. Thus Saigon's own Pentagon, itself a frustrated interservice bureaucracy far removed from the action it was supposed to control, could scarcely provide coherent strategic guidance through the greater bureaucratic jungle without, composed of the separate services and their diverse branches and innumerable subbranches.

This was the array of forces and system of command that waged the war in Vietnam. No ruthless enemy could have devised a better structure to ensure his own victory. Deadly encounters between the many different forces intersecting within Vietnam were usually avoided by a most intense effort of coordination by all those headquarters, and by highly elaborate communications. But no merely procedural arrangements and no electronic wizardry could impress a common purpose upon the many diverse forces. The men successively placed in Saigon to preside over bureaucratic rivalry and innocent confusion will not be celebrated names in military history—certainly not the hapless Westmoreland. But the quality of the man is of little consequence; even a Napoleon would have been paralyzed by the system. Each of the forces in Vietnam had its own preferred operational method, and the discipline of choice could not be imposed on them because any choice would have violated fiercely protected service, branch, and subbranch interests.

Faced with a village controlled by the enemy, the Infantry would plan

---

* For example, in 1968, the headquarters of the 1st Infantry Division at Lai Khe had an authorized strength of 486 in three HQ companies (divisional, artillery, and support); its three brigade headquarters accounted for another 366 slots. The 1st Cavalry Division (Airmobile) was even better staffed, with 520 at the divisional level and another 669 in the three brigade headquarters. (At their largest, in 1945, the Infantry divisions of the Second World War had a total of 270 in their headquarters.) Above the divisional level, the I Field Force headquarters at Nha Trang, equivalent to a corps, employed 432 officers and men in 1968, while II Field Force at Bien Hoa had 360, and XXIV Corps at Phu Bai had 367.[10]

a regular seize-and-clear attack, while the Air Cavalry would propose an airborne assault, to achieve surprise and thus reduce the enemy instead of merely driving him to the next village. Armor officers for their part deplored the casualties of the infantry attack and the lost helicopters of the airborne assault; foot soldiers and helicopter soldiers were quick to declare all sorts of terrain "impassable," but Armor knew better: it could storm the place in short order. The Artillery, for its part, would deem all assaults unnecessary, since one of its "time-on-target" barrages could pulverize the flimsy huts and all their inhabitants. Meanwhile, the Navy's surface branch would claim the task for its own bigger guns if the village had the good fortune of a seashore location, but the Air Force would insist that fighter-bombers could do it all faster and better—except that the SAC would deride their bombloads as petty compared with those of its own B-52s. The Army's "psychological operations" battalions might argue against all violence and suggest persuasion instead, to gain the villagers' loyalty for the government. The Special Forces would of course regard all other methods as clumsy and would offer instead its own technique of social infiltration and territorial control, consisting of free vaccinations, sweets for the children, farm tools for their parents, guns for a newly formed village guard, and a well-aimed killing or two. In the meantime, that entire other body of American officers, the advisers to the Vietnamese forces, would insist that any fighting could best be done by their own protégés, if only more and better equipment were provided. Naturally, some villages had the privilege of being the object of every one of those methods, in no particular sequence.

In theory, there should have been no problem. All modern military forces consist of diverse elements, each with its own operational method, and the country and the war varied so much from place to place and over time that there was some scope for each method at some time, in some place. In practice, however, there was no single and coherent strategy that would select the appropriate force for each time and place. Instead there was only the unified command system, which parceled out the territory and the targets "equitably" and then allowed each element to carry out its own standard operations, appropriate or not.

Lacking any true strategic guidance, the diverse forces nonetheless found a goal: to maximize their "production." Thus the three air forces achieved great efficiencies in generating the highest possible number of daily bombing sorties; the Artillery worked hard to fire as many shells as possible; the Infantry and Air Cavalry tried to obtain the most "contacts" to score the highest body counts in assaults, patrols, and sweeps; and all the other forces and service units did their best to produce the most, each in its own way according to its own measure.* Had the war been a contest of production, the North Vietnamese would have been hopelessly defeated. But of course much of what was produced with so much treasure and blood was simply irrelevant to the outcome: it is not by maximizing daily bomb tonnages or even body counts that wars can be won. The right bombing targets must be found (and they were very few), the right bodies must be killed, and even then victory was far from assured against an enemy that did have a strategy, which relied on the intangibles of subversion and covert terrorism, on elusive forces fighting in guerrilla style and on worldwide propaganda, none of which could be bombed or shelled effectively.

Among the leaders of the different services, branches, and subbranches, a solid pride in their own productive efficiency was mingled with a clear recognition that not enough was being done for victory. Many honestly believed that a war-winning strategy could be achieved only by expansion of their own forces to apply their standard methods, but on a far larger scale. Accordingly, they promoted their own strategies in the bureaucratic struggles of Saigon, Honolulu (home of the higher unified command for the Pacific), and above all Washington. In Saigon, the patriotic reward of any successful role expansion would be to bring victory that much nearer; the Washington payoff would be to achieve growth in the service or branch as a whole, with the attendant increase in funds, bureaucratic weight, and career opportunities. Thus patriotic dedication, bureaucratic urge, and even narrow personal inter-

---

* And of course the statistical indices devised by McNamara and his men in the Pentagon. In frontless war where there are no clear lines on the map to show victory and defeat, the only true measure of progress must be political and nonquantifiable: the impact on the enemy's will to continue the fight. This was much too vague for McNamara, who kept demanding statistics. Honest men in uniform were forced to collect all manner of misleading numbers (to count, e.g., the villages where the headman slept at home—which *could* mean that the village was secure, or else that the headman was himself with the Viet Cong). Some officers became intoxicated by the procedure. Major General Julian J. Ewell, commander of the 9th Division in the Delta, kept his men under pressure to maximize the numbers, not only the "body counts" (it was never quite certain which bodies were included in the tally) but also some downright absurd "civic action" statistics: man-days used in projects, dollar amounts of gifts, the number of orphanages assisted, the number of students in classes, etc.—without reference to the worth of the projects, the destination of the money, the size of the orphanages, or the political effect of any education imparted. Ewell's published memoir amounts to an exercise in unconscious self-parody.[11]

est were easily combined in the advocacy of all the different strategies. But when there are many strategies, there is no strategy—in Vietnam then, as in the making of peacetime military policy in Washington till now. So it was that *institutional* self-indulgence deprived the United States of any true chance of success. Indochina was full of trees and brave men, and mere force unguided by strategy could not prevail.

Another and quite separate consequence of the same structural defect was quite similar in its results to the camp diseases that afflicted the careless or unlucky armies of past centuries. Roman legionary troops were drilled in strict rules of hygiene, and the surveyors attached to each legion would site latrines most carefully; prefabricated wooden steps were to be used by the bucket crews when drawing water from rivers, to avoid fouling the stream. But after the Romans, dysentery became war's most loyal companion, and when prudent war leaders planned their campaigns they would recruit extra soldiers to allow for those who would be lost to disease. In Vietnam, excellent hygiene and advanced military medicine prevailed over the country's formidable tropical diseases; no allowance had to be made for the regiments of the sick. There was no such remedy, however, for the bureaucratic deformation that drastically reduced the true number of combat troops in the country to a fraction of the ostensible troop level. When General Westmoreland asked for another 206,000 troops in February 1968, only to be denied, Washington's refusal was explained by the natural reluctance to expose so many more men to deadly combat in paddy field, swamp, and jungle. But this concern was much exaggerated. Because of the multiplication of headquarters and their staffs, the lavish scale of service units of all kinds, and the profusion of very complicated equipment requiring maintenance by large numbers of depot troops, the soldiers actually left for close combat, weapon in hand, were only a small minority. At the end of 1968, with 536,000 American servicemen in South Vietnam, fewer than 80,000 served in infantry battalions, and the rest of all American troops in close combat—the Army's Air Cavalry flight crews and airborne troops, the Marines, Special Forces, and more— would not double that number. To be sure, the 40,000 or so in the artillery battalions were not less combat troops for being mostly secure in their well-protected fire bases. But even when the combat proportion is generously defined, it remains an exceptionally small part of the total. Vietnam called for simplicity, but the system imposed complication.[12] The country gave its men to be soldiers, but the system turned them into clerks and valets, mechanics and storekeepers, in huge and dispro-portionate numbers.

The notion of institutional self-indulgence may be new, but Vietnam was also the scene of a more familiar kind of self-indulgence. Its effects were felt neither in the impossibility of strategy nor in the loss of sol-diers but in the most basic of all the basics, the morale of the troops. This self-indulgence took many forms. One was the generosity with which officers gave medals to one another in huge, unprecedented, and uncounted numbers.* Judged by their medals, almost all officers sent to Vietnam must have been heroes. Even the Medal of Honor, far more carefully scrutinized than other medals and given to officers and enlisted men on an equal footing, was nevertheless depreciated: the Army of the Second World War, six million at peak, earned 294 in fighting truly formidable foes; the Army in Vietnam, never one-tenth as great, claimed 155.[14]

Not truly costly but very telling was the petty self-indulgence that prompted the issue of a special 9mm pistol to generals alone; helpfully engraved "GENERAL OFFICERS PISTOL," this weapon required different ammunition than the .45-caliber pistols issued to lesser mortals.[15] Far more serious was the self-indulgence that allowed the many desk-bound officers who found employment in the war zone, though far from com-bat, to live in surprising comfort, even outright luxury. Not only gen-erals but colonels had their own well-appointed clubs and well-stocked messes; permanently assigned personal helicopters were routine, and great ingenuity and significant resources went into the embellishment of living quarters. Personal staffs of aides, valets, drivers, and assorted flunkies became notoriously large.[16] When General Bruce Palmer, Jr., assumed command of his multidivision field command in 1967, he found that "at five o'clock every evening the senior officers flew by helicopter

---

* Interestingly enough, these are the only statistics that cannot be recovered from a war in which every triviality was carefully computed, though it seems that roughly half of the hundreds of generals who served in Vietnam received decorations for bravery (though only four were killed in action from 1961 to 1972). The officer/enlisted totals for all deco-rations suggest a rampant inflation: during 1968, when 14,592 servicemen were killed in action, 416,693 decorations were handed out. In 1970, when the number of servicemen in Vietnam had declined by 200,000 from the 1968 peak and the total killed in action was down to 3,946, the number of decorations *increased,* to 522,905.

This is one malpractice that has not ceased: after the Grenada operation the Army alone saw fit to issue 8,612 decorations (including more than 170 medals for valor) even though there were never more than 7,000 men on the island.[13]

to their quarters, a complex of villas and compounds in the nearby city of Bien Hoa. . . . [T]he . . . tactical operations center was simply not operational at night. . . .'' And in Vietnam, of course, night combat was of the essence.[17]

Partly because they were not confined to a remote front line far removed from the larger headquarters but instead moved into and out of large base camps, the impact on the Army's combat troops was devastating. After days in the field, the troops ''. . . returned to [bases] saturated with officers . . . well-fed and cared for . . . [they] . . . naturally came to believe that large numbers of their officers [did not] suffer any deprivation whatsoever.'' [18] It was a guaranteed prescription for the breakdown of morale, and it worked: after 1968, resentment and demoralization were manifest in the daily conduct of the troops. Although very high, the desertion statistics actually understate the problem, for in Vietnam, the deserter could not blend into the population nor easily leave the country.* Sometimes there was outright violence, the ''fraggings'' of evil memory; by the Army's formal accounting, ''Assaults with Explosive Devices'' numbered 788 between 1969 and 1972, mostly aimed at officers.[20]

Far more striking, however, is the fact that so many troops nevertheless obeyed and fought bravely in the face of intense provocation and in an increasingly unfavorable climate of domestic opinion.[21] The real question of continuing significance is the cause of the officers' highly visible misconduct, the breakdown of elementary professional craft. Officers in every armed force must find ways of inducing their men to fight and risk their lives—a most unnatural activity. Formal powers of command are not sufficient and never have been, except during tactical eras when the fighting was done by rank and file in rigid formation, under the watchful eyes of officers empowered to execute the unwilling. In modern warfare, where automatic weapons, artillery, and air power impose dispersal, men can rarely be pushed into combat; they must be pulled by the prestige of their immediate leader and the officers above him. Combat expertise that the soldiers recognize and personal qualities of authority are important, but so is an evident willingness to share in the hardships and deadly risks of war. Caesar retained both concubines

---

* In 1944, when many Army troops found themselves in France as well as Italy and Belgium, all places then poorly policed, quite hospitable, and undoubtedly attractive, the Army's desertion rate reached 63 per 1,000 before declining to 45.2 in 1945. During the Vietnam war the rate per 1,000 increased year by year, from 29.1 in 1968 to a peak of 73.4 in 1971.[19]

and catamites in his rearward headquarters, ate off gold plate, and drank his Samian wine from jeweled goblets, and he certainly exploited his campaigns for personal gain on a grand scale. But when Caesar was actually with his troops he ate only what they ate, and slept as they did —under a tent if the troops had tents, or merely wrapped in a blanket if they did not.

By Caesar's time this was already an old war leader's trick, the easiest way of evoking the devotion of the troops. Patriotic officers in all armies have made great use of the technique for their country's sake; those merely ambitious have done so to pursue advancement by battlefield success. Actually, it is not necessary to share hardship: Napoleon lived in great comfort in full sight of his adoring troops, and Montgomery—far better in leadership than in the other arts of war—slept in a comfortable caravan while his troops shivered in the desert night. But the risks of combat must unfailingly be shared whether it is tactically necessary to do so or not, and junior officers cannot do all the sharing.

If soldiers see that their immediate leader is exposed to risk while his superiors stay away from combat, they will be loyal to the man but disaffected from the army. Then they might still fight well—but only when shirking would endanger their own officer. In Vietnam, the mere fact that officers above the most junior rank were so abundant and mostly found in well-protected bases suggested a very unequal sharing of the risk. And statistics support the troops' suspicion. During the Second World War, the Army ground forces had a full colonel for every 672 enlisted men; in Vietnam (1971) there was a colonel for every 163 enlisted men. In the Second World War, 77 colonels died in combat, one for every 2,206 men thus killed; throughout the Vietnam war, from 1961 till 1972, only 8 colonels were killed in action, one for every 3,407 men.[22] And of course these numbers understate the contrast: in the frontless Vietnam war, with its terrorism and guerrillas, higher officers should have been much more exposed to risk than in the Second World War.

Military officers respectful of their profession would have known better. If for no other reason than the sheer morale effect, colonels and even generals should have spent enough time in places of combat to induce the feeling that they were fully participating in the risk. There was no need for Douglas MacArthur, then seventy years old and very much the commander-in-chief, to land at Inchon on September 17, 1950, when North Korean tanks were still counterattacking nearby. There was no need for him to drive beyond the burning town to the ridge where a Marine regiment was in close combat, climbing on foot to reach it under fire. (His transparent excuse was that he wanted to decorate an officer who happened to be there.) There was no need for him to go even nearer to the enemy to see the burning wreckage of a tank ambush on a slope exposed to enemy snipers where, as it happened, North Korean troops were still in hiding.[23] Perhaps it was all done for vanity's sake, but by showing himself to the troops as he did—to all the troops in Korea, in due course, for press photographers were with him—MacArthur increased his true authority as a war leader. Having shared in the risk, he could more easily ask the troops to accept further risks.

American officers have not always been highly regarded as tacticians, but they certainly tend to be brave. It was not because of any personal cowardice that so many in Vietnam made no effort to expose themselves to the risks of war. Crowded as they were in a grossly overofficered structure, the colonels and the generals became so fully absorbed in bureaucratic processes and office politics that even the most elementary aspects of the profession of arms receded beyond their horizon.

Normally, when armed forces go to war the bureaucratic encrustations of peacetime are quickly worn away. Elaborate peacetime procedures and complicated paperwork are soon displaced by war's urgent informality. There is a changing of the guard: the skillful memo-drafters who do so well in the bureaucratic battles of peacetime give way to the tacticians and leaders who can win battles of the real kind. In Vietnam, however, the very opposite happened: the sheer complications of the multinational, multiforce structure, the unprecedentedly elaborate logistics, required procedures even more elaborate, with yet more paperwork. There was no changing of the guard: the managers and office politicians were very much in their element.

But all this was trivial compared with the tactical self-indulgence that became routine: the jet-fighter bombing raids against flimsy huts that might contain a handful of guerrillas or perhaps none; the fair-sized artillery barrages that silenced lone snipers; the ceaseless firing of helicopter door gunners whereby a million dollars' worth of ammunition might be expended to sweep a patch of high grass. The grossly disproportionate use of firepower became the very theme of the war—and its imagery on television was by far the most powerful stimulus of antiwar sentiment.

The justification was that American lives were worth more than the ammunition fired with such abandon. But American lives were in danger because a war was being fought; the best way of ending the casualties was to win the war, and that could be done only by successful tactics that would implement successful operational schemes derived from a successful strategy. It is impossible to prove that the war could have been won by this or that strategy or any strategy at all; some wars simply cannot be won, and Vietnam may have been one of them. It is entirely certain, however, that the relentless use of firepower was not compatible with any conceivable war-winning strategy.

The one unalterable requirement of success was to enlist the active cooperation of the population at large in resisting the guerrillas and the infiltrated North Vietnamese regulars. Only if villagers would report their presence instead of giving them information, only if villagers would deny them food instead of supplying them, only if villagers would reject recruitment and desert if impressed could the native guerrillas be extinguished and the North Vietnamese left isolated and exposed. Much would have been needed to achieve all this—perhaps too much, from political, social, economic, and administrative reforms to the creation of an effective militia in every town, village, and hamlet. American forces, with their swift helicopter mobility and excellent communications, could then have been an indispensable ingredient in the overall strategy by promptly intervening to help local militias under attack and successfully attacking isolated enemy forces. All manner of tactics could then have been employed, but restraint in the use of firepower would have been their common denominator. On a lucky day, a sizable body of enemy forces might be caught in the open, thus providing the opportunity for a well-aimed air strike; sometimes a battery or two of the artillery might be employed—for example, to break up an assault against an American or Vietnamese outpost.

But that is not how firepower was used in Vietnam. During the peak years, the Air Force would fly three hundred sorties a day against targets in South Vietnam, the Marine air wings another two hundred, and the Vietnamese air force a hundred more—and those were only the *preplanned* strikes, launched against places that *could* contain enemy forces, in addition to civilians. There would also be unplanned "reaction" sorties, to reach a total of 750–800 per day.[24] Moreover, to reduce losses from ground fire, Air Force pilots were strictly forbidden to bomb at low altitude to ensure accuracy; 3,500 feet was the minimum, unless they were giving close support to the ground forces.[25] From such altitude, at jet speed, the frequent bombing of the innocent was inevitable. As for the artillery, it was used not by the battery in well-aimed and carefully judged fire, but by the battalion in barrage style.

Armed helicopters, or "gunships," with increasingly powerful weapons were also used on a huge scale, becoming the very symbol of the war: between 1966 and 1971 they flew no fewer than 3,952,000 attack sorties.* Firepower in such profusion, so devastating and futile, could have only one effect in Vietnam: to demoralize and antagonize first the population whose active goodwill had to be secured, and then the American public.

The gross overuse of firepower was thus merely the most visible symptom of the inability of the American military institution to formulate a coherent strategy that would focus and control the means of war. No failure of military competence could be more complete.

---

* During those same years there were also 7,547,000 Air Cavalry sorties. Incidentally, both attack and assault sorties, along with 3,548,000 cargo sorties, accounted for much less than half of the total of *36 million* sorties recorded between 1966 and 1971. The greater part of those flights were due to the use of helicopters as flying command posts or mere taxis, by all but the most junior officers. It was truly a luxurious war.[26]

CHAPTER TWO

☆

How the Lessons of Defeat Remained Unlearned

The customary reward of defeat, if one can survive it, is in the lessons thereby learned, which may yield victory in the next war. But the circumstances of our defeat in Vietnam were sufficiently ambiguous to deny the nation the benefit of a well-understood military failure. Because the senior officers in charge were not forced into retirement after their failure in Vietnam but were instead promoted to the very highest commands,* there could be no earnest reappraisal of the war. Junior officers who had seen combat were often bitterly critical of what had been done, but with the senior men still in control they could do nothing to expose the defects of structure, let alone achieve reform. Instead the defeat was blamed on the civilian authorities, and American society at large.

☆

White House civilians were blamed because they chose a fundamentally flawed defensive policy that prohibited a war-ending march on Hanoi in classic style, and then compounded their error by setting hesitant limits on the reprisal bombings of the North. Congressional civilians were blamed because they refused to issue a formal declaration of war, to make Vietnam a truly national endeavor. Pentagon civilians were blamed because of their interference in military decisions large and small, often on the basis of numerical analyses that excluded all the

---

* Most conspicuously General William C. Westmoreland, who became Chief of Staff of the Army.

essentials of war merely because they could not be conveniently measured. Media civilians and the entire "new class" around them—liberal
academics, journalists, publicists, writers, artists, and demi-intellec-
tuals in office employment—were blamed for having willfully misrep-
resented the war to glorify the enemy and denigrate our purposes.

There is much justice in all these charges. Certainly the national
policy shaped by the intersecting powers of the White House and Congress, and later the antiwar media, conceded the initiative to North
Vietnam. Plainly unthreatened by invasion, not seriously bombed till
December 1972 (and then only to secure a face-saving treaty long after
any mandate for victory had been lost), Hanoi's leaders could take as
much or as little war as they pleased. Not having to hold back their
forces to defend their own borders, they could instead send them against
the South, when and where they chose, infiltrating or invading, attacking or retreating as they saw fit. This left little room, perhaps not
enough, for a successful American military strategy. It was the military
institutions, however, that ensured the misuse of whatever opportunity
remained.

Of all the accusations, the one of most enduring consequence is the
charge of civilian interference in the detailed conduct of military operations. The political leaders of the critical Vietnam years have departed,
and the media, as powerful and as irresponsible as ever, remain impervious to any discourse of strategy. But there is still a Defense Department containing officials empowered to intervene in military decisions.
They, just as much as the military leaders, have learned to deplore the
sort of interference that did harm during the Vietnam war—namely, the
attempt to control the details of military operations, not for operational
or tactical reasons but rather in pursuit of fanciful policies.

The example best remembered was the selection of targets in the
bombing of North Vietnam. The list was limited each time for the sake
of a "graduated escalation" policy, whose key assumption was that the
members of Hanoi's Politburo were prudent and calculating men much
concerned with their people's welfare, in effect rational bookkeepers
who would weigh the benefits of continuing the war against the costs of
the bombing. Each target in North Vietnam was chosen by civilians,
sometimes ignoring professional estimates of its physical vulnerability
to the specific bombs, rockets, and missiles that could be used and of
the strength of local air defenses.

It is now the common view that this controversy was immaterial to
the outcome because, it is said, the bombing of the North could never

have won the war anyway. Hanoi imported all but a fraction of its arms and ammunition, so the war certainly could not have been won by destruction of North Vietnam's small and miserable industry. Because no Americans of any importance, civilian or military, would allow it, the most important target—the entire population with its youth of military age, which fueled the war—could not be bombed. And because no weapon could physically destroy it, the fanatical resolve of the war leaders in Hanoi could not be attacked either.

This left only one set of promising targets, precisely the ones that were not attacked during the critical years because of the interference of civilian officials: the tunnels, viaducts, bridges, roads, and rail lines that made up Vietnam's overland supply lines from China, and the ports where Soviet war supplies arrived in such vast amounts. When those targets were finally attacked, along with Hanoi itself, following the courageous decision of Nixon and Kissinger in December 1972 (described as the "Christmas bombing" in manipulative headlines that relayed Hanoi's atrocity propaganda), the effect was powerful and almost immediate. By then, of course, any fear of Chinese intervention or a powerful Soviet reprisal had been extinguished by Nixon's and Kissinger's well-crafted diplomacy. Their predecessors, who had no such assurance, can be excused for their inhibitions, though not for their further and much narrower self-imposed limits which "graduated" the bombing in a way that did nothing to shock Hanoi, while giving it ample warning to disperse its forces and depots and strengthen its air defenses. On that matter, the military complaint is amply justified.

It must be recognized, however, that the interference of the civilian officials of the Pentagon and White House had only a most superficial scope. Civilian officials mostly set limits on combat operations *outside* South Vietnam, and thus scarcely affected the far greater part of the fighting. The civilians certainly did not prescribe the structure of forces or their system of command, let alone the practice of rotation for officers and men.

It was not the civilians who created the "unified" structure of command in Saigon that displaced strategy to make way for corporate harmony. It was not the civilians who insisted that the war be shared among all the bureaucratic segments of the armed forces. It was not the civilians who then allowed each force to perform in its own favored style of war-making—relevant or not, or even counterproductive. It was not the civilians who willed the hundreds of daily sorties of the fighter-bombers and the almost *4 million* helicopter-gunship sorties of 1966–1971, whose bombs, rockets, and cannon shells would have destroyed all the armies of history had even a small fraction been aimed at worthy targets. It was not the civilians who likewise made unworthy use of the artillery in huge amounts. It was not the civilians whose poverty of operational thinking and atrophied tactics were revealed by such futile use of so much firepower. It was not the civilians who condemned the enlisted men to fight and die among strangers by making every unit a mere transit pool for individual soldiers, each on his own twelve-month Vietnam tour. It was not the civilians who laid down six-month duty tours for unit commanders, thus ensuring "equity" of combat exposure for future promotion, but also the constant renewal of inexperience as well as the automatic contempt of veteran soldiers for leaders just beginning their tours, sometimes with fatal effect—as when first-week enthusiasts and medal-hunters pushed their troops too hard. It was not the civilians who impeded the improvement of the Vietnamese forces by denying promotions to officers who chose to serve as advisers instead of "punching their tickets" in the customary sequence of command slots needed for career advancement. Finally, it was not the civilians who decided that every service unit and base, every headquarters and depot, be built on a lavish scale and administered by crowds of desk-bound officers, so very few of them concerned with any aspect of warlike endeavor, whether tactics or leadership, operational planning or strategy.

A new conventional wisdom now threatens to make a paralyzing myth out of the true but narrow evils of civilian interference in the conduct of the Vietnam war. When the crisis of Central America began to acquire a military aspect, because of the military buildup of Nicaragua instigated, or at least encouraged, by Cuba and the Soviet Union (which certainly provided weapons and advisers in numbers unprecedented for the region), Secretary of Defense Caspar W. Weinberger piously assured Congress that he would not allow his officials to intervene in the "detail" of military decisions over Central America. This was said even as the unreformed military structure and command system were already displaying their characteristic malpractices in El Salvador and Honduras. For there was no agonizing reappraisal after Vietnam, no reform of any kind, let alone the drastic reform so obviously needed.

In the absence of a most forceful civilian intervention, the system could only perpetuate itself. Below the unified Joint Chiefs of Staff, six "unified" commands still control all the deployed forces of the Army, Navy, and Marine Corps, as well as tactical air units. There are separate unified headquarters for Europe, the Pacific, the Atlantic, and Latin America (Southern Command, in Panama), in addition to two overlapping commands in charge of home-based forces. (The Air Force, however, retains the space, air-defense, strategic bomber and missile as well as the long-range airlift forces under four "specified" commands of their own.) Inside each of the unified commands, all the syndromes manifest in the Saigon headquarters continue unchanged till this day.

The true and disinterested patriotic concern of many individual officers in these commands—who are the first to recognize the fatal defect—can achieve nothing. Each is powerless to change practices and rules created over time by bureaucratic pacts, large and small, among the service institutions. Temporarily assigned to the Joint Chiefs organization or to one of the unified commands, overseas or at home, each officer is compelled to represent the interests of his parent service in the carving out of roles, and in appointments to desirable posts.[1] Neither the Joint Chiefs nor any of the unified commands offers a career track, for the United States has no unified general staff. Only the parent services can award promotions, and any lapse in loyalty is all too likely to be swiftly reported by fellow staff members and duly punished by the thwarting of career advancement. Thus the path of self-reform, which a healthy institution would achieve informally by an entire pattern of disinterested decisions, is rigidly blocked.

It is by the wholly unstrategic procedures of the Joint Chiefs that the form and content of any new forces and commands are decided, and also the planning of war operations, large and small. Thus when the Joint Chiefs were directed in 1977 to establish a rapid-deployment force, mainly for possible use in the Persian Gulf, it was again suggested that the "specified" model be used, with the Marine Corps in charge. Because the new force would have to be sent out at short notice instead of being based abroad, it was clearly expeditionary—and the Marine Corps is *the* expeditionary service, trained and equipped to operate on its own, far from any main bases. The new force would also have to rely mostly on sea transport, because the air delivery of heavy equipment is ruled out over the extreme distances to the Persian Gulf—and the Marine Corps is the branch most attuned to sea transport. Finally, it seemed very likely that the force would in large part intervene amphibiously—and that, of course, is the specialty of the Marines.

Thus the case for a "specified" Marine Corps command, with subordinate Army and Air Force elements as needed, seemed quite conclusive. But the Joint Chiefs could accept no such result. It would mean that the Marines would have the power to allocate any new funds provided for the rapid-deployment mission, and that very few new high-ranking posts would be created, all of which the Marines would keep for themselves. Accordingly, as in Vietnam, a unified structure was imposed. But it turned out to be no easy matter to carve out the new command "equitably," and it was not until January 1983—almost six years after the first directive of Secretary of Defense Harold Brown—that the new Central Command was finally unveiled, under an Army general, with all other posts carefully shared out among the services. In response to criticism, the then Chairman of the Joint Chiefs, General David C. Jones, explained that the participation of all services was in fact most desirable because each could contribute its own peculiar capabilities to the new force. On that argument he should also have included the Coast Guard (as oil-spill specialists), or for that matter an oil company or two (for oilfield repair). The price, once again, was an overstaffed headquarters, incapable of swift and unequivocal decision.

While the rapid-deployment-force controversy was still unresolved, the "unified" system had another opportunity to prove its worth in combat, if only on a very small scale. When the time came to plan the Iran rescue attempt—which would eventually culminate in the burning sands of the "Desert One" landing zone on April 25, 1980—the structure and the system faithfully repeated the Vietnam model in miniature. Not one of the services (except the Coast Guard) could be deprived of its share; the Army, Air Force, Navy, and Marine Corps were all present in the rescue force.[2] British, French, and Israeli commando experts were astonished: having mounted dozens of successful and sometimes most daring operations during the past two decades alone, they had learned long ago to avoid any mixture of men from diverse units, not to mention different services. Specialists might be attached as needed in small numbers, but even units of the *same* service cannot be combined without long joint training—let alone units of different services. Commando operations are just like normal combat operations, only more so. All the circumstances that make a cohesive unit far superior in combat to any improvised group—even if its members are individually more talented—are present in stronger form under the high stress and compressed tempo of commando operations. Any differences in jargon or procedure, any lack of deep mutual trust born of long familiarity can be fatal in critical moments—as it seemingly was at Desert One, when Marine helicopter pilots in need of refueling from Air Force tankers apparently feared that the tankers might take off too soon. This or a misunderstanding of procedure resulted in the collision in which eight died.*

Next, under the "unified" model there could be no single commander, no matter how small the force, for that would defeat the whole purpose of the system. So there was an Army commander with his ground assault force, a Navy commander who "owned" the helicopters but whose own helicopter never reached the site, and of course an Air Force commander, as well as a landing-zone commander who was actually in charge at Desert One. This arrangement violated the basic rule of "unity of command" that applies to all combat but is utterly essential for any commando exploits.[4] When the unexpected happened, as it usually does in war, in the form of a busload of Persians who blundered into the landing zone, a debate ensued over the captives. While the commanders argued, the bewildered Persians were first taken aboard an aircraft for evacuation and then removed; then they were boarded again, only to be removed again. The raid never proceeded beyond the first phase of mere transportation; one can only speculate as to what might have happened under all the pressures of combat, when still other "elements" were to take part.

Finally, the Iran rescue had to be controlled through multiple layers of authority. The Chairman of the Joint Chiefs, General David C. Jones, controlled the operation from the National Military Command Center in the Pentagon—even though there was little to command. The traditional middle layer was a special "unified" task-force headquarters set up in Egypt, under an Army major general with an Air Force deputy.† Nevertheless, when the one command decision of the raid—to withdraw in failure—had to be made, responsibility was thrust down the chain of command to the luckless man on the spot, Army Colonel Charlie A. Beckwith.[5]

As of this writing, when the United States is engaged in Central America to assist friendly governments in El Salvador and Honduras, a multiservice command is once again in charge, the "unified" Southern Command in Panama. And once again, the role-playing of all comers is given full license.

---

* If the Marine pilots of the Navy helicopter that collided with an Air Force C-130 transport hurried overmuch, they can be excused for their mistrust, for it was apparently shared by the ground commander, Colonel Beckwith.[3]

† Major General James Vaught. After the debacle Vaught was promptly promoted to lieutenant general and appointed commander of the U.S. Army Corps in Korea; this was only fair, since all those who reached Desert One actually received decorations.

When a military exercise was staged in September 1983 to intimidate the Cuban-aligned Sandinista regime in Nicaragua, the presence of Navy ships off its coasts and a pointedly symbolic Marine amphibious landing on a nearby Honduran beach might perhaps have persuaded the Sandinistas to moderate their policies. But Southern Command could not possibly reserve all the action for just the Navy and Marines, cutting out the other services. Accordingly, exercise "Big Pine II" became a much broader affair, with much of the action in Honduras itself. The total number of the U.S. troops involved did not exceed 3,500, yet it was deemed necessary to employ both a Navy construction battalion (the "Seabees" of popular renown) and also the Army's engineers to dig a few water wells and cut out a small airstrip. Both the Marines and the Coast Guard were called in to train a few Honduran troops in the handling of some small boats not larger or more complex than those used by pensioners to fish on calm lakes. And Southern Command found it necessary to call on three different services—the Army's Special Forces, the Navy's SEALs, and Air Force Special Operations—to provide counterguerrilla training for a single Honduran battalion. Nor was the plain Army overlooked; officer-advisers from the Infantry branch were sent in to provide antitank training for the Hondurans.[6] With so many diverse forces involved, logistics and communications became greatly complicated, so much so that 1,500 more men had to be sent in to support the 3,500.[7] Such duplication and triplication clearly had its uses, for it could justify the large multiservice Southern Command headquarters in Panama: much staff work was undoubtedly needed to coordinate all the different forces of the different services. (Naturally, Southern Command promptly requested a *permanent* increase in its staff.)

The result of this typical malpractice was that the entire purpose of "Big Pine II" was compromised. The complicated arrangements and elaborate planning of the exercise generated so much bureaucratic noise, so many trips by senior officers to and from Honduras, that some in the media came to the conclusion that what was being planned was no mere exercise but rather a full-scale invasion of Nicaragua. When Congressmen intervened to demand information, the White House had to issue a formal denial, explicitly ruling out an invasion. Thus, long before the exercise actually took place, there was no longer any possibility of intimidating the Sandinistas—as there might have been had the Navy been left alone to achieve a sinister convergence of its ships on both the Atlantic and Pacific coasts of Nicaragua.

As for the declared purpose of "Big Pine II," to provide training for the Hondurans, the effect of the multiservice circus staged by Southern Command was predictably confusing. In the course of a few days, the very simple Honduran Army was exposed to a bewildering variety of diverse service procedures and competing methods.

There was no invasion of Nicaragua and no war. But had war erupted —a possibility very remote, perhaps, but one that military men should presumably include in their thoughts—the small Nicaraguan Army would have had the very great advantage of fighting not a combat formation 3,500 strong, but rather a veritable salad of forces, each with its own noncompatible communications and its own service and branch procedures.

The second effect of bureaucratic overcomplication is manifest in the provision of military assistance to El Salvador. As in Vietnam, the people involved are so absorbed in the internal labyrinth of competing military bureaucracies that they scarcely notice the external reality beyond their offices in Washington and Panama—in this case the specific nature of the guerrilla war in El Salvador and the extreme poverty of that country's army. With Congress unwilling to allow more than a miserable trickle of military aid (less than $81.3 million in 1983), it was especially important to choose the right weapons and ancillaries. But the military bureaucracies obdurately refused to adjust their standard tables of equipment to fit the local situation, as if the very complicated, very delicate equipment of the richest armed forces in the world just happened to be right for the very poor and ill-trained troops of El Salvador. The same M-16 rifles built to millimetric tolerances out of fancy alloys and plastics that proved too delicate in Vietnam were duly issued in El Salvador, along with the M-60 machine gun which will promptly jam if the ammunition belts are dirty.* And for a poor army that has very few radios to begin with, the issue of the standard man-pack radio with its disposable, nonrepairable handsets is a disaster; by the cost accounting of the U.S. Army it is cheaper to replace the handsets than to repair them, but in El Salvador repair work is cheap, while the dollars needed to buy new handsets are often unobtainable. Had it not been for the bureaucratic syndrome, the United States could have produced a rifle made out of plain steel and wood—such as the ubiquitous Soviet

---

* The U.S. Army supplies the ammunition belts in closed boxes, delivered to the troops by helicopters or trucks; the Salvadoran troops march on foot and can carry the belts only *bandito* style, draped across their chests; as dust accumulates on the sweaty belts to form hard dirt, the feed mechanism is jammed.[8]

AK-47—that can fire even if quite dirty, and a similar machine gun and radio too. Yet though it is the declared policy of the United States to assist Third World countries under attack, no effort has been made to produce suitable equipment.

Even more disastrous was the refusal to adapt tactics and methods to the local reality of a desperately poor army. The standard American methods of counterguerrilla warfare rely very heavily on abundant helicopter lift, instant communications, and powerful gunship aircraft. With them, small patrols can go out by night to look for guerrillas, ready to call in swift reinforcements to trap and defeat them. Those are the tactics that were preached to the army of El Salvador by deskbound staff officers in Washington and Panama, and in speaking with the American press, those officers were very willing to criticize the Salvadoran officer corps for resisting their advice. But when radios are very scarce, helicopters hardly ever available, and gunships nonexistent, a small patrol will be defeated when it encounters guerrillas, and in any case there is no possibility of flying in battle forces and gunships to exploit any sightings it might make. Under great pressure from the Pentagon and Southern Command, the Salvadoran Army did try its own version of "search and destroy" tactics, removing troops from guard duties and sending infantry columns to look for guerrillas. Naturally troops marching on foot caught no guerrillas, but the latter found it easy to attack the towns, villages, bridges, and bases that had been left unguarded.

Insurgencies have been defeated throughout history without radios, helicopters, or gunships by the traditional method, which combines a great deal of patient static defense with the occasional ambush of a betrayed guerrilla band and the harsh punishment of civilians who help the guerrillas. In El Salvador the method could work well enough—and so could the more humane American method, if all the necessary equipment were actually supplied. But the combination of very sophisticated tactical advice and grossly inadequate equipment can result only in futile compromises, whereby the guerrillas are not caught and their targets are left unprotected. In the meantime, the insistent suggestion that the Salvadoran Army was simply incompetent made it yet more difficult to obtain Congressional approval for military aid for El Salvador.

The tendency to gigantism—so spectacularly manifest in Vietnam— was mostly kept under control in Central America by Congressional stringency, but promptly erupted as soon as the opportunity presented itself. When a camp had to be established in Honduras to train rotating groups of Salvadoran as well as Honduran troops, 7,400 acres were deemed necessary, as if vast maneuver grounds were needed to train young peasant soldiers in the cleaning of weapons, basic marksmanship, the siting of light machine guns, the digging of field latrines, and the simplest squad and platoon tactics. Seventy-four acres would have made an ample training camp; 740 acres would have allowed space for an airstrip or two, and much more. Instead, quite unnecessarily, many productive acres were most injuriously removed from Central America's poorest agriculture, evoking great resentment.

There was one military malpractice in Vietnam that was most fully recognized afterward, and universally denounced by the military itself: the short tours of duty of one year or less. ("We were not in Vietnam for thirteen years, but only for one year—thirteen times.") One would have thought, therefore, that at least that one malpractice would not be repeated in El Salvador—where detailed knowledge of the country, specific personalities, and the intricacies of factional politics are especially important. But the bureaucratic urges of the unreformed military system are apparently irresistible: during the four years of the first term of the Reagan Administration (1981–1984), no fewer than four different officers served as commanders of the El Salvador Military Assistance Group: Colonels Eldon C. Cummings, Moody E. Hayes, John D. Waghelstein, and Joseph S. Stringham.* Four different officers slowly learned the truths of that complicated country in the course of their one year or so, only to take their knowledge with them, leaving a new man to start off again raw and untaught. Information on paper, schematic knowledge, numerical data, and all that can be contained in files count for little in a guerrilla war compared with the intuitive feel for a country and its people that can come only from personal experience.

When Congress insisted on limiting the total number of American military advisers in El Salvador to just fifty-five, including the commander, one would have thought that the Joint Chiefs and Southern Command would reserve those scarce slots for Infantry and Special Forces men, for the war is essentially an infantry and guerrilla struggle. And one would have thought that ordinary personnel practices would be bypassed in order to ensure the selection of a crack team, our very best Spanish-speaking samurais. But apparently there is no strategic conscience at work to resist bureaucratic priorities: the Military Assis-

---

* Replaced in turn by Colonel James J. Steele, who is to serve for two years.

tance Group positions were duly shared out, with both the Air Force and the Navy successfully claiming some of the slots for their "representatives." Nor was any great effort made to preserve the remaining positions for the very best men who could be found. Instead, officers and sergeants were assigned just as if El Salvador were Germany or Korea, where servicemen serve by tens or hundreds of thousands.[9] And to further dilute the value of the entire effort, duty tours were often as short as one month. This came about because the highly complex and diversified American military establishment deemed it necessary to provide all sorts of specialized expertise to the forces of El Salvador, instead of concentrating on the basics of fieldcraft, squad tactics, and weapon skills. Thus "mobile training teams" were sent to El Salvador for a month or so to teach such things as brigade staff procedures or civil-action theory, thereby displacing the sergeants who might have taught the simple skills actually needed. One would have welcomed some interference by civilian defense officials in the "detail" of the American military-assistance effort in Central America.

The three episodes of war of the closing months of 1983—the terrorist bombing of the Marine headquarters in Beirut on October 23, the seizure of Grenada on October 25, and the Navy bombing strike in Lebanon on December 9—revealed once again the deep structural defects of the military institutions.

The commission, chaired by retired Admiral Robert L. J. Long, convened by the Secretary of Defense to investigate the circumstances of the Beirut bombing was perhaps intended to explain away the 241 deaths as an unavoidable tragedy. (Certainly Secretary Weinberger has steadfastly refused to countenance any criticism of the military on this or any other subject.) If so, the commission's report must have come as a great disappointment, because it sharply criticized the conduct of the commanders involved, for failing to take elementary security precautions, for concentrating approximately 350 servicemen in a single building (with a mere battalion landing team involved, 1,250 men in all, the headquarters element was, as usual, disproportionately large), and for giving inappropriate, unmilitary instructions to the guard force (whose weapons were kept unloaded, by order). The more fundamental defect of the system itself was not explicitly pointed out in the commission's report, but it emerged all the same. The commission's brief was to investigate the single episode in Beirut and not the manner in which the armed forces of the United States are commanded. Nevertheless, the telling evidence was the commission's finding that the chain of command "did not initiate actions to ensure the security of the USMNF [the Marines] in light of the deteriorating political/military situation in Lebanon. The Commission found a lack of effective command supervision." [10]

It was not that the battalion landing team was left to fend for itself under the sole command of its Marine colonel. On the contrary, literally dozens of generals and admirals in several layers of large headquarters had their say: orders and instructions came down from USCINCEUR, the "unified" headquarters for the Commander-in-Chief U.S. Forces Europe, to CINCUSNAVEUR, headquarters for the naval forces in the European theater (to which Lebanon belongs); to COMSIXTHFLT, the fleet headquarters in charge of Navy and Marine doings in the Mediterranean; to the command of CTF 61, the amphibious task force to which the Marines were attached; to the commander of the Marine amphibious unit, who also served as Commander U.S. Forces Ashore, Lebanon; and finally to the battalion commander. [11] It is perfectly obvious from a reading of the commission's report that with so many officers involved, responsibility was hopelessly diluted; here and there some officers would pass this or that instruction to the Marine battalion, but none of the headquarters intervened to examine the entire situation and to make sure that the proper security measures were enforced. (See Chart 1.) It was the finding of the commission that security precautions remained inadequate even *after* the October 23 bombing; the combination of Marine bravado (and ill-taught distaste for fortifications) and an unchanged command structure that still obscured specific problems and specific solutions in the paper shuffle of overstaffed headquarters had left the door open for further attacks. Only when the members of the commission actually visited the scene and complained in person was "a series of actions . . . initiated by the chain of command to enhance . . . security." [12]

The invasion of Grenada, Operation "Urgent Fury," which began at 5:36 A.M. on October 25, 1983, could not fail as the Iran rescue had failed: a complete Marine amphibious unit of 1,250 men heavily armed and two Ranger battalions, [13] backed up by the fighter-bombers of the aircraft carrier *Independence* battle group and also Air Force gunships, could scarcely be defeated by 679 Cubans and those few Grenadians who were actually willing to fight. [14] Actually, 636 of the Cubans were only construction workers with no more than conscript military training; not more than 43 were professional soldiers, including 22 officers. [15] Nor was Grenada protected by any kind of air defense system, of the sort

CHART 1

Operational Chain of Command
for the 1250-Man Marine Battalion in Beirut
(October 23, 1983)*

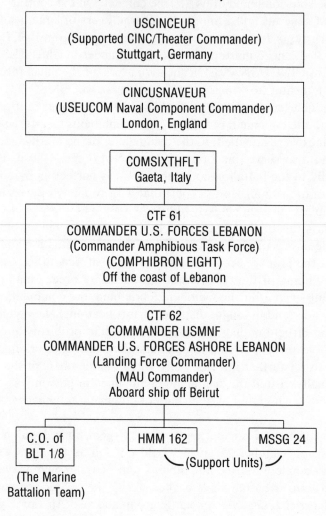

USCINCEUR
(Supported CINC/Theater Commander)
Stuttgart, Germany

CINCUSNAVEUR
(USEUCOM Naval Component Commander)
London, England

COMSIXTHFLT
Gaeta, Italy

CTF 61
COMMANDER U.S. FORCES LEBANON
(Commander Amphibious Task Force)
(COMPHIBRON EIGHT)
Off the coast of Lebanon

CTF 62
COMMANDER USMNF
COMMANDER U.S. FORCES ASHORE LEBANON
(Landing Force Commander)
(MAU Commander)
Aboard ship off Beirut

C.O. of
BLT 1/8

HMM 162

MSSG 24

(Support Units)

(The Marine
Battalion Team)

* Source: Report of the DoD Commission on Beirut International Airport Terrorists Act, October 23, 1983, p. 52, figure 3–1.

increasingly common even in the smaller Third World countries; there was not a single combat aircraft or antiaircraft missile on the island. As for the Cubans, commonly described in official reports as "heavily armed," they did not have a single tank or any artillery. In fact, they had nothing greater than a few wheeled armored cars and some light antiaircraft weapons.

Nevertheless, against such feeble opposition, the initial invasion forces had to be reinforced on the second day, October 26, by two battalions of the 82nd Airborne Division. On that day, the Chairman of the Joint Chiefs, General John Vessey, was quoted as saying: "We got a lot more resistance than we expected." [16] The extra troops did not suffice either, and by October 28, the third day of the invasion, more paratroopers of the 82nd Airborne had been sent in.

It was obvious by then that instead of a swiftly successful takeover, the invasion had degenerated into a series of drawn-out slogging fights. One result was that 224 of the students to be rescued, those at the Grand Anse campus of St. George's Medical College, were not reached by American troops until the late afternoon of October 26, the second day of the invasion. [17] By then they had spent a full day, a night, and much of the next day at the mercy of the Cubans and their Grenadian allies. Had the Cubans so desired, they could have taken those students hostage, or killed them—and they could have done either with political impunity, in the circumstances of their desperate fight against the invasion.

Because the invasion began with Marine and Ranger landings at opposite ends of the island, independent commando teams had to be employed for the urgent missions of "Urgent Fury," whose targets were in the central part of the island, around the capital of St. George's. One commando group, apparently the Delta force, was sent to reach and safeguard the political prisoners believed to be held in Richmond Hill prison. Another team was sent to seize and shut down the island's radio station, and a third was sent on the most important mission of all, to rescue Sir Paul Scoon, the Queen's representative as Governor-General of Grenada. As a known opponent of the murderous faction that had seized power in Grenada, Sir Paul was in acute danger in his official residence on a hill near St. George's. He was urgently needed safe and well in American hands to declare to the world media his authoritative approval of the invasion.

A team of SEALs (the Navy's own elite troops) was sent ashore in the predawn darkness on October 25 to reach and rescue Sir Paul before the overt invasion began. Landing in small boats on a nearby beach, twenty-two SEALs made their way up the hill to the Governor's residence. Sir Paul and his family were waiting to welcome them—but so were some Grenadian soldiers with three Cuban-manned BTR-60 armored cars. Very poorly protected, the BTR-60 can be penetrated and destroyed by even the lightest of hand-held antitank weapons; but the SEALs had only small arms with them. They were pinned down and trapped in the residence along with Sir Paul and his family. Eventually all but one of the SEALs were wounded.[18]

Vice Admiral Joseph Metcalf, the invasion commander, and Major General H. Norman Schwarzkopf, his hurriedly appointed deputy, did not use helicopters to send a platoon or two for a quick rescue. Instead they chose to stage an amphibious landing by a Marine company of 250 men, with five M-60 tanks and thirteen other armored vehicles, even though the amphibious shipping had to be moved halfway around the island to land near St. George's. The Marines and their tanks reached the beach at Grand Mal, just north of the capital, at 8 P.M. on day one, more than twelve hours after the initial calls for help from the Governor-General's residence.[19] By then two Marine Cobra helicopter gunships that had tried to provide supporting fire for the beleaguered residence had been shot down. But there was no rescue even then, because a second Marine company was awaited. Originally landed by helicopter in the initial assault of the invasion, this second Marine company did not arrive at the Grand Mal beach until 3 A.M. on day two.[20] It was not until 4 A.M. that the Marine force set out toward the Governor-General's residence. The rescue of Sir Paul, his family, and the SEALs was finally achieved at 7 A.M.; by then they had survived a twenty-four-hour siege, having received the protection of an Air Force AC-130 gunship during the night. The secret Delta force of elite Army commandos sent to rescue the political prisoners in Richmond Hill prison also failed in its mission. The force suffered (unlisted) casualties and was also rescued by the Marines.[21]

Nor were the larger actions—which simply could not fail—at all elegant in execution. With American elite-type forces—Rangers, paratroopers, and Marines—fighting Cubans (who are not Germans, nor Syrians) and even less impressive Grenadians, each engagement should have been swiftly victorious. It was not. The Rangers who parachuted onto the infamous airstrip under construction at Point Salines (whose excessive length suggested a Cuban strategic purpose) were thrown in front of the enemy's guns by a bad plan, had a hard fight, suffered casualties, and earned medals. The other initial move of the invasion, the helicopter landing of two Marine companies at Pearls airport and the nearby village of Grenville, encountered no trouble because the place was virtually undefended,* but when the 82nd Airborne paratroopers intervened, they encountered "stiff" resistance from Cuban forces at Frequente and Calvigny, as did the Marines who had landed at Grand Mal when they attacked Fort Frederick (the Pentagon of Grenada) after the rescue of Sir Paul Scoon.

By the end, 18 American servicemen had been killed and 116 wounded, several helicopters had been destroyed and more damaged, and the liberal use of A-7 Navy fighter-bombers, AC-130 gunship aircraft, and armed helicopters had inflicted much damage on Grenada and the Grenadians. There were also many accidents: 4 Navy SEALs drowned in an overturned boat, several Rangers were killed when two helicopters collided, 14 soldiers were wounded by an errant air strike, and 21 Grenadians were killed by a bombing error.[23]

In spite of all that had gone wrong, the military chiefs and of course Secretary Caspar Weinberger presented the outcome as a military triumph; the commander of the operation, Vice Admiral Metcalf, was quoted as saying "We blew them away."[24] Insofar as any problem at all was acknowledged, Metcalf's superior, Admiral Wesley L. McDonald, complained that the opposition had been underestimated by poor intelligence. (The CIA, it was said, "had no operation on the ground at all.") It was then claimed that instead of 500–600 Cubans, there were "as many as 1,100 Cubans with heavier weapons and better training than had been expected."[25] That turned out to be untrue two days later.[26] The more general excuse was that "Urgent Fury" had been planned so hurriedly that there was no time for proper intelligence collection or planning.

There is merit in that excuse, and it is also clear that the Rangers at least fought as true elite troops, showing great courage and dash. Nevertheless, if "Urgent Fury" is viewed in the perspective of Vietnam, the Iran rescue attempt, and even the Beirut bombing, the familiar structural problems begin to emerge. First, although every aspect of "Urgent Fury" was land combat, the operation was planned and commanded by naval officers, solely because Grenada is geographically located within the boundaries of the Navy-dominated Atlantic Command in Norfolk,

---

* A total of two 12.7mm machine guns were captured at Pearls airfield; the Marines were supported by formidable Cobra gunships.[22]

Virginia. Its chief, Admiral Wesley L. McDonald, thus served, in effect, as the "front" commander, while Vice Admiral Joseph Metcalf served as his operational commander. Two men expert in supervising the stately rotation of aircraft carriers between the Atlantic and Mediterranean, and in the planning of antisubmarine warfare and convoy escort, were thus placed in charge of the land operation based on airborne assaults and commando rescues.

To be sure, there are Marines in each naval command, and McDonald's "unified" Atlantic Command includes an Army and Air Force element. But because the Command is in effect "owned" by the Navy, the representation of the other services is small and of low rank. Similarly, Vice Admiral Metcalf had the Army's Major General Schwarzkopf to serve as his deputy. (He came in a package deal with the Rangers.) But there was no single command for the ground forces, as a Senate hearing was to reveal; apparently the Army and Navy could not agree on the matter.[27] Cosmetics aside, "Urgent Fury" was naval through and through, even though there were no ships to fight, no submarines to hunt, nor indeed any sea warfare at all; the Navy merely provided transportation and some carrier-launched air strikes that should not have been necessary at all.

The bureaucratic distortion that "navalized" the encounter deformed the entire *concept* of the operation. Because the entire operational area, the island of Grenada, amounted to only 133 square miles (twice the size of the District of Columbia); because the enemy had no ability at all to reinforce its troops, which lacked heavy weapons; and because of the very high political costs of any prolonged fight to the United States, "Urgent Fury" should have been planned as a *coup de main,* a sudden descent in overwhelming strength that would begin and end the fighting in one stroke. It is rarely possible to employ this method, for it demands an abundance of strength and permissive circumstances, but both were very much available in the case of Grenada.

In a *coup de main,* bodies of troops large enough to suppress opposition quickly are simultaneously placed directly on each target by the appropriate technique: airborne landing, parachuting, amphibious assault, and infiltration. Then there is no need for tactical movement on the ground or for airlifted vehicles, nor for coordination on the ground. And in a *coup de main* the enemy is prevented from any serious resistance by the sheer magnitude of the attack and also by the fact that its headquarters and commanders are attacked at the very outset.

Had bureaucratic boundaries been ignored, had "Urgent Fury" been planned by Army officers competent in land warfare, their natural tendency would have been to stage a *coup de main,* using as many battalions of the 82nd Airborne Division as could be airlifted, as well as the Rangers. As it was, Navy and Marine officers naturally opted for a "nibbling" approach, to establish bridgeheads in the expectation of subsequent advances, in the style of the Normandy landings. The operation as originally planned featured the Ranger and Marine assaults at opposite ends of the island, with the two forces advancing toward each other. In other words, the central part of the island would be reached only at the end of the operation. Since that part contained the capital of St. George's, the Grenadian leftist leaders, the Cuban command post, the radio station, the Governor-General's residence, and the military headquarters, the *sequence* of the operation virtually guaranteed prolonged fighting, since the Grenadian leaders and the Cubans were left undisturbed to organize resistance.

In the meantime, to deal with the urgent targets in the central part of the island, the SEALs were sent into action, along with the Delta force. It was characteristic of the admirals' coarse-grained understanding of ground warfare that they thought of the SEALs as "commandos," merely because they do a great deal of jogging and some unarmed combat. Commandos do that too, but their training is focused on combat operations, typically assaults—for which they will always strive to carry disproportionately heavy weapons to enhance the shock effect of surprise attack. SEALs, by contrast, are trained for stealth and infiltration; their task is to collect intelligence by acting as versatile swimming and parachuting scouts. To penetrate hostile naval bases and explore invasion beaches, they are accustomed to act in twos and threes, carrying only the lightest weapons, purely for self-defense. The team sent to the Governor-General's residence was therefore already large by SEAL standards, and it is not surprising that it came without any weapons beyond small arms. A perfectly good instrument was thus misused by remote headquarters that dealt in bureaucratic categories rather than the specifics of warfare.

The most disheartening aspect of the entire Grenada episode was the ease with which the performance of the armed forces was accepted as satisfactory, even praiseworthy. There was much satisfaction over the decisive conduct of the Reagan Administration, which indeed deserved great credit for seizing the opportunity offered by the plea of the Organization of East Caribbean States for help, even though it came in the immediate aftermath of the Beirut terrorist attack. And of course, the outcome was successful. Nevertheless, the quality of the overall planning, the agonizingly slow pace of the operation, and the dismal failure of two out of three "commando" actions against fourth-rate enemies should have prompted a most earnest investigation.

The same is true of the final and much smaller war operation of 1983, the Navy's attempt at a punitive air strike against targets in the Chouf and Metn mountains east of Beirut on December 4, 1983. In a place where others bombed both before and after with great effect and without suffering any losses, the Navy's carrier-launched air strike resulted in the loss of 2 aircraft out of 28, an A-6 light bomber and an A-7 fighter-bomber; another A-7 was heavily damaged.[28] The Navy's combat aircraft are, as a group, the world's most expensive and sophisticated, and the A-6 is the most elaborate of all (its unit cost exceeds $50 million). Nor did the Navy have to cope with an organized air-defense system: ever since June 1982 the Israelis had prevented the installation of any full-scale antiaircraft missiles in Lebanon. Thus the Navy aircraft faced only guns and the smallest missiles, SAM-7s and SAM-9s, both limited to low altitudes and both requiring visual detection and aiming—in daylight. Because the A-6 is fully provided with night-vision and precision-bombing equipment, and because any daylight overflights of the area attracted a great deal of enthusiastic firing by PLO and Druse gunmen, a night raid was obviously called for. Alternatively, an ultralow-altitude approach might have worked, with generous use of countermeasures to spoof the heat-seeking missiles during the bombing itself, for which the aircraft must briefly climb.

In fact, heat-seeking missiles such as the SAM-7 and SAM-9 can nowadays be spoofed by infrared flashers and hot balloons—but no longer by simple Vietnam-era flares. It turns out, however, that the Navy lacked such countermeasures, even though they are very much available and used by the Air Force and by some foreign air forces. In a classic distortion of its priorities, the Navy refused to purchase the devices in order to preserve its funds for more ships and more aircraft —in other words, for *institutional* growth. Thus the facade is kept up, more units and more command positions are created, but the genuine fighting edge is sacrificed.

Actually, even without modern countermeasures, the Navy could have avoided its humiliating defeat by a minimum of tactical ingenuity, in the form of a predawn strike using night-vision bombing, or an ultra-low-altitude strike, or even a surprise strike that would follow a circuitous approach. Undoubtedly the Air Wing officers on board the carrier offshore, who could see with their own eyes the intensity of the ground fire aimed at each passing aircraft, would have chosen one of those tactical solutions. But they did not have the authority to plan the attack of their own squadrons. In the perverse practice by now institutionalized, the lower-ranking officers in place who actually know the situation count for nothing: the plan was framed by a complex series of negotiations among the large and remote headquarters over them, the Joint Chiefs in Washington, the European "unified" command (USCINCEUR) in Germany, the Navy's own European headquarters (CINCUSNAVEUR) in London, and the Sixth Fleet headquarters (COMSIXTHFLT) near Naples. This committee of committees acted in true committee style, excluding all operational craft, tactical ingenuity, and plain cunning from the plan. The attack was launched in the best conditions of visibility, at 8 A.M., when the morning mists over the mountains had dissipated; this meant that the A-6s with all their sophisticated electronics were placed on the same footing as the Syrian troops and PLO gunmen who aimed their weapons by the naked eye. Moreover, the aircraft gathered at 20,000 feet to await sequential takeoffs from the decks of the carriers, ensuring that the Syrians would have full warning to alert their gun and missile crews and those of their Palestinian allies. Finally, the aircraft descended to 3,000 feet to launch their attack, thus placing themselves within the lethal range of the SAM-7s and SAM-9s.[29]

No competent officer would have deliberately prescribed such a self-defeating plan. But of course there was no single military mind behind the plan but rather the lowest common denominator of all those crowded headquarters. No doubt it was the Joint Chiefs of Staff who ruled out a night attack for fear of inflicting damage on innocent civilians —for that most unmilitary organization is highly sensitive to the fancied foreign-policy repercussions of military action in the Arab world. Sixth Fleet and CINCUSNAVEUR probably insisted that 8 A.M. was the best time because the chances of helicopter recovery for any downed pilot would be maximized when the visibility was best, and all the headquarters probably agreed that 3,000 feet was just the right altitude to achieve precision while staying clear of the mass of small-arms fire. Rear Admiral Roger Box, commander of the aircraft-carrier battle group, later explained that the orders for the air strike were "dictated by a higher chain of command than the Navy." He complained that the timing of the strike was wrong. "The sun was highlighting our aircraft while the missile sights were in the shadows, and we lost two aircraft."[30]

After the death of two pilots and the capture of Lieutenant Robert

Goodman, navigator of the A-6 that was shot down, after the destruction of two costly aircraft (more were damaged), the usual excuses were heard. Navy spokesmen did not hesitate to complain in public about the supposedly inadequate intelligence they had received, and there was much surprise about the intensity and accuracy of antiaircraft fire. Actually, conditions in Lebanon were unusually permissive for the air strike: owing to Israel's repeated attacks, the Syrians did not have a single radar-controlled antiaircraft missile in Lebanon, and neither did they have a proper radar warning net.

Civilian action—or, if one prefers, "interference"—might have saved lives (and the prestige of American arms) in the skies over Lebanon by overriding the Navy's bureaucratic reluctance to purchase modern countermeasures. Interfering civilians also might have saved the Marines in Beirut, if only by cutting through the labyrinth of higher commands to send a qualified antiterrorism expert to perform a security audit of the tragic building; such an expert could have spotted the fatal vulnerabilities overlooked by various visiting high-ranking officers, including Paul X. Kelly, then Commandant of the Marine Corps. And civilian interference would certainly be needed to expose the grave errors of the Grenada operation, now shrouded in secrecy, professional shame, or even fatuous self-satisfaction.

But that is not how things should be done. Instead of looking to a myriad of separate civilian interventions for each of the many malpractices that flow from the very nature of the military structure, the structure itself should be carefully examined and then radically remade, to debureaucratize the armed forces and reintroduce the discipline of strategy into their decisions. After one great civilian intervention to achieve structural reform, further interference would be unnecessary. In the meantime, the same self-defeating structure that deforms combat operations is also silently at work in peacetime, rejecting simplicity, ingenuity, and economy in favor of complex high-cost solutions burdened by the multiple demands of multiple authorities.

The very abundance of talent, dedication, and disinterested patriotism among our officers is definite proof of the impossibility of reform from within, for otherwise all those talented, dedicated, and patriotic officers would themselves have accomplished all the necessary reforms long ago, after Vietnam if not before. As it is, the more patient among the many officers who see very clearly the defects of structure, both in the higher commands and in the separate services, endure in order to contain the damage; the less patient, with bitterness in their hearts, simply leave their places in mid-career to the time-servers and the complacent.

Quite recently, a newly retired military officer publicly warned the nation that the very core of the system, the Joint Chiefs, is incapable of waging war successfully, and is most wasteful in peacetime. This was not some colonel disgruntled over denied promotions, nor some radical misfit forced out in mid-career, but rather General David C. Jones, Chairman of the Joint Chiefs of Staff until 1983.[31] His denunciation of the system he had headed for four years, and in which he had participated for more years as Air Force Chief of Staff, was an urgent appeal to the nation for fundamental reform—which evidently not even the nation's most senior military chief could achieve from within.* Similarly, some years before, Admiral Elmo R. Zumwalt, Jr., who retired as the Navy's chief officer, published a graphic account in his memoirs of the grave structural defects of the Navy's own organization—which he too had been powerless to correct.[33] Others of lower rank but not inferior in expertise have issued their own warnings about bureaucratic deformations in each of the services and the defense establishment as a whole. But such is the paralyzing effect of long-decayed military bureaucracies that even the widest consensus on the need for reform does not yield any substantial remedy.

The decay of the system should not be surprising: the military structures still with us today were shaped by legislation, policy, and chance events during the foundation years of 1945–1950, in the immediate aftermath of the Second World War. Since those days, nuclear weapons have evolved from a scarcity of fission bombs, almost exclusively American, to an abundance of fusion weapons altogether more powerful, far more accurate, and in Soviet hands too. Military equipment has become much more varied, so there are more choices to be made; weapons have become relatively much more costly, so there are greater penalties for error; weapons have become more complicated, so there are greater technical uncertainties, and, to an increasing extent, modern military equipment no longer fits the traditional distinctions between

---

* General David C. Jones: "Despite past and recent efforts [to reform the system] institutional resistance to change remains enormous . . . the likelihood of a successful initiative emerging from within the system is extremely low. As Admiral Mahan, the noted naval strategist, once wrote, a military service can not be expected to reorganize itself; pressure must be exerted from outside the organization."[32]

ground, air, and naval armaments, so that ownership boundaries between the services have become increasingly irrational.

The international political environment has also been transformed: by the recovery of Europe and the rise of disorder in the former colonies, so that there is less need for continental forces but more need for expeditionary forces; by the fall of Indochina and the altered stance of China, and by the rise of a self-reliant South Korea but also of Soviet oceanic strength, so that there is less need for ground forces in eastern Asia but more need for air and naval forces in the Pacific; and by the two transformations of the Middle East—which went from the safe playground of the British Foreign Office to a central strategic zone in the 1970s (when the Vietnam-shocked United States was in no position to act), only to start another cycle of decline in the 1980s under the impulse of native fanaticism—so that American military power was first unnecessary in the Middle East, then unready, and then unwanted.

The American political mood has also turned several times, from the 1945 demobilization fever to the surprisingly eager acceptance of responsibility for the defense of Europe and Japan a few years later. (Korea came in the package.) And then the mood turned again, from the enthusiasm for Kennedy's global containment in the early 1960s, to the longing for retreat after Vietnam in the early 1970s, to the rejection of continued retreat under Carter a few years after that, and back again to containment—but of uncertain scope.

Since the foundation years, the technical and tactical texture of military power has undergone great changes, invalidating many of the 1945–1950 assumptions that still shape the present military structure. Some things are much less important now than they were—for example, the payload capacities of bombers and fighter-bombers, because of fusion and precision weapons, respectively. Other things have become much more important than they used to be, such as electronic warfare in all its forms. Some things have become far more vulnerable, such as all *light*-armor vehicles, while other things are far less vulnerable than they were in 1945, such as submarines, because of nuclear propulsion. Some forms of military power that seemed very useful, such as the specially trained, specially equipped amphibious forces of the Marines, can be employed only rarely nowadays, and have a good and cheaper substitute in the helicopter delivery of ordinary forces. Other forms of military power are now much more useful than they seemed to be in 1945, such as high-quality *light* infantry, while the fighters and fighter-bombers that had only each other to fear in 1945 are now hemmed in by powerful air defenses based on surface-to-air missiles and radar-guided guns. Some things that were very rare and very expensive in 1945, notably military computers, have become very cheap, while other things that were very abundant and did not strain the 1945–1950 budgets, notably military manpower, have become very expensive.

Most important of all is the change in the very conception of war. A long global war fought by mobilization of 10 or more million men, which was universally envisaged in 1945–1950, no longer seems plausible. To be sure, *planning* for mobilization still makes sense—in order to discourage a Soviet "quick-win" strategy—but in that case a greater emphasis should be placed on the reserve forces of civilian part-time soldiers, sailors, and airmen. Above all, the equipment of the armed forces, from warships to rifles, should be drastically simplified, because much of today's ultrasophisticated equipment is simply not producible in the numbers required to arm forces of ten million men, or five million, for that matter.

Some changes that have overtaken the 1945–1950 assumptions were happily accepted by the military bureaucracies; for example, the advent of computers. Others were simply too powerful to be resisted. However, when a genuine response to change would have violated strong bureaucratic interests, the response was suppressed, or the change simply ignored. For example, the arrival of precision air-to-ground missiles and modern wide-area munitions should have induced the Air Force to switch funds from the combat aircraft themselves to the new weapons, in order to buy them in quantity. But the pilot-dominated Air Force bureaucracy will not reduce the number of aircraft that pilots can fly, merely to make the force as a whole far more effective. Instead the money still goes for aircraft and their upkeep. So few of the much-advertised wonder weapons have actually been purchased that they would be used up in a matter of days in the event of a large war; after that, all the action would revert to the old-fashioned "iron" bombs still stocked in quantity.

Similarly, the fixed geographic facts and the new military facts that make the Soviet Union much less vulnerable to amphibious landings than Japanese or German territories were during the Second World War should have resulted in a sharp reduction in funds and manpower for that particular form of warfare. But in the absence of any central strategic direction, the Marines have been able to preserve their 1945 status in the shared-out military bureaucracies. Because of this and the active loyalty of ex-Marines in politics, the Corps has been able to obtain year after year funds for the upkeep and costly renewal of a large quantity of amphibious shipping, landing craft, and armored vehicles, even though the Soviet empire has no exposed coasts like Normandy vulnerable to invasion, and no vital island shields like Iwo Jima to protect.

On a still larger scale, the great share of total military spending claimed by the Navy reflects much more its self-perpetuating 1945 status than present strategic realities. During the Second World War, Japanese military power was totally dependent on the use of the oceans to connect the imperial territories and supply the home islands of Japan with petroleum and essential raw materials, and Germany could be both blockaded and attacked from the sea. The Soviet Union, by contrast, could invade Western Europe, reduce China, and neutralize Japan without sending a single ship to sea; its war economy could survive indefinitely without any maritime communication; and its own territory is shielded from the oceans by the full depth of Europe, India, and China, while its own open-ocean coastline is quite short and scarcely vulnerable. Thus even a complete American naval supremacy would count for little against the Soviet Union, even in a protracted nonnuclear war, and in peacetime, American naval power counts for far less in the balance of international politics than equivalent land forces would—for they would immediately affect the security of Europe. To be sure, the Navy and Marines can do much in the "Third World—but that cannot justify their great share of the budget.*

The house of our defense, based on a 1945 design, with foundations and walls built with the tripled defense budgets that came with the Korean war, has been altered, patched, and extended many times. As lesser changes continued, the basic structure became more and more ill-fitting. As a huge new dining room only makes a small kitchen more inadequate, as extra bedrooms in the attic stand empty while aged and now childless residents lack a needed bathroom on the first floor, the structure of the house of our defense remains antiquated under the brand-new paint of each Administration's slogans and self-described "strategies." In peacetime, delusions of adequacy persist; but ever since Korea, each test of combat has revealed gross deformations in the making of strategy, in the absence of operational art, and in tactics made willfully clumsy.

* The Navy's aviation could be very useful for Europe as well (land bases are highly vulnerable), but only if its so-so "attack" aircraft were replaced by advanced "stealth" fighter-bombers.

Could it be, however, that a structure so seriously defective in the conduct of war is nevertheless effective in the peacetime tasks of national defense? After all, the everyday business of the Army, Navy, Marine Corps, and Air Force, of their civilian secretariats, and of the Defense Department civilians is not to wage war or mount commando raids, but rather to recruit and train manpower, both military and civilian, commissioned and enlisted; to select, purchase, and assimilate new arms and equipment; to research and develop future weapons and all that goes with them; to repair and supply equipment and forces already in hand; to maintain installations and build new ones; to provide military assistance, in both equipment and training, to lesser allies; and finally to engage in the deployment, exercise, and routine operation of combat and ancillary forces, both in full-time active units and in the part-time reserves, both nuclear and not, home-based and overseas.

Neither combat leadership nor tactical ingenuity, neither the operational art of war nor military strategy, seems at first sight very relevant to all these peacetime tasks. None looms large in the administration of shopfront recruitment offices, in the procurement of boots or ballistic missiles, in the direction of scientific research programs, in the running of repair shops or fighter squadrons, or in any other of the thousand different things that must be done to manage the daily workings of the defense establishment. So it is tempting to think that it is all a question of managerial ability, bureaucratic skill, technical expertise, and political talent, all qualities that are generously abundant in the officer cadres of all the services, among the civilians appointed by successive Presidents to head the Defense Department, and in the civil service too. If that were truly so, then the distortions that increase costs would be our only worry, at least in peacetime.

But that is an illusion. Managerial abilities, bureaucratic skills, technical expertise, and political talent are all necessary, but they can be applied only to goals that have already been defined by military policies, broad and narrow. And those policies can be only as good as the strategy, operational art of war, tactical thought, and plain military craft that have gone into their making.

At present, the defects of structure submerge or distort strategy and operational art, they outrightly suppress tactical ingenuity, and they displace the traditional insights and rules of military craft in favor of bureaucratic preferences, administrative convenience, and abstract notions of efficiency derived from the world of business management. First there is the defective structure for the making of military decisions, under the futile supervision of the civilian Defense Department; then come the deeply flawed defense policies and military choices, replete with unnecessary costs and hidden risks; finally there come the undoubted managerial abilities, bureaucratic skills, technical expertise, and political talents, all applied to achieve those flawed policies and to implement those flawed choices. By this same sequence was the fatally incomplete Maginot Line built, as were all the Maginot Lines of history, each made no better by good management, technical talent, careful accounting, or sheer hard work.

Hence the futility of all the managerial innovations tried in the Pentagon over the years. In the purchasing of weapons, for example, "total package" procurement, cost plus incentive contracting, "firm fixed-price" purchasing have all been introduced with much fanfare, only to be abandoned, retried, and repudiated once again. And each time a new Secretary of Defense arrives, with him come the latest batch of managerial innovations, many of them aimed at reducing fraud, waste, and mismanagement—the classic trio endlessly pursued by eager officials within the Defense Department and endlessly denounced in Congress, even though they account for mere percentage points of the total budget, and have no relevance at all to the failures of combat. The persistence of the Administrator's Delusion has long kept the Pentagon on a treadmill of futile procedural "reforms" that have no impact at all on the military substance of our defense.

It is through strategy, operational art, tactical ingenuity, and military craft that the large savings can be made, and the nation's military strength greatly increased, by achieving long-overdue structural innovations, from the central headquarters to the combat forces, from the overhead of bases and installations to the current purchase of new weapons. Then, and only then, will it be useful to pursue fraud, waste, and mismanagement, if only to save a few dollars more after the billions have already been saved. At present, by contrast, the Defense Department administers ineffectively, while the public, Congress, and the media apply their energies to such petty matters as overpriced spare parts for a given device in a given weapon of a given ship, overlooking at the same time the multibillion-dollar question of the money spent for the Navy as a whole instead of the Army—whose weakness diminishes our diplomatic weight in peacetime, and which could one day cause *us* to resort to nuclear weapons in the face of an imminent debacle. If we had a central military authority and a Defense Department capable of strategy, we could cheerfully tolerate much fraud, waste, and misman-agement; but so long as there are competing military bureaucracies organically incapable of strategic conduct, neither safety nor economy will be ensured, even if we could totally eliminate every last cent of fraud, waste, and mismanagement.

☆

CHAPTER THREE

The Labyrinth:
The Enormity of the Defense
Establishment

*If it is true that the very structure of our national defense is defective,
how could this have been overlooked for so long? The Pentagon is
subjected to such relentless scrutiny by Congress, the media, and the
public that it scarcely seems possible that any malady so basic would
not have been uncovered long ago and remedied. The first barrier to
understanding and reform is the sheer size of the defense establishment: there is simply nothing in American civil society that begins to
compare with its awesome dimensions. But an even greater barrier
is its inordinately complex structure, in which the lack of any national military authority has led to the multiplication of overlapping
functions.*

☆

In most countries, everything having to do with defense policy and the
armed forces remains shrouded in secrecy, except for what little may
be publicized through propaganda or carefully staged military parades.
In the United States, things are very different. Instead of secrecy, there
is a huge amount of information on virtually every aspect of the nation's
military power. Every year toward the end of January, the Secretary of
Defense goes before Congress to present his department's *Annual Report,* a bulky volume whose three hundred or more pages describe the
armed forces of the United States, define their tasks, and review the
military threats that might be ranged against them, all in order to justify

the defense budget for the coming fiscal year.* Everything is presented in great detail, complete with statistics, charts, and graphs. One version, for the Pentagon's internal use and for the Armed Services committees of the House and Senate, is classified "Secret," but the public version is almost as complete.

Every Washington bureaucracy produces reams of paper in a ceaseless flow of books and booklets, statements and memoranda. Few attract widespread attention, and a great many reach the wastepaper basket still unread. The *Annual Report,* however, is in a class by itself: even the censored public version is greatly in demand. The military attachés of a hundred embassies eagerly await their copies, and soon thousands of intelligence and defense officials overseas will be reading very carefully each line of the text, and between the lines too, because sometimes "classified" gaps can be reconstructed from the public text. On Capitol Hill, the large band of staff experts of the appropriations, armed-services, and budget committees, and the still larger number of staff assistants of individual Senators and Representatives, stand ready to study their copies, sometimes to interpret the broad policy contained in the document, but much more often to see how the detailed decisions might affect contractors or military bases in the home districts of their masters. Defense contractors pay even closer attention: their profits and perhaps their survival may depend on what is and what is not in the budget. The press receives its copies too, and within a matter of hours, headlines will be made by the first hurried readings. In the days, weeks, and months that follow, those initial impressions, all too often misleading, will be followed by many detailed stories and a great flood of editorials.

And the *Annual Report* is merely the first of a great number of annual reports, of narrower scope but greater detail, presented before the Congress by the Secretaries of the Army, Navy, and Air Force, the Chairman of the Joint Chiefs of Staff, the chiefs of the four services, the two undersecretaries for policy and engineering, the fifteen assistant secretaries and deputy undersecretaries, the directors of defense agencies,

---

* The document's full title (for this year) is *Annual Report to the Congress: On the Fiscal Year 1985 Budget, Fiscal Year 1986 Authorization Request and Fiscal Year 1985– 89 Defense Programs.* In it the Defense Department informs Congress of spending plans for the next five years—always subject to change, of course; actually asks for money for the forthcoming fiscal year; and presents a reasonably firm estimate of the intended request for the year after that. In parallel with the *Annual Report,* the Joint Chiefs as a body publish their own much shorter and altogether less informative report on the current fiscal year, *United States Military Posture.*

the service assistant secretaries, the "project managers" in charge of major equipment purchases, and more. Beyond this great mass of paper, there are "hearings" during the months that follow before a variety of Congressional committees. With the defense specialists on their staffs to help them, Senators and Representatives can probe matters in greater detail, requesting additional information "for the record," when—as frequently happens—the officials before them cannot answer all their questions.

In the end, when the "hearings" of the various committees are published, the combined texts run to tens of thousands of pages, hardly reduced by the few deletions that remove the most secret information, almost always narrowly technical. The hardy souls who read every page must be few indeed, but anything dramatic will have reached the public months before in the daily press, and much more will eventually appear in articles and commentaries.

A great deal more about every aspect of defense is revealed by the Congressional Research Service and Congressional Budget Office, both of which publish in-depth studies of particular issues in defense; by the General Accounting Office, which naturally concentrates on the financial aspect; and by a number of specialized magazines that are so well informed and reliable that their information might as well be official. (*Aviation Week and Space Technology* is famous for the detail of its revelations.) And finally there are the press leaks, usually the outpourings of disgruntled officials who intend to undermine government decisions that they happen to oppose; the extra bits and pieces thus reported are not always trivial. Yet despite all this abundant and detailed information the true nature of our difficulties is scarcely illuminated.

As of this writing, the Defense Department employs a total of 2,127,422 full-time servicemen (and women) on active duty. The Army, with 781,648, remains the largest service; the Navy has 555,269, and the Marine Corps, under the Navy Department but in every way a separate service, 198,574. The Air Force, the youngest of the services (formed only in 1947) but with the largest budget, has 591,931.[1] The part-timers who are paid to attend training drills and exercises in the "selected reserve" of the Army National Guard and Air National Guard of each state, and in the reserve forces of all four services, add another 1.005 million, and the civil employees of the Defense Department number more than 1 million,[2] with at least another 80,000 foreign nationals employed overseas. A total of roughly 4.5 million are thus employed by the defense establishment.[3]

Counting only barracks and depots of significant size, arsenals, firing ranges, office complexes, and defense laboratories, as well as full-scale military bases, the Defense Department controls 911 properties within the United States—some of huge dimensions. There are another 25 in U.S. overseas territories, mostly islands in the Pacific, and 334 in some twenty-one foreign countries. Within the United States alone, the Defense Department retains 24,192,253 acres for its use, an area more than three times the size of Belgium, and roughly equivalent to the combined territories of Connecticut, Massachusetts, New Hampshire, Rhode Island, and Vermont, with enough room to spare for two Delawares.[4]

Out of this vast infrastructure come the armed forces themselves. The category conventionally described as ''strategic'' (meaning long-range nuclear strike forces and continental air defenses) includes 1,000 Minuteman intercontinental ballistic missiles housed in underground launchers within the United States, 550 of them Minuteman IIIs, with multiple warheads. (Up to 100 MX ballistic missiles are to be acquired in 1987–1988, after a decade of hesitations.) The bomber force consists of sixteen squadrons, each with fifteen B-52s, large but old aircraft now equipped with very new cruise missiles, as well as four squadrons with a total of fifty-six FB-111A light bombers. To provide air refueling for the 10,000 and more miles of two-way bombing missions, there are 615 large tanker aircraft, mostly in the active Air Force but some manned by the Air National Guard and the Air Force Reserve. And the new B-1B bombers will begin to join the force in 1986. Finally, there are at present 480 ballistic missiles fitted on board *Poseidon-* and *Ohio*-class nuclear-powered submarines. In all, these intercontinental forces hold a total of more than 9,000 nuclear bombs and missile warheads.[5] An additional 572 nuclear-armed ballistic and cruise missiles whose range is less than intercontinental are being based in Europe, along with some more on Navy ships worldwide.

Traditionally the neglected stepchild of the strategic forces, continental air defenses are now reduced to a mere five squadrons of active Air Force fighter-interceptors (eighteen aircraft each), with another ten slightly smaller squadrons in the Air National Guard. Responsibility for the air defense of North America is still shared with Canada, and all interceptor squadrons are controlled by the joint U.S.-Canadian command post (NORAD) built deep within Cheyenne mountain. In addition to this meager force, there is a vast array of early-warning radar and optical detectors, which maintain constant surveillance against bombers and missiles in all directions and up into space. There are also special warning satellites, equipped with infrared sensors to detect hostile missile launches by their characteristic hot exhaust.[6]

The forces that our defense bureaucrats describe as "general purpose"—namely, the classic combat forces, which may use nuclear weapons (several thousand artillery shells, demolition devices, missile warheads, and bombs), but are primarily trained and equipped for conventional war—account for four-fifths of our defense expenditures, and take up a still larger share of the manpower. The "active"—that is, full-time—forces include sixteen (incomplete) Army and three Marine divisions of 17,000–20,000 soldiers each, one new 10,000-man light division of the Army, and about three more divisions' worth of separate brigades and cavalry regiments, armored and airborne (each with up to 5,000 soldiers). Outside the division/brigade structure—which contains the armored, mechanized-infantry, "straight-leg" infantry, and airborne forces, all trained and equipped for regular warfare—are the Special Forces, with three active "groups" of several hundred each, four more reserve groups, and two Ranger battalions. Above the divisional level are the corps and "army" supporting forces, which include the heaviest (8-inch) artillery, multiple rocket launchers and short-range nuclear missiles, as well as combat engineers, military police, and more. Nine Army National Guard divisions and one Marine Reserve division are supposedly deployable after mobilization, along with 25 separate Reserve brigades and some 3,000 lesser units, mainly of the Army National Guard, which range from combat battalions (one-tenth of a division) to highly specialized service companies (one-fourth of a battalion) such as oil-pipeline and MASH units.[7]

The air power described as tactical (as opposed to "strategic") includes twenty-six active "wings" of Air Force fighters, fighter-bombers, and attack aircraft—ground-attack, that is, for the aircraft in question are not meant for air combat. To provide maintenance and spares, each wing requires some 100 aircraft to keep 72 operational in three squadrons of 24 aircraft each, and the force is now somewhat understrength. The Air National Guard has twelve nominal wings with thirty squadrons and 660 fighter-bombers and attack aircraft, and the Air Force Reserve adds another ten reduced squadrons.[8]

The Navy has its own carrier-based fighters and attack aircraft, with a total of sixty-three squadrons (730 aircraft) distributed in the active carrier wings, with ten more squadrons of the Naval reserves. The Marine Corps has twenty-eight squadrons of fighter-bombers and attack aircraft (a total of 345) within its own mixed "wings," one for each of three active divisions, and another eight squadrons in the reserve air wing of its reserve division. Counting all the "tactical" combat aircraft of all the services, active and reserve, there is a total inventory of some 4,000 actually operational and in squadron service, with more in the maintenance float; there are also several hundred more aircraft in a variety of supporting roles, for electronic countermeasures, airborne early warning, reconnaissance, light observation, and air refueling.[9]

The squadrons of the Military Airlift Command, Active Guard, and Reserve operate 328 large and ultralarge (C-5) air transports of intercontinental range and some 500 medium-sized aircraft of lesser range, with all the service and maintenance units required by this largest of all American airlines.[10]

Aside from its 14 very large aircraft carriers, the Navy has 203 cruisers, destroyers and frigates, 10 of them in the reserves; 98 attack (i.e., not ballistic-missile) submarines, all but 5 of them nuclear powered; and 60 amphibious ships of all sizes (the 5 largest exceed 40,000 tons of displacement). Counting all the other apples and oranges, including missile boats, mine-warfare ships, under-way-replenishment tankers and transports, and all sorts of auxiliaries, the Navy's total ship count increases to 546—still short of the much-desired "600-ship" Navy. At any given time there are roughly 200,000 Navy men and women actually afloat on the oceans of the world. Not all the Navy's aircraft are carrier based;[11] its rather imposing land-based air force includes twenty-four active squadrons (220 aircraft) and thirteen reserve squadrons of long-endurance patrol aircraft used for ocean reconnaissance as well as submarine detection and attack.

If we examine the armed forces not as a mere inventory but rather by their geographic deployment, the outline of their purposes begins to emerge. Our deployment overseas resembles geological layers, each the enduring residue of some past crisis or war, now hardened into a "commitment"—the customary word for deployments that may no longer yield any tangible benefits to us, but whose removal might embolden enemies and dishearten allies, and thus possibly cause either war or appeasement.

It sometimes seems as if the military power of the United States is scattered across the globe. But aside from the Navy, which gets into all sorts of places, and the occasional expeditions of rather small Army or Air Force contingents, our foreign deployments are essentially centered in two defensive garrisons, one in central Europe, the other in Korea. In each case, the accompanying panoply of air power is more broadly based, but it too plans and trains mainly to defend the same frontiers the ground forces are watching.

The largest concentration of American forces overseas is in Europe, where 333,319 Americans are now serving. Although all four services are represented in twelve different countries and afloat with the Navy, the Army in West Germany accounts for two-thirds of the total, with 209,897 at the last count.[12] Having arrived in 1943 and 1944 to liberate Italy, France, Belgium, and Holland from the Germans, the armed forces of the United States have remained ever since, to help protect many more countries than were ever liberated. But it is only in Germany, the "central front" in NATO's language, that the United States provides direct physical protection, by guarding part of the frontier territory. The West German border with East Germany and Czechoslovakia, which is also the frontier between NATO and the Warsaw Pact, is divided into eight "corps" sectors. The United States is responsible for two of these, with its V Corps and VII Corps, which together form the U.S. Seventh Army, which has two armored and two mechanized divisions (out of sixteen active divisions worldwide), two armored-cavalry regiments, and three separate brigades, as well as a special brigade, mainly of infantry, in West Berlin.

This garrison, which can be reinforced by airlifted troops in any serious crisis (a most fragile assumption, which depends on fragile airfields), has the support of a complete air force, "United States Air Force—Europe," whose bases and area of operations extend far beyond Germany, from Spain to Turkey. It has twenty-eight fighter squadrons (out of seventy-eight active worldwide), two ground-attack squadrons, two reconnaissance squadrons, and two airlift squadrons.[13]

In Norway, one of the two NATO countries that share a border with the Soviet Union (the other is Turkey), there is no American garrison. But there are provisions for the deployment of a Marine brigade that would be transported from the United States; its air support would come from part of a divisional Marine "air wing," or from the Navy's carrier aviation. In Turkey there is no American garrison either, but there are Air Force bases, again with possible air reinforcement from the Navy. The only other ground forces in Europe are a single paratroop battalion based at Aviano in northern Italy but primarily meant for quick inter-

CHART 2

Major Army and Marine Combat Forces (Active Duty) Worldwide (as of March 31, 1983)

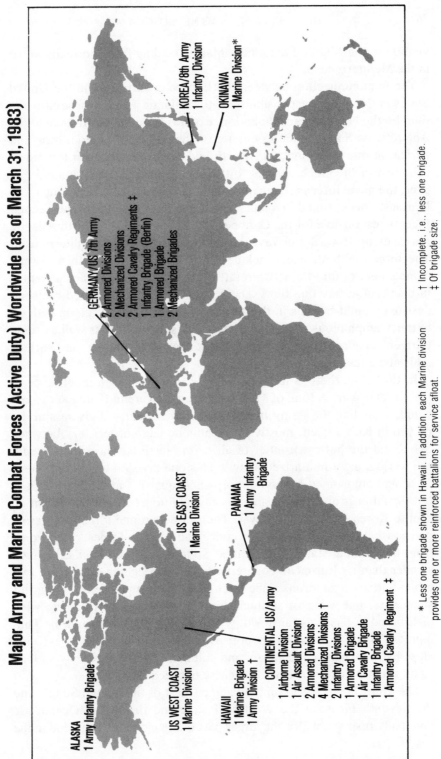

KOREA/8th Army
1 Infantry Division

OKINAWA
1 Marine Division*

GERMANY/US 7th Army
2 Armored Divisions
2 Mechanized Divisions
2 Armored Cavalry Regiments ‡
1 Infantry Brigade (Berlin)
1 Armored Brigade
2 Mechanized Brigades

ALASKA
1 Army Infantry Brigade

US WEST COAST
1 Marine Division

HAWAII
1 Marine Brigade
1 Army Division †

CONTINENTAL US/Army
1 Airborne Division
1 Air Assault Division
2 Armored Divisions
4 Mechanized Divisions †
2 Infantry Divisions
1 Armored Brigade
1 Air Cavalry Brigade
1 Infantry Brigade
1 Armored Cavalry Regiment ‡

US EAST COAST
1 Marine Division

PANAMA
1 Army Infantry Brigade

* Less one brigade shown in Hawaii. In addition, each Marine division
provides one or more reinforced battalions for service afloat.

† Incomplete. i. e., less one brigade.

‡ Of brigade size.

vention in the Middle East, and a Marine landing force normally afloat in the Mediterranean.

The vital connection between the European garrison and the United States is the major responsibility of the Atlantic Fleet, whose jurisdiction, by the Navy's grand definition, extends from the North Pole to the Antarctic, within boundaries cut across the middle of Siberia, Iran, and Africa on one side, and both North and South America on the other. (The rest of the globe belongs to the Pacific Fleet.)[14] In practice, however, the naval forces are organized into two fleets, with their embarked Marines, concentrated in a much smaller slice of the ocean: the Second Fleet is responsible for the Caribbean and the traditional North Atlantic sea-lanes up toward Norway; the Sixth Fleet is in the Mediterranean. The forces of both fleets include six aircraft carriers with a normal complement of up to ninety aircraft each: at least one of the carriers is in overhaul at any one time. There are roughly one hundred cruisers, destroyers, and frigates in the Atlantic zone as a whole, along with up to thirty amphibious ships and sixty attack submarines, as well as some thirteen squadrons of land-based long-range patrol aircraft, and various odds and ends, mainly supply ships.[15]

In East Asia there is the other American garrison, an inheritance of the Korean War. A total of 41,273 servicemen were in Korea at the last count, including the Army troops of the one infantry division still deployed in Korea itself, mostly in the 50-mile band of territory between Seoul and the hottest frontier of all, with North Korea—undoubtedly the world's most militarized state.[16] This one division has the privilege of being commanded by both a corps headquarters and the 8th Army, but the latter is also responsible for any additional troops that might be sent to Korea in the event of war. The nearest ground force is a Marine division based in Okinawa, but conceivably other forces could come from the United States. The United States Air Force Pacific is much smaller than its European counterpart, with ten fighter squadrons, two ground-attack squadrons, one reconnaissance squadron, two airlift squadrons, one wing of strategic bombers, and an air-refueling wing distributed in bases as far afield as Korea, Japan, Guam, and the Philippines. There is more air support available from the Marine air wing close by in Okinawa and Japan, and still more from the Navy—so long as its aircraft carriers are not otherwise engaged.[17]

The Third Fleet, based on the Pacific Coast of the United States, and the Seventh Fleet, in the Western Pacific and the Indian Ocean, are nominally responsible for the larger part of the globe not included in the

CHART 3

The US Navy: Major Ship Locations (Active Duty Only) Worldwide (as of March 31, 1983)

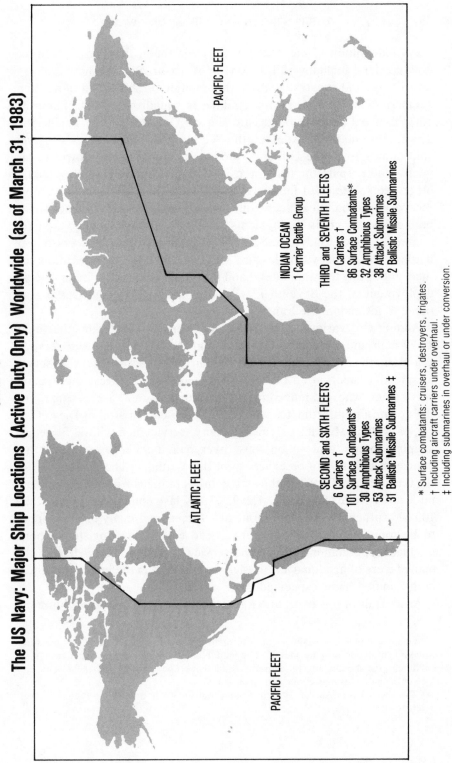

PACIFIC FLEET

PACIFIC FLEET

ATLANTIC FLEET

SECOND and SIXTH FLEETS
6 Carriers †
101 Surface Combatants*
30 Amphibious Types
53 Attack Submarines
31 Ballistic Missile Submarines ‡

INDIAN OCEAN
1 Carrier Battle Group

THIRD and SEVENTH FLEETS
7 Carriers †
86 Surface Combatants*
32 Amphibious Types
38 Attack Submarines
2 Ballistic Missile Submarines

* Surface combatants: cruisers, destroyers, frigates.
† Including aircraft carriers under overhaul.
‡ Including submarines in overhaul or under conversion.

Navy's definition of the Atlantic. Between them, they have seven aircraft carriers, including at least one in overhaul; almost ninety cruisers, destroyers, and frigates; some thirty amphibious ships; and thirty-eight submarines, as well as eleven land-based squadrons of patrol aircraft, and the usual panoply of logistic ships.[18] One fleet in the Pacific (the Third) and one in the Atlantic (the Second) work up the crews as each ship comes from the building yard or dry dock, shake down the air wings, and prepare the task forces and replenishment groups, while the other fleets, deployed far away (the Seventh and Sixth, respectively), receive these building blocks only when they are ready for action. In both cases, the crisis deployments of yesteryear have become the fixed commitments of today: the Sixth Fleet originated in a 1946 episode of battleship diplomacy (to reassure Turkey, which the Soviet Union was then attempting to intimidate),[19] and the much more recent Indian Ocean deployment of the Seventh Fleet dates back to President Carter's attempt to intimidate the Iran of the fanatics.*

Adding the various odds and ends overseas—including the lucky 1,759 men and women of the Navy and the 95 Marines who serve in Bermuda, the even luckier Air Force man (or is it a woman?) who serves in splendid isolation on beautiful Antigua, the rather less lucky 2,313 servicemen who are fenced inside the Guantánamo base in Cuba, and the downright unfortunates who serve in the barren atoll of Diego Garcia, as well as Marines on embassy duty, servicemen with U.S. peacekeeping forces, and so on—just over half a million Americans are overseas: 517,069, to be exact, as of this writing.[20] The greater part of the remaining 1,600,000 in the active forces remains within the continental United States (actually, 1,299,513, as last counted).† Fewer than 100,000 suffice to man the "strategic" forces, and many of the rest are to be found in the very large overhead of training, logistic-support, intelligence, communications, and service commands, as well as in the many layers of headquarters in each service, and in the joint commands, both "unified" and "specified."[22]

As a result of this overburden, the Army's 474,883 soldiers within the

---

* Gunboat diplomacy is always most attractive for those who would like to use force without fighting, because no shot need be fired to obtain results. But if the natives remain indifferent, the shooting must then start—and if there is no heart for that, the next appearance of the gunboats may evoke no response at all.

† The balance is in Alaska, Hawaii, Guam, Johnson Atoll, and Puerto Rico; in transit; or afloat with the Navy.[21]

continental United States yield only a total of ten divisions' worth of actual combat troops. They serve in one airborne division (the 82nd) and the helicopter-rich 101st "air assault" division, both primarily suited to rapid deployment; two armored and four mechanized-infantry divisions meant for the reinforcement of the Army in Germany, which already have three of their eighteen brigades over there; two infantry divisions nominally usable anywhere, but in fact fit for combat only where no strong armored forces are likely to be encountered; and three separate brigades—of armor, air cavalry, and infantry—as well as a brigade-sized armored-cavalry regiment.

The Marines, who are the most widely scattered, seem to do their scattering in very small doses, because out of a total of 198,574, roughly 142,000 Marines are kept within the continental United States. They man the two divisions deployed in California and North Carolina, along with the air wing of each, as well as the Marine overhead—which is not small. (The third Marine division, in Okinawa along with its air wing, accounts for most of the Marines overseas.)

The Air Force, with 433,466 men and women within the continental United States, is second only to the Army, and not by much; but its overhead is by far the largest. The Strategic Air Command of the Air Force operates nine missile "wings," which control the Minuteman missiles; nineteen wings that group all the long-range bomber squadrons; and two strategic-reconnaissance wings, as well as air-refueling-tanker wings. These are in effect the intercontinental nuclear forces of the United States, along with the Navy's ballistic-missile submarines.

The forces of the Tactical Air Command are all primarily meant for the reinforcement of air power overseas, and this central reserve—by far the most important "swing force" in the entire panoply of American military power—consists of thirty-nine fighter squadrons (with another thirty-nine in the Guard and Reserve), three close-support squadrons, three reconnaissance squadrons (with another eight reserve), and a variety of lesser forces. The Military Airlift Command, which is a joint command, though "specified" and thus Air Force property, includes seven airlift wings. The Aerospace Defense Command, also specified, controls the very small force of five active interceptor squadrons, not much augmented by the ten more interceptor squadrons of the Air National Guard. One more interceptor squadron is based in Iceland, under a nominally separate organization but in fact integrally connected with the defense of North America.

CHART 4

Major Combat Units US Air Force, Navy Aviation, Marine Air Wings (Active Duty Only) Worldwide (as of March 31, 1983)

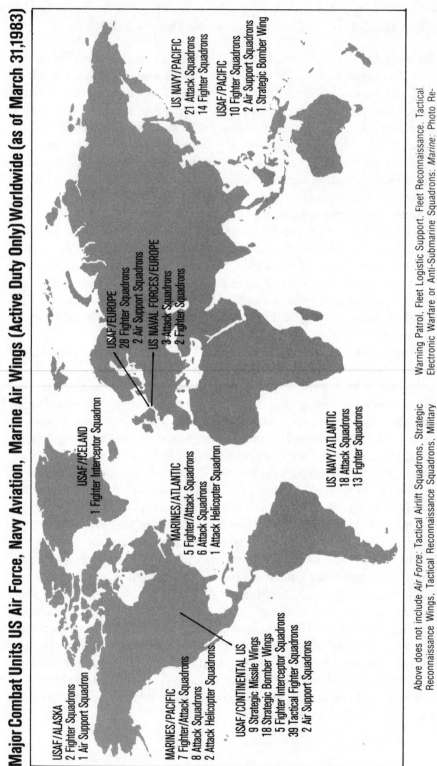

USAF/ALASKA
2 Fighter Squadrons
1 Air Support Squadron

USAF/ICELAND
1 Fighter Interceptor Squadron

USAF/EUROPE
28 Fighter Squadrons
2 Air Support Squadrons

US NAVAL FORCES/EUROPE
3 Attack Squadrons
2 Fighter Squadrons

US NAVY/PACIFIC
21 Attack Squadrons
14 Fighter Squadrons

USAF/PACIFIC
10 Fighter Squadrons
2 Air Support Squadrons
1 Strategic Bomber Wing

MARINES/PACIFIC
7 Fighter/Attack Squadrons
8 Attack Squadrons
2 Attack Helicopter Squadrons

USAF/CONTINENTAL US
9 Strategic Missile Wings
18 Strategic Bomber Wings
5 Fighter Interceptor Squadrons
39 Tactical Fighter Squadrons
2 Air Support Squadrons

MARINES/ATLANTIC
5 Fighter/Attack Squadrons
6 Attack Squadrons
1 Attack Helicopter Squadron

US NAVY/ATLANTIC
18 Attack Squadrons
13 Fighter Squadrons

Above does not include *Air Force:* Tactical Airlift Squadrons, Strategic Reconnaissance Wings, Tactical Reconnaissance Squadrons, Military Airlift Wings, Air Refueling Wings, Air Refueling Groups; *Navy:* Early Warning Patrol, Fleet Logistic Support, Fleet Reconnaissance. Tactical Electronic Warfare or Anti-Submarine Squadrons; *Marine:* Photo Reconnaissance, Tactical Electronic Warfare. Helicopter Lift Squadrons.

Outside the continental United States but still on U.S. territory there are two small garrisons—in Alaska and Hawaii. The Army keeps a rather specialized winter-warfare brigade in Alaska, and the Air Force has a separate command there with two fighter squadrons, a ground-attack squadron, a tactical-airlift squadron, and an important strategic-reconnaissance wing, which does much flying near the Soviet Union. In Hawaii the ground forces are more of a reserve than a garrison, and both the one Army division and the one Marine brigade are earmarked for duty in Korea or elsewhere in Asia. Finally, the Army keeps a brigade in Panama tuned for jungle warfare, much as the Alaska brigade is a winter force and the Berlin brigade is somewhat specialized in city warfare.

In this outline of the major combat units we do not do justice to the true dimensions of the American defense establishment and its numbing complexity. Aircraft carriers have been mentioned, but not the Navy's construction battalions, nor its worldwide network of communications and electronic-warfare forces. Armored divisions have duly been counted, but not the Army's large fleet of medium helicopters, nor its ballistic-missile defense force. Much has been said about the Air Force without mentioning its special operations force, a separate body for counterguerrilla action, commando raids, and air-land rescue, or the small airline's worth of large airborne command aircraft, wherein our President and quite a few generals can fly about to control the firing of nuclear weapons in brief safety.

With all these combat forces come their commanders, headquarters, and staffs. At the very top are the joint, multiservice commands. But below them, each service has its own stepladder of commands, with increasingly elaborate staffs and headquarters. The service chains of command run from the *basic units*—the companies, battalions, brigades, and divisions of the Army (and Marine Corps); the ships, air squadrons, flotillas, and carrier "wings" of the Navy; and the squadrons and wings of the Air Force—to the *higher formations,* namely the corps and numbered "armies" of the Army, the task forces and numbered fleets of the Navy, the numbered "amphibious forces" of the Marines, and the "air forces" of the Air Force. Above them all come the *geographic commands* in charge of all forces of that particular service in a given area. Thus all the Army forces within the continental United States come under the Forces Command in Fort McPherson, Georgia, whose overseas counterparts are the "U.S. Army, Europe" headquarters in Heidelberg, Germany, and the far smaller commands in

Hawaii (Western Command) and Japan (U.S. Army, Japan)—where there is also a corps headquarters, even though there are no Army troops in Japan. (In Korea, by contrast, the troops come under the numbered Eighth Army.)

The Navy keeps all its transports under a *functional* headquarters, the Military Sealift Command, but assigns all combat forces worldwide to one of three commands, "Pacific Fleet" in Hawaii, in charge of the Third and Seventh Fleets; "Atlantic Fleet" in Norfolk, Virginia, which controls the Second Fleet; and "U.S. Naval Forces, Europe," in charge of the Sixth Fleet and the Bahrein-based Middle East Task Force from its remote London headquarters. The Marines have parallel commands, "Fleet Marine Force, Pacific" in Hawaii and an Atlantic counterpart in Norfolk.

The Air Force too has its Hawaii headquarters for "Pacific Air Forces" (just recently elevated to four-star rank) and a much larger command, "U.S. Air Forces, Europe" in Ramstein, Germany, as well as a much smaller Alaskan Air Command. Within the continental United States, the Air Force does not have a single all-forces command; it divides its forces among three *functional* commands, Strategic, Tactical, and Military Airlift.

The higher levels of these service hierarchies—which ultimately reach the Chiefs of Staff of the Army and Air Force, the Navy's Chief of Naval Operations, and the Commandant of the Marine Corps—are not supposed to be operational. In theory at least, the one-service chains of command are responsible only for the upkeep of the forces, by way of training, exercises, discipline, and maintenance, while the *use* of the forces, both in peacetime deployments and in combat, is controlled by joint, multiservice commands that report to the Joint Chiefs of Staff. Thus, the typical Army chain of command runs from battalion to brigade, then to division and corps, then to one of the numbered armies, which usually belong to one of the Army's geographic commands. But that command receives its operational orders not from the Army's own Chief of Staff but rather from one of the joint commands—which may or may not be headed by an Army officer.[23]

Six of these joint commands, all "unified" and thus supposedly shared out equally between the services, divide the planet among them. The most truly unified of these commands is the European Command in Stuttgart, Germany. Always headed by an Army officer, who serves concurrently as the chief of U.S. Army, Europe, this command is also in control of a great deal of air power under U.S. Air Forces, Europe,

CHART 5

The Unified and Specified Commands

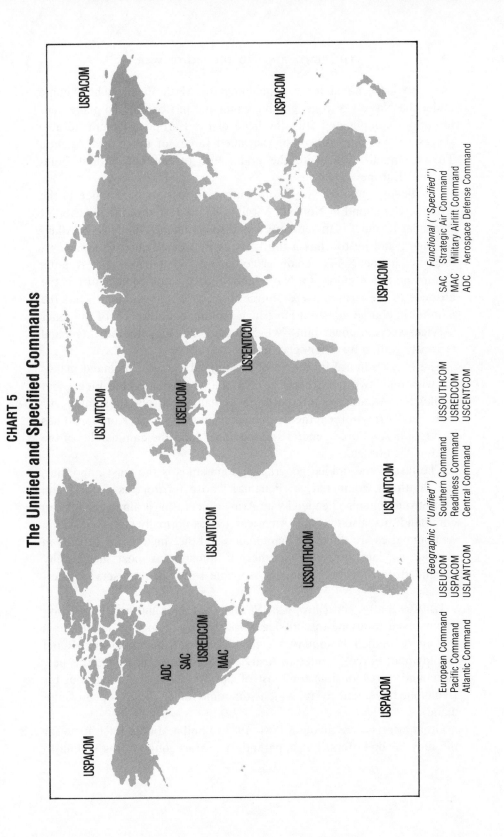

Geographic ("Unified")

European Command   USEUCOM
Pacific Command   USPACOM
Atlantic Command   USLANTCOM

Southern Command   USSOUTHCOM
Readiness Command   USREDCOM
Central Command   USCENTCOM

Functional ("Specified")

SAC   Strategic Air Command
MAC   Military Airlift Command
ADC   Aerospace Defense Command

and also large naval forces (including the Sixth Fleet), which come under the Navy's own geographic command in London. To make matters more complicated still, the head of the European Command also serves as the chief officer of the allied forces of the North Atlantic Treaty Organization, with the grand title of Supreme Allied Commander, Europe.

Identically "unified" in theory but much less so in practice is the Atlantic Command in Norfolk, Virginia, lately tested in the invasion of Grenada. Its chief is the admiral who also commands the Navy's Atlantic Fleet, and he too has a third hat as Supreme Allied Commander, Atlantic, in the NATO chain of command. What makes the Atlantic Command much more of a Navy fiefdom than a unified structure is the absence of the Army and Air Force from its watery domain. Thus the admiral in charge does not have high-ranking counterparts of the other services serving under him—which means that the Atlantic Command is poorly staffed by other services.

The Navy admiral in charge of the unified Pacific Command makes do with only two hats (he is also in charge of the Pacific Fleet), but unlike his Atlantic counterpart, he actually controls substantial Air Force and Army forces, the two divisions in Hawaii and Korea, and has a four-star Air Force general serving under him, the commander of the Pacific Air Forces.

The last of the unified geographic commands is the least important, the Southern Command, in Panama, whose territory is Central and South America; also headed by an Army officer, this is almost an orphan command, because the only American forces normally stationed within its boundaries are those in Guantánamo and the single Army brigade in Panama. Of late, however, Southern Command has most successfully expanded its role, by organizing a whole series of multiservice exercises.

Until recently, the European, Pacific, Atlantic, and Southern Commands used to divide the outside world among them, but now there is one more unified headquarters, the "Central Command" (ex–Rapid Deployment Force). Under an Army officer for the time being, this new command is responsible for most of the Middle East (though not for Lebanon, Israel and Syria, which still come under the European Command).

Great efforts were made in 1981–1983 to find a Middle East home for the new headquarters, but apparently no Arab country was willing to offer its territory for the purpose.[24] Central Command thus remains within the United States at McDill Air Force Base in Florida, which, notwithstanding the excellent climate, is a most uncomfortable location from a bureaucratic point of view since it is also the home of Central Command's great rival, the unified Readiness Command, which controls all Army and *tactical* Air Force units within the continental United States. Although headed by a four-star Army general, the Readiness Command is a mere asteroid among the planets of the *overseas* unified commands, because it serves only as a holding tank: as soon as its forces are sent into action anywhere overseas, they automatically come under the control of one of the overseas unified commands. The sphere of the Readiness Command has been further diminished because the new Central Command is a headquarters without forces of its own (since the United States has no bases in the Middle East); its role is to plan and eventually command expeditionary forces mostly drawn from the Readiness Command. The troopless four-star Army general in charge of Central Command must obtain his forces from the four-star Army general in charge of Readiness Command—who no doubt feels that all expeditionary planning could be done just as well by a three-star reporting to him; friction between the two commands has been chronic.

The Air Force assigns its *tactical* air power (fighters, fighter-bombers, and shorter-range transports) to the overseas unified commands headed by Army or Navy officers, or to the Readiness Command at home, but keeps all the big stuff—the strategic bombers and missiles, air-defense and space radars, and fighter-interceptors—in three *functional commands* under its own four-star generals. As with all other combat forces, these forces also must come under joint command, and the Strategic Air Command, Military Airlift Command, and Aerospace Defense Command are at least nominally "joint" and include Army, Navy, and Marine staff officers. The three commands are not "unified," however, but "specified"—i.e., controlled (overtly) by a single service. In practice, the three commanding officers are merely the equivalent Air Force commanders in charge of the Strategic, Space (not Aerospace), and Military Airlift Commands.

The great anomaly of this system is that the unified and specified commanders actually have no central headquarters above them fit to issue military orders. Their own service chiefs are of course officially cut out of the chain of command, while the President is only a nominal commander-in-chief most of the time. To be sure, the advent of instant

worldwide communications now permits all sorts of phenomenal interventions direct from the White House,* but regardless of his constitutional powers, and the limitless reach of the White House switchboard,
the President has no expert military staff—and even Napoleon needed
a staff to exercise command. In theory there is no vacuum of authority,
because the unified and specified commanders come under the Secretary of Defense, who has the Joint Chiefs of Staff to give him military
advice, while the Chiefs in turn have the Joint Staff to work out the
details for them. But in practice the Joint Chiefs are merely a weekly
gathering of gentlemen each of whom has his own service as his first
concern, while the Chairman has no one to serve him except the Joint
Staff, whose members the Chairman cannot promote or demote, and
who belong to their own services rather than to him.

Aside from the Joint Chiefs of Staff organization, which the sharing-
out system makes quite ineffectual, the Secretary of Defense has no
staff of his own capable of dealing with operational matters. Thus the
great body of the armed forces has no commensurate head, and behaves
accordingly: except in the truly unified European Command, the service
limbs move of their own accord, each according to the service's institutional urges.

In sharp contrast to the weakness of its strategic and operational
brain, the body of American military power is lavishly serviced and
supplied by the auxiliary and supporting forces of each service, and by
the all-service Defense Agencies. The entire array of the *combat* forces,
active and reserve, home-based and overseas, makes up only half of the
total forces: out of 2,127,422 men and women in uniform on active duty,
the combat forces account for 1,095,400.[25] All the rest, along with more
than a million civilian employees, are employed in supply depots, repair
shops, arsenals, dockyards, and scientific laboratories, in training centers, schools, academies, and war colleges, in hospitals and prisons, in
the many management offices, large and small, in computer centers,
meteorological stations, and all sorts of other facilities—a vast understructure that makes the combat forces look simple.

Moreover, the combat forces as officially defined—i.e., the strategic,
tactical, and "mobility" forces—already include much built-in overhead, partly because of the ample service units at each level, and partly

---

* During the 1975 *Mayagüez* incident, President Ford spoke directly with Navy pilots
actually over the target, to make tactical decisions in minute detail.

because of the proliferation of administrative and clerical work down to the basic units. Even ships at sea have become floating offices, to judge by the amount of paperwork they produce.* In fact, when we examine the official classification of "skills and specialties" for all *enlisted* personnel, we discover that out of 1,817,856 men and women, a mere 257,553 are listed as having "combat" skills, as opposed to the 371,999 with electrical and mechanical skills and 290,353 clerks and administrators, among other categories.[27]

Of the 1,032,022 men and women in uniform who are *not* in combat forces, one-third, or 301,000, serve in the purchasing, development, supply, and maintenance organizations of each service ("Base Operating Support"), under the Army's Matériel Command, the Navy's Material Command,† and the Air Force Logistics and Systems Commands (which also employed a good many of the additional 23,500 servicemen whose function was listed as research and development). A large part of the 429,510 civil servants employed by the Army, the 344,602 employed by the Navy, and the 256,107 employed by the Air Force (as well as 150,000 contract employees) are also employed by the many outfits of these huge commands, each one of them as large as a major industry.[28]

Another 151,400 are employed in running training facilities of one kind or another, from boot camps to all sorts of specialist courses,[29] to the war colleges where future generals are trained. Eleven major Defense Agencies belonging to the civilian side of the Defense Department (even though they are mostly headed by senior military officers) provide all sorts of things to all the services on a centralized basis, from code-writing and code-breaking (the National Security Agency) to audiovisual aids and legal work, from nuclear-weapons handling to mapping, from Intelligence to contract auditing, as well as centralized logistics, foreign military assistance, and all-service communications. Among them, these agencies, which make up the executive arm of the Defense Department, employ 134,300 servicemen, as well as many of the 83,923 civil servants (aside from contract employees) not employed by any one service.[30] An additional 43,500 men and women in uniform, including an always insufficient number of doctors, are assigned to the clinics and

---

* It has been estimated that 66,000 forms are filled out every day Navy-wide for aircraft maintenance alone.[26]

† Since the publication of the first edition of this book, perhaps not coincidentally, the Navy's Material Command has been disbanded.

hospitals that care for servicemen and their families, and another 31,800 are assigned to the rather opaque category labeled "personnel support."

Finally, 39,500 serve in "management headquarters"—typically the Pentagon itself—and an interesting group of 29,000, mostly officers, are on loan to other agencies of government, including the lucky handful who serve in the notoriously career-enhancing National Security Council of the White House, where four-star generals have been made out of mere colonels in the span of a few years.

The reader skilled in arithmetic will have detected something missing, because all the servicemen and women included in the supporting understructure (737,900), plus all those listed as being in the combat forces (1,095,400), do not add up to the total of 2,127,422 in uniform at the last count. In fact, there are 312,200 servicemen and women who do not serve either in the combat forces *or* in the supporting structure; they are listed instead in a most dubious and unmilitary category: as "individuals." [31] This is a substantial proportion of all military manpower— no less than 14.7 percent, to be unnecessarily precise. Of these, 11,800 are the unfortunates listed as patients, prisoners, and "holdees" (an interesting bureaucratic description for those who are destined to become prisoners, unless they are lucky enough to become "releasees" instead). Next, 75,800 are listed as transients—i.e., in the process of moving between bases or functions, between here and abroad. Finally there is the largest and most questionable group, the students and trainees—211,100 of them. [32] There is nothing questionable about young soldiers undergoing the hardship of basic training; but there are not 200,000 of them—or at least, there should not be, in the supposedly long-service "all volunteer" force of military professionals. There is nothing questionable either about the odd officer who is studying Japanese at some language school, or attending one of the war colleges. But very questionable indeed is the high propensity of the system to drain manpower away from organized units, in order to send officers and men to all sorts of specialist schools that may enhance the individual but do much less for the organization. As it is, many of those in uniform seem overeducated in all sorts of things, from high-energy physics to rat psychology, and neither the Defense Equal Opportunity Management Institute at Patrick Air Force Base, Florida, nor the Joint Military Packaging Training Center in Aberdeen, Maryland, is likely to impart the strategic, operational, and tactical teachings that the armed forces so badly need.

Each service has its own noncombat commands to manage all the auxiliary and support functions, and to handle its "individuals." Aside from the huge matériel commands, each service has a training command under various descriptions, a communications command, and an electronic-security command, with more variety beyond them: only the Army includes a Criminal Investigation Command among its major commands (as well as the more respectable Corps of Engineers); only the Navy would have use for its Oceanography Command; and the Air Force—always at the leading edge of technology—obviously needs its Systems Command to handle the research and development that the Army and Navy keep under their matériel commands. The individual service chiefs and their Pentagon staffs, who are officially excluded from the operational chain of command, would be most fully employed by the attempt to supervise the enormously variegated activities of the supporting commands; mostly they do not even try.

Under the present system, by now very widely criticized, civilian functions within the Pentagon are most unevenly split between the secretaries of the Army, Navy, and Air Force on the one hand (each with his undersecretary, his assistant secretaries, and their staffs), and the Secretary of Defense on the other, who has his own undersecretaries, assistant secretaries, assistants, directors, and advisers, each with his or her staff, sometimes very large. In theory, all that belongs to the upkeep of one service is supposed to be decided by the Secretary of that service in the first instance, while the use of forces, and any decisions that affect all services, belong to the Secretary of Defense. But in fact his own vast organization (modestly known as the Office of the Secretary of Defense) now reaches into all matters, leaving virtually nothing in the hands of the service Secretaries exclusively.

In practice this means that for most matters, there are at least three layers of *higher* management: the appropriate uniformed command at the service level, the Secretary's staff for that service, and then one or more parts of the Office of the Secretary of Defense. If a clever engineer imagines a new weapon for the Air Force, and if the research-and-development office specializing in that class of weapons approves of the idea, funding for its development must first be authorized by the Systems Command, then by the Air Force Assistant Secretary for Research and Development, and then by the staff of the Undersecretary of Defense for Research and Engineering.

Actually, this grossly simplifies the process. The Office of the Secretary of Defense includes a Director for Program Analysis and Evaluation, with his own large staff, skilled in mathematical techniques of analysis designed to uncover unnecessary or excessively costly "programs"; the engineer's clever idea may not survive their scrutiny, especially if its virtues cannot conveniently be presented in numerical form. And then of course there is the overall budget to consider—and for that the Secretary of Defense has an Assistant Secretary–Comptroller, and he too has a large staff empowered to overrule all who come before them. If the engineer's idea has any international implications—because, say, the new weapon would compete with a foreign product, made by a valued and needy ally, whose purchase had already been promised—the Under Secretary of Defense for Policy will also be forced to intervene, and he too has a staff inclined to be very active. All this takes place, of course, before the project is submitted for approval to the Congress, which will also appraise, investigate, and second-guess.

All these hurdles are a formidable barrier to innovation, yet we know that a great many new weapons are successfully brought from research to production. But the process takes a very long time—so many years that the armed forces rarely receive the full benefit of American scientific advancement: by the time a new weapon actually reaches service use, it is usually no longer new, and its Soviet counterpart and counter-measure are not far behind. Thus our insistence on overmanagement has much the same effect as all the restrictions of Soviet life have on the creativity of Soviet scientists.

And the multiple layers of management, the diffusion of authority, also have another effect: they greatly complicate everything that goes through the system. Only very rarely does the clever idea become a clever weapon of simple and economical ingenuity; as it obtains the approval of office after office, more and more requirements are specified, layer by layer, each adding cost and complexity. The F-16 fighter-bomber of the Air Force—which is now filled with electronic devices and costs more than $25 million a copy—started off as the "lightweight fighter" idea, a simple, cheap, but lethal fighter strictly for air combat, with no radar, no computer, and the smallest possible airframe built around the most powerful engine available for maximum agility.[33] But the Air Force has a Systems Command to write out the specifications—a huge organization with 34 general officers, 11,077 other officers, 15,000 other ranks, and tens of thousands of civilians in 1984, all dedicated to the pursuit of engineering excellence in every way.[34] Had the original idea (it came from the Air staff) simply been approved for development and production, none of the office directors, managers, and experts of Systems Command would have had a role in the proceedings—a very serious matter, since nowadays the Air Force designs a new fighter only once in a decade.

But a few thousand officers did have their say. Some insisted (successfully) that the new fighter should be a little larger to carry bombs as well, not just air-combat weapons; others demanded (successfully) the fitting of a radar; others still required (successfully) that their pet new-technology devices be included as well, beginning with a computer. By the time each level of the Systems Command had approved the idea and sent it up to the Pentagon staffs for review, the F-16 was no longer simple and cheap, and it became even less so as more military and civilian officials had their turn. The outcome is not a bad fighter—in fact, it is quite good, though far more expensive than it should have been—but the Israeli Air Force, the only one to have used the F-16 in combat, has found it a very poor bomber and believes it should have remained the pure air-combat machine originally intended.

An overcomplicated system usually overcomplicates needlessly; but it always delays, and sometimes prevents innovation altogether. When it comes to weapons, the powerful American passion for technological advancement helps greatly in overcoming the bureaucratic barriers. But when the new has no technological content, when it is organizations and procedures that need change, there is no such help. Then the layering of authority can become an absolute obstacle to the new. That is the fundamental cause of the present decrepitude of the defense establishment as a whole: the organization cannot renew itself because too many within have the power to stop change—and no change has been imposed from without.

Standing back from the details, the broad outlines of the structure have now emerged: as we saw, the combat forces of each service are supposedly controlled by "unified" or "specified" joint service commands, but they still respond first and last to their own service fiefdoms, which train, equip, and maintain them with their own supporting commands, under the supervision of their own service chiefs, who alone decide the fate of each officer's career. Over each service there is a civilian Secretary with no power at all in operational matters, but who is free to use his own staff to supervise the supervisors.

Over the services and their civilian secretariats, and over the all-service defense agencies, there is the Secretary of Defense, who has his formidable Office to help him supervise and manage, at least in matters of research and development, foreign policy, health and welfare, manpower and logistics, public relations, legal questions, intelligence oversight, and above all, finance and accounting. With their help, the Secretary of Defense oversees the preparation of the annual defense budget and monitors its outlays during the year, striving always to be a good manager. And the Secretary needs much help to manage more than four million men and women, 1,270 military installations worldwide, the spending of $285 billion and the upkeep of military alliances with forty-odd countries.

Only in one regard is the Secretary of Defense ill served: he has no source of disinterested and expert military advice; no central military staff to help him examine, evaluate, and perhaps change the operation of the armed forces or improve the military strategy he works so hard to manage. Some Secretaries have simply ignored the entire question of strategy; hardly any have tried to focus on the operation of the armed forces—to question, say, the obsession of the Marines with classic amphibious landings in the Iwo Jima style, or the refusal of the Air Force to give up its role of close air support, notwithstanding today's proliferation of antiaircraft weapons, or the Navy's entire concept of aircraft-carrier operations, for which less glamorous missions (e.g., mine warfare) are persistently sacrificed. These are all intricate questions, very hard to investigate, especially when there is only the shared-out Joint Chiefs organization to help in the work, instead of a central military staff independent of service fiefdoms. Thus the successive Secretaries of Defense have tended to seek the largest possible budgets for the armed forces, and they have tried to achieve economies and efficiencies while doing little or nothing to improve operations, or to reappraise the overall military strategies. This tendency, exemplified by the current holder of the post as of this writing, brings to mind the proverbial man in a hurry who believed that he could best reach his destination by driving as fast as possible, without wasting time to find the right road.

Historically, to be sure, it was by driving as fast as possible that the United States won its wars, by building up forces that could win by sheer matériel superiority and brute-force methods, regardless of poor tactics and clumsy operations, and with only the most prosaic of strategies. Unfortunately, the Soviet Union cannot be simply outgunned, as Germany and Japan were by 1944; a reliance on sheer matériel superiority is disastrous when the other side has more of everything. Hence for the first time the United States needs strategic coherence, operational craft, and tactical ingenuity—all things quite unobtainable from the present military establishment.

CHAPTER FOUR

☆

A Greater Enormity: The Military Power of the Soviet Union

The second great barrier to understanding and reform is the counterpart to the immensity of our own armed forces, the still greater magnitude of the forces ranged against them. Our own armed forces are difficult enough to comprehend, but to reach sensible conclusions about our defense we have to understand the true nature of the military power of the Soviet Union, and that is even more difficult.

☆

It is impossible to grow up in America without being conscious of the vastness of the land and the unique dimensions of its wealth. Not much given to arrogance and quite devoid of any imperial sense of superiority, Americans nevertheless approach the outside world with a presumption of material superiority—and with good reason: the United States remains by far the world's richest country. Others may have better restaurants, or even better universities; others may have outpaced the United States in productivity in some industries or many; and nowadays there are several foreign countries in which average incomes exceed the American level. But these are all new developments not yet fully absorbed into the minds of most Americans, and the United States still produces and consumes much more than any other country, and almost twice as much as the Soviet Union. Our minds therefore resist the notion that, large as the American military forces undoubtedly are, those of the Soviet Union are larger still, and in some ways much more powerful.

During the 1970s, when our perpetual debate over national defense was greatly concerned with rival computations of the American–Soviet military balance, it was still possible to believe that leftover advantages in such weapons as heavy-bomber squadrons, the B-52s of the Strategic Air Command, outweighed the new Soviet advantage in ballistic missiles based on land, or that the dozen large American aircraft carriers built during the 1950s and still in service were somehow a greater force than the many nuclear attack submarines the Soviet Union was building. The debate was never settled, because apples cannot be compared with oranges, but even as the futile arguments continued, matters were evolving in a direction that was all too clear. American forces were declining as the post-Vietnam reductions continued year after year, while Soviet forces were steadily increasing. Thus after much statistical disputation, the debate was finally overtaken by changing realities. By the end of the 1970s the debate over the "military balance" was over: only the size of the gap remained in dispute. That unhappy outcome received due recognition during the presidential elections of 1980, when both President Carter and Candidate Reagan advocated increased defense spending, disagreeing—and not by much—only over the amount; and the same was true of the 1984 elections.

During the last few years, a fairly large American rearmament has taken place amidst so much controversy that the average citizen can be excused for having formed a greatly inflated notion of its dimensions— certainly of the amount of spending that has been taken from social programs and shifted to the Pentagon.* In any case it would take more than a few years of increased budgets to reverse an imbalance of forces that had grown during the entire 1968–1980 period, when the sharply declining and then very slowly rising American defense effort was intersected by the Soviet buildup, which increased steadily until 1977 or so, then rising at a slower pace, though still exceeding the American rate of increase until 1981.

* In 1982, with the Reagan rearmament in full swing, defense took up 25.7 percent of the federal budget, as compared with 51.2 percent for all social services and welfare payments; in 1979 under President Carter the figures had been 24 percent and 52.3 percent.[1]

The Investment Gap

All measures of the gap are treacherous. No comparison even remotely valid can be made between defense spending in rubles and in dollars.[2] For one thing, the Soviet Union does not reveal its defense budgets. Each year some amusingly small figure is duly published, but not even full-time Soviet propagandists seriously pretend that it actually states the real amount of military expenditure.[3] And even if we could see the actual budget figures used by the inner circle of the Soviet Government, we would still know very little, in part because we cannot easily compare dollars and rubles (there is no such thing as a real exchange rate, as there is, say, between dollars and Belgian francs), and partly because we cannot know the true cost of Soviet weapons produced in state factories. Our only comfort is the certainty that the gentlemen in the Kremlin also have no precise figure for the cost of their own military forces. The price billed to the Soviet Defense Ministry for the latest nuclear submarine might be set at 5 rubles or 5 billion rubles, but either way it would make no difference, since neither of those numbers would measure the real cost in the way that the dollar price of an American submarine does—by telling us what other things we must give up in order to have that weapon.

For those who are not content with the very visible evidence of the several thousand Soviet tanks, the hundreds of aircraft and missiles, and the dozens of warships built each year during a period when the United States was producing its own tanks by the hundred, aircraft by the dozen, and warships by the handful, there are two pairs of statistics that might be worth inspecting: the military investment of the United States versus that of the Soviet Union, and the military investment of the United States plus NATO plus Japan versus that of the Soviet Union plus the Warsaw Pact countries. Excluding all the manpower and operating costs that can scarcely be compared at all, these statistics measure each side's annual investment in equipment, research and development, and facilities, with everything priced at the current American cost. Although the rate of rubles to dollars is always imprecise, and though there is still ample room for error in estimating production costs, since our industry is different, and we *never* have production runs as long as the Soviets', the comparison of military investments is unaffected by the huge discrepancy between well-paid American military men and the mass of Soviet manpower, conscripts who receive only a few rubles a month of pocket money.

The Soviet and American investment figures were roughly equal in 1970, at just over $80 billion (in 1984 dollars). By 1975 the Soviet figure was more than $100 billion, while the American was under $60 billion.[4] At that time, American defense budgets were going down in current dollars, and the value of each dollar was also going down fast, because of high inflation. But pay and benefits were increasing sharply—to attract all those "volunteers" to the all-volunteer force. As a result, there was not much left for the purchase of equipment or for other investment. It was only in 1978 that the American investment figure rose above $60 billion, and by then the Soviet figure was nearly twice as great, at $110 billion. The gap did not begin to close—and then only slowly—until 1980.[5] By then the Soviets had an eleven-year lead, and the extra American rearmament effort would have to continue for years and years to make up the difference.

The United States would not, of course, have to face Soviet military power on its own, unless it were caught in some expeditionary conflict all by itself—as in the Persian Gulf, for example, where there are no real allies, and where no European ally could send large forces. Otherwise, certainly in Western Europe and the Far East, the United States can count on rich and fairly well-armed allies. As it turns out, during 1968–1980, the long dark night of American underspending by choice and by inflation, the European allies in the North Atlantic Alliance and Japan did rather better in keeping up military investment, though not well enough to make up for the American decline. If we compare investment for the United States and its allies (NATO plus Japan) with the Soviet Union and its Warsaw Pact satellites, we discover that the lines did not intersect until 1971–1972, after which the Warsaw Pact total quickly rose above the U.S./Allied total. By 1976 the Soviet side was nearly $110 billion, while our side was at roughly $90 billion; after that, the gap began to close, much more rapidly than the U.S.–Soviet gap.[6] But as late as 1981 it was still $15 billion, with just under $120 billion on our side and roughly $135 billion on the Soviet side.[7] The difference, therefore, was no longer huge, and it has diminished further since then. Were it not for the fact that the West relies on better equipment to offset its numerical inferiority, the entire question would be of scant importance. As it is, the accumulated imbalance in military investment is the chief concern of the Alliance.

Western Quality Versus Soviet Quantity

Retreating from financial statistics, which after all measure only what is put in, and not what comes out in weapons and forces, we can examine the introduction of the larger and more visible weapons in detail. During the years 1974–1983, the Soviet Union and its Warsaw Pact allies added 27,850 new battle tanks; the United States and NATO added 10,450. For "tactical" combat aircraft, the numbers are a round 10,000 versus 7,300; for intercontinental ballistic missiles, 2,035 (all Soviet) versus 346 (all American); for major surface warships, 107 versus 172 (more than half belonging to our allies); for artillery, mortars, and rocket launchers, 29,500 versus 3,575; for ballistic-missile submarines, 33 (all Soviet) versus 5 (of which three are British and French).[8]

When we look at the Soviet production figures for these major weapons, we have the feeling of things already seen, but only once before—when the United States was producing big weapons in big numbers during the Second World War, when President Roosevelt kept his pledge to create an arsenal for democracy.

Western weapons, to be sure, are usually more elaborate, much more costly, and, one hopes, more powerful than their Soviet counterparts—but not always. For example, within the light-armored-vehicle category (55,400 versus 17,500), the Soviet Union builds well-armed BMP combat carriers in large numbers, while aside from a few hundred American Bradleys (600 in 1984), most Western vehicles are mere troop carriers.[9] In any case, the Soviet numerical advantage is so large in many classes of weapons that it easily overcomes the quality advantage of the West, which has diminished very greatly in recent years. In part the gap narrowed because much of the Soviet investment went into research and development. To a greater extent, however, the sheer volume of Soviet production also made a difference in *quality*. Because most of the new weapons have been used for replacement rather than to expand forces that are already very large, the high rate of production has resulted in a faster renewal of the total inventory, thus translating quantity into quality (very appropriately, for that conversion is a much stressed one in the Marxist faith).

Thus our very latest first-line fighters are still distinctly superior to their Soviet counterparts, but when we assess the fighter forces as a whole, we are comparing American aircraft that are more than nine years old on average [10] with Soviet aircraft that are five or six years old on average. As long as we continue to rely on so many ten-year-old fighters, twenty-year-old tanks, and thirty-year-old ships, the technological edge of the United States is converted into military power at a very slow rate. So it is misleading to compare American and Soviet weapon engineering, because in many cases the American engineering of many years ago is competing against much more recent Soviet technology.

Engineering Quality and Combat Effectiveness

In any event, quality as defined by engineers does not always translate directly into combat effectiveness. War is not fought by blueprints and factories, and technological superiority does not always yield advantages in combat. Certainly advanced materials and advanced processes may be negated by poor design. Any layman can tell at a glance that the American M-16 rifle is *technologically* much superior to the Soviet AK-47: the American rifle is made of advanced plastics and sophisticated light alloys, while the Soviet has only plain steel and wood; the M-16 has a precision finish, while the AK-47 is a result of the roughest methods of mass production. But although the M-16 costs more (roughly twice as much), its engineering superiority yields no perceptible advantage in combat. Indeed, many practical soldiers insist that the AK-47 is the better weapon by far: it jams less easily, and has a much better feel than the flimsy M-16.*

Still, technological advancement usually does yield a benefit; the open question is whether the superior quality of Western weapons in many categories can still offset Soviet superiority in numbers. In military history there are many cases of battles and even wars decisively won because of more advanced weapons. Certainly in late-nineteenth-century colonial battles, the breech-loaded rifles and early Gatling machine guns of the British Imperial infantry slaughtered African warriors by the thousand as they charged with their spears; at the start of the Second

---

* Unmeasurable in the computers of the weapon-purchasing bureaucrats, "feel" affects morale and is therefore of the greatest possible importance; the AK-47 is handy but reassuringly solid; the M-16 feels like a large toothbrush.

World War, Polish cavalrymen had no better fortunes when they charged German panzers;* and in 1941, Japanese Zero fighters shot down cloth-and-wire British biplanes over Malaya with impunity. Nowadays it is possible that quiet-running American nuclear-powered submarines may have a decisive advantage over their noisier Soviet counterparts; in the underwater struggle of the blind, the silent boat can stalk its prey undetected. (But the latest Soviet submarines reportedly can dive deeper, and could gain an advantage from their much higher speed, noise and all.)

But just as the complete misuse of advanced technology, as in the M-16 rifle, is quite unusual, so is the opposite extreme. Most often, the higher quality of Western weapons yields only a modest advantage in combat, a matter of fractions and degree—not the absolute advantage of machine guns against spears. Contrary to many claims, it is a delusion that the spectacular recent victories of the Israelis over the Syrians prove otherwise. When American-built jet fighters in Israeli hands destroy Soviet fighters in Syrian hands by the dozen, with no loss of their own (the 1982 score was 87:0), the encounter is really between the two air forces—each with its own institutional approach to air warfare, its own pattern of selecting and training pilots and ground crews, its own Intelligence, good and bad, and above all, its own operational methods. The Israelis have developed in concept and by most intensive training their own version of an aerial task force made out of airborne radars (E2-Cs), large fighters for interception at medium ranges with radar-guided missiles (F-15s), and smaller fighters for dogfighting with guns and infrared missiles (Kfirs and F-16s).

In the past, the Israelis did very well in air combat against the Syrians, regularly shooting down twenty or thirty aircraft and losing only one or two. But until they had their task force assembled and trained to work together, Israeli fighters already absorbed in dogfights would sometimes be caught by surprise by Syrian fighters that reached the scene undetected. With the task force, the airborne-radar aircraft could detect and track each Syrian fighter from the moment of takeoff; the large F-15 fighters could be employed to break up formations by sending their radar-guided missiles into them; and the light fighters already in the air could be disengaged in time to meet the approaching Syrian fighters. Syrian pilots, or Soviet ones for that matter, would have suffered great losses even in straight individual combat with their exceedingly accom-

---

* Largely a legend, of course, but it did happen, if only once or twice.

plished Israeli counterparts. Moreover, the average, mass-deployed MiG-21 and MiG-23 Soviet-built fighters flown by the Syrians were certainly inferior to the latest and best American fighters flown by the Israelis.

If the air forces of the Western alliance could reproduce in Europe the successes of Israeli air power, then the technological advantages of American and European aviation would be translated into a broad air supremacy that would have a large impact on the total military balance. But that is a distant hope. In the first place, the Soviet Air Force has its own version of an aerial task force. Its elements and training may not be up to Israeli standards, but Soviet fighter pilots would not find themselves fighting on their own, like the Syrians, against a well-concerted array of radars, missiles, and razor-sharp dogfighting pilots. Second, the fighter forces of the Alliance are not equipped predominantly with the latest and best aircraft but rather with a mixture of older heavy fighters (F-4s), older light fighters (Mirages and F-5s), and fighter-bombers of low air-combat performance (Jaguars), as well as the Tornado strike-fighter, which is brand-new, but not designed for air combat.* Thus in mass deployments the quality advantage of the Western fighter force as a whole over the newer Soviet fighters is far smaller than the unit-quality advantage that the Israelis have enjoyed. Third, only the U.S. Air Force has a really integrated aerial task force; the other air forces have only some of the parts. Finally, because of funding restrictions on flight hours, but also because of crippling safety rules, the fighter pilots of the Western alliance are not as well prepared for combat as their Israeli counterparts.

Once the special advantages that the Israelis have enjoyed in their air combat with Soviet-built aircraft are removed from the comparison, it is possible to make a realistic assessment of the worth of Soviet combat aircraft. The MiG-21, still widely deployed in the Warsaw Pact in a variety of versions, some greatly improved, is a formidable dogfighter, fast and agile. In Vietnam, American fighters found it difficult to defeat earlier versions of the MiG-21: during the entire war, from 1965 to 1973, only 87 MiG 21s were shot down by Navy, Marine Corps, and Air Force fighters, and Vietnamese MiG-21s managed to shoot down 47 American fighters.[11] A total of 106 older MiG-17s and MiG-19s were also shot down in air combat, but even those older machines inflicted a total of

---

* The Royal Air Force is acquiring an air-defense version of the Tornado, suitable for the interception of bombers, even if not for the "air superiority" role against more agile fighters.

34 losses on American fighters.[12] The overall ratio against Vietnamese pilots of so-so quality was therefore 193/81, or 2.38:1—by no means a splendid success.[13] That is solid evidence of the worth of Soviet jet fighters even then.

The MiG-23, absent from Vietnam and now in standard deployment, is a less racy machine than its predecessor, but more powerful all around, with more range and payload and much more elaborate electronics. Its ground-attack variant, the MiG-27, is clearly superior to its nearest Western equivalent, the much older Anglo-French Jaguar. The high-altitude fighter-interceptor-and-reconnaissance MiG-25, whose basic design is now twenty years old, remains the fastest fighter in the world (Mach 2.8) and has old-fashioned but very powerful electronics. The newest MiG fighters, the MiG-29 and MiG-31, are both heavy fighter-interceptors with radars that attempt the hardest of all tasks, detecting targets flying close to the ground. Finally, the new Su-27 light fighter is certainly very agile and may turn out to be the successor to the classic MiG-21.

None of these aircraft, not even the latest, is as good as the best American-built jet, just as the Anglo-German-Italian Tornado is a better aircraft than its Soviet equivalent, the SU-24 light bomber. But the average quality of Western fighters, old and new, is not much better than the Soviet average in mass deployment, and the same is true of the air-combat missiles of both sides: the (very costly) latest American models are much superior, but the depots of the Alliance are still filled with older missiles.

Similar considerations apply to Western technological superiority in ground combat. If the Western alliance could do to the Russians in Europe what the Israelis did to the Syrian Army in the Vale of Lebanon during those three days of fighting in 1982, then the Alliance would have little to worry about in defending its frontiers against the forces of the Warsaw Pact. But it would be pure delusion to interpret the outcome in Lebanon as proving the superiority of Western armaments.

First, the Israelis were not outnumbered, as the Alliance would be in Europe; on the contrary, they had the numerical advantage, as a four-division Israeli armored corps fought a total of about three Syrian divisions, of which one did not arrive until the last day.[14] Second, the Israelis were not armed with a representative array of Western ground weapons but rather with their own peculiar hybrids, conversions, and purely domestic weapons, whose quality is superior on average, even in the small arms. For example, the rifles that the Alliance predominantly uses, the American M-16 and the Belgian FN, are also much used by the Israeli Army, but mainly to equip the truck drivers of supply columns, service troops in the rear, clerks and women soldiers, overage infantry used only for static defense, and elderly home guards; most front-line troops had the far superior Israeli Galil automatic rifle.

The Israeli artillery, with its combination of locally produced and American weapons, was not better equipped in 1982 than the Alliance, but in Lebanon the Israelis had many more guns and howitzers than the Syrians—on top of complete air supremacy. Western forces, by contrast, would be outgunned by a large margin in a European war. The Israeli armored forces, which make up the bulk of Israel's ground army, were also numerically superior and had a large quality advantage, too. On the face of it, the tanks of the Israelis were much inferior to those of the Alliance: most were Centurions, a British-built tank designed before 1945 and long since phased out by the British Army; many of the rest were American M-48s or early-version M-60 Pattons, as well as captured Soviet T-62s and older T-55s. Not more than two brigades (roughly 200 tanks) had the new Israeli-made Merkava, itself not well regarded by many armor fanciers because it is very heavy (60 metric tons) and rather underpowered. By contrast, the tank forces of the Alliance in Europe have ultra modern American M-1s and West German Leopard IIs, well-protected British Challengers and Chieftains, and a mass of still quite respectable Leopard Is, French AMX-30s, and American M-60s, all of more recent vintage than Israeli average.

But appearances deceive, and it is worth considering the difference between a war-ready force such as the Israeli Army (and no doubt the Afghanistan-tested Soviet Army) and the armies of the Alliance, which have never quite emancipated themselves from their origin as largely symbolic forces, mere trip wires for nuclear retaliation. On closer examination, it turns out that almost all the Israeli tanks were heavily modified hybrids by 1982—uniformly up-gunned to the 105mm standard and supplied with Israeli armor-piercing ammunition of exceptional penetration; powerfully up-engined with new American diesels; and fitted with ultramodern laser range finders for accurate long-range shooting. And the Merkava turned out to be a far better tank than its known specifications could have suggested: very comfortable, to keep its crews fresh and alert; surprisingly maneuverable, for all its weight; and exceptionally well protected. But what made the Israeli tanks superior to the Western average was not these visible upgrades, which merely offset the defects of older tanks, but the many small modifications, a variety of gadgets and novel protection devices—built-in mortars, revolutionary active-armor plates, vertical searchlights, electronic fire suppressors—all the products of battle experience and highly focused research and development. They are all absent from the tanks of the Alliance: such modifications do not involve enough advanced technology to excite the interest of the research-and-development bureaucracies; they are too cheap to activate the contractor/union lobbies that influence Western purchasing; and often they are simply too small to attract the attention of defense managers. But they make all the difference in combat.

It is therefore unnecessary to insist on the superior quality of Israeli ground forces and their commanders to reject the analogy between Lebanon and Europe that would be so reassuring to the Alliance. Contrary to the misleading impression created by the tank battles of 1982, the most modern Soviet tanks are powerful machines whose armor is hard to penetrate, and are especially dangerous at the short and medium ranges likely in Europe—where any inferiority in Soviet gunnery electronics would count for little, while the very large 125mm guns of Soviet tanks would be devastating. As it is, the Soviet T-72s in mass deployment are at least equal and most likely superior to the average, predominantly older Western tanks, few of which have a gun as powerful and most of which are less well armored. Likewise, the new Soviet T-80 should hold its own against the American M/1 and the West German Leopard II; probably somewhat inferior in quality, it will also be much more abundant.

As for the rest of Soviet ground equipment, nobody can dispute the quality of Soviet small arms, which are at least as good as the latest Western weapons and distinctly superior to the average. Similarly, Soviet guns and howitzers have long been recognized as not less than excellent. Though formerly fielded as classic towed weapons, in recent years they have been mass-produced in self-propelled versions, mounted on tracked and armored vehicles—thus eliminating one more long-standing Western advantage. Certainly the United States has no technological superiority in all such prosaic armaments, and attempts to introduce advanced technology within ancient tube weapons (by producing laser-guided shells, for instance) have had disappointing results.

One category of Soviet ground equipment that fortunately remains untested in the Middle East could turn out to be decisive in an East–West war: chemical weapons and chemical defenses. Nobody disputes the Soviet advantage in this area, which is not even the product of advanced technology but simply a matter of will. Confusing ethics with mere aesthetics, Western parliaments (and the U.S. Congress) oppose chemical weapons—or at least, politicians who know better do not like to be seen approving their production, as if there were a difference between death by bomb or bullet and death by poison. And military bureaucrats do not press the point because there is no institutional cult for chemical weapons as there is for the sleek jet fighters of the air forces, the majestic ships of the navies, and the formidable tanks of the armies. Thus, one more imbalance is unnecessarily created: Soviet ground forces are fully equipped for chemical war, while most Western armies do not even have sufficient supplies of defensive masks and suits, let alone the gas-filled shells, bombs, and warheads that the Soviet army stocks in great quantities.[15]

One consequence is that the Soviet Army could achieve victories in the field by the *mere threat* of using its chemical weapons, conveyed by sinister but harmless smoke barrages. Western troops outfitted in their clumsy and exhausting chemical suits would be greatly hampered in trying to defend the front against Soviet forces that retain the initiative in using chemical weapons and could therefore fight unencumbered till they chose otherwise. And unprotected Western troops (as many are) are likely to panic and break at the merest sign of what seems to be a chemical attack. Ironically, the weakness of Western chemical armaments could thus trigger the use of far more terrible nuclear weapons in the urgent circumstances of an imminent collapse of the front.

Even more fundamental is the difference that prevents us from translating to the Soviet–Western balance the results of the June 9, 1982, Israeli strike against the very large array of Soviet-made equipment upon which the Syrians relied for their antiaircraft defenses in Lebanon. Of all the Israeli military successes since 1948, none was as dramatic as the utter destruction of the dense network of missile batteries and radar-controlled mobile guns that provided multiple layers of overlapping coverage for the air defense of the Biqa, the Vale of Lebanon. All competent observers had fully expected that the Israelis would eventually prevail in this "defense-suppression" campaign. None expected them to knock out *eighteen* missile batteries (the United States has some fifty worldwide) and many guns in a couple of hours, without losing a single aircraft in the process. There is no doubt that if this result could be reproduced in Europe, the consequences would be of decisive strategic importance. The major Soviet strength is on the ground, not in air power. Soviet armored forces—advancing to break through the Western front line to reach deep into the rear, in order to cut supply lines, overrun air bases, and "hug" cities (to dissuade nuclear strikes)—would mainly have to fear air attacks against their long road columns, and their defense against air attack is provided by the same mobile antiaircraft missiles and guns that the Syrians used in the Biqa. To be sure, Soviet and Warsaw Pact fighter-interceptors would also be fully engaged to blunt the impact of Western air attacks against the ground forces, but they would be much more effective on the Soviet side of the front, where the ground radar network could offer good coverage of the air, thus allowing the control centers to direct the fighters effectively.

If it could be shown that Soviet air-defense missiles and guns could easily be neutralized, it would follow that Soviet armored penetrations of the Western front would be fatally exposed to air attack. If that were so, then the entire threat to the Alliance would be greatly diminished, for the Alliance is far better placed to fight a war of attrition on the front line itself than to cope with fast-moving armored columns penetrating into its very vulnerable deep rear. Hence the eagerness with which the Israeli strike of June 9, 1982, was studied by the experts of East and West alike.

Unfortunately, the results were most disappointing to those eager to replicate the Israeli method. As it turned out, the Israelis had used some American electronic countermeasures, but also much homemade equipment of their own, including pilotless observation mini-aircraft. Still, all the equipment employed in the strike is either already in hand or could easily be acquired by Western air forces. But the fatal obstacle to replication has nothing to do with equipment: it is the broader circumstances that cannot be repeated. The Israelis had the Syrian air defenses close by, a mere 40 kilometers or less down the road from their positions, and they did not hesitate to exploit this proximity. For many months before the strike they frequently overflew the Syrian batteries and kept their pilotless observation aircraft overhead for hours at a time; they monitored all transmissions, even the trivia of administrative messages; and they sent scouts to watch the Syrians as they trained and operated the equipment.

This produced a far richer intelligence picture than even the United States can obtain by its satellite cameras and electronic receivers. By June 9, 1982, the Israelis knew not only the number, type, and locations of the weapons and the frequency and power of the radars but also the working habits and rotation times of the crews, the tactics of the control centers, and more. Through their long observation, the Israelis even had a feel for the confidence and expertise of particular crews and controllers. Having thus studied the Syrian array in intimate detail, the Israelis could design their methods to exploit very specifically each weakness they identified, while evading the strengths of a potentially formidable system. Proximity also enabled the Israelis to employ some ground-launched rockets to distract and attack the Syrian defenses.

By contrast, the Soviet and Warsaw Pact air defenses are not confined to a small area such as the Biqa. The antiaircraft units of the Soviet ground forces that are now kept ready opposite the Western "front" are deployed in depth across East Germany and Poland, Czechoslovakia and Hungary. Moreover, these units are not on their own. The missile belts and fighter-intercept zones of the *territorial* air defenses (as opposed to the mobile antiaircraft units attached to the ground forces) stretch back for hundreds of miles, eventually blending into the air defenses of the Soviet Union itself. The mobile air defenses that a successful Soviet breakthrough would bring into the Western rear could therefore remain silent and inactive during a prewar period, thus denying Western intelligence the benefit of listening to their radars and transmissions.

In any event, the vast array of both mobile and territorial air defenses of the Warsaw Pact cannot possibly be investigated in the depth and detail that the Israelis achieved in their anatomy of the Biqa defenses. Nor can the Western alliance violate the Warsaw Pact's frontiers on a continuous basis, as the Israelis did, to monitor the inner workings of the antiaircraft forces and territorial air defenses.

Finally, there is one difference that dominates all others. The Israeli ground offensive had been under way for three days when the strike was launched. The Israelis could not, therefore, catch the Syrian air defenses by surprise; by then it was perfectly obvious what would happen next. But the Israelis could and did devote their full resources and complete attention to the defense-suppression strike and the concurrent air combat, without having to worry about the air-support needs of their own ground forces. The Western alliance, by contrast, would have to confront the task of attacking the air defenses during the first and most traumatic days of war—when the outnumbered and surprised ground forces would most probably be flooding the air headquarters with desperate calls for assistance, and when a good many fighters would be engaged in air combat with the Soviet and Warsaw Pact air forces. In such circumstances, precisely coordinated, finely tuned, and deliberate strikes in the Israeli style of June 1982 would simply be out of the question.

Once all these matters are duly considered, it is possible to make a sober and realistic assessment of the true worth of Soviet air-defense weapons. Of the fixed-site missiles, the older version of the SAM-2, by now internationally known, was quite effective at the higher altitudes in Vietnam, until electronically countermeasured. It was then greatly improved and worked reasonably well in the Middle East, until countermeasured again. Now modernized once more, it remains in service in huge numbers (400 sites at the last count) in the territorial air defenses of the Soviet Union and the Pact countries. Not much newer but also upgraded, very much larger, and with an exceptionally long reach for an antiaircraft missile (almost 200 miles) is the SAM-5, long in service in the Soviet Union and now forward-deployed in Eastern Europe as well.[16]

The main effect of these higher-altitude weapons is to dissuade hostiles from trying to fly over the defenses, and thus to make them vulnerable to the greater number of lower-altitude weapons—SAM-3s, SAM-4s, and the versatile SAM-6 of Middle East fame (which wrought havoc with Israeli air power in 1973, only to be ignominiously countermeasured by 1982, and then upgraded). These weapons in turn drive hostile aircraft into low and very low altitudes—not merely when they actually strike but also when they are in transit to the target. And at the low altitudes Soviet weapons are present in still greater numbers: the hand-portable SAM-7, the sophisticated radar-guided SAM-8, the simpler, more abundant infrared SAM-9, the much more costly and more advanced SAM-10, and the yet more modern (but less ambitious) SAM-11, and SAM-13, as well as antiaircraft guns by the thousand, large and small, radar-guided and not, armored and self-propelled, towed and static.

Even the simplest of these weapons, without radar guidance, sufficed to destroy two Navy aircraft over Lebanon on December 4, 1983. When these weapons form a concerted array with overlapping capabilities, they are formidable. Since the United States relies heavily on air power to make up for the weakness of its ground forces, the strength of Soviet antiaircraft forces weighs heavily in the overall military balance.

The Soviet style in weapon design—stressing raw performance (speed in aircraft, range in artillery, etc.); an absence of embellishments, but also of useful gadgets and valuable comforts; a severe economy in manufacture, oddly combined with a bold use of advanced materials—is faithfully reproduced in the ships and submarines of the Soviet Navy. American ships have long been designed not as weapons but as flexible containers for well-housed crews, elaborate electronics, and a changing cast of weapons. Generous unused space for future add-on weapons, and large storage areas for long endurance, result in warships with excess tonnage for the weapons they carry; hence their characteristic clean decks and boxy superstructures. Soviet warships are by contrast crowded with weapons, their superstructures are much smaller, and their bows cut a rakish angle.[17] Soviet warships still crowd in many more weapons per ton than their American counterparts, but in recent years there has been a definite convergence in design: the latest Soviet warships have much more endurance and crew space than before, though still less than their American counterparts.[18] One critical aspect of Soviet design remains largely unknown: the extent and quality of damage-control features. Nothing is more easily overlooked in peacetime estimates; nothing is more important in war, for ships do get hit, and what counts is how far the fires and flooding then spread.

The latest Soviet warships of each class—the *Koni* frigates, the *Sovremennyy* and *Udaloy* destroyers, the *Krasina* and *Kirov* cruisers (the latter nuclear powered), and the *Kiev* medium aircraft carriers—are all quite obviously well-built and of sound design, at least in their known specifications.[19] Certainly in their weapons and sensors, and also in their observed conduct at sea, these newer warships, as yet present in small numbers, are comparable to their American counterparts. That was not true of most of their predecessors—the older cruisers, destroyers, and frigates, which are far inferior to their nominal American counterparts and still account for much of the Soviet Navy. For obvious reasons, promoters of American naval rearmament have been fond of straight numerical comparisons, in which the sadly inadequate *Kynda* (5,700 tons, of 1962 vintage) ranks as a cruiser, along with American ships twice its size; the makeshift *Kashin* (4,500 tons, 1963) and *Kotlin* (3700 tons, 1954), or even the pathetic *Skory* (3,080 tons, 1949) destroyers are compared to American ships much larger and superior;[20] and, most blatantly misleading, the large number of Soviet missile boats are boldly listed as though they were full-scale warships.

There is, of course, a fundamental strategic asymmetry that could excuse and even justify all such comparisons: the United States absolutely needs the oceans to maintain the vital link with its forward defenses in Europe and East Asia, and to reach expeditionary theaters such as the Persian Gulf. The Soviet Union, by contrast, can mount overland offensives into those theaters, and has no need to send a single ship to sea in order to conquer. The American Navy must therefore strive for sea control, while the Soviet Navy need worry only about sea denial, a far easier task. Moreover, all the shortcomings of its older warships would count for little if the Soviet Navy were to start off a naval war by a surprise attack. Because American and Soviet warships are frequently intermingled in times of crisis, as both sides deploy to the same coasts, a concerted missile strike could be devastating. Against all this is a plain geographic fact that makes it difficult to create a great naval power out of the Russian lands: the Soviet Union is mostly landlocked, its coastlines icebound, hard to reach, confined by straits, or all of the above.

The Soviet attack-submarine fleet—which has the Soviet surface fleet's advantage of numbers, with few of its disabilities, and is less affected by an unfavorable geography—is unambiguously a most powerful force. Important enough to warrant a very large effort even in the later 1950s, when the rest of the Navy was visibly neglected, the Soviet submarine fleet has been treated well in recent years. The latest attack submarines are extraordinarily ambitious in design, though they are produced in smaller numbers than their simpler predecessors (12 were produced in 1979, but only 7 in 1982).[21] That is just as well, since the two most recent nuclear-powered types have formidable specifications: the huge *Oscar* of fifteen thousand tons (the size of a cruiser), fitted with twenty-four cruise missiles for attack against ships; and the ultrafast and very deep-diving *Alfa,* by far the largest structure ever made of the costly metal titanium.[22] Moreover, though the older surface warships of the Soviet Navy are very unimpressive, the older attack submarines that are present in larger numbers—the cruise-missile Charlie Is and IIs and the torpedo Victor IIs and IIIs (all nuclear powered)—remain very effective. The Soviet Navy has also continued to produce diesel submarines (torpedo-firing Tangos and earlier Foxtrots), and these too are effective, certainly against merchant ships.

What makes the Soviet attack-submarine fleet so dangerous, quite apart from its numbers and quality, is the great increase in the vulnerability of the Western fleets as a whole, both military and commercial. A huge growth in the size of ships has brought about a drastic decline in their numbers. A 50,000-ton tanker was considered very large in the 1950s, when the oil trade was served by thousands of tankers; today a 250,000-ton tanker is common, and fewer than two hundred tankers carry most of the oil used by the Western world. During the Second World War, when German U-boats could scarcely attack warships, the Allied navies had 2,000-ton destroyers, 6,000-ton cruisers, and 30,000-ton aircraft carriers in large numbers. Today, each of those tonnages has doubled or trebled, the numbers are very small, and submarines can definitely attack them. It was a heroic feat for the diesel submarines of the Second World War—with their short-range torpedoes and 9-knot underwater speeds—to attack a warship; but it must be routine for 40-knot nuclear-powered submarines, especially if armed with cruise missiles. Thus the economically beneficial increase in the size of commercial ships has been disastrous for the West, from a naval point of view; and the insistence of the American Navy on building very large ships in each category—not merely carriers, which perhaps must be large, but all other ships—reveals a greater regard for the peacetime advantages of size than for prudence in the face of threats from the deep.

One last category of Soviet naval weapon that is entirely absent from the American Navy is also the most dangerous threat to its survival in any nonnuclear war: the long-range land-based naval bomber.[23] Under an agreement among the services that dates back more than thirty years, the American Navy is prohibited from having its own land-based strike aircraft—all such aircraft must belong to the Air Force. But the latter places a very low priority on antiship bombers, for ships are the Navy's business.* The Soviet Navy is under no similar restriction and relies heavily on land-based aircraft—far cheaper pound for pound than those fit for carriers, and unlimited in size.

Armed with missiles powerful enough to disable any ship, fast enough to reach quickly even distant waters, the *Backfire* naval bombers have a huge advantage over the American naval task forces they would seek out. In their normal operation, aircraft carriers and their air-defense cruisers rely on powerful radars.† But these are like giant flashlights in the dark; their beams can easily be detected and traced back with simple receivers. Attacking Soviet bombers can therefore keep their own radars silent and gain a major advantage in the electronic war that decides

---

* Now that large bombers can patrol the oceans, and loiter over them with air-refueling, it is only the Navy's bureaucratic interest that prevents "sea-control" by land-based aircraft. Certainly, the future "Stealth" bomber should make a formidable aerial cruiser, in addition to its other roles.

† Carrier task forces can operate in radar silence using the passive receivers of their E-2C aircraft to detect the radars of approaching hostile aircraft. But Soviet bombers too can approach silently, relying on satellite information to find the task forces.

the outcome. A great part of the strength of American Navy carrier task forces is already used up for their own protection; eventually, as each increase in the strength of Soviet naval-strike aviation evokes a greater defensive effort, American carriers and their escorts will be largely self-serving—very powerful in some theoretical sense, very difficult to attack, almost invulnerable perhaps, but also virtually useless because so much of their strength will be needed for self-defense.*

When that happens, it will be because of the bombers more than the submarines. In the meantime, American naval superiority remains a fact, but so does the Soviet Union's substantial immunity from naval power in any form, except for sea-launched nuclear weapons.

Are the Soviet Armed Forces Competent, or Merely Well Armed?

One thing is quite obvious: the recent military record of the Soviet Union compares very well with that of the United States; it contains neither small debacles, nor—so far—any failure in protracted war.

The powerful urge to see a Vietnam in Afghanistan remains frustrated: the guerrillas are not suppressed, but neither do they threaten the Soviet occupation. One small fact is enough to cut through all the justifiably proud claims of the Afghan guerrillas, to deny the hopeful analogy: fewer than *5 percent* of all Soviet Army troops, no more than five divisions, are in Afghanistan; many more divisions are idle at home. More than one-third of all American Army troops were in Vietnam by 1968, by contrast, and because of the large immovable overhead in the United States, that third was really more than one-half of the deployable strength. What we see in Afghanistan is not a frantic attempt to win and go home by Christmas, Easter, or the next election, but instead a leisurely imperial pacification. The Soviet Union controls the towns, from the police to the schools. Afghans thus have a choice: to accept Soviet rule and learn to live in the newest province of an empire that already has many provinces, or else to live out a hunted and miserable life roaming the mountains. It is the classic formula, once used most successfully by the Romans.

---

* This outcome could be mitigated if the offensive content of the carrier air wings were increased; the Navy is reportedly considering the introduction of advanced "stealth" fighter-bombers, a major improvement if modern munitions are also provided.

Perhaps in the years ahead the Soviet Union will withdraw all the same, in return for Afghanistan's neutralization under a government respectful of Soviet desires. Or else the country will become one more province, or at least a firmly held satellite. Either way, there will be no hurried evacuation, no abandonment.

In the meantime, to estimate the competence of the Soviet armed forces one should recall how the Soviet invasion began. On the night of December 27, 1979, elite airborne troops of the 105th Guards Airborne Division, reinforced with troops from two more such divisions, as well as KGB special assault detachments, moved into Kabul, the Afghan capital, to seize the Presidential palace, the telephone exchange, the radio and television station, the defense ministry, military headquarters, and the guarded refuge of the Afghan President in the Darulaman fortress.[24] Of course Afghanistan had been thoroughly penetrated and subverted long before the invasion. Still, it was by no means an easy operation. All the many things that can go wrong in warfare will go wrong, and more easily, in a commando operation in which everything must be done swiftly. Moving at night through a strange city, Soviet assault teams had to find specific buildings and even specific rooms under tight time schedules to achieve surprise simultaneously at each place, under very precise coordination to avoid fratricidal encounters.

By then Afghanistan was being invaded overland by five Soviet divisions, and the country's fate was sealed. If, however, Kabul had not been seized right from the start, then Afghan President Hafizullah Amin would have had the opportunity to muster some sort of defense with still loyal regular forces, which would have delayed the Soviet conquest and inflicted some losses. Much more important, Amin could have used radio and television to arouse an easily aroused people to armed resistance, and to call for foreign help. No country in the world, and certainly not the United States, could have intervened usefully, but Amin's appeal, by publicizing the fact that the venture was a blatant aggression, would have cost the Soviet Union much. Hence the considerable value of the Kabul operation, and the Soviet acceptance of considerable risks to pull it off. A mere handful of tanks drawn from the nearby Afghan division could have turned the Soviet landing areas into fields of massacre. And any serious delay in the overland linkup by the mechanized forces driving from the Soviet border over easily blocked mountain roads could have endangered the lightly equipped airborne forces. Boldly planned and well executed, the Kabul operation revealed tactical competence of a high order. It was also proof of a new military self-confidence never before seen in the conduct of the Soviet Army.[25]

In fact it was an operation very much in the German style: elegant, full of risks, and most profitable—very different from the heavy-handed, slow, and costly methods that once marked the Soviet military style (like the Russian imperial style before the revolution). Certainly the Soviets could not have redeemed failure during that bloody night in Kabul by pouring in more troops—their traditional solution to all military problems. In the past, the Kremlin leaders were visibly dissuaded from using their military power in the Third World because the Soviet armed forces had only sledgehammers in their tool kit. Now they have sharp blades as well.

Still, for all its historic significance in marking a new stage in the military evolution of the Soviet Army, the Kabul operation may be disregarded as a measure of military competence because it was carried out by elite forces against Afghan forces that were primitive to begin with and caught by surprise. (Though in Grenada, elite Rangers, Marines, and Airborne troops took three days and more to defeat ill-armed, ill-trained Cubans and Grenadians.) The combat value of the mass of the Soviet armed forces remains untested by the terrible urgencies of war. But it is possible to estimate their organizational, operational, and tactical competence—if not their fighting spirit—by observing exercises, which show quite clearly that the Soviet armed forces can now execute complicated military operations on a very large scale.

Specifically, we know that the Soviet Army can assemble, supply, and send out its long columns of armor and considerable artillery to defeat enemy fronts not in a steamroller action of costly head-on attacks, as in the past, but rather in quick probes—to find gaps and weak sectors, and to follow with fast-paced penetrations into the rear to achieve great encirclements; to overrun forward air bases, depots, and command centers; to "hug" cities to inhibit nuclear attacks; and to seize large extents of territory by so doing.

At the same time, raiding forces of the airborne divisions, of the special helicopter assault brigades, of the "diversionary" and commando units of both military and civilian Intelligence can fly into, parachute into, or infiltrate the deep rear in order to seize nuclear-weapon storage sites, attack headquarters and communications centers, sabotage aircraft in their hangars and fire across crowded runways, ambush road convoys, and spread havoc by their mere presence—

and by the inevitable tide of false reports about their doings and undoings.[26]

We know that the Soviet Air Force has enough aircraft, enough bases, and enough quality in men and machines to deny air supremacy to whatever Western air forces it might meet in Europe, the Persian Gulf, or East Asia. Its fighter-interceptors, along with their antiaircraft defenses, could keep Western air forces from doing much harm to the Soviet Army; its long-range strike fighters could reach and bomb Western airfields even in the deepest rear; and its fighter-bombers and ground-attack aircraft could disrupt if not seriously reduce Western ground forces.[27] In theory, Western air forces could eventually prevail in the contest for air supremacy—if the Soviet ground forces had not by then overrun their airfields. One thing is certain: Western air power can give little help to the ground forces in the first days of a war—precisely when air support would be needed most urgently.

We know that the Soviet Navy can send out its aircraft, group its ships, and deploy its attack submarines in a concerted worldwide action to stage simultaneous missile strikes on American carrier task forces at sea, certainly in the Indian Ocean, eastern Mediterranean, and northeast Pacific, and possibly in the Atlantic and eastern Pacific as well. Though lacking the floating air power that remains the costly centerpiece of the American Navy, the Soviet Union can nevertheless soberly estimate that *if* it attacks first, it could destroy the main fighting strength of the American Navy actually at sea. In any event, Soviet attack submarines will endanger the sea connection between the United States and American forces overseas.

Motivation, Morale, and Discipline

Entire books have appeared which argue that the Soviet armed forces are much weaker than they seem. Citing refugee accounts or personal experience, they depict the pervasive technical incompetence, drunkenness, corruption, and bleak apathy of officers and men.[28] Drunken officers and faked inspections, Turkic conscripts who cannot understand orders in Russian, drownings in botched river-crossing tests, the harsh lives of ill-fed, ill-housed, and virtually unpaid Soviet conscripts, and a pervasive lack of adequate training fill these accounts.[29]

It is odd how all these stories (each true, no doubt) contrast with the daily evidence of the routine operations of the Soviet armed forces. Merely keeping its warships seaworthy and supplied in distant and often stormy waters demands a great deal of discipline and expertise from the officers and men of the Soviet Navy. Even more skill is needed to carry out successfully the missile launches and gunnery trials that are also part of the Soviet naval routine. Likewise, we have the daily evidence of Soviet air operations; they too require a great deal of competence, both in the daily training sorties of the fighters and in the long-range flights of the bombers and transports. Nor can the Soviet Army fake all the disciplined maintenance, tight planning, and skills needed to assemble, move, and operate the many thousands of complicated armored vehicles, hundreds of helicopters, and countless smaller weapons used in its exercises. It takes only a little drunken inattention or technical incompetence, or mere apathy by maintenance crews, to cause an aircraft to crash; a little more can sink a ship; and the delicate gearbox of a battle tank is easily wrecked. Many refugees can no doubt honestly report having seen many soldiers and officers drunk; each of them who has served in uniform has no doubt encountered incompetence at all levels. But there is much less in these accounts than meets the eye.

Very similar stories of gross incompetence can be heard from anyone who has served in the armed forces of any country, even the most accomplished. When one assesses the actual record of war, not from official accounts but rather from those who were there, it becomes quite clear that battles are won not by perfection but rather by the supremacy of forces that are 5 percent effective over forces that are 2 percent effective. In peacetime, when all the frictions of war are absent, when there is no enemy ready to thwart every enterprise, effectiveness may reach the dizzy height of 50 percent—which means, of course, that filling in the wrong form, postings to the wrong place, supplying the wrong replacement parts, assigning the wrong training times, selecting the wrong officers, and other kinds of errors are merely normal. Matters cannot be otherwise, because military organizations are much larger than the manageable groupings of civilian life that set our standards of competence; and because their many intricate tasks must be performed not by the life-career specialists who run factories, hospitals, symphony orchestras, and even government offices, but by transients who are briefly trained—short-service conscripts in the case of the Soviet armed forces.

Actual alcoholism, in the severe, clinical sense, is now epidemic in the Soviet Union, where so many lead bleak lives, no longer alleviated by the once vibrant hope of a fast-approaching bright future. So drunkenness is no doubt pervasive in the Soviet armed forces. But Russians have always been great drinkers. Drunk they defeated Napoleon, and drunk again they defeated Hitler's armies and advanced all the way to Berlin. All these stories of corruption are also undoubtedly authentic. But no great military empire is likely to be undone by generals who procure villas by corrupt dealings, nor by sergeants who take the odd ruble off a conscript; Anglo-Saxon morality makes much of these things, history much less.*

On the question of loyalty even less need be said. Should the Soviet Union start a war, only to experience a series of swift defeats, it is perfectly possible that mutinies would follow against the Kremlin's oppressive and most unjust rule. But if the initial war operations were successful, it would be foolish to expect that private disloyalty would emerge to undo victory and disintegrate the armed forces. There will always be a small minority of lonely heroes with the inner resources to act against the entire power of the world's largest and most complete dictatorship. The rest of us weaker souls stay in the safety of the crowd —and the crowd will not rebel against a uniquely pervasive police system at the very time when successful war is adding to its prestige, and the laws of war are making its sanctions more terrible.

Only one claim can be allowed: it is true that the ethnic composition of the Soviet population is changing, with non-Russians making up an increasing proportion of the total. This creates problems of loyalty that are unknown in the United States, because in the Soviet Union, distinct nationalities persist with their own languages, ethnic sentiments, and sometimes strong antagonism to the Russian master-people.[30] As the proportion of non-Russian conscripts increases, language problems also increase, and because many of these conscripts come from backward nationalities, they are harder to train in modern military skills, even if they do know the Russian language. There is also a greater potential for ethnic strife, already manifest in barrack-room fights.

In the *very* long run it is possible and even likely that the non-Russians, or at least the larger non-European peoples—the Uzbeks, Kazakhs, Tadzhiks, and so on—will demand full national independence and struggle for it, eventually causing the dissolution of the Soviet empire, which is the last survivor of the European empires that dominated

---

* Corruption in the higher ranks can demoralize the troops—but not if it is accepted as a normal part of life.

much of the entire world until a generation ago. Demography is indeed a powerful and relentless force, but slow in effect.[31] In 1970, out of a total Soviet population of 242 million, 74 percent were Slavic and 53 percent actually Russian. (Some of the fiercest antagonisms are between Russians and other Slavs.) In that year, there were 35 million of Muslim origin (mostly Turkic), just under 15 percent of the Soviet total. By the year 2000 it is projected that the Muslims will account for more than a fifth (21–25 percent) of the total population of 300 million, with Russians at 47 percent and all Slavs at 65 percent.[32] Naturally, the change will be felt sooner and more strongly in the younger groups of military age. For example, out of the 2.1 million males projected to be at the conscription age of 18 in 1985,[33] the non-Slavs will account for more than 35 percent, and quite a few of them will not know enough Russian to obtain the full benefit of training.

But of course the armed forces of a multinational empire know a thing or two about managing diverse nationalities. Those with a high percentage of dissidents, such as the Estonians, western Ukrainians, and Jews, are safely employed in military-construction battalions, which are virtually unarmed, or in other support units far from combat; those with many illiterates or conscripts whose Russian is poor, such as the Kirghiz, Turkmen, and Tadzhiks, are placed in the undemanding mechanized infantry of second-line divisions. There are problems, but they remain quite manageable. The real threat of national self-assertion is for the distant future.

Estimating the Military Balance

So far nothing precise has been said about the most obvious attribute of the Soviet armed forces: their sheer numerical strength. The gross totals are well known, and mean little. As against the 30 large divisions of the U.S. Army and Marine Corps, active and reserve, the Soviet Army has 194 divisions, smaller by a third on average but just as heavily armed. One-third are fully manned, one-third are half and half, and the rest rely mostly on reservists—but all Soviet divisions are fully equipped, even if not with the latest and best, and all have a full-time professional cadre, even when their line units are to be filled by reservists.[34] The Soviet tactical air force has some 6,000 strike aircraft, fighters, and fighter-bombers, less advanced on average but also of more recent vintage than the 5,600 or so equivalent aircraft of the U.S. Air Force, Navy, and Marine Corps.[35] Another 1,250 interceptor-fighters serve in the territorial air defenses (along with more than 9,600 antiaircraft missiles), and the Soviet Navy's land-based aviation also includes some fighter-class aircraft.[36]

For the Soviet Navy, one ship list prepared by the U.S. Navy shows 1,324 "surface combatants," as against its own 285 surface warships; 367 submarines, as against 99; and 770 auxiliaries, as against its own 105 logistic and support ships. The figures are, of course, grossly inflated, but even the most sober count that excludes the old, the inactive, and the small would still list 290 major Soviet surface warships, 119 nuclear and 157 diesel attack submarines, and 360 land-based naval bombers, of which 100 are modern machines of transoceanic range.[37]

No true military balance is made of mere lists, however. The place and the time, the allies present on each side, and the circumstances of the conflict and of the particular theaters of war will govern what can be achieved, and indeed what forces can be deployed at all. No estimate can be made for expeditionary ventures in undefined theaters of hypothetical war—except to say that the power of the Soviet forces wanes drastically as the distance from the Soviet Union increases: much more so than does that of the American forces, which are far better equipped to reach and fight in faraway places. But we can make rather solid estimates for the continental theaters of war directly adjacent to the Soviet Union—in Europe, the Middle East, and Northeast Asia. The results are grim.

In the five possible war theaters of the North Atlantic Alliance—northern Norway, the "central" front in Germany, northeastern Italy, the Thracian frontier of Greece and Turkey with Bulgaria, and the Turkish border with the Soviet Union in remote eastern Anatolia—it is clear that the ground forces of both the United States and its allies, those already deployed in peacetime and those to be mobilized, would be outnumbered or outgunned, or both. By adding absolutely everything on the books—including Turkish infantry and the American National Guard, in addition to the manned forces actually in place—the total number of Alliance divisions for the five theaters rises to 144, as against a combined Warsaw Pact total of 170.[38] That is scarcely a catastrophic imbalance, and the situation looks even easier for the Alliance when we recall that the Warsaw Pact total includes 56 divisions of rebellious Poland, unwilling Hungary, restive Czechoslovakia, doubtful East Germany, and uncooperative Romania.[39] If we make a somewhat finer comparison, however, including only tank and mechanized divisions on the Alliance side, thus removing a mass of ill-armed and immobile infantry forces of low military value, while at the same time eliminating *all* the non-Soviet forces of the Warsaw Pact, 80 divisions of the Alliance remain, while the Soviet army alone has 109—*after* leaving 78 Soviet divisions to face the Chinese border, occupy Afghanistan, and control Iran's long border.[40] These 109 Soviet divisions are smaller than the Western divisions, but no longer by much,[41] and they do belong to one army under one central authority, whereas the Western total is split among the armies of the United States, Canada, Britain, Norway, Denmark, West Germany, Holland, France, Portugal, Italy, Greece, and Turkey—and the French divisions are not under Alliance command and not necessarily available, the Greek divisions are of uncertain allegiance, and the American reserve forces must first be mobilized, then filled out and updated in training, then transported across the ocean.

If we include the nonmechanized forces of high military value (such as the American and Soviet airborne divisions), and exclude Alliance forces not rapidly available for reinforcement, the realistic Alliance count is on the order of 56 divisions; the Soviet, 114.[42]

The situation in the air over the European fronts is similar: by the fullest count, the Soviet Union alone could muster 4,700 fighters, fighter-bombers, and interceptors, without reinforcement from other theaters; the Western air forces in Europe hold a total of 3,045, of which not more than two-thirds can be considered modern, including all the 594 American fighters and fighter-bombers.[43]

To consider the military balance in the Persian Gulf, with Iran as the possible theater of war, no computation is even needed: against a maximum of 4 or 5 American divisions that could eventually be deployed with great difficulties and greater risk, the Soviet Union could send 20 with great ease.

On the last of the "continental" fronts, which cuts across the peninsula of Korea—where sudden war is all too possible, but where a large Soviet intervention now seems most unlikely—it is the Korean forces on both sides that now make the balance. But should Moscow choose to do so, it could add much more to the North Korean strength than the United States could add to the South.

Thus on every possible major front we encounter the powerful arithmetic of the Soviet Army. By integrating reserves with active units and providing full equipment, the Soviet Army is a very effective producer of armor-mechanized divisions. Not at all suited for overseas expeditions, dependent on rail transport for large movements between the different fronts separated by several thousand miles, these divisions are nevertheless powerful instruments of offensive war usable wherever the Soviet Union may seek to enlarge its empire.

With Western air power now offset to a large degree by Soviet air defenses, and with naval power relevant only in the less critical theaters remote from Europe, the Middle East, and East Asia, it is the ground forces that are the basic currency of East–West strategy. Because of the Soviet Union's energetic countering efforts, its advantage in ground forces can no longer be offset by Western strengths in other forms of military power, including nuclear.

So far, not a word has been said about the entire subject of Soviet nuclear weapons. This segregation and implied downgrading of the matter corresponds to the strategic logic of the Soviet position against the West. Moscow's protestations of reluctance to use nuclear weapons against the West (China is another matter) may be perfectly sincere. Just as the invader is always peaceful—for he seeks only to advance and not to fight, while it is his victim who causes war by resisting—so the Soviet Union has every reason to avoid nuclear war, because it is now stronger than the West in the nonnuclear military forces. Fully able to invade Europe, Iran, or Korea without having to use nuclear weapons, the Soviet Union now needs its nuclear weapons mainly to neutralize the nuclear deterrence of the United States, Britain, and France. Just as it is always the victim who must make war to resist aggression, so the West must rely on the fear of nuclear war to obtain security, by threatening nuclear attacks against invading Soviet forces if they cannot be stopped by nonnuclear means.

To deter such "tactical" attacks—that is, to inhibit the first level of the Western nuclear deterrent in order to restore the full value of its armies for intimidation or actual invasion—the Soviet Union has built up its own "tactical" nuclear forces, in the form of artillery shells, rockets, short-range missiles, and bombs for fighter-class aircraft and strike bombers. The Soviet Union can therefore reply in kind should its invading armies have their victories spoiled by nuclear attacks.

If the West begins to strike at invading Soviet columns with tactical nuclear weapons, the Soviet Union can, in a simple military calculation, use its own tactical nuclear weapons to blast open paths through the Alliance front, so that even badly reduced and shocked invasion columns can continue to advance, eventually to reach and "hug" the cities

—thereby forcing the Alliance to stop its nuclear attacks. In the far more meaningful political calculation, the mere existence of large and very powerful Soviet tactical nuclear forces should inhibit to some extent the Western use of those same weapons. But the Alliance has a most significant advantage that arises from its purely defensive character: at this first level, the entire onus of beginning a war rests on the Soviet Union; it is by *its* decision that the movement of the armies would begin; it is by *its* decision to continue invading Western territory that tactical nuclear weapons would be used against its forces, raising the conflict to the second level. Hence the Soviet tactical-nuclear forces are not sufficient to deter Western use of the the same weapons. The Soviets could use them only to achieve physical results (blasting gaps through the front) that would not begin to remedy the catastrophic deterioration of their position from a successful nonnuclear invasion to a nuclear conflict in which no good result could be achieved.

Therefore, to inhibit much more powerfully the Western tactical nuclear forces, the Soviet Union maintains another category of nuclear weapons of longer ("intermediate") range, which threaten the cities of Europe, as well as large military targets in the deep rear, such as air bases. At present, the celebrated SS-20 ballistic missile is the main weapon in this category, which also includes Soviet strike aircraft such as the Su-24 (*Fencer*). With these weapons the interaction between Soviet and Western military power reaches its third level.

Of late the Alliance has begun to deploy "intermediate-range" cruise and Pershing II missiles in Britain, West Germany, and Italy (more are to be deployed in Belgium and Holland). Because they are widely regarded as an entirely different category of weapon, they *are* different politically: the huge controversy surrounding their deployment may enable the cruise and Pershing II missiles to have a counterintimidation impact, since public opinion views them as an answer to the SS-20s. To that extent, they are *politically* distinct from the far more abundant aircraft bombs and all the other nuclear weapons officially described as tactical. In addition, the new missiles may be more reliable in reaching their targets than strike aircraft with nuclear bombs.

But *strategically* the cruise and Pershing II missiles are not different from the tactical nuclear weapons of the Alliance: they too serve to neutralize the nonnuclear strength of the Soviet army, and they too are neutralized in turn by the Soviet nuclear counterthreat against the cities of the Alliance. As a matter of physical fact, the cruise and Pershing II missiles do not threaten anything not already threatened by Alliance weapons classified as tactical; specifically, they do not threaten Soviet cities any more than the tactical nuclear bombs of longer-range Alliance strike aircraft. Both those aircraft and the new missiles could reach cities in the western part of the Soviet Union; neither is meant to be used against those cities; for both, the relevant targets are the Soviet military forces and their bases and command centers. To neutralize the Soviet third-level threat against the Alliance cities in Europe, the new missiles would have to counterthreaten Soviet cities with an equal certainty of complete destruction; because of their vulnerability and range limits, the new missiles cannot do that. Hence the new missiles cannot take the strategic interaction to a fourth level, where the Soviet invasion potential is once again neutralized. The third level thus leaves the Soviet Union in control of the situation, because with or without the cruise and Pershing II missiles, the Alliance can protect its frontal defenses only at the risk of provoking Soviet nuclear attacks against the cities that those same frontal forces are supposed to protect.

It takes a fourth level to restore a war-avoiding balance, in which this Soviet third-level nuclear threat is itself deterred by American intercontinental nuclear forces capable of inflicting catastrophic destruction on the Soviet Union. Thus the Western "tactical" nuclear forces can once again deter a Soviet (nonnuclear) invasion, so that the Soviet Union's invasion potential yields neither war options nor the power to intimidate the European allies of the United States.

The Soviet response has been to seek a fifth level of strategic interaction, at which the American deterrent is neutralized by the threat of destroying all the intercontinental nuclear forces if any are used against Soviet military forces, and American cities if any Soviet cities are destroyed. If the United States Government would withdraw its threat of a nuclear attack on the Soviet Union in response to a Soviet attack on European cities, or if American intercontinental nuclear forces could not plausibly threaten the Soviet Union, the strategic interaction would revert to the third level, at which the Soviet threat against the cities of the Allies inhibits the West from using its tactical nuclear forces, thus making the world safe for the Soviet Army.

One hears it said endlessly that the competition between American and Soviet intercontinental nuclear forces is not only costly and dangerous but also futile, because each side can already destroy the population of the other "many times over." That, however, is a vulgar misunderstanding. It is not to destroy the few hundred cities and larger towns of each side—easy targets neither protected nor concealed—that intercontinental nuclear forces continue to be developed. The purpose is not to threaten cities and towns already abundantly threatened, to "overkill" populations, but rather to threaten the intercontinental nuclear forces themselves: the missiles in their fortified housings, the bomber bases and missile-submarine ports, and the centers of military command and communication for all those forces. Thus there are several thousand targets, as opposed to a few hundred cities and towns, and many of those targets can be destroyed only by very accurate warheads.

At the fifth level of interaction, each side strives to reduce the nuclear attack strength of the other, by defenses when possible (notably antiaircraft, against the bombers), but mainly by offensive weapons accurate enough to destroy the weapons of the other. And it is not enough to be able to threaten the destruction of the weapons: to make the threat effective it is also necessary to demonstrate the ability to destroy them without at the same time destroying the nearby population centers. For if that happens, then all strategy and all rational purposes come to an end, as the victim will respond by launching his surviving weapons (there will always be some, perhaps many) against the cities of the attacker. For the United States, the competition at this point is driven by the goal of keeping the strategic interaction at the fourth level, where the Soviet army stands deterred; for the Soviet Union, the goal is to reach the fifth level, where American nuclear deterrence is itself deterred.

Because of the goals now pursued, intercontinental nuclear weapons, contrary to widespread belief, are steadily becoming *less* destructive in gross explosive power. The goal of each side is to make the forces more accurate and more controllable so that they can destroy small and well-protected targets, and no more. During the 1960s, the United States was still producing weapons of 5 and 9 megatons, while the Soviet Union was producing 20-megaton warheads; nowadays, most new American warheads have yields of less than half a megaton, while most Soviet warheads are below 1 megaton.[44] As new weapons replace old, the total destructive power of the two intercontinental nuclear arsenals is steadily declining. (A "freeze," incidentally, would put an end to that process.)

The state of the American–Soviet intercontinental nuclear balance is the basic index, the Dow Jones of world politics. Directly or through sometimes subtle hopes and fears, it shapes much of what American and Soviet leaders feel free to do in world affairs. Two things are quite obvious about the current intercontinental nuclear balance. Each side can easily destroy the cities and larger towns of the other. And neither can launch an all-out strike that would fully destroy the other's weapons. The competition is now between these two extremes, as each side seeks to protect as many of its weapons as possible while threatening the other's weapons.

Although the United States is by no means inferior across the board, category by category, it is impossible to extract an optimistic estimate from the numbers. There are 1,398 Soviet intercontinental ballistic missiles in underground housings, as against 1,000 American Minuteman missiles; some of the latter have been modernized and others have not, but the Soviet missiles are much larger, with many more warheads (almost 6,000 versus 2,100), of which the more modern are no longer less accurate than their American counterparts (as was the case till quite recently).[45] No expert disputes the accuracy and reliability of the more modern Soviet ballistic missiles—the four-warhead SS-17 (150 in service), the huge SS-18, with as many as ten warheads (308 in service), and the slightly less modern but more abundant six-warhead SS-19 (330 in service). The combined Soviet force clearly outmatches the 450 one-warhead Minuteman IIs and 550 three-warhead Minuteman IIIs.[46] Specifically, the Soviet land-based missiles could now destroy all but a fraction of their American counterparts, while the latter could not hope to do the same to the Soviet force.

The remaining defect of the Soviet land-based ballistic-missile force is that its warheads are not yet small enough to make the threat of a "clean" disarming strike believable. (The smallest warheads are of half-megaton size, and some are almost a full megaton.) The Soviet Union is now developing an entire new group of land-based ballistic missiles: undoubtedly they will be more accurate, and their warheads will be smaller. The new American MX missiles now in production are also more accurate, although their original purpose was greater survivability —which they cannot achieve because they will be placed in fixed housings, though built for mobility.

The Soviet force of submarine-carried ballistic missiles is also much larger than the American, with 980 missiles as opposed to 480, but the quality difference is still so great that the American force remains superior.[47] In the first place, most Soviet submarine-launched missiles are still one-warhead weapons, while their American counterparts have multiple warheads. As a result, the Soviet Union has fewer than 1,000 separate warheads in its submarine force, as against more than 5,000 (much smaller) American warheads.[48]

A greater defect in a force that is, or should be, the ultimate strategic reserve, the best protected of all in the intercontinental category, is the fact that all the Soviet submarines, except perhaps the very latest, are much noisier and thus more easily detected than their American counterparts.* This is all the more striking because the Soviet submarines are much newer on average: between 1974 and 1984 the Soviet Union built 35 *Delta*-class submarines and one huge *Typhoon,* as against just 4 *Ohio*-class submarines built by the United States. On the other hand, the latest Soviet submarine-launched missile, the SS-N-20, has such a long range (8,300 kilometers) that it can reach most targets without requiring the submarine carrying it to leave the safe waters near the Soviet northern coasts.[50]

Throughout the long years of strategic competition, the Soviet force of intercontinental bombers remained much smaller, and its aircraft much inferior, though this may be about to change. In the latest count, the 297 American bombers, mostly ancient but much-modernized B-52s, can be compared with a total of 273 Soviet bombers, including roughly 130 *Backfires* that are modern and supersonic, but not quite sufficient in range (5,500 kilometers), as well as a greater number of Tu-95s, an aircraft as old as the B-52 but much inferior in every way.[51] Only recently has the Soviet Union started producing a true modern intercontinental bomber, the *Blackjack,* which is externally similar to the new American B-1B, and is destined to be electronically less advanced but also much faster.[52]

For all their technical inferiority, Soviet bombers are still formidable, simply because the United States has very weak air defenses. While American bombers would have to contend with 1,250 Soviet interceptor fighters and almost 10,000 antiaircraft missiles to reach their targets, Soviet bombers would virtually have a free ride against 90 Air Force and 180 Air National Guard interceptors, and not a single missile.[53]

The Soviet Union's destruction of the Korean airliner (KAL flight 007) on September 1, 1983, has been interpreted by some as proof of the incompetence of the Soviet territorial air defenses. In one version, which assumes that the attack was made in error, the Soviet radar network is judged grossly incompetent for having failed to distinguish

---

* Among the 80 Soviet ballistic-missile submarines in service, some 22 are ancient diesel and early-vintage nuclear boats that have every right to be noisy, but these account for fewer than 60 of the 980 missile tubes. The bulk of the force should be much less noisy than it is, raising some interesting questions about Soviet design or perhaps Soviet strategy.[49]

between KAL 007 and the very much smaller RC-135 electronic-recon-naissance aircraft (supposedly the intended victim). In a second version, the mere fact that KAL 007 was not actually shot down until two and a half hours after it first entered Soviet airspace over the Kamchatka Peninsula is treated as a failure of the system, regardless of whether the aircraft was correctly identified.

These interpretations illustrate very well the difficulty of making op-erational judgments in a vacuum; the plain facts that the Korean airliner *was* found and reached by a Soviet fighter, that a missile was launched correctly, that it detonated and destroyed a large aircraft are simply taken for granted, as if these were easy things. And indeed they should be for any air-defense system at war, operating day in and day out, with all the habits of combat operations. But on September 1, 1983, until KAL 007 arrived on the scene, Soviet air defenses were at peace, as they have been for almost forty years. To monitor the airspace closely, to have the fighters ready at the end of the runway, to have pilots find the target, to have missiles fully operational—and to have all that when the action suddenly starts after decades of inaction is not easy at all.*

Even a delay of two and a half hours would not be significant. But as it happens, the delay was nowhere near as long; KAL 007 first pene-trated and then left Soviet airspace (over Kamchatka) before reentering it (near Sakhalin). The aircraft's first penetration was very brief, a mat-ter of minutes and forgivable even by the Soviet Union. Its second led to its destruction in short order.

The misidentification theory takes for granted that a 747 can very easily be distinguished from an RC-135. That is simply not the case; identification depends on, among other things (size, aspect, type of radar and displays), atmospheric conditions. But as it happens, it is certain that the Soviet air-defense controllers knew exactly what they were destroying; this is one case in which the negative evidence pre-vails. As in the Sherlock Holmes story, the dog that did not bark is definite proof: though Soviet air-defense controllers could have con-fused the KAL 007 radar image with that of an RC-135, the scheduled Korean Air Lines flight from Anchorage, Alaska, to Seoul, Korea, which Soviet radar would routinely track, had to be *somewhere* on the

---

* The interception of KAL 007 should be compared with the noninterception by Amer-ican air defenses of more than one Cuban airliner that violated U.S. flight corridors on the Havana–Mexico City route.

radar screens. If it was not, only two possibilities remained: either that KAL 007 had inexplicably crashed into the sea without any signal at all, or else that the aircraft being intercepted was in fact KAL 007. So to believe in the misidentification theory, we have to assume that Soviet air-defense controllers not only confused the two radar images but believed that KAL 007 had mysteriously fallen out of the sky without even a few seconds in which to transmit a "mayday" call. Thus once again we must resist the seductive urge to believe in Soviet ineptness.

The Soviet Union continues to make a large effort in strategic defense, maintaining costly forces to fight what can be fought (the bombers and cruise missiles), doing all it can to develop anti-ballistic-missile defenses, and keeping up a nationwide civil-defense program which mingles elements both highly realistic and merely symbolic arrangements, from shelters to evacuation. The United States, by contrast, is pursuing innovation in offensive weapons and is exploring many highly advanced defensive schemes based on satellite-mounted weapons, but has no serious civil defense.

One could add details and nuances to the estimate of the Soviet Union's intercontinental nuclear strength and homeland defenses, but the result would not change, for the two forces do not have the same task. The United States must rely on believable threats to use its intercontinental nuclear forces to offset the Soviet Union's nonnuclear superiority and "tactical" nuclear parity. Otherwise matters would stand at the third level, where there is nothing to stop Soviet military intimidation of America's allies—which then could scarcely remain allies. The Soviet Union, by contrast, need only make the American intercontinental nuclear threat unbelievable in order to recover the invasion potential of its armies, thus restoring their power to intimidate or actually invade. To do that the Soviet Union does not even need the intercontinental nuclear superiority, which it is striving so hard to achieve. But the United States does need a margin of intercontinental nuclear strength merely to keep the overall military balance balanced.

Hence "parity" (shorthand for strategic-nuclear parity) is or should be fundamentally unacceptable to the United States. Any true parity between the intercontinental nuclear forces of each side must leave the United States militarily inferior in all the continental theaters where the Soviet Army can muster its power—namely, Europe, Iran (and thus the Persian Gulf), and Korea. And that is the situation which now prevails, the cause of today's anxieties for world peace.

Soviet Military Power and American Military Reform

The present dimensions of Soviet military power mean that we cannot take seriously the most common remedy for the high cost and visible excesses of the American military establishment: we cannot simply cut the defense budget. If we merely reduce funding across the board, without first achieving radical reforms which would enable us to spend the money much more wisely, we are likely to have ample reason to bitterly regret the savings.

The formidable military power of the Soviet Union should be the chief incentive to reform. But that is not so. The very opposite is the case. One problem is that precisely those who know best all the problems and deficiencies of our military institutions are also the ones who understand best the Soviet Union's military power (including the fact that the Soviet Union's much-advertised mechanical and human weaknesses do not seriously diminish its invasion potential). Many of these experts, who would otherwise be the first to inform the public about the need for reform, are instead fully engaged in the struggle to persuade their fellow citizens of the pressing need to counter the Soviet Union's military power through steady and serious rearmament. It is very difficult for them to argue both that we should devote greater resources to our defense and that the military establishment is crippled by fundamental defects.

In Congress, where any reform must finally be accepted and made into law, the reality of the Soviet Union's military power has a paralyzing effect on reform. When well-informed and serious Congressmen examine our own military establishment and begin to see its profound defects, their interest in reform is awakened. But once they confront the sheer enormity of Soviet military power, our forces begin to look small, even dangerously insufficient, and rearmament becomes their dominant priority.

As in those trick illustrations that yield one image when first seen, only to reveal quite another when our angle of observation changes, two radically different perspectives are in collision in the public debate over national defense—the inner-regarding perspective on the sheer size, cost, and defects of our defense establishment, and the outer-regarding perspective on the Soviet Union and its greatly increased military strength.

Many political leaders and much of the press choose the first perspective to denounce the great cost of the armed forces, and to probe for fraud, waste, and mismanagement in the Pentagon. Other political leaders and many of the best-qualified experts choose the second perspective and demand a broader and faster rearmament. Loud voices are thus at cross-purposes, yielding only confusion that is faithfully reproduced in the mass of information that reaches the public.

In theory the two perspectives are fully compatible, and careful examination of speeches and articles on "fraud, waste, and mismanagement" reveals the odd phrase about the need to strengthen the armed forces precisely by cutting "the fat in the military budget." Likewise, those who stress the formidable military power of the Soviet Union will also advertise their determination to root out fraud, waste, and mismanagement. Thus in theory the two sides differ only in their priorities. But in practice each side's prudent disclaimers are drowned out in the barrage of the public debate.

In what follows, reform is the subject, but the pressing reality of the Soviet Union's ascent to military primacy affects every aspect of it. To do less in the name of reform is much worse than no reform at all.

CHAPTER FIVE

☆

The Materialist Bias: Why We Need More "Fraud, Waste, and Mismanagement"

The public is flooded with information about the Pentagon; the media, often careless and almost always uninformed, are at least alerted to scandal. Congress reviews and investigates the armed forces every year in "hearings" conducted by the Budget, Armed Services, Appropriations, and Intelligence Committees of the House and of the Senate, with yet more committees active in particular areas. In 1982, Pentagon officials testified for a total of 1,453 hours before Congressional committees.[1] And the hearings are only the beginning; in 1983, just one of many Pentagon staffs, that of the Chief of Naval Operations, had to prepare 37 formal reports ordered by Congress, answer 2,900 information requests by individual members, and provide 245 briefings and 4,500 written replies to questions for the record following a total of 110 hearings.[2]

The great mystery, then, is how reform remains unachieved. The answer is to be found in the old joke about the man who was looking for his house key one night, not on the doorstep, where it had slipped from his hands, but across the way under a streetlamp—because, he explained, it was much too difficult to find a small key in the dark. In the matter of our national defense we too have been looking hard and long on the wrong side of the street.

☆

When confronted with immensity, the normal impulse is to focus on the particular: the soldiers on leave recently seen at the airport, the warship visited in harbor on a Sunday outing, or perhaps the "controversial" fighter aircraft whose costly purchase was discussed at length in the newspapers. The pathologist who examines a tiny sample of human tissue under a microscope to identify a disease follows exactly the same procedure, but his professional training enables him to know what the sample represents, so that a bruised toe is not easily confused with a brain tumor. By contrast, the ordinary citizen's attempt to focus on the particular is defeated by complexity: if those soldiers at the airport were sorry specimens, are there many like them, or only a few? Were they the very best of an elite force, or merely washed-out recruits on their way home? That warship seen in harbor may have looked most impressive, heavily armed and spotlessly maintained, but would its missiles actually work in combat?

And what can we conclude from those newspaper stories seemingly so conclusive in denouncing fraud, waste, and mismanagement? If much more was spent for the development of a weapon that had been planned, was it due to mismanagement or fraud at the taxpayers' expense, or was it because a higher performance unexpectedly became feasible, or perhaps because defects possibly catastrophic were successfully uncovered by honest testing? The fact that some weapons become controversial during their development and production, while others do not, means nothing. For example, hundreds of newspaper articles and at least one full-length book[3] were written to denounce the F-111 heavy fighter, which was certainly much more costly than planned and which was afflicted by all sorts of technical defects. In the end the number bought was greatly reduced, and indeed the aircraft barely survived outright cancellation. Yet today, some twenty years after the controversy, the F-111, in its second decade of service, remains the most valued of all Air Force aircraft, always the first to be sent overseas in a crisis, because it is almost immune to most antiaircraft weapons and is capable of reaching its targets in almost all weather conditions and at night.

By contrast, quite a few weapons that attracted no hostile comment at all during their entire span of production have turned out to be almost worthless when placed in service—for example, most of the radar-guided missiles provided for Air Force and Navy fighters between the 1950s and the late 1970s. For most of two decades, these costly missiles were regarded as the very embodiment of advanced technology successfully applied (they were the first of the "smart" weapons), and there was no controversy about their cost or technical development. But even the best of them, the Sparrow, rarely worked properly when used in

Vietnam.[4] More recently, the equally uncontroversial Dragon antitank missile turned out to be grossly inadequate in its very design; its limited range puts its users within the lethal reach of enemy machine guns—a crippling defect in its class of weapons.

There is no mystery in all this: a reliable way to avoid trouble within the defense establishment, funding cuts by Congress, and controversy in the press is to complete the development of a weapon on time and within the planned budget—even if serious defects persist.

Actually, there is a powerful bias built into Congressional scrutiny and media coverage that defeats any attempt to understand the broader picture from the steady crop of complaints about fraud, waste, and mismanagement. The Pentagon purchases millions of items (3.8 million in 1984), but it is the very large and most visible that attract almost all of the attention—the $2-billion aircraft carrier, the $40-million aircraft, the $2-million tank. The sheer magnitude of such numbers suggests wasteful overspending;[5] yet it is precisely the acquisition of major weapons that is most carefully controlled. The grossly overpriced $50 helmet or $20,000 jeep passes unnoticed, merely because the *unit* cost is not impressive. Yet it is in the great mass of minor items and spare parts that fraud, waste, and mismanagement are much more likely. And the little things count for a lot in the total expenditures. If every one of the "controversial" weapons funded in 1984 had been cancelled—the Air Force's MX ballistic missile and B-1B bomber; the Navy's Aegis CG-47 cruiser, F/A-18 fighter-bomber, and Lamps III antisubmarine helicopter; the Army's Bradley infantry combat vehicle, AH-64 attack helicopter, and DIVAD armored antiaircraft gun and its entire antiballistic-missile defense program; and the Marines' vertical-takeoff AV-8B Harrier fighter-bombers—the grand total saved would have amounted to $25.6 billion, just over one quarter of the $94 billion requested for all procurement in the 1984 budget.[6]

In fact, in those rare cases in which we can actually make valid comparisons between American and foreign military purchases, we discover that foreign-made fighter aircraft, warships, and tanks tend to be more expensive than their American equivalents, while the foreign armed forces' smaller and more prosaic things are less expensive. Obviously the problem is that the elaborate contracting procedures, the complex cost accounting, and the minute specifications that work well enough in the purchase of major weapons are now indiscriminately applied to all purchases, frightening away cheaper suppliers and burdening the hardy survivors with disproportionate costs for documentation, bookkeeping, and lawyer's fees, not to mention redesign costs to meet exacting specifications. Thus we create the $2 paper clip, tested in both arctic and tropical conditions, which comes complete with a hundred-page contract and whose production is fully documented to show compliance with all current cost-accounting regulations; environmental rules; and minority-employment, handicapped-employment, and small-business "affirmative-action" goals.

There is, however, a much stronger and more pervasive distortion that makes many of our controversies over the Pentagon misleading. In searching for mismanagement and waste, we naturally compare what the Pentagon is doing with commonsense civilian notions of efficiency. This seems reasonable; after all, efficiency measures output against effort, and *in*efficiency can scarcely be a Good Thing. The trouble is that the outputs that count in war are very particular and very different from the outputs that count in peacetime, and when civilian notions of efficiency are applied, the difference is routinely overlooked.

Take the case of two corporations bidding on the production of the same battle tank under a standard cost-plus-fee contract. One offers to produce each tank at a cost of, say, $2 million, while the other demands $2.3 million for the same tank, identical in every detail. Surely the Pentagon would be wasting the taxpayers' money if it chose to buy from the costlier producer. Congress should promptly intervene to repudiate such a contract, and perhaps a grand jury should probe for corruption. But not necessarily. It could be that the higher-cost producer simply intends to pocket the difference by disguising profit as overhead. And it is possible that the cheaper supplier has a better work force and a more alert management. But the difference could also be in the efficiency with which the plant and machinery are used, with one company planning to work day and night in three shifts to produce the monthly lots of tanks with a smaller and cheaper plant, while the other intends to provide a much larger plant and many more machines that will work only one eight-hour shift. If the contract is signed with the more efficient producer, the taxpayer will get all the tanks that are actually funded for less money. But if the less efficient corporation gets the contract, albeit at higher cost, its much larger plant will also contain the potential to increase production quickly by working more shifts in an emergency— a very valuable bonus. We are, after all, purchasing tanks to deter war, and an army that cannot quickly obtain more tanks when it needs them is a poor deterrent.*

So inefficiency acquires quite a different meaning, and seems a prudent investment rather than a source of waste. In fact, we may conclude that the Pentagon should seek out underused plants when awarding its contracts, to keep *them* in business rather than their three-shift competitors. This conflict between business notions of efficiency and military effectiveness is not unusual. On the contrary, it is very much the rule.

Consider the entire question of diversity versus standardization in military equipment. Congressional and media complaints about "duplication" are a constant theme in our defense debates, and Congress has often stepped in to forbid the purchase of different weapons with similar or overlapping functions. And the supposed need for more standardization is the great standby of pious comment on the North Atlantic Alliance—whose members are guilty of "triplication" and worse, as each country tries to develop as many of its own weapons as possible. There is no doubt that there is much duplication in the Alliance especially, but also in our armed forces, and there is no doubt that the parallel research and development of the same class of diverse weapons is very costly, and that the shorter production runs of each are less economical. In the world of civilian business that would settle the matter; but in the realm of strategy things may be quite different.

Any well-run business that uses machines will make every effort to standardize on the smallest possible number of models in acquiring its machines. If a single type of passenger aircraft, truck, or machine tool can be used instead of two, three, or ten, all the costs of stocking spare parts, of repair rigs and tools, of operator and maintenance training can be reduced accordingly. But well-run businesses do not go to war, and they do not have to contend with enemies whose tactics are specifically designed to exploit the shortcomings of any particular piece of equipment. Airliners must fight gravity, trucks must overcome the road's friction, and all machinery must prevail over the passive resistance of materials. But gravity, friction, and the rest are not live, intelligent beings actively seeking to outmaneuver and defeat what the airliner, truck, or machine is built to achieve. But of course action and reaction,

---

* At present, sixty M-1 tanks are produced each month;[7] in the 1982 Lebanon war, as in the 1973 Arab–Israeli war, even the victorious Israelis lost more than sixty tanks *a day* on bad days; most were repairable, but not immediately.

deliberate resistance, and outmaneuvering attempts are the very essence of conflict: thus standardization becomes much less attractive in combat. If, for example, our forces use a single, standardized type of antiaircraft missile for the sake of efficiency, enemy pilots will be able to underfly its minimum operating altitude or overfly its maximum ceiling, and the enemy's electronic wizards can devote all their efforts to countering its specific detection and guidance systems. If efficiency is sacrificed and a second, different type of missile is added with higher or lower altitude limits, or merely different electronic specifications, the enemy's pilots will find it that much more difficult to avoid both missiles, while the enemy's electronic countermeasures must cope with two different challenges.

When diversity increases, unit costs must also increase, because of all those different spare-parts and training needs. But less standardized military forces are more resilient. Whereas the civilian concept of efficiency calls for maximum standardization, ultimately yielding one-gun/one-tank armies, one-fighter air forces, and one-ship navies, military effectiveness demands diversity to resist the enemy's outmaneuvering effort.

The conflict generally between business notions of efficiency and sound military practice shows how unwise it is to worry overmuch about the diversity of armaments within the forces of the Western alliance and, indeed, our own. It is in the use of military personnel, however, that this conflict is at its sharpest: civilian efficiency calls for placing each individual where his skills are most needed; military effectiveness demands stability, to promote solidarity among those who will need to trust one another with their very lives in combat. In a civilian factory it would be foolish to keep a skilled lathe operator driving a truck, while training a perfectly good truck driver in the machine shop. But that is precisely what must be done in military life, where in ship crews or infantry companies, fighter squadrons or artillery batteries, it is much more important to preserve the delicate fabric of cohesion than to obtain a perfect match between individual skills and specialized tasks. As people in uniform enter or leave the service, as they acquire this or that skill on the job or by formal instruction, as they rise in rank, any attempt to preserve optimum efficiency in the placing of every individual must lead to constant turbulence, in which each unit of the armed forces becomes a mere transit camp for strangers coming and going. Thanks to the advent of the computer, a constant stream of transfer orders can preserve maximal efficiency, but strangers cannot be expected to risk their lives for one another, and the effectiveness of the unit will suffer accordingly, as soon as there is any fighting to be done.

The divide between efficiency and effectiveness is at its deepest in combat. What are the most effective military operations? In very general terms, they are operations in which the enemy is *not* outfought by greater firepower, greater numbers, greater bravery, and greater sacrifice of lives, but instead surprised and then outmaneuvered and disrupted, and thus never given a chance to fully employ his fighting capacity in the first place.

And what is the common denominator of such operations? Inefficiency.

Consider surprise. How is it achieved? By deception—unless the enemy is merely apathetic or unobservant, and therefore outclassed to begin with. And how is deception achieved? By doing the unexpected. And what is the unexpected? Something other than the sensible, normal, and efficient. Thus an offensive fully prepared—for which all the appropriate forces are assembled and all the necessary arrangements are carefully made to position each unit and each force at exactly the right place—cannot possibly catch the enemy by surprise, simply because in seeking to use all available means as efficiently as possible, we would broadcast all possible warning signals of the coming offensive to the enemy. If there is to be any hope of achieving surprise, some preparations must visibly be left incomplete, and some forces must remain unready or ill positioned; to add to the inefficiency, some forces and much effort must be put into camouflage, decoys, simulations, feints, and diversions.

How is the enemy outmaneuvered? By action that proceeds at a faster pace than the enemy reaction, whether in actual tactical movements, as in the classic case of ground forces' seeking to find uncovered flanks, like two wrestlers circling each other, or in operational schemes that place entire armies in the enemy's rear, or fleets where they can intercept enemy resupply ships, or in the development of weapons.* And how is the advantage obtained? By the deliberate acceptance of inefficiency. In the case of the competitive development of weapons, for example, efficiency in the use of resources demands a deliberate pace

---

* For this kind of maneuver, which entails no movement, the phrase "relational maneuver" is suggested.

in research, to avoid wasting funds on dead ends while searching for the best possible weapon configuration. Then one or more custom-made prototypes are needed, to test the design concept carefully or perhaps compare alternative designs. Next, the test results must be evaluated and costs compared just as carefully, before a specific weapon is actually engineered in detail—and that too should be done in a careful and deliberate fashion to avoid overtime charges and all the errors that come from urgency. Only when the weapon is fully specified in every detail does work begin on production tools and jigs, and then, finally, the weapons should be produced at a steady and economic rate.

Speed, by contrast, demands a broader and much less efficient research effort in which all the alternatives are explored concurrently, rather than one after another. Detailed engineering must begin as soon as a design is in hand, without the delay of a prototype stage; work begins on the tools and jigs just as soon as each part is engineered; and the first tests are conducted on weapons that are already at the preproduction stage, even though this will mean that any necessary modifications will be very costly, because some tools and jigs will have to be scrapped and made anew. Finally, production will be as rapid as possible, without regard to efficiency in using manpower (costly overtime) or equipment (multiple tooling; extra machines). Broad-front research, concurrent at each stage, and crash production rates are both inefficient, very wasteful of resources—but they may yield a weapon that is *decisive* in conflict, not merely a better weapon but one that the enemy cannot cope with at all, and which therefore can disrupt his *entire* force with a narrow but shattering impact.* In due course, countermeasures will emerge, limiting the span of the decisive advantage, but a slower development may mean that there is no period of decisive advantage at all.

If we consider a more prosaic example of the surprise/outmaneuvering/disruption sequence, a penetration and envelopment by mobile forces, we see inefficiency clearly revealed. To begin with, perfectly good fighting forces are not allowed to fight against the enemy immediately in front of them, but are instead sent on a roundabout approach in order to reach the enemy's rear. More generally, the structure of each formation—originally balanced among combat echelons, support

---

* Nowadays it is electronic warfare above all that offers such opportunities, for example in making an entire aircraft-carrier task force useless, not by fighting its destroyers, cruisers, and protective aircraft individually, but rather by successfully masking a single cruise missile diving onto the flight deck.

forces, and supply units, to obtain maximum efficiency in the use of each—is willfully disrupted, as slow-moving elements are left behind for the sake of speed. In the end, after the enemy is fatally disrupted by the successful envelopment, the *entire operation* can be said to be most efficient, when the results achieved are compared against the losses, but till then there is only inefficiency, deliberately accepted.

This, therefore, is the supreme irony: the public, media, and Congress deplore, criticize, and punish inefficiency. Managerial-minded Secretaries of Defense—like Caspar Weinberger and, far more clamorously, Robert S. McNamara—insistently promote new managerial schemes whose goal is to increase efficiency. What all parties desire and preach is a more "businesslike" Pentagon. But conflict is not like civilian business and efficiency is the wrong goal to pursue: efficiency in making a radar or refueling a ship, of course; efficiency in making radar*s*, or refueling ship*s*, no, for efficient economies of scale in purchasing radars lead to a single mass-produced radar that will be more easily countermeasured, and efficient refueling leads to a few large fleet oilers that are more easily intercepted and destroyed by the enemy. (Each of our majestic aircraft-carrier task forces is now dangerously dependent on a single, very large, very efficient resupply ship.*) Conflict *is* different.

It is not surprising that lawyer-Congressmen and businessman-Congressmen should persist in applying the wrong criterion in their examination of military matters, for efficiency is the right criterion in so many spheres of civilian life. The greater damage to the armed forces is self-inflicted. Under the guidance of civilian officials—many of whom care little about their ignorance of strategy, operational craft, and tactics, and present themselves as managers capable of managing all things regardless of their content—the military establishment itself long ago accepted the pursuit of business efficiency as its supreme goal. And that goal is by no means uncongenial to the great number of demilitarized military officers whose professional outlook is managerial anyway, who simply do not think in warlike terms (not even the most ferocious business competitors exploit the inherent vulnerability of concentrated assets to sabotage), and whose greatest personal accomplishment is a graduate degree in business administration, management or eco-

---

* Aircraft carriers must be large because a flight deck cannot be cut into two or three segments distributed on different ships; but there is no justification for the 52,500-ton "Fast Combat Support Ships" (AOEs) which carry fuel and ammunition to the carrier task forces. Obviously efficient, such overconcentration is also obviously vulnerable.

nomics.* With the passing of the generation that fought and won the Second World War, and then took on the war in Korea, the military understanding acquired by painful experience has been extinguished, leaving a vacuum in which misapplied civilian notions can flourish.

The Importance of Intangibles

Actually the displacement of *conflict* effectiveness by business efficiency is merely part of a much larger phenomenon—the pervasive materialistic bias that distorts our entire approach to defense policy and military matters in general. With few exceptions (as when nuclear weapons are at issue), Pentagon officials, military chiefs, Congress, and the media all focus their attention on the measurable, material ''inputs'' that go into the upkeep and growth of the armed forces—i.e., the weapons and supplies, maintenance and construction, salaries and benefits. Spelled out in dollars and cents, these inputs are very important considering the federal budget and the entire relationship between the military establishment and the nation's economy. But the purpose of the armed forces is to make the nation secure and powerful, and for that it is the ''outputs'' of military strength that count. In the generation of electric power or in the accumulation of savings for retirement there is a very direct relationship between what we put in and what we get out in return. We can focus on the material inputs and work to increase them if we desire more output. But when it comes to military power, the relationship between material inputs and desired outputs is not proportional; it is in fact very loose, because the making of military strength is dominated by nonmaterial, quite intangible human factors, from the quality of national military strategy to the fighting morale of individual servicemen.

The first of the intangibles standing between the inputs we pay for and the outputs of military capability that we can actually obtain is the quality of strategy at all levels. If we make the wrong choices between different forms of military power in shaping our *national military strategy,* such as overfunding the Navy at the expense of the Army, then we may spend a great deal and yet remain weaker than we should be. If we

* There are ten with such degrees for each history graduate in the officers corps; one hundred for each graduate in military history.

make the wrong choices in our *force* strategy, such as overstressing armor and artillery for the Army at the expense of light infantry, then our ground forces may be strong by some abstract measures of fire-power and yet weak in fighting the smaller wars that actually come our way. If we make the wrong choices in our *theater* strategy, such as placing too many of our European-based forces on the forward line instead of keeping an elastic reserve, then our ability to deter the wars that the Soviet Union may actually intend is correspondingly diminished. At each of its levels, strategy thus determines the "outputs" of deterrence and fighting strength that we can actually obtain from the inputs we pay for. And even the most minor errors of strategy can easily cost much more than all the fraud, waste, and mismanagement that Congress and the Pentagon seek to reduce.

Next comes the subtlest of the intangibles: *organizational* quality, the structural appropriateness or lack of it—of the service structures and the boundaries between them, of the higher command headquarters, of the branches, and of the combat units themselves. The armed forces are made of thousands of organizations, large and small, each set up in its present form in response to needs felt in the past, possibly many years ago. If these organizations were continually recast to ensure a perfect fit between structures and changing needs, the resulting chaos would dwarf any possible benefit felt within each unit and command, each branch and service. On the other hand, if the powerful bureaucratic preference for keeping things as they are, or mere habit, results in the preservation of structures that have become more and more outmoded, the quality of strategy at all levels will help us less and less, because material and human resources will then be increasingly misapplied.

For example, the American air bases in Europe are undefended, because the U.S. Air Force has no antiaircraft or ground-combat units such as those of the Royal Air Force Regiment, while for the U.S. Army the protection of rear areas is a distinctly secondary mission warranting no special effort.* For many years, this organizational gap was of no great importance because the Soviet Union had no long-range aircraft suited to "counter-air" strikes, or any other means of attacking the air bases. Besides, until 1967 the strategy of the Alliance still relied on nuclear retaliation for any serious attack, and all aspects of conventional defense were little more than symbolic. Now that the Soviet Air Force does have in the Su-24 *Fencer* a very good airfield-attack aircraft, and

---

* A most belated effort to remedy this problem has now been announced.[8]

the Soviet Army has substantial commando-type forces for deep raiding, the failure to close the mission gap between Air Force and Army could lead to disaster. Even if the damage inflicted by surprise air attacks and commando raids could be repaired in a couple of days, the entire defense of the Alliance in Germany could collapse if American air power were immobilized during the beginning stages of a war, for it is then that the ground forces would most need air support to hold the front.

More generally, the organizational structure of forces greatly influences their war-effectiveness. An army of one million men can yield fifty divisions or half that number, according to its organization. To be sure, the difference need not be significant if it is due only to the differing *sizes* of those divisions; other things being equal, twenty-five divisions of 20,000 men each should be no less effective than fifty divisions of 10,000 each. If, however, one army has twice as many divisions because its better-organized overhead consumes much less of its total strength, then the difference would be significant. Hence the importance of updating the structures of the forces, to make the most of their total resources.

The most purely professional of the intangibles is the quality of the operational methods and tactics embodied in the training and plans of the armed forces. If they contain no ingenuity, no "art of war," if they are nothing more than managerial procedures for the use of equipment and men in great quantity, then success, at best, can be expected only in combat against enemies whose ingenuity is no greater, and whose resources happen to be fewer. And in all such contests of mutual attrition, it is not only the material resources that are expended but also lives.

Similarly, if our operational methods and tactics are fixed routines that are not specifically attuned to the nature of enemy forces, while the latter use "relational" methods and tactics that are tailor-made to exploit our weaknesses and circumvent our strengths, then our wisest strategies may be undone by operational and tactical failure—and by then deterrence will already have failed.

One intangible that comes close to being measurable—at least indirectly, by way of the training that goes into its making—is skill, or rather the thousands of different skills needed by modern military forces. But when one is dealing with *combat* skills, as opposed to military cooking or military music, mechanical or clerical skills, the costs and duration of training no longer predict the results actually obtained.

When a worker is taught how to operate a new machine in civilian industry, there is no need to worry about the *realism* of his training: either he knows what to do or he does not. But the fighter pilot's skill in air combat or the rifleman's skill must be exercised under the terrible urgencies of deadly danger, and then the realism of the training counts for much more than mechanical know-how.

Training time and training costs are measured easily enough. For example, twenty flight hours per month seem to be the international norm required to keep jet-fighter pilots combat ready, and the cost can be calculated down to the last cent on the basis of the cost per flight hour, which varies from $1,000 for the cheaper fighters to $3,000 for the most elaborate. What really counts, however, is *how* those hours are flown. Are they gentle evolutions well within the safe margins, or do the pilots "pop the rivets" in high-energy maneuvers and combat acrobatics? Similarly, in preparing Army recruits for combat, twenty-two weeks of basic training (as in the British and Israeli armies) should be better than fourteen weeks or nine, and the cost difference can be measured very closely. But the seriousness of the training—which cannot be measured at all—is far more important. What really matters is not what the soldier knows, but rather what he is actually conditioned to do in the reality of combat.

One very serious obstacle to the proper training of the armed forces is the often exaggerated regard for safety rules that are already very conservative to begin with. At present the incentives for supervising officers are lopsided: accidents and, of course, deaths will attract fierce criticism from media and Congress, and can easily ruin a career, while there is no equivalent reward for realistic training. For a great many skills required by the armed forces, from oceanography to aluminum welding, from radio repair to truck driving, safety rules are prudent and necessary and do not diminish the value of the training in any way. But in preparing ground forces for combat in large field maneuvers or elite troops by means of endurance marches, in preparing warship crews for bad-weather operations, or in sharpening the dogfighting edge of fighter pilots, the value of the training directly depends on realism, and realism is dangerous.

When 50-ton tanks with powerful engines and slow-acting brakes are exercising across country at night without road lights, any foot soldiers nearby are in danger; when sailors are manning their posts on a rolling destroyer deck in high winds, they are in danger; and when fighter pilots go to the limit in steep dives and fast turns, and in high-speed bombing runs 30 feet off the ground, they too are in danger. Because all such activities are indeed dangerous, there must be safety rules, and the rules must be properly enforced. But when the successive outcries that follow occasional accidents over the years lead to more and more restrictive rules that sacrifice a larger and larger portion of realism, the ultimate consequence could be much worse than any number of peacetime deaths, should a war occur.

In war, tank columns must always move at night without any visible lights, and in the fragmented terrain of woods and cities the infantry must dismount from its armored carriers to give close escort against any enemy foot soldiers with antitank weapons. If this procedure has never been realistically practiced because of stringent safety rules, either there will be *many* accidents when it must be done for the first time in war, or else tanks will be destroyed because of their lack of proper escort. And it is one of the ironies of war that even as combat aircraft become more and more automated and their crews have less and less to do, the few functions that still depend on the eyes, brains, and hands of fighter pilots loom larger and larger in importance—and so does pilot training, in quantity and quality. In the air battles fought between Arabs and Israelis (in which 644 Arab aircraft were shot down between 1967 and 1982 as against perhaps 14 Israeli fighters[9]), in the entire Second World War, in Korea, and in Vietnam (where 193 Vietnamese fighters were shot down, as against 81 Air Force, Navy, and Marine aircraft[10]), pilot quality has been *the* decisive factor, more important than any but the grossest differences in aircraft performance. And pilots of high quality are made first by severe selection and then by training that is both intense and realistic—and thus inevitably dangerous. If pilots are branded as gung-ho cowboys for trying out risky maneuvers, if officers are penalized in their careers for accidents that will occur in any realistic training program, the entire fighting edge of the forces will be dulled over time.

Finally there are the classic human intangibles of war: leadership, group cohesion, and individual morale. Leadership at all levels comes first because it is also the main influence on the other two. Of subtle origin and very fragile, leadership is easily damaged, especially by the pursuit of corporate-style goals in the education and "career management" of the officer corps. Once again, what is good for business is not good for deadly conflict. For example, because personal ambition drives effort it is much valued in business; but in the military only a little ambition can be tolerated, because men in combat must never suspect that they are being exposed to greater risk for the sake of another man's career. Similarly, the corporate world has good reason to be unfriendly to personal eccentricities in dress, speech, manner, and style because any unusual trait may irritate a customer or a banker in the casual encounters common in business, perhaps losing a sale or hampering a loan; hence the smooth organization man does best with safely conservative dress and inoffensively conventional style. But an officer's important dealings with those below him and those above him are not casual; first impressions are not the last, and therefore, within the limits of regulations, outward eccentricities should be tolerated, especially because a man brave enough to lead in combat is also likely to be brave enough to defy convention, and is quite likely to want to do just that. (The matter is not trivial: leadership is a delicate thing.)

The importance and even the true meaning of cohesion are not quite so obvious as those of leadership and morale, both of which are experienced in everyday civilian life. It is only when we visualize the terrible stress of combat, in which survival and success so often depend on the willingness of fighters to take risks for one another, that we can appreciate the crucial importance of "buddy solidarity" in the myriad of units, teams, and crews that make up the armed forces as a whole. The cohesion of all those groups is a key determinant of combat strength, and it is fragile. The pursuit of manpower efficiencies by the frequent moving of individuals from unit to unit, in order to fit each one into his own best slot as qualifications and seniority change over time, achieves one-man efficiencies at the price of weakened group solidarity. To say that warfare is a team effort is a mere commonplace, and yet the need to make teams and keep them together is frequently overlooked.

The supreme intangible among all the human factors is individual fighting morale: it has no measurable input cost at all, yet it is the greatest single influence on the output of true combat strength. Quite probably not one of the thousand and more generals and admirals in the four services would deny this, but in the reality of their day-to-day decisions they act otherwise. For example, while vast sums are spent to obtain sometimes very small improvements in equipment by research and development, there is hardly any systematic research in morale questions. Thus the Army never bothered at the time to investigate the morale effect of its individual-rotation system in Vietnam, which left the troops in a state of solitude before the enemy. Nor does the Air Force, which spends hundreds of millions of dollars to obtain a 10-percent thrust increase in a jet engine, devote any real effort now to find out what it takes to make a really sharp fighter pilot.* Similarly, while billions are spent to obtain better equipment for the forces, only the most feeble provision is made for the practical, social, and emotional needs of service families whose husbands and fathers are serving away from home on "unaccompanied tours" or at sea. At the same time, the military mail works very well (as a material process, it is treated very seriously), so that word of each domestic problem can swiftly damage the morale of the servicemen, who often feel impotent and captive when they hear of plumbing in need of petty repair, or of a son on drugs.

Especially in a society where many have become persuaded that happiness is a right, the attention given to morale is a clear indication of its true priority. The British Army has regiments that still operate today very much as tight tribal families; the Soviet Army is harsh but has commissars with little to do except look after the morale of the troops; the American Army has social workers as well as MPs to look after the troublemakers, but nothing much for the merely troubled and lonely. To be sure, ever since the so-called "all-volunteer" force replaced the draft, the service chiefs have been very much concerned to keep pay and benefits competitive with civilian earnings. But important as that is, the emphasis on pay and benefits is nevertheless an expression of the materialist bias, because so little is done to attract and retain servicemen by social means. In an alienated society, the armed forces, if only they organized accordingly, could offer ready-made extended families to the recruits—an old military trick, much used by successful armies (as by the wartime German Army, which was noted for its exceptional morale), and which costs little or nothing.

What is extraordinary about the habitual neglect of all these intangibles by the American military establishment is merely that it persists virtually unremarked, notwithstanding all the failures in war that the gross overemphasis on material inputs has caused ever since Korea, and in spite of the most basic lessons that can be extracted from military history. In considering the familiar evidence of the Second World War, the victory of Germany over Poland could be superficially attributed to material superiority alone—but how then is one to explain the successful resistance of the Finns against Stalin's invasion? (As compared with the Finns, the Polish Army was lavishly equipped and scarcely outnum-

---

* Neither Air Force nor Navy will train pilots unless they have already completed four years of college education; therefore many are likely to be married and with children before they ever sit in an operational cockpit. But do we really want college-trained fathers as fighter pilots?

bered.) Similarly, except for air power, any comparison of numbers and weapons would have shown the Anglo-French forces of May 1940 as much stronger than those of Hitler's Germany—on the eve of the battles that left France invaded and Britain under siege in a mere six weeks. Most notably, the French alone had more and better tanks, but the Germans used their tanks in the *Blitzkrieg* to spearhead front-breaking invasion columns, while the British and French mostly used theirs merely as support weapons for the infantry line. In this case the dominating intangible was the superior war craft of the German army.

Six months later, a thinly armed British army of 31,000 men easily defeated a much larger Italian army in the first week of the North African offensive of December 1940, capturing 38,000 prisoners at a cost of 133 killed, 387 wounded, and 8 missing.[11] Except for a few well-employed tanks, the British advantages were all intangible, mainly a superior operational method (a quick copy of the German *Blitzkrieg*) and much better junior leadership and troop morale. Similarly, the German armies in the summer and autumn of 1941 were inferior in numbers to the Soviet armies they so roundly defeated, and it was only in the air that the Germans had higher-quality equipment; otherwise their superiority was all in the intangibles. Hitler's strategy violated the only principle of war that Field Marshal Montgomery would endorse (invade neither Russia nor China), but Stalin, who would trust no other man, insisted on trusting Hitler and refused to allow a full mobilization against the attack that came in June 1941—for fear of provoking a war that Hitler had long planned. It was again the German method of armored warfare, as well as fine tactics and carefully nurtured junior leadership, cohesion, and morale that defeated more than two hundred Soviet divisions during the first year of war.[12] But ultimately nothing could remedy Hitler's defective *national strategy,* which first made Germany very strong, but only for short wars, to seize countries in one bound, and which then sent the German Army to invade the only country of Europe too deep to be captured in one bound. Sheer distance had already defeated the Germans, by overstretching their supply lines—before the first snow and before the first Russian counteroffensive.

When the Japanese swiftly conquered Malaya and Singapore immediately after Pearl Harbor, they were most surprised to capture many more British troops and much more equipment than they themselves had in the entire theater of war. The Japanese did have air superiority, but their bombing capacity was so small that it was their outmaneuvering jungle tactics and fast-paced operational tempo that decided the outcome—unmeasurable intangibles that had not appeared in any pre-war comparison of the military balance. Earlier, the attack on Pearl Harbor had come as a complete surprise, in spite of successful code-breaking, partly because Japanese combat skill and tactical ingenuity had been grossly underestimated. Unaware of the unique quality of Japanese naval aviators, of their ability to fly accurately at long range and then prevail in air combat against fresh pilots, of their deadly pre-cision with bombs and torpedoes, the Americans who were reading the Japanese diplomatic cables thought that the Philippines might be in-vaded, but could not imagine that the U.S. Navy's fleet at Pearl Harbor was in imminent danger.

Half a year later, the Japanese made the same mistake about the Americans, whose abilities they rated as very low after the clumsy American performance at Pearl Harbor and defeat in the Philippines. Very much aware of the huge armaments effort under way in the United States, the Japanese feared for the future, when all those new warships and aircraft would reach the Pacific, but they felt very confident of defeating the remnants of the prewar American fleet in the meantime. The decisive defeat of the materially superior Japanese fleet in the great naval battle near Midway island in June 1942 owed everything to the intangibles, and virtually nothing to the belated war mobilization of American industry. It was because of that most rarefied of all intangi-bles, secret intelligence obtained by code-breaking, and because of lead-ers willing to risk its use that the U.S. Navy was able to ambush the Japanese attempt at a surprise attack. And it was primarily because of the distinct American advantage in the obscure skills of shipboard dam-age control that successful air attacks caused far greater loss to the Japanese than to the American Navy.

It was only in the last two years or so of the Second World War that the material factors seemingly began to dominate, and the outcome of battles and campaigns supposedly became the predictable result of nu-merical and weapon advantages. The claim of Germans and Japanese at the time was that their military virtues were simply overwhelmed by the sheer size and material means of the Allied forces. Though seemingly plausible or even self-evident, this explanation is nevertheless an optical illusion. It is true that after 1942 the Allies had an ever-increasing su-periority in numbers and equipment in virtually every theater of war and every form of warfare. But in fact these material superiorities be-came decisive only because quality differences between the two sides became smaller and smaller as the hurriedly mobilized Allied forces gradually matured, their combat skills steadily improved, and their leaders became more adept.

By 1944 the Soviet Army not only had many more tanks than the German, but also troops properly trained by then in using their weapons, well-led units cohesive enough to fight, and a new generation of young generals altogether superior to the Stalin cronies and political hacks who had presided over the catastrophic defeats of 1941 and 1942.

By then the armies of the United States and the British Empire had acquired many able junior leaders and millions of well-trained troops. Had the GIs who landed in Normandy on D-Day fought like the hapless beginners caught at the Kasserine Pass two years earlier, no victory could have been won in France, even against battered and depleted German forces. The naval officers and sailors of the Anglo-American fleets were obviously highly competent, and by 1944 the fighter pilots of all British and American services were usually superior to their German counterparts, and totally outclassed the raw cadets whom the desperate Japanese were sending into air combat.

The great upsurge of war production by the United States, the Soviet Union, and Britain therefore masked the more important ingredient of their victories of 1945. It was indeed a colossal achievement to produce all those tanks, aircraft, warships, and everything else; but the *decisive* achievement was the training of vast armies, navies, and air forces, the development of sound methods and tactics that suited the new forces, the creation of a vast yet competent mass of officers out of minuscule peacetime cadres (in the American case especially), and the formulation of sensible strategies for the use of all those forces. Whenever the Allies tried to prevail by sheer superiority of matériel with inadequate tactics, as in the battles of Monte Cassino of 1943, and as late in the war as the Arnhem operation of 1944 ("Market Garden"), they were defeated.

Likewise, the results of the fighting between Arabs and Israelis since 1948 reveal the dominance of intangibles. In the early summer of 1948, at the beginning of the first all-out war (desultory guerrilla fighting had begun long before), Israelis who had hurriedly formed into makeshift battalions—armed with little more than rifles but strong in morale and with spirited junior leaders—managed to contain the invading Arab forces of well-armed infantry, which had artillery in support, quite a few armored cars, and even some tanks. By the end of 1948, the new Israeli Army—which was already fighting in brigades and had a few dozen aircraft for its air corps, a handful of tanks, and some two hundred half-track carriers to spearhead its truck columns—had expelled the invaders and was stopped from larger conquests only by British and American pressures.

In June 1967 the Israelis were once again faced by Arab armies with superior equipment, and once again they won decisive victories on three fronts, conquering much territory in the process. Highly effective operational methods—in both the deep-penetration offensives of the armored forces and the all-out surprise air strike against Arab airfields—were added to the long-standing Israeli advantages in morale, combat skill, leadership, and tactics. At the time, some said that the Israelis won because they attacked by surprise on June 5, 1967, in the fourth week of the crisis that began when Egypt sent its army into the Sinai. But in October 1973, when it was the Egyptians and the Syrians who achieved surprise, the Israelis won all the same, counterattacking with great force after the first few days of confusion and defeat, and winning more territory than they had lost. Finally, in June 1982, when the Israelis—with both superior numbers and superior equipment on their side —fought the Syrian Army and Air Force in Lebanon, their victory was swift and utterly crushing. After a mere forty hours of actual fighting, the Syrians were forced to ask for a cease-fire (in very humiliating circumstances, for the Israelis would give no respite to the PLO), and by then they had already lost great quantities of advanced equipment and several thousand dead.

In those rare cases when the intangibles are more or less evenly matched, as in the war between Iran and Iraq, a stalemate is the usual result, even if there is a great difference in the material inputs—equipment and numbers. Abundantly armed with a full selection of the latest Soviet weapons and also a variety of Western weapons, the Iraqis advanced at the very beginning of the war in September 1980 and seized the southwestern fringe of Iran virtually unopposed. But soon they were barely holding their ground against the counterattacks of the Iranian revolutionary militia and rather small bodies of regular troops. In 1981, the Iraqis were expelled from most of the Iranian territory they had taken, even though they remained conspicuously superior in armor and firepower, equipment and logistics. As the war continued year after year, the Iraqi forces received further large supplies of the latest Soviet equipment as well as French jet fighters and assorted hardware from the world arms market (e.g., Brazilian armored cars). Nevertheless, they remained very much on the defensive, precariously holding a long front against the attacks of Iran's three-part army, made up of lightly armed volunteers with the simplest infantry training; surviving fragments of the Shah's army and air force, still equipped with the remnants of a once magnificent arsenal; and new units still raw and poorly armed with a hodgepodge of freshly imported weapons (North Korean tanks, Spanish mortars, and more). Partly because of this three-part division, Iranian logistics remained chaotic, capable of little more than conveying the major ammunition to the battle fronts. To judge by the material inputs on each side, Iraq should have won the war long ago—but as usual, it was the intangibles that dominated.

Actually the Iran–Iraq conflict is a most interesting example of how the intangible of *theater* strategy can be of exceptional importance. The Iraqis were defeated from the start by an incoherent strategy. When Iraq's sole ruler, Saddam Hussein, started the war in September 1980, he did so by surprise (which is the clever thing to do, tactically) and with very modest war aims (which is the clever thing to do, politically), but he overlooked the contradiction between the two. With Iran in revolution and its military forces in disarray, Iraq had emerged as the remaining strong power in the region, according to all the usual comparisons of force inventories and weapon lists. But when he sent his forces to attack and invade, Hussein asked Iran only to evacuate three tiny and uninhabited islands in the Persian Gulf (seized by the Shah in 1972) and to make some very minor adjustments to the common border, restoring the 1913 demarcation line along the Shatt-el-Arab estuary. Consistent with these very limited war aims, when the Iraqis attacked they did not mount a full-scale invasion that would take them all the way to Tehran; they merely crossed the border and settled down to occupy their modest conquests. In international politics, modest war aims are usually the key to success, and surprise is always of great tactical value. So Saddam Hussein undoubtedly was most surprised to discover that in the paradoxical realm of strategy, two war-winners can add up to a loser. A surprise attack is desirable *only* if it is the prelude to all-out invasion; but if, as in this case, there is neither the will nor the capacity to follow the initial attack with a total invasion, then surprise can easily lead to strategic defeat. Had Hussein not attacked by surprise, had the Iranians been warned of the coming attack and mustered their forces to meet it, the Iraqis would have had to fight hard at the beginning, instead of crossing the border almost unopposed. But then they would also have had a chance to defeat the Iranian forces. With the road to Tehran wide open, Saddam Hussein might have been able to advance that far, to negotiate from strength a satisfactory end to the war.

By their surprise attack, the Iraqis were assured of an easy success at the start, but all they achieved was the seizure of some square miles of Iran's vast territory. Far from being defeated, Iran's slow-moving forces were not even on the scene. The Iranians had been provoked but not decisively weakened; they began to muster their forces to attack, with increasing strength. From the immediate aftermath of the invasion till this writing, Iran has had the initiative. Having lost long ago their easy conquests, the Iraqis remain hard-pressed, on the defensive and facing endless war.

The Links of the Chain

An intellectual's prejudice would rank strategy in its various levels as the most important of the intangibles that go into the making of military power. But actually strategic coherence is no more important than any other of the intangibles, for at least a modest adequacy in each of them is an absolute requirement of military success. Without fighting morale there is no military power, but even high morale counts for little without at least a minimum of trained skill. Both are of little avail if cohesion is lacking, and all must be for nought if there is no adequate leadership to direct the fighting. And what high-morale, skilled, cohesive, and decently led forces can actually achieve in combat will depend on the quality of their tactics.

If forces fight with the wrong tactics or simply defy tactics by attempting the unfeasible, all the other qualities will only multiply casualties, as in those doomed infantry charges of 1914 in which the attempt was made to overwhelm 500-rounds-per-minute machine guns with the 3-miles-per-hour momentum of advancing infantry. Adequate tactics in each facet of the fighting are therefore necessary, but they are not sufficient. If the operational methods of war that the tactics serve are fundamentally wrong in concept, there can be no success. In 1940 many of the French forces holding segments of the Maginot Line fought very well indeed, contrary to legend, but their stubborn defense merely ensured their captivity, because in the meantime the entire Line was being circumvented and outflanked. Finally, even the best of operational methods combining valid tactics ably carried out by motivated, skilled, cohesive, and well-led forces will only make failure more agonizing when one or more of the levels of strategy prohibit success.

It is not controversial to note that the troubles of our armed forces and of the entire defense establishment derive more from defects in the intangibles than from any possible inadequacies in the material inputs listed in each year's defense budget. Obviously, therefore, the best energies of Pentagon officials and military leaders alike should be devoted to the advancement of our strategy at each level, to the improvement of operational methods, to tactical innovation, and to the enhancement of morale, cohesion, and leadership.

But there is a great and obvious obstacle: while the material inputs are all hard facts, costs precisely stated in dollars and cents, the intangibles are difficult even to define and mostly cannot be measured at all. All those involved in defense policy-making will readily admit that strategy and all the other intangibles are of decisive importance, but they continue to neglect them. Recoiling from the complications of strategy, unwilling to make the effort needed to seriously examine tactical and operational matters, reluctant to immerse themselves in the infinite mass of details of leadership, cohesion, and morale, Pentagon officials and far too many military men happily cooperate in focusing on the inputs, the costs and material details that can be understood and argued about in perfect certainty. Then there is no need for strategic wisdom, nor for any serious study of military craft; the lowly skills of the bookkeeper are quite sufficient.

Certainly Congress is greatly to blame. To an ever-increasing extent, not only the Pentagon's civilian officials but also its military chiefs are forced to devote much of their time and energy to "Congressional relations"—to appear before the committees, to answer official and unofficial inquiries, and to prepare formal reports. Inevitably, Congressional priorities become their priorities, shaping not merely their timetables but also their outlook—and Congress focuses almost exclusively on the material inputs. Anyone who cares to read the "Hearing" books that record the sessions of the Armed Services Committees of the House and Senate discovers that those bulky volumes contain page after page of dialogue between senior defense officials and Congressmen on the exact costs and exact specifications of each weapon, lengthy argument about every other measurable input—and little or nothing about the strategic intangibles that actually determine what armed forces are needed in the first place, and in what form.

When admirals, officials, and Congressmen gather to examine the Navy in each year's review of the budget, ten minutes of desultory chitchat disposes of the entire question of naval strategy—i.e., the purpose of the Navy, its major tasks, and the chosen operational formats

—before all concerned settle down to many weeks of scrutiny, in great detail, of every single item of expenditure. As naval strategy is slighted, so are air strategy and ground strategy, as are military strategy as a whole and all organizational questions (other than the creation of posts for political appointees). Debate on each service's chosen operational concepts of war, which actually determine their equipment needs, is almost unknown, and all agree that tactics are not worth discussing— even though often enough capabilities acquired by very costly research and development programs could have been achieved far more cheaply by the devising of better tactics instead.

Similarly, Congress is vapidly superficial in dealing with human factors and all personnel questions—except in regard to the measurables of pay, benefits, and pensions. The general in Okinawa who sends his favorite poodle to its favorite doggie-hairdresser in Beverly Hills by four-engine military jet, the servicemen guilty of using drugs, the incompetent surgeon in uniform who has butchered a whole string of patients —all attract eager denunciations and offer scope for rich rhetorical fulminations, and that virtually exhausts the subject as far as Congress is concerned. The quality and seriousness of training, the stability of manpower in the single units, the professional competence of officers, and the education of officers reaching the higher echelons of command are never debated in Congress, or not seriously, at any rate, even though they make a far greater difference to the real military strength of the nation than the purchase or nonpurchase of any one of the warships or aircraft deemed worthy of the most obsessive scrutiny.

It is consistent with this wholly misplaced materialistic bias that Congress is much more tolerant of lethal incompetence than of mere venality. The general who loves his poodle too much or the admiral who may have asked a sailor to paint his fence during duty hours is harshly criticized, while their colleague who planned a debacle that humiliated the entire nation and killed several soldiers is easily forgiven. There is no procedure, or seemingly even the desire, to root out military incompetence. When the Army chose to promote the commander of the 1980 Iran rescue task force to lieutenant general almost immediately after the debacle, there was no protest from Congress. When the Long Commission, appointed in the wake of the Beirut bombing, called for the punishment of the negligent, Congress did not intervene, even though the officers in question lacked the good grace to resign, their service chiefs failed to act, and the Secretary of Defense chose to issue only the mildest form of reprimand.

To be sure, it would not be easy for Congress to address the questions that really matter. It would mean engaging in serious strategic discourse and reasoned discussions about the operational and tactical aspects of modern war. Much time would have to be devoted to the subject of morale, the stability of units, officer education, and the selection of our generals and admirals, and even more perhaps would have to be devoted to the appraisal of theater-strategic plans for the Alliance defense of Europe and for Korea and the Persian Gulf, and of force-strategic plans for the use of naval, air, and nuclear forces. And of course the national military strategy above both sets of plans would make a still larger subject for lengthy investigations.

Even though a great many other very intricate subjects are deemed worthy of the most exacting scrutiny (natural-gas pricing, farm subsidies, Social Security revision, and more), the proper examination of the intangibles of military power is much less congenial to most Congressmen, whose lawyerly minds are trained to deal in very specific facts. And it is just as uncongenial to military officers of the bureaucratic kind, and even more to the senior defense officials whose skills and interests are administrative or political. Therefore, by common agreement it is simply assumed that the outputs will somehow correspond to the inputs, that numbers and firepower, accuracy and lethality, speeds and payloads, survivability and supply, and all such material inputs will translate into the outputs of deterrence and actual fighting strength. The intangibles are left to take care of themselves—or more precisely, some are left at the mercy of mere habit and mindless continuity, while others are controlled by military officers not especially selected by their own services nor supervised by the Presidentially appointed senior defense officials. After all, in a military establishment where the battles of the budget—among the services and then with Congress—count for everything, while strategy and the rest of the intangibles are deemed too vague and inconclusive to warrant serious attention, it is inevitable that they should be left to the second-stringers and also-rans.

If the United States is ever again to use force successfully on any serious scale, against any serious enemy, if we are ever to improve the relationships between the dollars we spend and the military strength we actually get, ways must be found to elevate strategy and all the other intangibles above the bookkeepers' idea of what is important. Obviously such a transformation of priorities cannot be achieved by mere preaching. It can be done only by a recasting of incentives in the promotion of military officers, in the advancement of bureaucrats, and above all in the machinery of Congressional review. So long as Congress continues to regard the upkeep of morale, the realism of training, the stability of units, the cultivation of operational talent in selecting senior officers, and, above all, strategy at each level as mere trivia, while giving all its earnest attention to the individual "line" items of the budget, the military establishment will do exactly the same thing.

Of course the *total* defense budget and its *broadest* choices do deserve serious examination by Congress and the public, because of their large economic consequences. But what should follow that necessary first step is a serious appraisal of the intangibles across the board, instead of an obsessive scrutiny of the material inputs in minute detail, as is now the case. It is, of course, the interest of their constituencies that compels Senators, Representatives, and their staffs to pay serious attention not merely to the material inputs in general but to the individual line items. If they fail to do their bit (or at least make a very good show of trying) to ensure funding for the weapons purchase that will in turn provide employment for the local defense contractors, if they fail to prevent the closing of the local military base that is perhaps useless militarily but very important to the local economy, they will certainly lose votes and may lose their seats.

There is nothing shocking or anything very damaging about Senators and Congressmen who thus represent the interests of their electors. Rising standards of public morality have already liberated Congressmen from much of the compulsion to provide jobs for their constituents, by replacing a good many political appointees with civil servants, by setting firm limits on the dams that can be built and on the pork-barrel contracts that can be handed out. If the staffs of individual Congressmen continue to hunt for local advantage in the single-line items of the defense budget, no great harm is done; the trouble is that having catered to the needs of their own electorates, the members of Congress then fail to do their duty to the nation by proceeding to a serious examination of the intangibles, which cannot be computed or computerized but which can most certainly be studied, debated, and improved. With four well-staffed committees in the Senate and another four in the House now active in reviewing military matters, it should be possible to devote at least one committee in each house to the strategy that should guide the budget, and another to the actual military *content* of all those separate line items.

Only then will it become possible for the higher officials of the Pentagon and the military chiefs to redirect their attention, opening the way for fundamental improvements of strategy and military organization that will be far more beneficial than any possible reduction in fraud, waste, and mismanagement.

The present priorities may have achieved some small savings at the margin. They also erode our security by giving us much less military power than we pay for, and they have certainly hurt our higher strategic interests, and also our self-esteem, by yielding a long record of military failure, ever since the Korean war.

CHAPTER SIX

☆

The Officer Surplus and the Research Merry-Go-Round

In spite of the greater visibility of the civilian Pentagon officials, the greater power of decision remains with the armed forces. To a large extent, the civilians merely administer decisions already made within each separate service. The service chiefs shape the structure of the forces, even if Congress determines their size by setting budgets. They choose the design of weapons, if not their number, and they control the operational conduct of the war, even if it is the civilians from the President down who decide what wars are fought, for how long, and within what limits.

Obviously, therefore, the quality of American officers is crucial. At present, the fact that so many of them are highly educated and strongly dedicated is of little benefit to the nation. The grossly excessive number of officers above middle rank drowns the undoubted talent and dedication of individual officers in the mediocrity of the crowd. And the diffusion of decision-making power among the many separate military bureaucracies that have proliferated over the years to accommodate all those officers defeats the pursuit of any coherent policy in peace or war. The consequences of the officer surplus for the peacetime management of the military establishment are widespread and surprisingly harmful. By far the least important of those consequences is the cost of officer salaries and benefits.

☆

When we compare the officer cadres of today with those of 1945, when the United States was more fully mobilized than ever before or since,

157

with more than 12 million under arms, the result is quite remarkable. The first point to note is that there is not now and there never has been any surplus of *junior* officers (from second lieutenant to captain, or Navy ensign to lieutenant). On June 30, 1945, when the enlisted total in all services was 10,795,775, the number of junior officers was 1,031,523 —a little more than a 10:1 ratio.[1] Considering the large number of junior officers serving as individual specialists—pilots or meteorologists, surgeons or surveyors—and allowing for junior officers serving as staff aides and administrators, a 10:1 ratio is the highest that will allow the required number of commanders for small units, platoons, and companies, small boats and ship departments, aircraft squadrons, ground crews, and so on.

Even if there had been a surplus of junior officers over the number needed to fill all the posts in the 1945 table of organization, that would not have been evidence of excess. As commanders of 30-man platoons or 100-man companies in the ground forces, as fighter pilots and in bomber crews, aboard warships or actually in charge of torpedo boats, junior officers in the fighting echelons notoriously suffered high casualties.

Moreover, a pool of spare officers was needed for the frequent relief of those actually engaged in combat. When first sent into action, junior officers who were platoon commanders, fighter pilots, and so on performed better and better as they acquired more combat experience. But they were also absorbing more and more stress. In some cases, the outcome of cumulative stress was a sudden breakdown, usually triggered by some incident that was trivial in itself. Usually the effect was more subtle: a growing fatalism masked by the casual attitude that comes with expertise. Eventually this could result in outright apathy, even in the midst of combat. Unless relieved, at least for a while, men who were thus afflicted would become a danger to themselves and everyone with them. Thus some surplus of junior officers was certainly needed, during the Second World War, to allow for spells of rotation out of combat, and would become necessary again in any serious fighting.

On June 30, 1950, five days after the outbreak of the Korean war, the strength of the American armed forces was—not by coincidence—at its lowest point ever between the end of the Second World War and today. At that time the enlisted total was 1,269,891, and the number of junior officers stood at 117,928, almost an 11:1 ratio. It was widely believed then that the invasion of South Korea by Communist North Korea was merely the opening move of a general Soviet offensive against Western Europe. Some feared that the North Korean attack was a calculated act of misdirection whose purpose was to draw into the remote Korean peninsula the very small combat-ready forces of the United States. Nor were such fears so farfetched: with its conventional forces very weak, and with all its European allies except Britain virtually disarmed, the United States was relying very heavily on the atomic bomb, but its monopoly had just been lost. (The Soviet Union detonated a fission device in September 1949; the North Korean invasion followed nine months later.)

In any case, the response of the Truman Administration was not confined to Korea but instead took the form of a very broad and fast rearmament of all the services worldwide.* By 1952, the number of enlisted men had almost tripled, reaching a total of 3,245,310 by June 30 of that year, while the number of junior officers had increased less than proportionally, to 254,905. The ratio had thus risen further, to almost 13:1, and there was a distinct shortage of junior officers, certainly in the combat units of the ground forces.

By the time the Eisenhower Administration took office in 1953, fears of an imminent third world war had evaporated; the war in Korea had become exceedingly unpopular, as casualties mounted with no victory in sight; and there was acute concern about military spending and the deficit. The soldier President accordingly set out to reduce the number of soldiers—or rather, the costly conventional forces as a whole. His "bigger bang for the buck" defense policy relied on a sharper nuclear deterrence, supposedly much enhanced by the newly developed hydrogen bomb. Under the new strategy of "Massive Retaliation," the United States would supposedly punish any major aggression by nuclear bombing, instead of relying on conventional forces. Therefore there was no need for the powerful and very costly array of ground, air, and naval forces that the Truman Administration had been building up. But there was no drastic demobilization of officers and men; instead, their numbers slowly declined during the remaining years of the decade, from 3.55 million in 1953 to 2.47 million in 1960.

In a third abrupt reversal of basic military policy within little more than a decade, the Kennedy Administration set out in 1961 to rebuild American military power across the board, both to strengthen nuclear

---

* Between 1950 and 1952, the defense budget increased by 407 percent—an increase three times as great as the 1981–1983 Reagan rearmament.[2]

deterrence *and* to adopt a more flexible strategy in which the use of nuclear weapons would be the last resort, instead of the first move. The number of enlisted men and junior officers thus began to increase—a process that greatly accelerated when the new strategy was overtaken by Vietnam.

By December 31, 1968, at the peak of the American intervention in Hanoi's thirty-year struggle for regional supremacy, the enlisted total stood at 2,977,093, and there were 254,457 junior officers in the four services—a lower ratio* than in 1952, but still above 10:1. Following the withdrawal from Vietnam, the armed forces steadily declined in size as well as in funding throughout the 1970s, and the modest Reagan buildup that began in 1981 did not come anywhere near to undoing the results. At the last reckoning, on May 31, 1983, the enlisted total was 1,821,315, and there were 175,186 junior officers, so once again the ratio remained a little above 10:1.[3]

Thus throughout the post–World War Two period there has been no increase in the ratio of enlisted men to junior officers. In fact, not all the junior-officer posts in the official tables of organization of the combat forces are filled at present, and there is an actual shortage in some cases.

When we consider the middle ranks (from major to colonel or Navy lieutenant commander to captain), the picture is radically different. In 1945, there were 143,558 officers in the middle ranks, 1.3 of them per 100 enlisted men. There was much for those officers to do then—with some ninety Army divisions and some forty corps, and army, Army-Group, and theater headquarters in need of staffs; with a Navy so large that it included one hundred aircraft carriers; with the naval air forces numbering ten times as many aircraft as the Air Force has today; and with a great many positions to be filled in the worldwide logistic networks of the forces, in the military governments of occupied Germany, Italy, and Japan, and within the entire support structure at home and abroad.

But the proportion of middle-ranking officers was phenomenally altered by 1950, the historical low point in the strength of the armed forces. There were then 51,241 middle-ranking officers, 4.0 of them per 100 enlisted men—a more-than-*300-percent* increase over the ratio of 1945. That was a deliberate result of key decisions made before 1945 by the chiefs of the Army, Army Air Forces, Navy, and Marine Corps. As

---

* My thanks to John M. Hendrik of Annapolis, Maryland, for clarifying remarks on the expression of ratios.

early as 1943, when the war against Germany and Japan was still being fought, selected staff officers were given the task of planning the structure and missions of their services in the postwar world.[4] Having personally experienced the massive disorder of the sudden, all-out mobilization that followed Pearl Harbor, and very much aware of its wasteful urgencies and makeshift improvisations, the planners made it their goal to prepare for another great mobilization that would bring the forces back to their 1945 dimensions, with 10 million or more in uniform. For the Navy, this meant keeping the ships built during the war in reserve, protected against rust and weather; for the Army, it meant keeping the war-expanded structure of training camps and depots; for the Air Force, more skeptical of long wars now that strategic bombardment had increased its efficiency with nuclear bombs, no physical preparations would count for much. But all the services did their best to retain the largest possible number of middle and senior officers.

Congress never formally approved the mass remobilization plans, and neither did the higher civilian officials. But there was no need for any such approval, because there was nothing controversial about those plans. In 1945 the Cold War had yet to begin, but it was already clear that the overriding task of the armed forces was to deter a war with the Soviet Union, and that the United States would have to maintain a believable capacity to remobilize in order to fight on a continental scale, as the Soviet Union could, with many millions bearing arms. The United States still had a monopoly over the fission bomb, but only a small minority of the officers in charge, mostly in the Air Force, believed that all threats could be nullified by the counterthreat of nuclear attack alone.

In the circumstances, the need for service structures specifically designed for quick remobilization seemed obvious. At any rate, there was no interference by civilian officials in the military planning of 1945–1948, in which the largest possible number of middle-ranking (and senior) officers were to be retained on active duty, in storage as it were, ready to take charge of greatly expanded forces in the event of another great war. While enlisted men and junior officers could be turned out quickly from the training bases and officer schools, their seniors obviously had need of far more prolonged career preparation.

This argument for remobilization was sound, and it remains sound today. But it does not necessarily lead to the conclusion that extra officers should be kept on active duty. One obvious alternative is to rely on civilian reservists. Selected junior officers who return to civilian life after completing their service could be given the opportunity to pursue a part-time vocation as military officers. Starting out with their original training and practical full-time experience in the more junior ranks, reserve officers could advance in rank by attending training courses at each stage and by taking tests and participating in exercises. The military experience of countries as diverse as Switzerland and Israel shows that part-time reserve officers can attain high competence in this way, with not much more than one month a year of courses and exercises, as well as occasional one-day refreshers. In the Israeli Army, reserve officers have successfully commanded battalions, brigades, and divisions in each war since 1948; as of this writing, one of the multidivisional corps (a very large force with as many tanks as the entire British Army) is also commanded by a reserve officer, albeit one who retired as a senior general.[5]

For men approaching middle age who can still enjoy some youthful diversions in uniform and who may also derive prestige from their second identity as officers of considerable rank, the attractions of a reserve scheme can be considerable. The Army National Guard and Army Reserve, the Air National Guard and Air Force Reserve, the Naval Reserve and Marine Corps Reserve offer just such an arrangement now. Though often short of enlisted men, technical sergeants, and junior officers, none of the reserve forces has ever lacked middle-ranking officers.

It is true that many active-duty officers have a low opinion of their reserve counterparts, especially in the Army National Guard. But even if the command of large formations is thought to be too exacting to be left to part-timers, they could certainly fill many staff positions in the combat forces, and even more in training, logistics, and administration. As for the specialist functions, reserve officers could certainly bring valuable civilian expertise to their mobilization assignments; business executives have many skills directly valid in every aspect of supply and transport, civilian engineers are well suited to serve as military engineers, accountants can staff finance departments and pay offices, academics can fill out Intelligence units, and so on, profession by profession.

As it is, many reserve officers have individual assignments, but at present they are treated as mere supernumeraries; they are added to offices already abundantly staffed, instead of running those offices on a rotating basis along with a skeleton crew of active-duty officers. That naturally affects recruiting; no capable, dynamic civilian executive or professional wants to serve as an individual reservist when he will be confined to make-work tasks during his annual stint in uniform. If suitable and essential work were assigned to reserve officers, each slot could keep twelve reservists in training (assuming one month of recall per year), with the ongoing work passed on from one reservist to another. Though impossible for many officer jobs, such as the command of active-duty forces, such a system is quite adequate for many other jobs in which civilian skills can be matched with military ones. And though it would be unattractive for the lone professional or small-business man who cannot just leave everything behind for one month a year, this system could attract many volunteers from among those who work in large organizations where work is handed around anyway.

In spite of its merits, the reserve-officer solution was rejected—if it was considered at all—by the planners of the postwar defense establishment. Instead, the extra officers who would be needed only in a large war were simply kept on active duty. Assuming that the middle-ranking officers of 1945 were fully employed in leading vast forces in combat, in running the headquarters of armies, fleets, and air forces, in managing logistics, all the way from the huge war-expanded production base to the immediate rear of the combat zones, their counterparts of 1950 must have been greatly underemployed. Had the surplus officers been allowed to remain at home, had their salaries and benefits been granted as sinecures, no great harm would have been done. A rich country can afford to keep some tens of thousands idle.

Unfortunately, the many middle-ranking officers not needed in peacetime did not remain idle. Instead, headquarters staffs, the supply organizations, and all the military bureaucracies expanded to absorb them, subdividing the work into thinner and thinner slices to keep everyone busy. Where there had been one set of officers running one department in 1945, several sets were employed in several new departments after the war, sharing one function among them. Then another higher office would be needed to coordinate their work, providing employment for even more officers, including at least one of higher rank.

By 1950 the process was far advanced, but relief was at hand. The Korean war and its considerable rearmament seemingly proved the foresight of the postwar planners. In 1952, the number of middle-ranking officers had increased to 94,425—almost twice as many as in 1950; but the number of enlisted men had increased by more than 250 percent, so there were 2.9 middle-ranking officers per 100 enlisted men—a considerable decline from the 1950 ratio of 4 per 100.[6]

Few of the additional officers had been promoted from more junior ranks. The majority were Second World War veterans recalled to active duty—a procedure that could have provided all the necessary expansion, instead of merely one part of it. Had there been no expansion at all in the middle ranks, had the 1952 forces remained with the middle-ranking cadre of 1950, there would still have been 1.6 of them per 100 men, comfortably in excess of the 1945 ratio (1.3), and undoubtedly sufficient. With more than twice that proportion, there was a distinct overabundance of middle-rank officers in 1952, presaging some of the syndromes of Vietnam.

It was precisely at that time that the military commands of the North Atlantic Treaty Organization were being formed, and its several new headquarters immediately absorbed large numbers of American middle-ranking officers. Until then there had been only a treaty, a declaration of intent; but when the Korean war triggered fears of a wider war that could engulf Europe, the United States took the initiative to endow the Alliance with an entire multinational command structure, headed by an American Army general serving as Supreme Allied Commander, Europe. Incidentally, because American officers serving in the Organization are supposed to have colleagues, subordinates, or superiors from each Allied country, the armed forces of the Allies were forced to match the great number of American officers, in order to obtain proper representation. For some of the Allied forces, as overofficered as our own or even more, the large number of additional officer posts in the Supreme Headquarters Allied Forces, Europe (then elegantly housed near Paris) and the regional headquarters for northern and southern Europe and the Channel area offered welcome relief. Other allies, however, strongly resented the necessity of expanding their officer cadres to match American proportions, and also the high cost of keeping so many officers living abroad. In any case, the various Alliance headquarters soon became overofficered, and in due course began to suffer from all the typical dysfunctions of overmanaged structures.

After the Korean war, during the Eisenhower years, when the official strategy of "massive" nuclear retaliation justified a diminished reliance on the conventional forces, the total number of enlisted men in the four services continued to decline, from 3.16 million in 1953 to 2.93 million in 1954, 2.57 million in 1955, and so on, eventually reaching a low of 2.16 million in 1961, on the eve of the Kennedy buildup. But the number of middle-ranking officers did not decline in parallel; in fact, after a small dip during the post-Korean demobilization, there was a steady growth in their number, so that the ratio of middle-rank officers continued to increase:

	Officers: Major–Colonel/ Lt. Cmdr.–Captain	Enlisted: All Ranks (E-1 to E-7)	Ratio: Mid-Rank Officers per 100 Enlisted
1954	92,890	2,931,220	3.2
1955	96,463	2,570,754	3.7
1956	97,673	2,445,287	4.0
1957	97,441	2,442,908	4.0
1958	96,957	2,264,527	4.3
1959	98,308	2,174,747	4.5
1960	101,537	2,149,060	4.7

Those were truly the formative years in the evolution of the American officer corps; it was then that the patterns of overmanagement which remain with us today were established.

The great number of middle-ranking officers could no longer be justified, as in 1945–1950, by the possibility of another mass mobilization that would bring several million more servicemen into the forces. The official strategy ruled out any such need: if a Soviet aggression did take place, it would be countered by nuclear attacks. It is true that strategies can fail, or can simply be abandoned, as Massive Retaliation indeed was. But if the services were taking out insurance, they should have done many other things as well, which they conspicuously failed to do —notably designing basic weapons suitable for mass production. By 1960 the number of middle-ranking officers was roughly 70 percent of the 1945 level; it was therefore sufficient for some 7 million enlisted men at 1945 rates—and moreover, by 1960 the jet fighters, supercarriers, and tanks were already too complicated and too costly to be produced in very large numbers.

In any case, the mobilization argument could only explain the high ratio of officers to enlisted men—it could not possibly explain the steady *increase* in the ratio that took place. As the years went by and the weapons became less easily producible, the ratio should have been going down if it had truly contained a large mobilization allowance.

There is another explanation for what was happening to the officer corps during the 1950s: rank inflation, the familiar "grade creep" of government bureaucracies, which substitutes for salary increases when Congress is not in a generous mood. While in no sense a valid justification, especially in those years, when the dollar held its value and prices increased only very slowly, rank inflation is not in itself greatly harmful. If colonels do exactly the same job that majors used to do, if Navy captains take over the functions of commanders, with no change in the structure itself, the only harmful result is that military spending increases by the very small amount of the salary differentials.

Unfortunately, this is not what happened. Aircraft carriers were commanded by Navy captains in 1945, and they were still under a captain in 1960, as they still are. Army battalions had a lieutenant colonel in charge in 1945, and they remained under a "light" colonel in 1960, as they do today. It is true that Air Force pilots tended to have gradually higher ranks, and in all the services there was some rank inflation here and there. But the greater number of middle-ranking officers were absorbed in this period by a process in which the military bureaucracies kept expanding, not merely by increasing the size of each command, headquarters, department, or bureau, but also by subdividing their functions to absorb the surplus officers in many new *separate* offices.

At first it may seem that no great harm is done by this cell-like process of expansion, aside from the actual cost of the extra salaries for the surplus officers.* But the far greater costs are indirect, as overstaffing leads to overmanagement, and its effects deform the entire conduct of the armed services and their bureaucracies.

Consider, for example, the role of the Air Force Systems Command, which has expanded and subdivided over the years to accommodate 10,524 officers, including no fewer than 34 generals, at last count.[7] The Systems Command is responsible for the acquisition of all the equipment that the Air Force introduces into service. It does not manufacture aircraft, missiles, or any other equipment; private contractors do that. Nor does it carry out any major research and development; that too is contracted out, although Air Force laboratories under the Command do perform some basic research. The Command does not build prototypes, nor does it engineer the "systems" in detail; that too is done by contractors. Its role is rather to define Air Force requirements for all classes

* Although that is not an entirely trivial amount. In 1984, for example, if the number of middle-ranking officers had been brought back to the 1945 ratio, which was already fairly high, the savings would have been on the order of $5 billion—a tidy sum by any standard, though still less than 2 percent of the total defense budget for the year.

of equipment, and then to supervise each stage of acquisition, including the final manufacture.

The central headquarters of the Systems Command at Andrews Air Force Base, just outside the border of the District of Columbia, which supervises the various divisions and offices of the Command that do the actual supervising, already forms a very large bureaucracy. Headed by a four-star full general (whose own inner-office executive group includes four colonels), with a three-star lieutenant general serving as vice commander, the headquarters is coordinated by a chief of staff who has his own well-staffed inner office. These officers supervise the sixty-eight "directorates" that divide the functions of the headquarters among them; mostly headed by colonels who report to eleven deputy chiefs of staff (who are mostly brigadier generals), these directorates cut the work into very fine slices indeed—and each slice provides employment for several officers.

In addition to the directorates—which supervise the supervisors in the divisions outside the headquarters—there are nine supporting officers that provide services for the Andrews complex, for administration and "history," communications and electronics (not the kind that go into aircraft, nor those that service the Systems Command, but rather the electronics needed by the headquarters themselves), public affairs, security police, and so on.

And that is only the central headquarters. The actual work of the Systems Command is distributed among four major divisions, each headed by a three-star lieutenant general—in charge of space equipment (in Los Angeles), electronics (at Hanscom AFB, Massachusetts), aircraft (Wright-Patterson AFB, Ohio), and armaments (Eglin AFB, Florida). In addition there are eight other lesser divisions and "centers." Each of the divisions has its own headquarters (very large in the case of the four major divisions), which coordinates and supervises the different functional offices and directorates, which in turn supervise the contractors and in-house laboratories. Whatever else may be said, the acquisition of Air Force equipment does not suffer from a lack of supervision.

The first consequence of this organization is that the Air Force will not purchase readily available civilian products, even when they are perfectly satisfactory in every way. With so many officers employed in specifying Air Force requirements—all anxious not to overlook some special feature that is or could be needed, or would be nice to have— and with all of these officers supervised several times over by the headquarters of their own divisions and then by the appropriate directorates

CHART 6
HQ Air Force Systems Command
January 1984

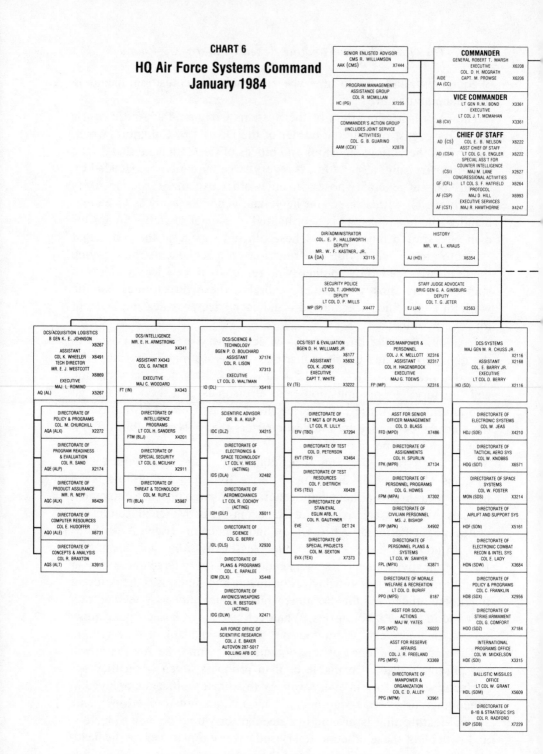

SENIOR ENLISTED ADVISOR CMS R. WILLIAMSON AAK (CMS) X7444	**COMMANDER** GENERAL ROBERT T. MARSH X6208 EXECUTIVE COL. D. H. MCGRATH AIDE CAPT. M. PROWSE X6206 AA (CC)
PROGRAM MANAGEMENT ASSISTANCE GROUP COL R. MCMILLAN HC (PG) X7235	**VICE COMMANDER** LT GEN R. M. BOND X3361 EXECUTIVE LT COL J. T. MCMAHAN AB (CV) X3361
COMMANDER'S ACTION GROUP (INCLUDES JOINT SERVICE ACTIVITIES) COL. G. B. GUARINO AAM (CCX) X2878	**CHIEF OF STAFF** AD (CS) COL. E. B. NELSON X6222 ASST CHIEF OF STAFF AD (CSA) LT COL. G. G. ENGLER X6222 SPECIAL ASST FOR COUNTER INTELLIGENCE (CSI) MAJ M. LANE X2627 CONGRESSIONAL ACTIVITIES GF (CFL) LT COL S. F. HATFIELD X6264 PROTOCOL AF (CSP) MAJ D. HILL X6993 EXECUTIVE SERVICES AF (CST) MAJ R. HAWTHORNE X4247

DIR/ADMINISTRATOR COL. E. P. HALLSWORTH DEPUTY MR. W. F. KASTNER, JR. EA (DA) X3115	**HISTORY** MR. W. L. KRAUS AJ (HO) X6354
SECURITY POLICE LT COL T. JOHNSON DEPUTY LT COL D. P. MILLS MP (SP) X4477	**STAFF JUDGE ADVOCATE** BRIG GEN G. A. GINSBURG DEPUTY COL T. G. JETER EJ (JA) X2563

DCS/ACQUISITION LOGISTICS
B GEN K. E. JOHNSON X6267
ASSISTANT
COL. K. WHEELER X6491
TECH DIRECTOR
MR. E. J. WESTCOTT X6869
EXECUTIVE
MAJ. L. ROMINO X5267
AQ (AL)

- DIRECTORATE OF
  POLICY & PROGRAMS
  COL. M. CHURCHILL
  AQA (ALX) X2272
- DIRECTORATE OF
  PROGRAM READINESS
  & EVALUATION
  COL. R. SANO
  AQE (ALP) X2174
- DIRECTORATE OF
  PRODUCT ASSURANCE
  MR. R. NEPF
  AQC (ALK) X6429
- DIRECTORATE OF
  COMPUTER RESOURCES
  COL E. HUDOFFER
  AQO (ALE) X6731
- DIRECTORATE OF
  CONCEPTS & ANALYSIS
  COL. R. BRAXTON
  AQS (ALT) X3915

DCS/INTELLIGENCE
MR. E. H. ARMSTRONG X4341
ASSISTANT X4343
COL. G. RATNER
EXECUTIVE
MAJ C. WOODARD X4343
FT (IN)

- DIRECTORATE OF
  INTELLIGENCE
  PROGRAMS
  LT COL H. SANDERS
  FTM (BLJ) X4201
- DIRECTORATE OF
  SPECIAL SECURITY
  LT COL G. MCILHAY
  FTI (BLA) X2911
- DIRECTORATE OF
  THREAT & TECHNOLOGY
  COL M. RUPLE
  FTI (BLA) X5987

**DCS/SCIENCE &
TECHNOLOGY**
BGEN P. O. BOUCHARD X7174
ASSISTANT
COL. R. LISON X7313
EXECUTIVE
LT COL D. WALTMAN X5416
IO (DL)

- SCIENTIFIC ADVISOR
  DR. B. A. KULP
  IDC (DLZ) X4215
- DIRECTORATE OF
  ELECTRONICS &
  SPACE TECHNOLOGY
  LT COL V. WESS
  (ACTING)
  IDS (DLA) X2482
- DIRECTORATE OF
  AEROMECHANICS
  LT COL R. COCHOY
  (ACTING)
  IDH (DLF) X6011
- DIRECTORATE OF
  SCIENCE
  COL G. BERRY
  IDL (DLS) X2930
- DIRECTORATE OF
  PLANS & PROGRAMS
  COL. E. RAPALEE
  IDM (DLX) X5448
- DIRECTORATE OF
  AVIONICS/WEAPONS
  COL R. BESTGEN
  (ACTING)
  IDG (DLW) X2471
- AIR FORCE OFFICE OF
  SCIENTIFIC RESEARCH
  COL J. E. BAKER
  AUTOVON 287-5017
  BOLLING AFB DC

DCS/TEST & EVALUATION
BGEN D. H. WILLIAMS JR X6177
ASSISTANT
COL K. JONES X5632
EXECUTIVE
CAPT T. WHITE X3222
EV (TE)

- DIRECTORATE OF
  FLT MGT & OF PLANS
  LT COL R. LILLY
  EFV (TBO) X7294
- DIRECTORATE OF TEST
  COL D. PETERSON
  EVT (TEV) X3464
- DIRECTORATE OF TEST
  RESOURCES
  COL F. DIETRICH
  EVS (TEU) X6428
- DIRECTORATE OF
  STAN/EVAL
  EGLIN AFB, FL
  COL R. GAUTHNER
  EVE DET 24
- DIRECTORATE OF
  SPECIAL PROJECTS
  COL M. SEXTON
  EVX (TEX) X7373

**DCS/MANPOWER &
PERSONNEL**
COL J. K. MELLOTT X2316
ASSISTANT X2317
COL H. HAGENBROCK
EXECUTIVE
MAJ G. TOEWS X2316
FP (MP)

- ASST FOR SENIOR
  OFFICER MANAGEMENT
  COL D. BLASS
  FFD (MPO) X7486
- DIRECTORATE OF
  ASSIGNMENTS
  COL H. SPURLIN
  FPK (MPR) X7134
- DIRECTORATE OF
  PERSONNEL PROGRAMS
  COL G. HOWES
  FPM (MPA) X7302
- DIRECTORATE OF
  CIVILIAN PERSONNEL
  MS. J. BISHOP
  FPP (MPK) X4902
- DIRECTORATE OF
  PERSONNEL PLANS &
  SYSTEMS
  LT COL W. SAWYER
  FPL (MPX) X3871
- DIRECTORATE OF MORALE
  WELFARE & RECREATION
  LT COL D. BURIFF
  PPO (MPS) 8187
- ASST FOR SOCIAL
  ACTIONS
  MAJ W. YATES
  FPS (MPZ) X6020
- ASST FOR RESERVE
  AFFAIRS
  COL J. R. FREELAND
  FPS (MPS) X3369
- DIRECTORATE OF
  MANPOWER &
  ORGANIZATION
  COL C. D. ALLEY
  PPG (MPM) X3961

DCS/SYSTEMS
MAJ GEN M. R. CHUSS JR. X2116
ASSISTANT X2168
COL. E. BARRY JR.
EXECUTIVE
LT COL D. BERRY X2116
HD (SD)

- DIRECTORATE OF
  ELECTRONIC SYSTEMS
  COL W. JEAS
  HDJ (SDE) X4210
- DIRECTORATE OF
  TACTICAL AERO SYS
  COL W. KNOBBS
  HOG (SDT) X6571
- DIRECTORATE OF SPACE
  SYSTEMS
  COL W. FOSTER
  MON (SDS) X3214
- DIRECTORATE OF
  AIRLIFT AND SUPPORT SYS
  HOF (SON) X5161
- DIRECTORATE OF
  ELECTRONIC COMBAT
  RECON & INTEL SYS
  COL E. LADY
  HON (SDW) X3684
- DIRECTORATE OF
  POLICY & PROGRAMS
  COL C. FRANKLIN
  HDB (SDX) X2956
- DIRECTORATE OF
  STRIKE-ARMAMENT
  COL G. COMFORT
  HOO (SDZ) X7184
- INTERNATIONAL
  PROGRAMS OFFICE
  COL W. MICKELSON
  HDE (SDI) X3315
- BALLISTIC MISSILES
  OFFICE
  LT COL W. GRANT
  HOL (SDM) X5609
- DIRECTORATE OF
  B-1B & STRATEGIC SYS
  COL R. RADFORD
  HDP (SDB) X7229

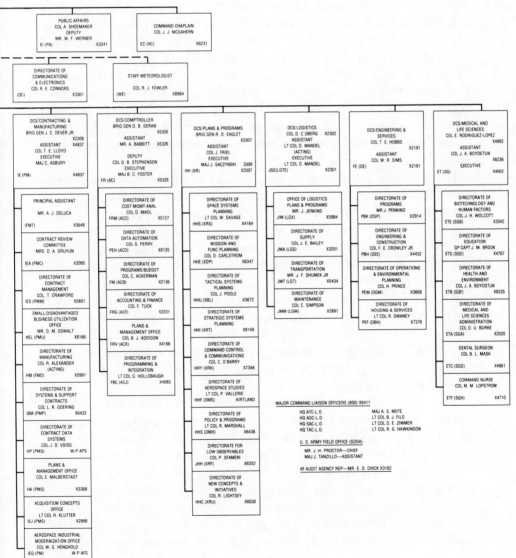

of the Command's headquarters, which among them will not fail to uncover further requirements if any have been missed lower down, the *other* officers of the Command, those who are in charge of the research and development of new products, will rarely be deprived of work by the straight purchase of ready-made items. Civilian industry does not, of course, sell ballistic missiles or bombers of its own design. But the natural tendency of a specification-writing bureaucracy is to insist on specially made products and to find inadequacies in commercial items that could just be bought off the shelf. Much of what is laboriously specified by the Systems Command and eventually developed under its supervision to meet all those specifications is readily available from civilian sources at lower prices—including $2,500 aircraft video re-corders that cost $7,000 for the special Air Force version, $14,000 diesel generators that cost the Air Force $56,000, and several hundred other products.[8] If it could get away with it, the Systems Command would no doubt write Air Force specifications for toothbrushes—and make them so unusual that not one of the hundreds of toothbrushes on the market would be found acceptable.

It is the equally natural tendency of a chronically underemployed research-and-development bureaucracy to welcome exacting specifications that impose the need for a research-and-development program every time the Air Force needs some product or other. Finally, it is also the natural tendency of an equally overstaffed supervising bureaucracy to impose all sorts of controls on manufacturers, and to demand mountains of paperwork.

Any Air Force Systems Command we might have, indeed any government buying outfit, would suffer from the same tendencies. But it is the great surplus of middle-ranking officers that has led to the luxuriant growth of the Systems Command bureaucracy we actually have, and then in turn to its grotesque overmanagement, which drives those natural tendencies to extremes.

Some years ago, another part of the Air Force, which wanted to buy not merely commercial toothbrushes or commercial video recorders but actual commercial aircraft, experienced the Systems Command syndrome at its worst. To reduce the very high fuel and operating costs of its fleet of heavy B-52 bombers, the Strategic Air Command came up with a major money-saving scheme; instead of flight-training its navigators by having them sit in B-52s, the Command wanted to use civilian executive jets fitted with B-52 navigation consoles. The executive jets would cost $2 million or $3 million each, but they are very cheap to keep repaired, and their small twin engines would burn less than one-tenth of the fuel consumed by the eight engines of each B-52. Having a large number of spare navigation consoles from scrapped B-52s in its depots, the Strategic Air Command wanted the Air Force to buy the jets and planned to employ its own technicians to install the navigation equipment and convert the seating. It was calculated that the savings under this "companion trainer scheme" would pay for the purchase of the executive jets in a couple of years, and then yield large savings each year thereafter.[9]

The Strategic Air Command is supposed to frighten the Soviet Union, but it completely failed to frighten the Systems Command. The "companion trainer scheme" was a direct threat, and it was treated accordingly. During the twenty-year period 1965–1984 (twenty years is the greater part of any officer's career), the Air Force has developed a grand total of only two bombers, one of them merely a converted fighter (the FB-111); only three fighter-class aircraft (two others, the F-4, and the A-7 were developed by the Navy and merely converted); only one transport aircraft; and a single trainer. In other words, the Aeronautical Division of the Systems Command at Wright-Patterson has suffered from chronic underemployment.

So the folks at Wright-Patterson were very sympathetic to the needs of the Strategic Air Command; the idea of a low-cost trainer for B-52 navigators clearly was excellent. Had they been asked to create a brand-new aircraft, their response would have been enthusiastic. But it takes some ten years for a new aircraft to go through the entire acquisition process, from the lengthy initial studies to Congressional approval and then manufacture; it also takes a great deal of money. The Strategic Air Command wanted a quick solution—the straight purchase of commercial jets, with minimal modification—and that was something the Systems Command could not possibly allow.

Still, the Strategic Air Command is a very powerful institution within the Air Force, and the Systems Command could not simply refuse its request. On the other hand, to avoid "fraud, waste, and mismanagement" and to apply all the available expertise, none of the three operational commands (strategic, tactical, and airlift) is allowed to write its own specifications for the equipment it needs, or to do its own purchasing; under Air Force procedures only the Systems Command can do that.

Under the expert scrutiny of the Systems Command, it soon transpired that all the commercial jets had grave defects that had somehow

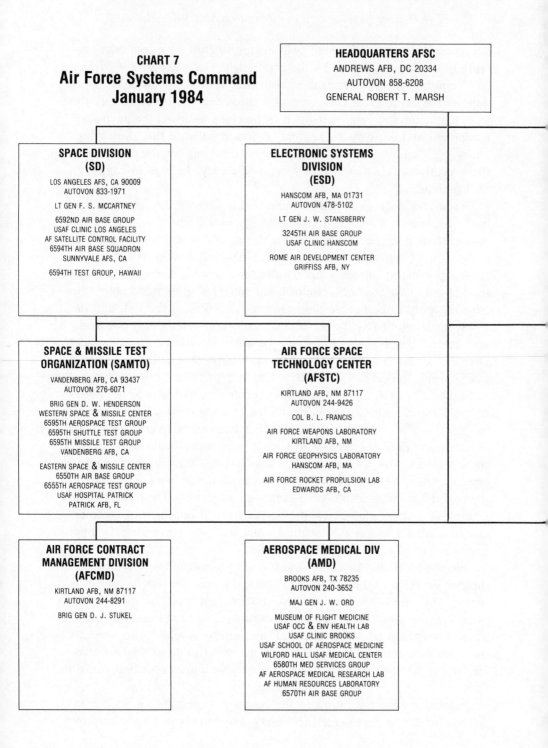

CHART 7
Air Force Systems Command
January 1984

HEADQUARTERS AFSC
ANDREWS AFB, DC 20334
AUTOVON 858-6208
GENERAL ROBERT T. MARSH

**SPACE DIVISION
(SD)**

LOS ANGELES AFS, CA 90009
AUTOVON 833-1971

LT GEN F. S. MCCARTNEY

6592ND AIR BASE GROUP
USAF CLINIC LOS ANGELES
AF SATELLITE CONTROL FACILITY
6594TH AIR BASE SQUADRON
SUNNYVALE AFS, CA

6594TH TEST GROUP, HAWAII

**ELECTRONIC SYSTEMS
DIVISION
(ESD)**

HANSCOM AFB, MA 01731
AUTOVON 478-5102

LT GEN J. W. STANSBERRY

3245TH AIR BASE GROUP
USAF CLINIC HANSCOM

ROME AIR DEVELOPMENT CENTER
GRIFFISS AFB, NY

**SPACE & MISSILE TEST
ORGANIZATION (SAMTO)**

VANDENBERG AFB, CA 93437
AUTOVON 276-6071

BRIG GEN D. W. HENDERSON
WESTERN SPACE & MISSILE CENTER
6595TH AEROSPACE TEST GROUP
6595TH SHUTTLE TEST GROUP
6595TH MISSILE TEST GROUP
VANDENBERG AFB, CA

EASTERN SPACE & MISSILE CENTER
6550TH AIR BASE GROUP
6555TH AEROSPACE TEST GROUP
USAF HOSPITAL PATRICK
PATRICK AFB, FL

**AIR FORCE SPACE
TECHNOLOGY CENTER
(AFSTC)**

KIRTLAND AFB, NM 87117
AUTOVON 244-9426

COL B. L. FRANCIS

AIR FORCE WEAPONS LABORATORY
KIRTLAND AFB, NM

AIR FORCE GEOPHYSICS LABORATORY
HANSCOM AFB, MA

AIR FORCE ROCKET PROPULSION LAB
EDWARDS AFB, CA

**AIR FORCE CONTRACT
MANAGEMENT DIVISION
(AFCMD)**

KIRTLAND AFB, NM 87117
AUTOVON 244-8291

BRIG GEN D. J. STUKEL

**AEROSPACE MEDICAL DIV
(AMD)**

BROOKS AFB, TX 78235
AUTOVON 240-3652

MAJ GEN J. W. ORD

MUSEUM OF FLIGHT MEDICINE
USAF OCC & ENV HEALTH LAB
USAF CLINIC BROOKS
USAF SCHOOL OF AEROSPACE MEDICINE
WILFORD HALL USAF MEDICAL CENTER
6580TH MED SERVICES GROUP
AF AEROSPACE MEDICAL RESEARCH LAB
AF HUMAN RESOURCES LABORATORY
6570TH AIR BASE GROUP

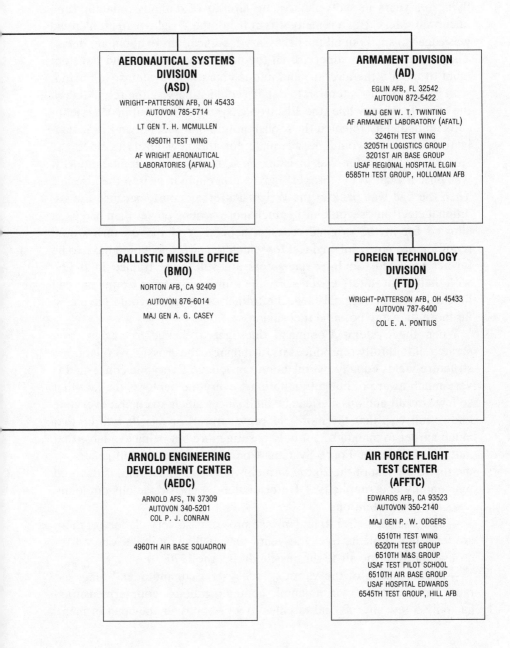

**AERONAUTICAL SYSTEMS
DIVISION
(ASD)**

WRIGHT-PATTERSON AFB, OH 45433
AUTOVON 785-5714

LT GEN T. H. MCMULLEN

4950TH TEST WING

AF WRIGHT AERONAUTICAL
LABORATORIES (AFWAL)

**ARMAMENT DIVISION
(AD)**

EGLIN AFB, FL 32542
AUTOVON 872-5422

MAJ GEN W. T. TWINTING
AF ARMAMENT LABORATORY (AFATL)

3246TH TEST WING
3205TH LOGISTICS GROUP
3201ST AIR BASE GROUP
USAF REGIONAL HOSPITAL ELGIN
6585TH TEST GROUP, HOLLOMAN AFB

**BALLISTIC MISSILE OFFICE
(BMO)**

NORTON AFB, CA 92409

AUTOVON 876-6014

MAJ GEN A. G. CASEY

**FOREIGN TECHNOLOGY
DIVISION
(FTD)**

WRIGHT-PATTERSON AFB, OH 45433
AUTOVON 787-6400

COL E. A. PONTIUS

**ARNOLD ENGINEERING
DEVELOPMENT CENTER
(AEDC)**

ARNOLD AFS, TN 37309
AUTOVON 340-5201
COL P. J. CONRAN

4960TH AIR BASE SQUADRON

**AIR FORCE FLIGHT
TEST CENTER
(AFFTC)**

EDWARDS AFB, CA 93523
AUTOVON 350-2140

MAJ GEN P. W. ODGERS

6510TH TEST WING
6520TH TEST GROUP
6510TH M&S GROUP
USAF TEST PILOT SCHOOL
6510TH AIR BASE GROUP
USAF HOSPITAL EDWARDS
6545TH TEST GROUP, HILL AFB

been overlooked by the hundreds of pilots who had flown them ever since they were first placed in service. In their ignorance, all those wealthy business executives, film stars, and plain rich folk had been flying for years in sadly inadequate aircraft of dubious reliability and uncertain safety. But a remedy was at hand: the Wright-Patterson crowd was eager to spell out all the necessary modifications in abundant detail. They were ready to supervise all the necessary research and development to modify the aircraft, and in due course the Systems Command, with its customary attention to detail, would supervise the rebuilding of the aircraft. Meanwhile, the Electronic Systems Division in Massachusetts immediately rejected the foolish notion that secondhand B-52 navigation consoles would be adequate for the new aircraft; since the Aeronautical Division was insisting on so many costly modifications, it was only logical to fit "proper" navigation equipment into the aircraft. Then the ball was back in the Wright-Patterson court, because the additional electronics would need much more cooling power than had been allowed for in the original redesign scheme, and that in turn would require more powerful engines, for which the airframe would have to be further modified. So B-52 navigators are still being trained in B-52s, with their eight thirsty engines. By the time the Systems Command had finished with the original idea, the trainer conversion would have cost far more than any possible fuel saving.

When the Systems Command does get a chance to design from scratch, it faithfully reproduces its own image: the grossly overelaborate structure yields equally overelaborate products. Everyone concerned is very much aware of budget limitations; everyone deplores the fact that so few aircraft and missiles can be built since each is so costly; everyone knows full well that the more elaborate aircraft or missile will be that much harder to maintain, not only costing more but being available that much less. The Air Force Systems Command, from the full general at the top to the last of the 26,077 airmen who serve under him, is devoted to economy and simplicity.[10] Unfortunately, a classic vicious circle defeats the good intentions.

—Because each aircraft and missile project is so very elaborate, there are very few projects over the years (one ballistic missile, one air-to-ground missile, one air-to-air missile during the 1970s[11]).

—Because each of the various "subsystem communities" (engines, radar, navigation, environmental, communications, countermeasures) has only a few aircraft and missiles to work on over the span of many years, each strives very hard to apply the full scope of its technological advances into those few aircraft and missiles.

—And that, of course, makes each aircraft and missile so elaborate that there are very few projects.

That outcome is manifest across the board, from missiles to lowly unguided munitions, but it is most dramatic in the case of manned combat aircraft. In Fiscal Year 1984, during the great Reagan buildup, Congress allowed the Air Force to purchase a grand total of 207 fighters, airlifters, intelligence aircraft (modernized U-2s), and bombers—not a colossal number by any standard.*

Most of the 207 were fighters—36 twin-jet F-15s and 144 F-16s, the latter being the famous, cheap "lightweight fighter" originally brought into existence by a brave band of dogfighting enthusiasts who successfully circumvented the Systems Command until the aircraft was very largely defined. The F-15, a perfect representative of the Systems Command way of life, came in at $42.4 million in 1984.[13] The price of the very cheap F-16—still widely regarded as sadly inadequate at Wright-Patterson, in spite of the many "enhancements" successfully added—was $17.7 million per copy.[14]

If a crew of skilled accountants were to explore the F-15 to find where the $42.4 million went, they would encounter everywhere the consequences of allowing the Air Force to employ so many of its surplus colonels in the Systems Command. The airframe is large and must therefore be costly—say, $10 million, including the overhead of the contractor, plush Washington offices, lawyers, consultants, and so on. There are two engines, which will not cost under $1 million each, with all their intricately crafted special metals. Then there are all the other parts—undercarriage, hydraulics, and more—to reach a total of, say, $25 million's worth. The rest is all in the "subsystems," each taken to the ultimate level of performance, technical advancement, and complexity. With so many officers dedicated exclusively to the advancement of radar technology, and with the F-15 the first Air Force fighter fit to carry a really powerful radar since the days of the F-111 in the early 1960s, the F-15 clearly *had* to have the ultimate radar with all the trimmings.

And so it went for each of the "communities" and its subsystems, from flight controls to electronic countermeasures, from the air-condi-

---

* In fact, not enough to prevent the aging of the aircraft fleets. Just to keep the inventory of fighter/attack aircraft of the active Air Force at the ten-year age mark, 260 aircraft should have been bought.[12]

tioning crowd (a separate "community") to the weapons-delivery people, and more. The F-15 is a wonderful aircraft in every way, and its "subsystems" have many virtues. But they also offer a lot of overperformance mostly unusable in combat, they require much maintenance, and, above all, they raise the cost so high that the Air Force can buy only very few F-15s (39 in 1983; 36 in 1984).[15]

Still, overelaboration merely costs money. The needlessly complicated product must be more expensive; its greater out-of-service time for maintenance means that more of the products must be bought to have any given number ready for use; and of course operating costs are higher. But a second consequence of keeping a grossly overofficered Systems Command is much more serious. For a rich country that is spending much less of its total wealth on defense than it did during the 1950s and '60s, the greater penalty of the Systems Command syndrome is the fact that important military capabilities are lost because some things are not produced at all.

It is certainly not that the Systems Command overlooks any category of air armaments. On the contrary, somewhere in the structure there are dozens of colonels investigating every possible air weapon, actual or imagined. The problem is rather the refusal of the research-and-development offices to put themselves out of business by actually declaring their work completed and ready for production.

True, in the case of combat aircraft, the eagerness of a pilot-dominated Air Force to fly new planes gives such a tremendous impulse to the development process that the entire cycle now takes no more than ten years or so, and sometimes less—a veritable miracle, given the dense layers of Pentagon overmanagement awaiting the aircraft project that has survived the Systems Command's own overmanagement. Similarly, the development of nuclear weapons is usually of great interest at the political level; it is true that Congress often delays those weapons, sometimes to the point of extinction (very few programs are cancelled outright). But the civilians of the Executive Branch have tended to push for rapid development, at least since the great turn in the strategic balance.

But when it comes to things that pilots cannot fly and that are nonnuclear—the tactical missiles, rockets, and bombs that combat aircraft are built to carry, and which in fact justify their very existence—there are no such countering impulses. Those policy orphans are left at the mercy of research-and-development bureaucracies, which have the strongest possible vested interest in *not* finishing their work. At Eglin

Air Force Base, home of the Systems Command's Armament Division, the usual hordes of colonels are to be found overseeing the research and development of tactical munitions. It is they who conduct all the studies, work out the detailed performance specifications, and supervise the Air Force laboratories and outside contractors that do the actual work. For Eglin and for the in-house Air Force labs, the completion of research and development for any one type of ordnance means that no more work can be expected in that line of business for ten or fifteen years. In spite of the phantasmagoria of "smart" weapons written up by the press, there are *very* few projects going (roughly one air-to-ground missile and one bomb type every ten years, a single air-to-air missile over twenty years), and underemployment is a chronic threat to bureaucratic survival.

The Eglin remedy is simple: having worked hard for as many years as possible to develop the best possible munition, instead of certifying the project as completed and ready for production, the Armament Division suddenly uncovers new and wonderful technical possibilities, wholly new thresholds of performance, and thus repudiates the ready-for-production munition as "less cost-effective," so everyone concerned can happily start at the beginning all over again.

But the comforting knowledge that a certain number of Air Force colonels will be guaranteed employment along with many more lab civilians must be balanced off against the military consequences, which are very serious. For example, for the crucial "counter-air" mission (the attack on Soviet air bases), the Eglin merry-go-round has deprived the Air Force of any runway-cutting controlled bombs like the French-made types employed by the Israelis as long ago as 1967. Normal "dumb" bombs are ineffectual against concrete runways because they slither about and usually leave only shallow and easily reparable holes; air-to-ground guided missiles are hopelessly expensive, and nowhere near enough of them could be delivered to do the job. Having simply remained without effective bombs for many years (it is almost as if pilots did not care for munitions, since they spoil the clean lines of their aircraft and slow down flight), the Air Force, under great civilian pressure, is now acquiring a suitable weapon, if only in token numbers—the *Durandal,* imported from France.

If one were to investigate the files of Systems Command, one would almost certainly find drawings of *Durandal*-type weapons dating back to the early 1960s, if not before—but they were never produced. The Command undoubtedly researched and developed version A of this most important category of weapon, only to cancel the project on the eve of production in order to start afresh with version B; then the game was repeated with C. No doubt on the eve of the *Durandal* purchase, not much of the alphabet was left—but the Air Force was still without any runway cutters.

A second crucial mission for the Air Force is to assist the ground forces against Soviet-style deep-column armored thrusts. The one Air Force air-to-ground missile in production, the IIR Maverick, is meant for direct attacks against single armored vehicles; in addition, of course, the Soviet-style invasion columns can be attacked with normal "dumb" bombs, rockets, and cannon, in true 1944 style. Unfortunately, the dense and effective air defenses of Soviet ground forces make all forms of *direct* attack very unprofitable, including Maverick attacks.*

For these reasons it has long been understood that the best way of opposing armored thrusts from the air is to attack not the vehicles doing the advancing but rather the movement itself, by dropping antiarmor *mines* in large numbers across the enemy's intended paths of advance. To achieve a tolerable economy, these mines must be very small ("mine-lets"), while still being effective—i.e., they must be miniature munitions of advanced design that can be dispensed in large numbers from cluster-type bombs or special pods attached to the aircraft.

Beginning in the late 1960s, when the concept was first proposed (by the German defense ministry), the Systems Command set out to design suitable minelets. It became clear early on that there was a very promising line of development based on small, light, yet powerful hollow charges. By the beginning of the 1970s, Eglin had a design ready for production, but the creators themselves rejected their creation, in favor of a second, more advanced design concept. Thus no mines were produced, and the research-and-development process started again. That second design gave way to a third, a very complicated active minelet (ERAM) that was intended to "sense" nearby armor movements, determine their range and direction, jump up by a controlled explosion, and then hit the target with a self-forging fragment capable of penetrating thick armor. Such complexity in a device needed in huge numbers was suspect, but with the need totally unmet, even this submunition was an attractive prospect.

It was not to be. Under the name "wide-area antiarmor munitions"

---

* That $150,000 missile is very accurate—if the launching pilot can see and identify the target. But if he sees the target, the target is likely to see him—and ground fire may cause the pilot to abort the attack even if his aircraft is not actually hit.

(WAAM) a research-and-development program continues year after year, with no production in sight. In his Fiscal Year 1985 "Annual Defense Report," Secretary of Defense Weinberger once again presented the WAAM program with the usual glossy prose, asking for $27.3 million of development funding and zero production funding. No production funds were requested for 1986 either.[16]

These goings-on should not be cynically accepted as bureaucratic inevitables. The systematic holding back of innovation in practice for the sake of greater innovations in theory has a serious impact on the overall military balance. Soviet numbers are supposed to be balanced by our more advanced technology; but only deployed weapons count, not blueprints and projects. In the summer of 1944 the Anglo-American tactical air forces hammered the German Army in France with their unguided rockets, unguided bombs, and gunfire; today, the U.S. Air Force would still have to rely on unguided weapons and gunfire, except for a few thousand Maverick missiles and laser-guided bombs of limited abilities. All the talk over a decade and more about "smart" weapons that would make our costly air power dramatically more effective remains just that—mere talk.[17] In the summer of 1944, with the Luftwaffe almost out of business over France, the German columns advancing to confront the Normandy landings and then retreating had only a few mobile antiaircraft guns and their small arms to ward off air attacks. Today, Soviet ground forces have their entire array of antiaircraft missiles and radar-controlled guns to protect them, in addition to a very large air force. The advances made in microelectronics and propulsion during the last two decades could have yielded the answer to Soviet antiaircraft power by developing guided dispensers for cluster munitions. Yet not one is in service, while the Eglin merry-go-round turns and turns again.

The very purpose of keeping a Systems Command is to harness the scientific and industrial potential of the nation to serve the urgent needs of the Air Force. What defeats that purpose is the way the Command is structured, as a layer cake of bureaucracies in which officers lose sight of the operational needs of the Air Force while pursuing the narrowest goals within the boundaries of their own offices.

The Air Force itself has at times obliquely acknowledged the resistance of its own technical bureaucracy to real innovation. When the need was really urgent, when dramatic innovation was required by insistent civilian officials, the entire Systems Command structure was bypassed. That was the case when the very innovative U-2 photographic-intelligence aircraft was needed during the later 1950s to achieve superhigh altitudes and very long ranges, and later when the much more spectacular SR-71 intelligence aircraft was needed during the early 1960s.* In both cases, the Lockheed aircraft company was allowed to insulate a small group of talented engineers in its secret "skunk works," and the Air Force let them work under loose supervision from the very top, without having to produce tons of documentation for the Aeronautical Division and its headquarters, and without having to satisfy the desires of each "subsystem community" and then each one of its directorates at Andrews. Nowadays the Stealth bomber is likewise being produced by Northrop and other contractors outside the official system, under a similar arrangement that also bypasses all the bureaucratic layers until the very top.

That is also how Marcel Dassault has produced his *Mirage* aircraft over the years, and how the pathbreaking aircraft of the Second World War were produced, notably the celebrated *Mustang*. This should not be surprising, for there is much art in the engineering of very advanced things, and no complex bureaucracy should ever be allowed to meddle with art. The message is clear enough; but to adopt a skunk-works approach for everything would leave dozens of generals and hundreds of colonels visibly redundant—and that, clearly, is the real obstacle to the one procedural innovation that would do wonders for real innovation.

The same corruption of purpose is manifest in the Navy and Army counterparts of the Air Force Systems Command. The air, electronic, and sea "systems commands" that come under the Navy Matériel Command,† with its 5,047 officers (typically of middle rank), 9,885 other Navy personnel, and 217,507 civilians;[18] and the research-and-development commands that come under the Army's Matériel Development and Readiness Command, which employs some 10,850 Army personnel (mostly officers), as well as 107,400 civilians, have also organized themselves as supercomplex structures that absorb many mid-rank officers who cannot be employed as unit commanders or staff officers, or in the supporting forces.[19] Between 10 and 15 percent of all mid-rank officers are so employed, with the highest percentage in the Air Force and the lowest in the Navy.

* It is still by far the fastest American aircraft in service, at Mach 3 + , and the only one that can fly supersonically for hours, instead of the minutes of which F-15s and F-16s are capable.

† See page 87 *n*.

Each of these overelaborate organizations shows the same preference for overelaborate weapons. In the Army, the tendency to pursue technological advancement for its own sake is most prominent, as with the gas-turbine engine of the M-1 tank, very advanced and very desirable in every way—except in combat. (For one thing, the jet efflux gives away the position of the tank and prevents escorting infantry from taking shelter behind its armor.) This bit of technological ambition endangered the entire M-1 program, and the fact that the risk was taken is proof of the sheer bureaucratic power of the research-and-development crowd; by the time the M-1 came along, the Army had lost two earlier opportunities to replace its very inadequate *Patton* tanks with the MBT-70 and the "austere" XM 803, both cancelled because of their grossly overambitious design.

In the Navy, the overdoing of everything is plainly manifest in the sheer size of the ships. While constantly complaining about Soviet *numerical* superiority, the Navy creates that superiority by designing ships so large that very few can be acquired, even with generous budgets. We are now up to 90,000 + tons for the aircraft carriers, 50,000 tons for resupply ships, and 8,000 tons for mere destroyers. The fourteen deployable carriers of the Navy are simply too few to cover the Atlantic, Mediterranean, Pacific, and Indian Ocean—but the Sea Systems Command has successfully blocked all proposals for "small" 50,000-ton carriers.* The Navy's destroyer fleet is much too small to provide decent convoy escort, but it was only the heroic determination of Admiral Elmo Zumwalt that overcame the Command's fierce resistance to the 3,500-ton frigates now in service, which were simply too small to accommodate all the bells and whistles of the different "subsystem communities."

Each of these chronically underemployed organizations shows the same tendency to suppress military innovation by keeping new weapons on the research merry-go-round. When a weapon is actually new in *concept,* when there is therefore no "user community" already in place within the armed forces to press for early production to renew its weapons, innovation is greatly delayed. But things are even worse when the new equipment threatens to reduce the role of well-established user groups.

That has been the fate of the enlarged model airplanes that are offi-

---

* Actually large enough to accommodate all current carrier aircraft, unlike the 20,000-ton British carriers, for example, from which only vertical take-off aircraft can operate.

cially known as remotely piloted vehicles. Thanks to advances in electronics, plastics, and small engines, these mini-aircraft can already substitute very advantageously for piloted craft used in reconnaissance, and they could easily be developed to serve as strike aircraft as well. But it is now clear that the potential military value of these mini-aircraft will never be realized if pilot-dominated bureaucracies continue to control their development.

During the Lebanon fighting of 1983–1984, the colossal firepower of the reactivated battleship *New Jersey* was largely wasted when it bombarded Druze and Syrian positions, because its guns were fired on map coordinates without concurrent target finding or correction. For fear of losing men, only rarely were spotters sent out with binoculars and radios into the hills beyond Beirut, while the Navy neither developed its own observation mini-aircraft nor saw fit to buy them ready-made from abroad. With them, the fire-control officers of the *New Jersey* could have seen the entire target area from above, focusing down at will to identify specific gun positions, rocket launchers, or hostile gunmen; the gunfire could then have been redirected as needed, shot by shot. It is not, of course, that the Navy's Air Systems Command has been ignorant of these possibilities. On the contrary, it has been researching unmanned aircraft for decades—but it seems that none was sufficiently perfect to be put into production, according to the pilots in charge.

The Army has an even greater need for remotely piloted observation aircraft to control artillery fire, but it too has none in service; over many years, it has continued to "develop," without any production. Thus the Army spent $317.4 million over the 1983–1985 period alone, when for half that amount, every active division of the Army could have been equipped with two sets of the ready-made Israeli product, which has the same payload and twice the endurance of the *Aquila,* currently proposed for production.[20]

But the rejection of "not-invented-here" equipment is one more consequence of grossly overmanned bureaucracies that are fiercely determined to keep for themselves whatever work is to be had. Weapons developed by other services will be accepted only under the strongest possible pressure from Pentagon high officials and Congress—and even then, the potential economies are usually lost because each service insists on major modifications. For example, when the Air Force was compelled in the early 1960s to accept the Navy-developed A-7 attack jet, it eventually gave in, but then its Systems Command insisted on "customizing" the aircraft, doubling its cost and reducing commonality with the Navy's A-7s to a mere 40 percent.[21] No matter how useful and economical, foreign weapons are not purchased except in very rare cases, nor are their licenses bought for production in the United States, nor will they even be copied at no charge.

Though present in all the systems commands, this tendency does the most damage in the Army. The United States is so advanced in aeronautics and missile work that it genuinely has little to learn from others. Naval technology is a middle case (every aircraft-carrier innovation of note, from the angled decks to the ski jump, has come from the Royal Navy). But certainly in ground weaponry, from small arms to tank design, the United States still has a great deal to learn from others. However, because of the protectionist instinct of self-serving bureaucracies, innovation from abroad can filter in only with great difficulty. While Congress is very often very willing to press the services to accept one another's equipment, its own protectionist tendencies lead it to tolerate the services' spurning of effective and economical foreign weapons. The outcome not only deprives the services, and especially the Army, of better and often cheaper weapons; it also does great damage to American relations with the European allies, which bitterly resent the trade imbalance in weapons.

But insult is added to injury when civilian defense officials try to compel the services to evaluate foreign alternatives to their chosen designs. The same systems-command people who would be put out of business if the foreign products were chosen are given the task of testing that product, and they know what to do—with results sometimes downright farcical. For example, when the Army was asked to choose a ready-made 9mm automatic pistol to replace the ancient (vintage 1911) .45-caliber buffalo-killer of inordinate weight (3 pounds, loaded) and minimal accuracy, it tested the Italian Beretta 92SB, the German P7A13, the Swiss P226, and the American Smith & Wesson 459M. All candidates were rejected after tests conducted in 1981–1982; none, it turned out, was sufficiently "reliable." That result was obtained easily enough: to pass the test, each pistol had to fire 800 rounds at a stretch. But the pistol is no more than an occasional self-defense weapon; statistics show that very few pistols are ever fired in earnest. In combat it is carried loaded, with one or two spare magazines; the firer might conceivably use another pair of magazines in very unusual circumstances. Thus 50 rounds might be fired at a stretch, once or twice during a long war. Under no imaginable circumstances would 200 rounds be fired nonstop, let alone 400—and 800 is an inconceivable number.[22]

But extreme and fanciful requirements are not the end of the story. When a weapon must be rejected, sheer cheating is not uncommon. Earlier, when the Air Force (which has no pistol-design community) tested the same pistols, the Beretta averaged 2,000 rounds without a malfunction in a 40,000-round reliability test.[23] Similarly, after the comparative evaluation of the M-1 and Leopard II tanks, the Germans complained that certain malfunctions noted during the tests had been contrived by the evaluators. The damage thus inflicted to Alliance relations is very serious; after so many disappointments, American offers of "two-way street" purchasing are met with well-justified cynicism.

Each of the major systems commands has enough middle-ranking staff to supervise the acquisition of *all possible* weapons—not only for all four services but for every armed force of the world, including that of the Soviet Union. Not one of the systems commands is capable of doing its assigned work speedily and economically. They are the ultimate case of too many cooks in one kitchen—or rather, of kitchens greatly enlarged to accommodate more cooks around fewer pots.

☆

CHAPTER SEVEN

The Officer Surplus and the Decline of Leadership

What is true of the systems commands is true of all the other sup-porting structures in charge of manpower, training, and administra-tion. In those vast noncombat organizations—which account for more than half the total manpower in uniform, along with transients —a myriad of separate divisions, offices, "centers," departments, and directorates have divided and subdivided each legitimate func-tion to the point where large coordinating headquarters are required merely to achieve a minimum of coherence.

☆

With the advent of the Kennedy Administration in 1961, the ensuing increase in enlisted manpower had to be balanced by an increase in the number of junior officers. But there was no need to increase the number of middle-ranking officers as well: the very high ratio of 4.7 per 100 enlisted in 1960 could simply have been allowed to decline to a more reasonable level. Had that been done, the proliferating bureaucracies would have begun to shrink, and their dysfunctions would have become less severe. But by then the services were geared for bureaucratically driven growth, so that even the fast buildup of the armed forces in response to the Berlin crisis caused only a slight dip in the ratio: [1]

	Officers: Major–Colonel/ Lt. Cmdr.–Captain	Enlisted: All Ranks (E-1 to E-7)	Ratio: Mid-Rank Officers per 100 Enlisted
1961	101,537	2,158,530	4.7
1962	109,127	2,452,468	4.4
1963	107,642	2,354,531	4.5
1964	106,751	2,338,153	4.6

From 1964 onward, the increasing American participation in the Vietnam war was reflected in the statistics:

	Officers: Major–Colonel/ Lt. Cmdr.–Captain	Enlisted: All Ranks (E-1 to E-7)	Ratio: Mid-Rank Officers per 100 Enlisted
1965	112,023	2,506,593	4.5
1966	118,380	2,969,743	4.0
1967	128,033	2,982,189	4.3
1968	133,246	2,977,093	4.5
1969	132,161	2,876,679	4.5

Two things are remarkable about this string of ratios, which begin and end at the identical level of 4.5:100. First, it completely explodes the rationale of keeping a mobilization allowance within the officer ranks. When the number of enlisted men increased, so did the number of middle-rank officers, and not much more slowly. Had there been no increase whatever over the 1965 number of mid-rank officers when the number of enlisted men peaked on December 31, 1967, the ratio would have declined only to 3.7 per 100—still a very comfortable level as compared with the 1.3 ratio of 1945. Obviously the habit of placing such officers in make-work positions, where their energies are absorbed in trivial tasks, was so deeply ingrained that it easily withstood even the impact of a fairly large war.

The second remarkable thing was that the Vietnam ratios were much higher than those of the Korean war (when the ratio was 2.9 at peak), in spite of the crucial operational difference between the two conflicts

—which should have yielded exactly the opposite result. In Korea, after all, the war was fought by regular forces in large formations engaged in conventional combat with a well-defined front; such forces obviously needed their quota of mid-rank officers and corresponding higher headquarters. In Vietnam, by contrast, the war was fought almost entirely by small groups of enlisted men and junior officers in the platoons and companies of the Army or Marines, in the small boats of the Navy's riverine fleets, or in crews for aircraft and helicopters. The larger-formation headquarters were sent out to Vietnam all the same (if only because of the pressure of senior officers hungry for a combat command), but the higher headquarters mostly played a merely administrative role. There was certainly not much scope for the operational planning, staff oversight, and medium-formation command that are commonly practiced by middle-ranking officers. Nevertheless, huge numbers of them were present in Vietnam all the same, greatly overstaffing headquarters and service organizations of all kinds, with disastrous effects on the tactical, operational, and strategic conduct of the war, and with an impact just as harmful on the morale of enlisted men, for whom the very authority of rank was irremediably trivialized.

After the withdrawal from Vietnam, with the introduction of competitively paid military service (the so-called "all volunteer force") and the resulting decline in the size of the armed forces, the ratio of middle-ranking officers to enlisted men increased still further. On April 30, 1973, with the American withdrawal from Vietnam completed, 112,290 officers of middle rank were in uniform as against 1,937,100 enlisted men—a phenomenal ratio of 5.8 per 100.

Clearly, there was a reluctance to dismiss officers in mid-career even if they were less necessary and useful than ever before; to put it differently, officers looked after one another in difficult times. The indulgence shown at that time toward loyal career men is far more understandable and acceptable than what has happened in all the years since then. After all, a decent proportion of middle-rank officers could have been obtained gradually—with no need to throw the surplus onto the street—by the natural progress of retirements.

Instead, at last count (May 31, 1983) there were 97,639 mid-rank officers in the four services, a ratio of 5.3 per one hundred enlisted—a very high ratio, *four times* as high as in 1945.[2] Because no global war involving millions is now being fought, the mass of these officers must be employed quite differently than were their counterparts in 1945, who provided leadership and administration for forces almost *six times* as large as those today, with a mid-rank cadre larger by only 47 percent. To be sure, the greater complexity of modern weapons might justify some of the increased ratio, but surely not much, because the Defense Department also employs many scientists and technical specialists among its 668,150 white-collar civilian employees.[3] Perhaps there is now a greater need for middle-ranking officers in organizations outside the services, including the defense "agencies," and still other justifications may be uncovered. But after a full allowance is made for all possible worthy employments, the number of middle-ranking officers is still grossly excessive and very harmful in both peace and war.

So far, the surplus of middle-ranking officers has been blamed for the bureaucratic diseases that have deformed the military institutions. But the ultimate cause of and certainly the entire responsibility for their proliferation must rest with their superiors—the flag-rank officers, from the one-star brigadier generals (or Navy commodores) to the four-star generals and admirals.

On June 30, 1945, there were 2,068 flag-rank officers, including seven five-star generals and admirals who had just earned in war their titles of "general of the army" and "fleet admiral." (When the last of them, Omar N. Bradley, died in extreme old age, the rank lapsed.) A good many of them were employed in direct command of almost one hundred Army and Marine divisions as well as a multitude of naval task forces and flotillas, air formations, and the corps, army, Army-Group, and theater headquarters for Europe and the Pacific. The supporting organizations for manpower and training, research and development, purchasing and transport, as well as the logistic networks that then stretched across four continents accounted for only a small part of the flag-rank total. With 10,795,755 enlisted personnel on active duty, the ratio of flag-rank officers to enlisted men was 1.9 per 10,000.

These generals and admirals certainly had much to do. Though there were no Alliance headquarters to fill, as there are now, the United States did fight the Second World War with allies. With the British there were many joint committees and also joint headquarters to run, while other senior officers were kept busy maintaining liaison with allies as diverse as the Soviet Union and Chiang Kai-shek's China, the Yugoslav partisans and the royal Italian Government, the Free French of Charles de Gaulle and the freer French of the internal resistance. It is also true that the equipment of 1945 was much simpler than today's, but there was so much more of it: the armed forces of 1945, numerically almost five times larger than today's forces, had more than five times as many units of equipment (aircraft, ships, tanks).

Finally, though nuclear weapons justify a more intensive high-level control of the armed forces than in 1945, the conduct of a global war entailed much work for senior officers that is no longer needed, including the military government of tens of millions under occupation. Yet there was no shortage of senior officers during the Second World War. On the contrary, it was already commonly noted that there were too many generals and admirals.

After the mass demobilization completed by 1947, the armed forces continued to decline in a manner that seemed to have no logical halting point, in spite of the rising tensions of the Cold War. By June 30, 1949, only 1,615,360 officers and enlisted men remained on active duty; one year later their numbers had further declined to 1,269,891. That was the year General of the Army Omar Bradley, Chairman of the Joint Chiefs of Staff, solemnly testified before Congress that he had accepted a $13.2-billion defense budget because to spend any more would "bankrupt the nation." At that point, 881 officers of flag rank remained on active duty, and the ratio stood at 6.9 per 10,000 enlisted.

Bearing in mind the still widely accepted mobilization assumption, that ratio was not yet grossly excessive. Except for the officers of the Strategic Air Command of the Air Force—who honestly saw no justification for the continued existence of the Army and Navy at a time when they could destroy Moscow, Leningrad, Kiev, and several more major cities at the very outset of a war, thus ending it victoriously as soon as it began—civilians and military alike were convinced that any war would result in a mass mobilization. And if several million men were added, the 881 flag-rank officers would indeed find themselves fully employed.

Moreover, the equipment in those days was still perfectly compatible with rapid mobilization. If the strength of the Army had to increase from the 593,167 of 1950 to 3 million or so, in order to field some forty divisions in Europe and the Middle East (Iran was a plausible theater), those forces could have been largely equipped with still-modern hardware taken from storage or else quickly producible in large numbers. The Sherman tank, designed in wartime for mass production, was still in service, and its emerging successor, the Patton M-47, was also producible. Very few wartime weapons of the ground forces had become obsolete, and in those days the research-and-development people were still habituated to move quickly. Thus when there was obsolescence to overcome (as in the case of the too-small wartime bazooka), the new weapon would be ready for production in months rather than years, and it too would be producible in large numbers.

The Air Force was not quite so well prepared for mobilization because after 1945, with the advent of jet propulsion, it had scrapped most of its wartime aircraft almost immediately. Still, it did have tens of thousands of still-fresh pilots who could be recalled for duty; the celebrated P-51 *Mustang* was still very much in service, and the most successful of the new jet fighters, the F-86 *Sabre,* was a one-engine, one-pilot 20,000-pound machine, simple enough to be produced in large numbers.[4] (In fact 6,353 were built, mostly in 1950–1953, as a result of the Korean buildup.)*

In 1950, the Navy would have had little to do even in a large war with the Soviet Union, except to escort convoys across the Atlantic. It certainly would have had no need to build any new ships; the vast fleet of still-new destroyers mothballed after 1945 would have provided for any conceivable requirements.

The Korean war did not trigger a full-scale mobilization, but the cadre policy was duly tested by the expansion of the forces, and it worked more or less as intended: in 1952, at the peak of the buildup, the ratio of flag-rank officers was down quite sharply, to 3.5 per 10,000 enlisted. There were then 1,142 flag-rank officers on active duty (including six surviving five-star officers), as opposed to 881 in 1950, when the ratio had been 6.9 per 10,000 enlisted. In other words, the number of generals and admirals had increased by less than 30 percent while the enlisted total had increased by more than 250 percent. Still, even then the number of senior officers was proportionately much higher than in 1945, and no sufficient justification for the increase is apparent.

During the rest of the 1950s and into the 1960s the spreading disease of bureaucratization was reflected in the ratio of flag rank to enlisted. Or rather, to place cause and effect in correct order, it was during those years that the increasing proportion of flag-rank officers resulted in the progressive fragmentation of the supporting functions, as each general and admiral kept himself busy by appropriating a slice of the work for himself. When we recall the context of each period, and the diminishing

---

* No current U.S. fighter could possibly be built at those rates; at the very most, perhaps 250 of the "cheap and simple" F-16 could be built in the first year of a buildup, and not twice that number in the second year, even though several hundred F-16s could easily be lost in a few days of intense fighting with the Warsaw Pact.

capacity of the forces to expand greatly in war because of the declining producibility of their equipment, we can recognize that the increased ratio encompasses the root cause of America's military decline.

	Flag-Rank Officers Brigadier General/ Rear Admiral +	Ratio per 10,000 Enlisted
1945: war	2,068	1.9
1950: large mobilization reserve in the officer corps	881	6.9
1952: mobilization partly achieved	1,142	3.5
1955: official strategy excludes mass mobilization	1,239	4.8
1960: no change in official strategy but weapons less producible, mobilization less feasible	1,260	5.8
1965: equipment no longer producible in large numbers; mass mobilization impossible	1,312	5.2

Because of the far more restricted mobilization potential of that period, the 5.2 ratio of 1965 implies a greater degree of bureaucratization than the 6.9 of 1950. As we have seen, it was from the mid-1950s that the surplus of higher-ranking officers began to deform the armed forces. Each general and admiral had to have his own command with his own executive officers and personal aides; with so few combat commands open in the diminished armed forces, the extra billets could be obtained only by the subdivision and then overlapping of the support structures of each service.

When the growing American involvement in the Vietnam war resulted in the expansion of the armed forces, the flag-rank ratio should have declined, because senior officers are not made as fast as recruits can be drafted. In fact it did, but not by much: in 1966 with a flag-rank total of 1,334, the ratio per 10,000 enlisted stood at 4.5; in 1967 it went down a shade to 4.45, and in 1968, the peak year, with 1,354 flag-rank officers on active duty, the ratio had increased again to 4.5, still almost two and a half times the 1945 ratio—and in Vietnam there was very little need for large-formation commanders and central staffs.

During the 1970s the flag-rank total declined more slowly than the size of the armed forces, so the ratio continued to increase. By 1980, with 1,645,100 enlisted men on active duty and 1,118 flag-rank officers, the ratio had increased again, to 6.4 per 10,000 enlisted, or more than three times the 1945 level. Since 1981 the number of flag-rank officers had been stabilized at 1,073—but not because of any restraint on the part of the armed forces. It was Congress that did it, and in 1983 it had to intervene once again to block an attempt to add more generals and admirals to the active rolls. (An increase of 27 flag-rank positions had been included in the Fiscal 1984 budget request.)

In combining one-star officers with those more senior, the flag-rank totals given above conceal an even more spectacular growth in the number of *senior* generals and admirals. in 1945, the 12 million at war were managed and commanded by a total of 101 three-star officers (lieutenant generals/vice admirals) and 38 full generals and admirals, including the 7 of five-star rank. In 1983, a total of just over 2 million in uniform enjoyed the attentions of 118 three-star officers and 34 full generals and admirals.[5] In other words, the number of these most senior officers *is now actually greater than in 1945,* even though command positions in the combat forces have diminished to roughly one-sixth of the 1945 levels.

Now the full dimensions of the problem are revealed. It must be recalled that there has been no rank inflation as such: three-and four-star officers command the same formations they commanded in 1945, and the number of these larger formations is much smaller today than it was then. Aside from a handful of senior officers serving outside the armed forces (for example, the 7 now in charge of "defense agencies"[6]), all the senior flag-rank officers who have no forces to command are to be found in the Joint Chiefs of Staff organization; the nine joint commands, both unified and specified; and, above all, in the support structures of each service, which have been duly expanded, subdivided, and then overlayered to accommodate them all. Unable to command, because only a fraction can be accommodated in bona fide command slots, all these senior officers must manage instead; but there is not enough management to keep them occupied, so they must overmanage and micro-manage, or else "coordinate" the massive complications that overstaffing has caused in the first place.

It is interesting to note that the most successful military organization of our day, the Israel Defense Force, has a much lower proportion of middle-ranking and senior officers. In fact, by American standards, the IDF is severely underofficered. There are no four-star generals at all, and only one three-star lieutenant general, officially described as "chief of staff" but in fact the professional commander (not the political commander-in-chief) of *all* the Israeli armed forces—ground, naval, and air. (Under the Israeli single-service system, there is no independent air force or navy, but instead the "air corps" and "sea corps" of the army, and the chief of staff is always a ground-force officer.)

Though a very large force by any standards, with almost as many combat aircraft as the Royal Air Force, the Israeli air corps is commanded by a single major general (the USAF has 120). Its own version of a systems command, staffed by a handful of colonels and headed by a one-star general, has in recent years successfully supervised the development of an entire range of advanced equipment, including air-to-air missiles, air-to-ground missiles, and pilotless aircraft, as well as the secret equipment employed in 1982 (alongside standard U.S. devices) to destroy the Syrian antiaircraft array in the Vale of Lebanon. Similarly, the Israeli "sea corps"—admittedly a very small force, though no longer insignificant with its powerful fleet of missile boats—is also commanded by a single two-star rear admiral. As for the ground forces, which have three times as many tanks as the British Army, in eleven well-equipped armored divisions, their command structure is run by 4 major generals (the U.S. Army has 140), and 5 more two-stars head the entire IDF-wide support structure for manpower, logistics, training, Intelligence, and planning. With 2 more two-stars in charge of the central headquarters, a military chief rabbi and chief judge, and also the defense attaché in Washington, the Israelis have a grand total of 16 major generals on active duty for their ground, air, and naval forces (the U.S. total is 362).

American military forces—more than ten times as large, distributed on three continents, serving worldwide at sea, and in need of senior officers for alliance commands in Europe and beyond, with many tasks totally unknown to the Israelis, such as the Army's ballistic-missile-defense program, and with nuclear weapons to keep—certainly need more than a proportionate number of senior officers. They could not possibly function with only ten times as many generals and admirals as the IDF. (Actually there are thirty times as many.) So any direct comparison would be foolish. Still, it is interesting to compare the workings of a deliberately underofficered structure with one that plainly has too many chiefs.

While officers in underofficered military forces must dispense with everything that is not urgent and essential, notably paperwork, their counterparts in an overofficered structure must constantly invent new functions and new administrative procedures to keep themselves busy, in spite of computerization and kindred threats to their full employment. In the former situation, mistakes will be made and lesser things neglected because each officer has more work than he can cope with; in the latter, the complexity of procedures and the dulling effect of the paperwork make it difficult to focus on essentials.

While officers in an underofficered structure must distribute their time among too many tasks, those in an overofficered structure must compete to obtain a share of too few tasks. In the former, each overburdened officer has no time, energy, or reason to claim more bureaucratic terrain than he already has, and he may not even be able to attend fully to the duties already his; in the latter, turf fights are endemic and much energy is consumed in bureaucratic warfare with other officers of parallel rank who head competing departments.

While officers in an underofficered structure will naturally focus on the immediate needs of the combat forces, simply because that is where most of them are serving most of the time, their counterparts in an overofficered structure will have few opportunities to command forces and will tend to pursue the actual priorities of their position: administrative refinements in an administrative command, technological advancement for its own sake in a systems command, logistic elaboration in a matériel command. In the former situation, there is always the risk that senior officers will neglect wider strategic questions and long-range technological possibilities while focusing on the basics of morale, training, cohesion, leadership, tactics, and the operational art of war; in the latter, the wider and longer view comes much more easily, but it is the basics of the military craft that are liable to be neglected.

Above all, an underofficered structure allows each officer a very wide area of activity and forces him to assume great responsibilities in his day-to-day work. In an overofficered structure, each officer, even of high rank, has only a narrow sphere of personal responsibility and has scarcely any opportunity to prepare himself for the moment of combat —when every officer must carry the supreme responsibility of life and death, even if his rank is quite low. In the former, officers must be bold risk-takers simply to carry out their day-to-day work in peacetime, because they have so little supervision from above; in the latter, risk-avoidance is the rule, because till the very top is reached there is always a more senior officer who is underemployed, eager to micro-manage, and on the lookout for errors that need his correction. In the former, the habit of large responsibility can easily bring with it a warlord mentality among senior officers, because each routinely does so much on his own; in the latter, the career-long lack of responsibility can easily yield senior officers who are unfit to exercise command when war and all its risks must suddenly be confronted.

It is the remoteness of so many officers from the day-to-day realities of the forces—the divisions and brigades of the Army and Marines, the ships and fleets of the Navy, and the squadrons and wings of the Air Force—that gives rise to most of the bureaucratic deformations we have encountered. (Most staff jobs are not within the forces but rather far above them—and a staff officer who serves in one of the Alliance commands, joint headquarters, or the Pentagon is an administrator, and has no real contact with the forces.)

The services ostensibly recognize the importance of preserving the vital link between their officers and the actual forces, whose upkeep is the purpose of all that manpower-management, research and development, procurement and supply. That is why officers are not allowed to make their career within any one specialized organization but are instead supposed to "rotate" into and out of combat forces between courses at professional schools, managerial jobs in the supporting structures, Pentagon staff positions, and administrative posts of one sort or another. In theory, rotation is supposed to make officers versatile and broadly knowledgeable about their own service and the military establishment at large—while allowing them to remain genuine combat professionals.

But the arithmetic of our armed forces—which have so few combat formations because their overhead is so large, and which have a disproportionate number of middle and senior officers—thoroughly defeats the aim of rotation. As officers rise in rank, there are fewer and fewer command or operational staff posts for them. The U.S. Army, for example, has 17 divisions on its books—i.e., 17 command slots for major generals, and only a handful of *operational* staff positions at that level. But the Army does not have 17 major generals, nor 34, nor 68: the number at last count was 140.[7] For each of them to get a division for a decent term of command, say two years, major generals would have to stay at their rank for 16.5 years—far more than is possible or desirable.

Similarly, the Navy has no fewer than 3,738 captains on its books—a rank that rates command of an aircraft carrier—but can scarcely place one in a hundred in a captain-rated command slot aboard ship.[8] The Air Force, most grossly overofficered of all, has 5,431 colonels, almost 30 for each squadron command. Even the Marine Corps, which so greatly prides itself on being lean in every way, has a total of 1,594 lieutenant colonels for only 182 command billets in its ground and air forces.[9]

Because the official myth still is that officers are combat leaders first and foremost, they must normally obtain "command tours" to be promoted; there is therefore tremendous competition to beat the numbers. One false remedy has been to make command appointments very short, in order to give as many officers as possible a chance to "punch their tickets" in a command position. By the time of the Vietnam war, a mere six or seven months had become quite normal for commanding officers of middle rank and above. This nefarious practice meant that commanders were relieved just about when they had learned their job, understood the war they were fighting, and begun to deviate from the textbook to devise methods of war attuned to the realities of the conflict. The fact that the forces were for much of the time deliberately placed in the hands of inexperienced commanders, for the sake of the career prospects of those same commanders, could only be demoralizing. Those who served under them, and especially the enlisted men, knew full well that they might have to pay with their lives for the errors of their ever-changing superiors. Even more demoralizing was the widespread suspicion that commanding officers were apt to place their units at excessive risk in order to show "career-enhancing" results during their brief turn in charge.

In peacetime the consequences of short command tours are less extreme, but the temptations, and the resulting demoralization of the men, are just as intense. In only a short period, officers cannot do very much more than pretty up their units for the visits of more senior officers, and above all for the inspections that result in the all-important "readiness" reports. If the training of the men happens to be badly outdated, if equipment or facilities need to be reorganized, if the unit has accumulated an excessive number of duds, the commander who honestly confronts the problems places his career in danger. Having inherited the unit from a commander who was obviously successful in sweeping problems under the rug, the conscientious officer is in effect challenging his superiors when he uncovers what is wrong. As soon as he reports truthfully, he exposes himself as a possible troublemaker, or at least labels himself as the man in charge of a problem unit—and he may not have enough time to clean up the mess and then wait for the results to show up in formal reports. The safer procedure is to keep up the facade, and let the next man take the rap if problems become too severe to be concealed.

Even though the short command tours were recognized as a scandalous malpractice by the time of the Vietnam war, it was not until 1981–1982 that the Army Chief of Staff, General Edward C. Meyer, finally prescribed minimum command tours of two years—after encountering much foot-dragging from the "manpower planners," for whom the extra months made the arithmetic of fair-shares-for-all even more impossible. And there was outright opposition from the officers—and their wives—who had to wait for their turn at command.[10] The Marines did not confront the problem until 1984 (i.e., after the report of the Long Commission); it was only then that the Commandant finally issued an order that specified battalion-level command tours of two years, allowing a reduction to eighteen months at the commanding general's discretion.[11] No doubt anticipating the pressures to come, the Commandant's edict stated that any shorter tours would require his personal approval. Naturally, Marine manpower planners complained that the new rule meant that fewer officers could be "rotated into command billets to gain leadership experience."[12] Obviously suggesting that in the past men ill suited for command had been given their turn anyway, the Commandant's order included the following by way of explanation: "[Marines] . . . who are required to go in harm's way deserve leadership of the very finest quality."[13] As of this writing, the Air Force and Navy have yet to act.

Actually the principle of career advancement by rotation is now wholly outdated. Because of the numbers, rotation can no longer achieve its basic aim of preserving a combat-minded officer corps, nor can it endow the officers with a useful variety of experience. By preventing officers from rising step by step in one of the specialized noncombat organizations, rotation prohibits the accumulation of true expertise, and many of the different outfits to which officers are now rotated have functions so intricate that any knowledge gained must remain terribly superficial. At the same time, because officers cannot rise step by step within a given battalion, brigade, and division, or ship, flotilla, and fleet, or air squadron and wing, with only professional courses and staff positions in between, rotation prevents the emergence of a solid regimental spirit, which can do wonders in keeping men together under severe stress.

The effect of rotation is instead to promote a nonexpert and thoroughly demilitarized officer corps. Instead of taking relatively brief educational intervals between years of genuine military duties, in genuine military settings, officers live three, four, or five years virtually as civilians—as mere office workers in uniform—for each year they spend with a combat force in the field or aboard ship, or with an air unit. In the Washington suburbs, where many of them live, in other suburbs around military bases all over America, and in the little Americas that have grown around bases overseas, officers live much as insurance salesmen, junior executives, high school teachers, or plumbers do. Just like them, these 9-till-5 officers fight traffic to get to work. More than most, they try to be good neighbors, active in the local PTA and timely in mowing their lawns as they enjoy the modest pleasures of suburban life and endure its petty travails.

The problem is compounded by the mechanics of promotion. Until the very highest ranks are reached, the "fitness report" prepared by an officer's immediate superior is essential for promotion. Right from the start, young officers learn that promotion goes to the polite, well-rounded man who can keep a tidy desk and avoid any eccentricity in taste or conduct. An overintense interest in the military arts is rated as an eccentricity and is thus to be avoided (except in the Army, the one service where self-reform is under way). In any case, the education received by many young officers at West Point, Annapolis, and the Air Force Academy certainly does not encourage such interest. In course lists crowded with economics, management, political science, mathematics, science, and above all engineering—electrical, mechanical, aeronautical, and electronic—military history is treated as a very minor subject, and there is very little teaching of tactics, operational art, or strategy. At West Point there are a department of chemistry, a department of electrical engineering, another department of engineering, a department of geography *and* computer science (!), a very large department of mathematics, a department of mechanics (more engineering), a department of physics, and so on—but no department of military history.[14] At all the academies, athletics are greatly stressed, as are formal good manners, in a somewhat old-fashioned version.

When America was young and primitive, it made sense to rely on

West Point to train engineers who could survey uncharted lands, build bridges and roads, ports and public buildings. And in a raw pioneer society full of frontiersmen, farmers, and immigrant laborers, it was right to believe that the status of the leader was best ensured by his instruction in social graces, bourgeois manners, and book knowledge. In our suburban society, however, where half the population receives some form of higher education, it is the skill and the aptitudes of war that are missing, and the academies certainly do not provide them. Their aim is quite clearly to educate not young combat leaders but future generals and admirals—not strategically minded, or tactically cunning, but technically sophisticated, bureaucratically adept, and politically sensitive, as our senior officers are.

But the academies that nowadays provide some 10 percent of all officers,[15] and a far greater proportion of the generals and admirals, do offer an excellent preparation for military careers in which the approved model is that of the corporate executive—or more precisely, the junior executive in a very large, very stable corporation, such as an electrical utility. The entire character of the academies seems almost calculated to attract young people of no great talent or curiosity, eager to find security in highly regulated institutions. That many of their graduates are nevertheless so gifted reflects the innate qualities of our youth, and not the education offered by the academies.

Thus the apparent demand of American society for a very civilianized body of officers, as far removed as possible from the dreaded image of an arrogant military aristocracy or a warrior fraternity, has now been fully satisfied. Very few of today's officers can be accused of being aristocratic in their outlook and still less in their tastes, if only because so few officers have private financial means. Even fewer officers can be accused of being infected with the warrior spirit. There is neither an officer caste nor, therefore, a brotherhood: because of their sheer numbers and modest position in society, military officers cannot feel that they belong to a proud, exclusive elite with strong solidarity and an attitude of superiority to civilians.

Yet elitism does have one very great virtue in military life. Feelings of mutual solidarity created by the consciousness of belonging to an elite serve to moderate the pursuit of career advancement. That would not be a virtue at all in the civilian world of the corporation, where— quite rightly—"careerism" is seen as a positive force that can harness for the employer all the energies that only personal ambition can release. But the military profession is fundamentally different in this matter, just as war is different from commerce. Among military officers the intensive pursuit of personal advancement is corrosive, and if careerism becomes the general attitude, the very basis of leadership is destroyed.

In the business world too there is leadership, but there the leader can rely on personal motivation, and financial rewards can be measured out quite precisely and awarded to deserving individuals. The military leader, by contrast, must always motivate the entire group, not just the sum of individuals, and he has no material rewards to offer. He must evoke the common interest of the entire group in order to lead it, persuading all concerned by word, deed, and personal example that it is by following his orders that the common interests of country, service, and unit are best served. If subordinates sense that the officer over them is using his command as a mere stepping-stone to his next posting, if they come to believe that they are being asked to strive for performance in peacetime or to risk their lives in wartime merely to justify claims of success by a commanding officer who is eager to leave them in order to be promoted, a sharp divide must emerge between the interests of the leader and those of the led. This in turn deprives the commanding officer of his principal resource, his moral authority. In peacetime, obedience can still be obtained without it, because men will follow rules and obey orders to avoid sanctions—but not in combat, when sanctions are reduced to insignificance in the face of deadly peril.

The officer who is sufficiently elitist to be moderate in his career ambitions, who manifests a visible reluctance to leave his present unit, even for promotion to higher rank, is far better placed to ask his men to perform for the sake of the group than the officer plainly eager to move on to bigger and better things. In the British Army, the elitist solidarity of each regiment is so strong that a posting to the "war house," the British equivalent of the Pentagon, is not welcomed but dreaded—even though it brings faster promotion, as it must, in order to overcome officers' reluctance to leave the regiment. Soldiers who serve under officers too elitist to be ambitious respond duly to the group loyalty they see affirmed by their commanders and the effect is compounded by the stability of the regimental group, and by long command tours.

The connections between elitism, group solidarity, and leadership are therefore very strong. The more that officers regard themselves as members of an elite, the less likely they are to disrupt its bonds by trying to push ahead of their fellow elite-members of the same generation, and this moderating barrier to careerism contributes greatly to the moral basis of their leadership. Thus the prejudice of civilian society against an elitist brotherhood—of the sort that runs forces as diverse as the British and Israeli Armies—is actually very harmful: where there is no elitism, only individual ambition remains, and corrosive careerism is the usual result. And an elitist officer corps does not imply a militaristic officer corps that would see merit in war for its own sake, as the forge of martial virtues deemed superior to all others, and which would seek to impose its own warlike priorities on civilian society at large. Far from it; elitism implies solidarity *within* the group, not the desire to spread martial ideals to society at large. The elitist British and Israeli officers are the very opposite of militaristic; if anything, they are distinctly less bellicose than their civilian fellow citizens. Both Britain and Israel went to war in 1982; in both countries, populist leaders reflected popular opinion in wanting to go to war, but the officers who led both forces to victory were distinctly less enthusiastic about the conflict than the publics which applauded their success.

But there is certainly no danger of militarism in America, at any rate not among the career officers. The very real danger is the opposite: that the officers are so "civilianized" by their entire career experience that they are ill prepared for the brutal urgencies of combat.[16] And the military institutions run by our civilianized officers may be more responsive to the civilian priorities of efficiency, honesty, and political obedience than to the requirements of strategy—both to avoid conflict by demonstrated strength and to wage war successfully if necessary.

If one considers the present workings of the military justice system, the outright domination of civilian priorities is very clear. Young officers soon discover that military justice is now geared to the fullest possible protection of individual rights, without regard to the morale and discipline of the group as a whole. Individual rights are sanctified in the Constitution, but the peculiar tension between amity and discipline that any good fighting unit requires has no such high protection. Knowing that even the most minor violation of individual rights can ruin a career, while successful leadership may simply go unrecognized, commanding officers devote extreme care and much time to laborious legal procedures in dealing with the small number of habitual troublemakers—even if they must thereby neglect the rest of their command.

Article 15 of the Uniform Code of Military Justice is supposed to alleviate this problem; it provides for the "nonjudicial" punishment of minor offenses (always subject to appeal, of course). The procedure is optional, with the accused having the choice; he can always opt for a court-martial. In theory, Article 15 should enable the commanding officer to dispense swift justice, acting on his experience, instincts, and personal knowledge of the accused. In practice, however, so many qualifications and complications have encrusted the workings of Article 15 over the years that military advocates must now be present—and instead of taking a few minutes, even petty cases can now go on for hours. In the meantime, the soldier, sailor, or airman who had problems that are more or less serious but nonlegal, and whose morale and performance could be restored by the caring advice and friendly direction from his commanding officer, will often find him too busy to help. In the armed forces of other countries that are just as democratic and attentive to human rights as our own, petty infractions of the Article 15 variety do not detain the unit commander, but are instead judged by noncommissioned officers without any formal procedure at all. That releases the time and energy of unit commanders to look after the majority, and also preserves the authority of the sergeants, corporals, and petty officers who form the backbone of most well-run military forces. The greatest cost of our civilianized system of military justice is that it erodes the authority of the first level of leadership, that of the noncommissioned officers, on which all higher leadership depends.

It is impossible to have any sustained contact with our armed forces without discovering that the individual quality of their officers is very high. The *average* officer one encounters is deeply dedicated, exceedingly well educated, and of sound moral character. In fact, inside the officer corps of each service, and certainly among the generals and admirals of each, there is enough potential talent to lead not merely the U.S. Army but several other large armies as well; not only the U.S. Air Force but all the air forces of the Western world; not just the U.S. Navy and Marine Corps but all the naval forces of the entire world. But the qualities of individuals who would be outstanding in other settings are now submerged in the crowd, and reduced to mediocrity in far too many cases. A capacity for initiative is eroded by excessive supervision. The tactical and operational abilities of individuals, and their strategic insight, are made quite irrelevant by the predominance of committee solutions reached in overstaffed headquarters. A native gift for leadership cannot be manifest in careers marked by so few opportunities for command. And the nobility of character that officers need more than expertise has no outlet or stimulus in lives so often trapped in banal office jobs and subjected to the standards of suburbia. Officers should always feel that they are among the few who have accepted responsibility for the protection of the many, with a rare and valuable dedication. And that is a feeling impossible to sustain when their vast numbers are kept busy only by the contrived and willful complications of grossly over-elaborate military bureaucracies.

CHAPTER EIGHT

☆

The Great Budget Game and the Cost of Weapons

One of the more recondite pastimes of American life is the annual controversy over defense spending. Its season begins at the end of January, when the President submits his budget requests for the next fiscal year, and does not end until September or even later, when Congress finally approves a new budget, often greatly amended. In between, a thousand discordant voices demand increases or, more often, cuts; attack or defend the merits of this or that weapon; and sometimes even present complete alternative budgets guaranteed to offer more "real" security for less money.

The public is most fortunate in having so many experts for its instruction: each member of Congress, and certainly the 140 legislators who serve on the Armed Services or Appropriations committees of House and Senate, claim superior knowledge, as do the paid spokesmen of the major pro- and anti-defense-spending lobbies, and any number of self-appointed gurus. A variety of research institutes offer their often very partisan views, while the lobbyists of the larger defense contractors need only speak in quiet undertones to have an effect. Hardly ever heard in public, but very powerful indeed, are the Congressional aides, neither elected nor publicly appointed, not specially trained nor expert, but in full command of the thousands of details that make up the budget. If only all this abundant energy and wisdom were applied to the making of our strategy and to the reorganization of our defense, spectacular improvement could be achieved. As it is, the substance of our defense is glimpsed only now and then through the veil of the numbers.

☆

Under the antique theory preserved in the Constitution, the armed forces of the United States have no lasting existence but are annually dissolved at 12 o'clock midnight on September 30, the last day of the fiscal year, only to be "raised" again on the following day, as if entirely new. By then Congress will have approved a new budget—or, if still locked in controversy, it will have passed a "continuing resolution," whereby most expenditures continue at the same rate and under the same categories as in the previous year. Because the Pentagon does not dismiss all its servicemen and civil employees at the stroke of midnight on September 30, or shut down and abandon all its offices, bases, and depots, because there is no dramatic ending and no visible beginning, the moment is easily overlooked.

But the fanciful procedure has one very real effect: it allows, indeed prescribes, a lack of continuity in Pentagon purchasing that brings with it huge hidden costs. The men and women who work for the Pentagon, in or out of uniform, need not seriously fear abrupt dismissal. Nor do the suppliers of standard commodities, such as jet fuel or bread, have much to worry about, because military purchases are only a fraction of their total sales. But the industries that must train manpower, maintain factories, and prepare tooling for products that only the Pentagon can buy have no such safety.

Until that day at the end of January when they can see their own products included in one or another of the several hundred "line" items of the budget request, defense contractors cannot be absolutely certain that their purchase will be authorized, and if so, in what quantity—even though they will have done their best during the preceding twelve months to follow closely and influence the officers and officials of the branches, services, and departments as the latter bargain within the Pentagon to accommodate competing desires within the total budget that the President and his men will submit for defense. If their product is safely included, it will meet its first test in the hearings and staff reviews of the Armed Services Committees of both House and Senate, which will recommend for or against authorization.

Anti-defense-spending spokesmen routinely dismiss both committees as mere rubber stamps, packed with uncritical supporters of the Pentagon and front men for the big contractors. But nowadays fewer than half of the programs go through without some serious question about costs or performance, arms-control effects or "constituency impact." And this is not idle chitchat: during 1983, of the 731 separate line items in the Fiscal 1984 Pentagon request, no fewer than 424 were changed by the House and another 450 by the Senate at the authorization stage.[1] It is true that the major programs are only very rarely cancelled outright, but a good many are reduced and a few increased, while the fate of lesser programs with weak constituency backing is much more precarious.

Next, the product that survives must receive its actual funding for the year from the Appropriations Committee of each house; of late their defense subcommittees have been reexamining many programs anew, recommending cuts more often than not. At that stage, the budget requests are further broken down into many more line items. Of the 1,129 separate requests in Fiscal 1984, the House changed 766 and the Senate 710. It was by that procedure that the President's request for a total of $280 billion* was reduced to something over $265 billion—a huge cut, equivalent to three-fifths of the entire British defense budget.[3]

By then the snows of Washington's winter are long gone; it is high summer, a year after the midpoint of the internal Pentagon disputations that finally resulted in the January requests. Even then, the contractor who must meet a payroll, maintain factories, and renew their tooling cannot be certain of his sales. When their appropriation decisions differ, as they often do, House and Senate committee members must meet in conference to shape a compromise, and some programs are changed yet again in the bargaining between the houses of Congress.

Then there is one final hurdle: a handful of programs are sufficiently controversial to remain unsettled until a final vote on the floor of House or Senate or both. But these are usually the very large programs (often nuclear weapons), upon which hundreds of subcontractors may depend.

In other words, the contractor who is relying on money from the first day of the fiscal year on October 1 cannot be certain of his sale until the very eve—and not even then if the final budget votes are delayed and the government is paid for under a continuing resolution.

Making long-term investments in plant or machinery in order to im-

---

* The Fiscal 1984 budget-authority request for the Defense Department was for $273,902 million; the total "National Defense" request (which includes the nuclear activities of the Department of Energy and some small transfer payments) came to a total of $280,503 million. The net total actually authorized, after Congressional reductions and supplementals, came to $258,654 million for the Department of Defense as such, and $265,316 million for "National Defense" as a whole.[2]

prove a product or reduce its unit cost, taking the long view and actually training manpower instead of poaching from others, retaining expert staff by offering the assurance of stable employment—all these are impossible or greatly discouraged by the present system. Faced with so much uncertainty, the prudent corporation in the defense business will "diversify"—i.e., use its profits to take over nondefense companies, instead of investing in its own production plant. As a result, defense contractors all too often end up manufacturing the most-advanced-technology products in the world by using so-so technology and less than modern machinery, unless each item can be billed to the government in a cost-plus contract (when everything can be greatly overdone). Faced with so many players who have some degree of power over their future, prudent defense contractors will also divert much money to their "Congressional relations" offices, their lawyers, lobbyists, and ex-military "consultants," whose cost adds nothing to their products but is still billed to the taxpayer in the form of larger overhead charges.

It is only since 1982 that Congress has made possible a minimum of continuity by allowing "multi-year contracting," whereby a certain level of purchases is guaranteed, in some cases by stiff penalty clauses. Hedged in by restrictions as it is, the privilege has been granted to only twenty-one programs till now, a mere fraction of total defense purchasing.[4] Otherwise the chronic uncertainty, and all its waste, continue as before.

Following a second antique convention, not significantly wasteful but greatly confusing, Congress does not consider the budget under strategic headings, such as the defense of Europe, the security of the sea-lanes, nuclear deterrence, and so on; nor by service totals, which would at least have the virtue of simplicity; nor by the type of force that is being maintained, say, intercontinental-nuclear, ground forces, submarine warfare, and so on. Instead, because of the internal arrangement of its subcommittees, which is not constitutionally prescribed but merely a habit, Congress requires that the separate line items be distributed service by service among a set of categories ("titles") wholly devoid of any strategic meaning:

Defense Appropriations Act
  Military Personnel
  Retired Pay
  Operation & Maintenance
  Procurement

Research, Development, Test, and Evaluation
Special Foreign Currency Program
Revolving and Management Funds

Military Construction Act
Military Construction
Family Housing & Homeowners Assistance Program

Trust Funds, Receipts & Deductions

The last category is merely a bookkeeping device, and another is inherently insignificant—the sinister-sounding "Special Foreign Currency Program," which covers some humble housekeeping functions funded in 1984 with the magnificent sum of $3 million (i.e., just over 0.001 percent of the total defense spending in that year).[5]

All the categories are misleading because of arbitrary classification: spare parts, for example, are listed under "Procurement" if they are deemed to be part of the initial purchase of the equipment, but under "Operations and Maintenance" later on—but not always, because if some modification, however slight, has intervened, the item moves from one category to the other.

Just about the only thing that can be learned by an examination of the numbers thus categorized is the less than earth-shattering discovery that when the budget becomes greater without any parallel expansion in the size of the armed forces, less of the total is eaten up by military pay:

Defense Expenditures for Personnel in Selected Fiscal Years
(in billions of dollars)[6]

	1972	1980	1984
Military Personnel (pay)	22.9	31.0	48.6
Total Budget Authority	75.0	142.6	258.2
Personnel as percentage of total	30%	22%	19%

Thus the budget increases of the Reagan buildup resulted in a more-than-proportionate increase in the amount of money for everything besides military pay—mainly weapons and other hardware, but also the training and operation of the forces.

But the sharp decline in the share of military pay was not entirely translated into greater expenditure for the hard stuff, because another item also increased: "retired military pay." One of the built-in deceptions of the so-called "all-volunteer force" is the reckoning of the cost of military pay, which is far from being the total cost of hiring the manpower for it does not include the promise of very generous pensions, now one of the most attractive lures of the recruiting sergeant. At present, all in uniform are entitled to retirement pay after twenty years; a great many pensions thus begin in the 38–42 age range, and are destined to be paid out for thirty years and more.

The cumulative amounts eventually to be paid out are therefore dramatically greater than in the case of ordinary civil pensions, which begin at age 65 and do not last much beyond ten years or so. We are in effect hiring half-million-dollar sergeants under the present system, and the accrued pension debt (as opposed to actual payouts) was not even listed in the budget until 1985. Although the immensity of the cost is not yet apparent, and will not be for more than a decade, any child with a ruler and a sheet of graph paper can project the long-term consequences:

Defense Expenditures for Retired Pay in Selected Fiscal Years
(in billions of dollars)[7]

1972	1980	1985	1989 (forecast)
3.9	12.0	17.6	24.0

By 1989, the cost of these pensions will approximate the present level of the entire British defense budget. Because there is no pension fund being accumulated by contributions to meet the growing bill—in contrast to all normal pension systems—and because the annual amount paid out is simply voted by Congress, this is one of those burdens that the present generation is irresponsibly leaving for the next one. As the great mass of today's higher-grade enlisted men (389,469 at E-6 and above) and officers begin to reach retirement age, the total cost of retired pay will increase from the present 6.4 percent of the defense budget to perhaps 10 percent or even more.

Still, the reckless accumulation of pension promises does not yet hurt. And in the meantime, the money available for Procurement, and for

Research, Development, Test, & Evaluation—the two categories that buy our present and future weapons—has increased by spectacular amounts lately:

Defense Expenditures for Hardware in Selected Fiscal Years
(in billions of dollars)[8]

	1972	1980	1984
Combined Total of Procurement and Research, Development, Test, & Evaluation	25.3	48.8	112.6
Total Budget Authority	75.0	142.6	258.2
Combined as percentage of total	34%	34%	44%

However, many voices in the defense debate do not take it for granted that spending on weapons and assorted hardware is a Good Thing. Their claim is that the Reagan Administration—in its eagerness to accumulate more aircraft carriers and bombers, tanks, and fighters—has neglected "readiness," i.e., the training and upkeep of the forces we already have, loosely covered by the Operation & Maintenance category of the budget. In fact, the critics compare the latter with the procurement category to make their case:

Procurement versus "Readiness" in Selected Fiscal Years
(in billions of dollars)[9]

	1972	1980	1984
Procurement	17.8	35.3	86.0
Operation & Maintenance	20.8	46.4	70.9
Total Budget Authority	75.0	142.6	258.2
Procurement as percentage of total	24%	25%	33%
Operation & Maintenance as percentage of total	28%	33%	27%

In the absence of any strategic view of the matter, both hawks and doves, defense-boosters and budget-cutters, aroused Congressmen and a most placid Secretary of Defense all seem to accept "readiness" not merely as one more Good Thing but rather as the supreme quality—as if there could be no such thing as too much readiness. With the criterion itself left unquestioned, this particular debate takes the form of rival claims and counterclaims about the true degree of current "readiness." The critics repeat horror stories about returning warships that have to rendezvous at sea with warships going out to the forward fleets in order to hand over missiles in short supply, and they make much of the fact that a number of Army forces are classified as not fully combat ready. The Pentagon replies by citing statistics showing that more money than ever is being spent for training, spare parts, ammunition stocks, and maintenance, thus increasing the readiness status of ships, aircraft wings, and ground units—that between 1980 and 1983, "ready" Navy and Marine Corps aircraft increased from fewer than 60 percent to more than 65 percent of the total; Army aircraft (mostly helicopters) increased somewhat less in readiness, from 74 percent to 76 percent; and Air Force fighter/attack (though not all aircraft) increased from 62 percent mission capable to 69 percent.[10] The critics reply in turn by citing other parts of the same official statistics to show, for example, that "only" 85 percent of the Army's troop carriers and 87 percent of the tanks are "fully mission capable,"[11] or that the waiting time for spare parts in the Navy remained at an average of 44 days at the last count (in 1983).[12] And so it goes, with one side earnestly claiming it is doing much to keep up the forces, while the other side charges that the Pentagon's "buying spree" is sacrificing real combat strength for the sake of the hardware.

Readiness is a Good Thing, to be sure, but much of it is also highly perishable. Except for the stocks of ammunition and spare parts, the rest of it—notably both training and maintenance—is like cut flowers: we must buy them every day for that day, and buy them again tomorrow and each day thereafter. And the more is spent on day-to-day readiness, the less remains to equip the forces and develop equipment for the future. Certainly the forward fleets, the Sixth in the Mediterranean and the Seventh in the Pacific, should be fully provided with trained men and both ships and aircraft in fighting trim; the Army and Air Force units in Germany, Korea, and other forward bases overseas must be ready for combat in every way, as must be the Marine battalions already afloat and those kept for immediate reinforcement.

Beyond that, however, the desired degree of readiness should be carefully calculated and by no means allowed to increase without limit —for one very effective way of increasing the nation's military power is precisely to keep much of it "unready." That is how the Soviet Army maintains the largest empire in history and also keeps both Europe and China under a weighty threat of invasion: its power is defined by the 194 divisions it could mobilize more or less quickly, not by the 60–70 kept ready on a permanent footing. And it is because of its even greater degree of unreadiness that Israel has a formidable army, with as many armored divisions as the active Army of the United States—at a mere fraction of the cost. With their manpower of civilian reservists not even in uniform, and their equipment in storage, most of the 11 armored divisions of the Israeli Army are totally unready most of the time. But when war comes, the bodies and the equipment are in place to be mobilized, quick refresher exercises update the training of officers and men, and speeded-up maintenance work takes care of the equipment.

What the Soviet Army or the Israelis choose to do is not appropriate for the United States, which must keep large forces overseas. But it is quite certain that no valid strategic purpose is achieved by a frantic attempt to keep each and every component of every ship, tank, and aircraft in perfect working order, and all the manpower fully trained all of the time. After all, for the large war that the United States seeks to deter, it is large forces that are needed, not fully ready forces of inadequate size. The Soviet Army itself would have to recall civilian reservists, refit equipment taken out of long-term storage, hold refresher courses, and shake down its units before starting a large war. On the other hand, in the much smaller combat that comes along from time to time, only a fraction of the total forces is employed in any case. Certainly the less-than-brilliant record of our armed forces in all recent minor combat was not caused by any lack of readiness of all the equipment, nor by any inadequacy in the training of all the manpower.

If anything, our forces now are too ready in general, even while dangerous shortages are allowed to persist in certain supplies that are absolutely critical in combat. The forward-deployed Air Force units in Europe, for example, are short of the most modern air-to-air missiles, the aircraft of the Sixth Fleet lack countermeasure equipment, and the Army does not have enough modern ammunition even for its tanks in Germany.[13] There is no need, by contrast, to keep all the artillery 90 percent ready, as is now the case, nor all the tanks at 87 percent, and even flying hours may be excessive.[14] For fighter pilots, twenty hours per month is the norm and more hours are better, and also great fun for the pilots; but at $1,500–$2,500 per hour, the extra time is very costly. In his 1984 Report to Congress the Secretary of Defense boasts that

Navy fighter/attack flight hours are so well funded by his policies that the average pilot will be able to fly 288 hours in Fiscal Year 1985, as opposed to 276 in the previous year—but nowhere is it explained why all the pilots need the extra hours, especially now that real flying can most usefully be supplemented by simulators.[15]

There is one more cost, which is the greatest of all: the unstrategic urge for ever more readiness has become one more factor in keeping the officer corps focused on mechanical, managerial, and logistic priorities at the expense of strategy, operations, and tactics. And likewise the civilian officials of the Pentagon are further encouraged to devote their energy to the procedural upkeep of the armed forces instead of reforming their organizational structures and alleviating the present malpractices.

If we now review the defense budget by reorganizing the standard categories under strategic headings, we can obtain some sense of the entire magnitude of the Reagan buildup and of its distribution:

The Defense Budget in Selected Fiscal Years (by budget authority, in billions of dollars)[16]

	1980	1982	1983	1984	[1985 request]
I. Manpower Costs:					
Military Personnel	31.0	42.9	45.7	48.6	70.5*
Retired Pay	12.0	15.0	16.2	16.6	[17.6]†
Family Housing, etc.	1.5	2.2	2.7	2.7	3.2
Subtotal	44.5	60.1	64.6	67.9	73.7
II. Running Costs:					
Operation & Maintenance	46.4	62.5	66.5	71.0	81.4
III. Investment:					
Procurement	35.3	64.5	80.4	86.0	107.6
Research, Development, Test, & Evaluation	13.6	20.0	22.8	26.9	34.0
Military Construction	2.3	4.9	4.5	4.5	7.2
Subtotal	51.2	89.4	107.7	117.4	148.8
IV. Bookkeeping:					
Special Foreign Currency Program	.007	.003	.004	.003	.009
Revolving and Management Funds	1.3	2.5	1.0	2.5	1.7
Trust Funds, etc.‡	(0.7)	(0.7)	(0.4)	(0.5)	(0.7)
Totals:					
Budget Authority	142.6	213.8	239.5	258.2	305.0
Constant 1985 $s:	192.1	242.2	260.4	269.8	305.0

  * The 1985 budget request for manpower includes—for the first time—the accrued retirement pay that will be paid in future years.

  † That is, the actual amount authorized to be paid to retirees for Fiscal Year 1985.

  ‡ Negative amounts—i.e., net receipts.

There has therefore been a great increase, though not as dramatic as many believe. Still, even when we compare the totals in "constant" dollars, in order to eliminate the effects of inflation, we see that in the five years from 1980 through 1984, the budget increased by 42 percent —a mere trifle compared with the 345 percent in two years of the Korean buildup, but very respectable when measured against the more recent past.[17]

The huge numbers are best set in context by a comparison with other numbers even more huge, the entire federal budget and the gross national product. In 1980, before the Reagan buildup, total Pentagon *outlays* amounted to 23 percent of total federal spending; 15.6 percent of total public spending—local, state, and federal; and 5.2 percent of the gross national product. In 1984, after five years of increases, defense outlays had grown to 27 percent of the total federal budget, 18.5 percent of total public spending, and 6.5 percent of the gross national product, then greatly depressed by economic conditions.[18]

In that context, comparing the Carter year of 1980 and the Reagan year of 1984, the shift in priorities seems dramatic and unprecedented. But if the context is broadened, a very different picture begins to emerge:

Defense Department Outlays, * Selected Fiscal Years*[19]

	1955	1960	1970	1980	1984
As a percentage of:					
Total Federal Outlays	51.3	45.0	39.4	23.0	27.1
Total Public Outlays	35.5	30.3	25.4	15.6	18.5
Gross National Product	9.2	8.3	8.0	5.2	6.5

* Outlays represent actual payments during the course of the fiscal year, as opposed to budget authority, which covers orders that have been authorized, on which payment will be made over time in accordance with deliveries.

Now we no longer see the unprecedented and inordinate Reagan buildup denounced by a thousand angry editorials, but only a modest and partial attempt to return to the pattern that was normal before the American military decline of the 1970s. Under President Eisenhower (who now enjoys a great reputation among people of liberal sentiments for having "stood up to the Pentagon"), more than 8 percent of the gross national product went for defense—*after* the end of the Korean war, and after the implementation of the "New Look" strategy that supposedly reduced the need for costly nonnuclear forces, by accepting a great risk of nuclear escalation. Under Presidents Kennedy and Johnson, the great worldwide economic boom of the 1960s should have resulted in a sharp decline in the defense share of the gross national product, at least until Vietnam—but it did not, because the defense budget was increased in proportion. Only in 1965, just before the Vietnam increases, was there a slight dip, and in that year defense outlays amounted to 7 percent of the gross national product. Reagan's 6.5 percent is therefore no more than modest, especially in a year in which the gross national product was greatly (and temporarily) depressed.

The Top Ten

What is being bought with all the money? In examining the budget we can relate the numbers to things, up to a point—and that point is the overhead in every category. To get some idea of the cost of weapons nowadays, the easiest connection to make is between the procurement funds and the equipment actually bought, because the bill for each "system" is separately published.

Take for example the "top ten"—the ten largest hardware programs requested from Congress for Fiscal Year 1985:

—The B-1B long-range heavy bomber of the Air Force, developed under Presidents Nixon and Ford, cancelled by President Carter (when it was a 212-aircraft program) and revived by President Reagan in a more modest design as a 100-aircraft program;

—The MX *Peacekeeper* intercontinental ballistic missile, 200 of which were to be produced under President Carter (for mobile deployment among more than 6,000 shelters arranged around 200 specially built ring roads) and 100 of which are now in production (for emplacement in existing "silos");

—The F-16 *Falcon* "lightweight" fighter, with one engine and a modest radar, which makes up the low end of the "high–low" fighter mix of the Air Force;

—The CG-47 *Aegis,* the Navy cruiser that houses the most complicated radar-computer system ever sent to sea, whose role is to protect aircraft carriers and their escorts from antiship missiles with its own surface-to-air missiles;

—The SSN-688, the very large nuclear-powered "attack" submarine (6,900 tons displacement), whose role is to hunt other submarines;

—The F/A-18 *Hornet* dual-role fighter and fighter-bomber for the Navy's carriers, whose cost has been particularly controversial because the aircraft was originally offered as a low-cost alternative to the larger F-14, but happened to enter production in years of very high inflation;

—The F-15 *Eagle* fighter, with two engines and all the trimmings, which forms the high end of the Air Force mix;

—The C-5B *Galaxy,* the largest transport aircraft, originally built at the end of the 1960s, whose production line has been reopened for the purchase of another 50 in a strengthened and updated "B" version.

—The M-1 Abrams tank, the first all-new Army tank in more than thirty years, which combines advanced technology with a conventional design;

—The *Ohio*-class submarine, a huge, cruiser-size (18,700-ton) nuclear-powered submarine, popularly known as "Trident," which is essentially a launch platform for 24 large-diameter ballistic missiles.

A mere glance at these numbers shows that our weapons are not cheap. Straight division can be tricky, because each year's buy may or may not include long-delivery components already bought in the past, or now being bought for future years. But because most of these "long-lead" items cancel each other out, we can more or less read off the 1985 cost of each weapon: fighter aircraft, for example, at $27.6 million each for the F-16, $31.9 million each for the F/A-18, and $46.1 million each for the F-15. The last of these, incidentally, serves as a good illustration of the costs of discontinuity. The contractor who produced the 36 F-15s actually purchased in Fiscal 1984 (which began on October 1, 1983) did not know how many he would be asked to produce until September 1983, when Congress finally decided to reduce the Pentagon's January request for 48 aircraft. Inevitably, the 36 aircraft actually bought had to carry exactly the same overhead of managers and offices, lawyers and scientists, consultants and factories, machines and tools as the 48 would have done—greatly increasing the cost of each one.

The high-overhead syndrome is chronic in the case of the Navy's fighters and "attack" aircraft (i.e., light bombers), which, except for the F-18, are bought year after year, off greatly underworked production lines, in numbers so small that the overall programs do not make it into the top ten. The Navy's own high-end F-14—with swing wings, two

Procurement Funding for the "Top Ten" Weapons
(in billions of dollars) [20]

	1983 (actual)	1984 (planned)	1985 (requested)
B-1B bomber			
Amount	4.0	6.1	7.7
Number	7	10	34
MX Missile			
Amount	0	2.2	3.2
Number	0	21	40
F-16 Fighter			
Amount	2.2	2.5	4.1
Number	120	144	150
CG-47 Cruiser			
Amount	3.0	3.3	3.2
Number	3	3	3
SSN-688 Attack Submarine			
Amount	1.7	2.1	3.0
Number	2	3	4
F/A-18 Fighter			
Amount	2.5	2.3	2.7
Number	84	84	84
F-15 Fighter			
Amount	1.5	1.5	2.2
Number	39	36	48
C-5B Transport			
Amount	0.8	1.4	2.2
Number	1	4	10
M-1 Tank			
Amount	1.8	1.7	1.8
Number	855	840	720
***Ohio* Submarine**			
Amount	1.8	2.1	1.8
Number	1	1	1

engines, two pilots, and the most powerful radar of any fighter—is a $40-million machine when produced at the rate of 2 per month ($976.9 million for 24 in 1985).[21] But its greatest distinction is in its main weapon: the F-14 can fire air-to-air missiles of the ordinary sort, and it has cannon too, but the missile it was actually designed to fire, and for which it was truly built, is the AIM-54 *Phoenix,* which obtains its long range (80 miles plus) at $1.18 million per copy ($472 million for 400 in 1985).[22] One wonders how many of them a fighter pilot is allowed to fire during his years of duty with F-14s, and one hopes that pilots will think twice before firing a million-dollar Phoenix at one of the cut-price Soviet fighters of the older sort that still equip many hostile air forces.

At 24 per annum, the F-14's production rate cannot be economical, but it is a dream of efficiency compared with the six-per-year rate of the Navy's A-6E light bomber. A modest subsonic aircraft in every way except in its electronics for night bombing (the one shot down in Lebanon was sent in full daylight), the A-6E was priced at $35.7 million in 1985.[23]

There is finally the AV-8B "Harrier" of the Marines, which is not modest at all in being our only vertical-takeoff fighter and fighter-bomber. Since this is a major innovation, predictably it did not come from the Air Force Systems Command nor from the Navy's Air Systems Command; it is instead a British product, further refined in the United States. At $25.7 million each in 1985, when 32 were requested (before the virtually certain Congressional cut to 27 or so), the Harrier enjoys reflected glory from the great air-combat successes of its British versions in the Falklands war, and it is the only air-fighting machine that is independent of airfields (prime targets in any war, though not so easy to shut down as one may suppose).[24] On the other hand, the extra machinery needed for the vertical takeoff eats greatly into the range/payload of the aircraft, and the delicate moment of transition to normal horizontal flight is a great cause of accidents. (In 1983, the rate of major accidents was 31.98 per 100,000 flight hours—almost four times the average for naval fighters.*[25])

Fighter aircraft are expensive—roughly thirty times as expensive as their vaguely comparable jet-fighter predecessors of thirty years ago (cars and houses are roughly ten times as expensive). But they are dirt cheap compared with the other aircraft on the list—the B-1 bombers at $227 million each (though long-lead items may have inflated that number somewhat) and the C-5B transports at $219 million.

The C-5 is a huge creature, to be sure (351,072 pounds—empty), but is only slightly larger than the commercially produced and commercially priced Boeing 747, which can be had for roughly $60 million each. It is not that the contractor is stealing the Pentagon blind (though that can happen easily enough) but rather that the making of the C-5, which after

---

* The British, however, strenuously insist that the problem rests with the Marine pilots and not with the Harrier. They may have a point, because the overall Marine major-accident rate for all aircraft, including helicopters, was 6.15 per 100,000 flight hours, as compared with 3.92 for the Navy and 3.7 for Air Force tactical aircraft.[26]

all is a transport and not a combat aircraft, pays the fullest tribute to the Air Force Systems Command way of doing things. Every normal part of a transport aircraft is present in the C-5B in a superelaborate form at unique cost; on top of that, there are special features absent from the 747, to enable the aircraft to operate from less developed airfields. That is a capability required of a military aircraft, but in the C-5 it is greatly overdone, considering that such scarce and supercostly aircraft would hardly ever be risked in precarious landings at exposed forward airstrips, a job for which we have lesser transports, such as the classic and much cheaper C-130.

The Systems Command, however, certainly cannot be accused of wanting to impose the new C-5 now being bought upon the nation. When the Defense Department decided to increase airlift capacity on an urgent basis because of the Persian Gulf crisis, the Command did not offer the present B version of the C-5, or any other ready-to-build aircraft, but rather a leisurely seven-to-ten-year research-and-development project for a future transport, the C-17. It was only because of the energetic intervention of then Deputy Secretary of Defense Frank C. Carlucci that the high-priority airlift funds linked to the "rapid deployment force" were not misused for more of the R & D merry-go-round. The Air Force characteristically tried to circumvent Carlucci with the help of friendly Congressmen; equally characteristically, the bureaucratic guerrilla fighters were bought off by the funding of a C-17 research project as well (at $129.3 million in the Fiscal 1985 request).[27]

Big aircraft are more expensive than smaller ones, but all aircraft are mere trifles compared with the Navy's warships. The 18,700-ton *Ohio*-class missile-carrying submarine costs $96,257 per ton; the 6,900-ton SSN-688 attack submarine, just over one-third in tonnage, comes in at $108,690 per ton. It is nuclear propulsion that is most expensive, and its cost does not subdivide easily as size goes down. Unlike today's jet fighters, which are at least loosely comparable to the fighters of thirty years ago (they too had jet engines and radars), the nuclear submarines cannot be compared to the much smaller submarines of the diesel age, which were not true underwater vehicles at all but rather small ships that could dive for a few hours at a time, to creep along at a few miles per hour.

The nuclear submarines inhabit a world that Admiral Hyman Rickover created out of nothing, during a career that violated all the rules of "career development" by a total absence of rotation from place to place or job to job. Everything is special in Rickover's world, meeting unheard-of standards of precision and reliability in men and machines. Certainly the industry that makes nuclear power plants and all that goes with them, including the boats themselves, has only the loosest relation to normal industry and the normal economy. A total of thirty years without a nuclear-power accident of any consequence is the bounty from Rickover's planet; a price per pound not far removed from that of truffles, caviar, and precious metals is the price we pay.

No aircraft carrier is included in the top ten of the 1985 budget request because all the carrier building for the decade was already authorized in 1983—the famous year of the two carriers for which the tidy sum of $7 billion was authorized.[28]

One argument often heard against carriers is that they are vulnerable. It is said that $3.3 billion worth of carrier and the 6,300 men on board could be sunk by a single spread of torpedoes fired by a single lucky submarine. But carriers are well-protected against submarine attack by two or three destroyers in close escort (roughly $500 million each), and also by an attack submarine, which usually tags along underwater. Moreover, carriers have their own antisubmarine helicopters for close-in defense and also a squadron of fixed-wing antisubmarine aircraft to patrol farther out.

A far greater danger to the carrier nowadays is the antiship missile— or more precisely, the simultaneous attack by many antiship missiles launched from Soviet naval bombers, surface ships, submarines, and even small missile boats. But the carriers are well protected against missile attack too, by their two squadrons of F-14s, built precisely to intercept bombers 200 or more miles away; by one or two antiaircraft cruisers in forward escort ($1 billion plus for the current type); and finally by their own antimissile guns. In any case, at more than 91,000 tons displacement for the latest *Nimitz* class, and with damage-control features built into everything, carriers are very hard to sink (though their flight operations can be knocked out much more easily).

Actually, all the talk about vulnerability misses the point. What is really wrong with aircraft carriers is not their vulnerability, but their *in*vulnerability—or more precisely, the burden of their protection. Each carrier must be escorted by several destroyers and cruisers, and the attack submarine too—and the nonnuclear ships need fleet oilers to follow along, in addition to the 52,500-ton supply ships that replenish the jet fuel and ordnance of the carrier air wing. Thus more than $6 billion worth of shipping, as well as salaries, benefits, and pensions for some 8,000 people are needed to keep one carrier wing of aircraft at sea, with some 90 aircraft in all.

But many of those aircraft are needed just to protect the carrier: 24 F-14s, 4 airborne-radar E-2C aircraft, 10 antisubmarine S-3 aircraft, and 6 antisubmarine SH-34 helicopters, on the average.[29] We thus reach a total bill of roughly $8 billion worth of ships and aircraft for the services of the remaining "attack" aircraft that fulfill the *positive* function of the carrier—to launch air strikes against targets at sea and on land. Because the decks of carriers have become more and more crowded with aircraft intended for their own self-protection, only 10 medium A-6s and 24 lighter A-7s can be accommodated, not exactly a devastatingly powerful force—even if the particular aircraft were better equipped with "smart" ordnance and modern countermeasures than they now happen to be. (The Lebanese gunmen bombed by A-6s and A-7s in the ill-fated 1983 air strike were certainly not impressed.) Thus the mighty whale gives birth to a sprat.

In the future, as threats to their survival continue to grow, the Navy could still keep its aircraft carriers well protected by adding more—or more powerful—escort ships,* and by offloading more "attack" aircraft to increase the number of carrier-protecting aircraft on board. The aircraft carriers could thus remain well protected, but they will mostly serve to protect only themselves.

Once upon a time, when carriers were one-third the size of today's 90,000-ton-plus nuclear-powered monsters, they were all business, with their decks crowded with torpedo-bombers, dive-bombers, and fighters that also dropped bombs. They were useful to strike at land targets, but were absolutely indispensable for superiority at sea, because no land-based aircraft had the range to attack enemy warships across the vastness of the Pacific, and only very slow and very vulnerable flying boats could make it across the Atlantic.

Now that very fast bombers can reach any point on the Pacific in short order, and even fighters can cross the Atlantic, the carrier is no longer essential for sea control. Therefore its strategic justification rests more than ever on its ability to "project" air power onto land. But the increasing burden of self-protection has outpaced the growth of the carriers, so that their net air power has actually diminished. Moreover, thirty years ago or even twenty, the air power that could be generated

---

* Lately, the billion-dollar *Aegis* CG-47 cruisers, discussed on p. 222.

off the deck of a single American aircraft carrier was more powerful than the complete air forces of most countries of the world. Nowadays, by contrast, a mere 34 attack aircraft are no match for the strong air defenses and large fighter strength of a good number of countries in the very regions that are the likeliest combat zones for our carriers.

The diminishing value of carrier air power has been masked in recent years by political malpractice. Presidents unwilling to actually use force, but equally unwilling to admit impotence, have developed the habit of sending aircraft-carrier task forces to regions in crisis, where American interests are in danger. The carriers go off, and the mighty armada is duly filmed in distant waters for the benefit of the nightly television news. The President, it seems, has acted. But the crisis continues to unfold just as before, and the natives do as they want with our interests in need of protection, quite unafraid of those 34 attack aircraft.

Nothing of value is therefore achieved; but the aircraft carriers and all their escorts are kept on station day after day, for weeks or months. Actually, there is one significant result from this parody of gunboat diplomacy: next time, upon the occasion of the next crisis, the sending of the aircraft carriers will intimidate even less. Of course, the maneuver could work—but only if the rule of gunboat diplomacy were strictly followed: if the natives refuse to behave themselves, the gunboats must open fire, if only to preserve their value for the next occasion. But that is not a rule likely to be obeyed when the whole point of sending out the carriers in the first place is not to act, but rather to avoid having to act. Nevertheless, in February of the year following each such maneuver, when the Secretary of the Navy presents his statement to Congress, he will stress how much the carriers were "used" during the previous year, and note their great utility for "crisis management."

Thus the aircraft carriers we are even now building at great cost may still be triumphant tactically in remaining well protected, and they may perpetuate the illusion of political worth. But all along they are becoming steadily more self-serving at the operational level, and they are also being outclassed at the strategic level.

Also included in the top ten is one of the escort ships that carriers nowadays need in order to survive. In fact, the most remarkable of the Navy's price stickers belongs to the billion-dollar CG-47 cruiser, which is not nuclear powered, not a floating city like the aircraft carriers, but merely a garden-variety destroyer filled with combat electronics and perhaps overloaded at 9,200 tons. One billion-dollar question is whether the ten-year-plus development time for these "Aegis" ships did not result in the sending to sea of ten-year-old computers—a lag equivalent to forty or fifty years for most other technologies. It may also be asked if it is sensible to concentrate so much value in just one hull.

The Navy's aircraft carriers and their escorts do need a multilayer defense against concerted attack by antiship missiles launched from Soviet naval bombers, surface ships, and submarines. It makes sense to insert a protective layer of medium-range missiles for fleet defense between the outer layer of protection afforded by F-14 patrols and the close-in protection of each individual ship with its own short-range missiles and guns. And to intercept many missiles at one time, out to medium ranges, powerful radars and even more powerful computers are needed to spot the real targets, burn through countermeasures, launch the defensive missiles, track them along with the targets, and guide them to intercept. But with modern radar techniques and today's compact and powerful computers, it should be possible to distribute the equipment and the job among several ships, thus avoiding the dependence of the entire task force on its one *Aegis* ship. (Because of its cost, only one is being built for each carrier.)

As compared with those of the Air Force and the Navy, the Army's weapons are cheap: a mere $2.4 million for each M-1 tank, the only Army weapon to make it into the top ten, and not more than $9 million or so each for the AH-64 *Apache* attack helicopter (144 requested in 1985 for a total of $1.3 billion), although the real cost of the *Apache* is not quite so small, because some of its costly weapons and sensors are billed separately.[30] The M-1 tank has been praised for its superior Chobham armor (a British innovation) and greatly criticized for its gas-turbine engine. There are also some serious questions about the vulnerability of its ammunition, carried high behind the turret in a box with a blow-off top, which may blow off too easily.

On the other hand, many complaints about the M-1 have confused ordinary teething troubles with terminal defects, or else plainly show an ignorance of armor warfare, notably in denying the importance of long-range accuracy for the gun, and therefore the value of the tank's admittedly costly night-vision devices, laser range finder, and ballistic computer.*

---

* To fight Soviet armor advancing at, say, 20 kilometers per hour, a computerless range of only 1,000 meters means that there will be only three minutes of fighting time to hold the line against the attack, during which three or four rounds can be fired. With all its gear, by contrast, the M-1 has nine minutes and more, unless visibility is particularly bad, permitting the successive engagement of as many as ten enemy tanks.

Perhaps the weightiest and most valid criticism of the M-1 is simply that after almost fifteen years and several billions of dollars' worth of research and development, a totally ordinary design finally came out—with the same old rear engine, high turret, and low hull layout that goes back to the 1920s. The Swedish turretless S tank of the 1960s, the far superior Swedish turretless tank now being built, and the exceptionally well-protected Israeli *Merkava* with its front engine, high hull, and low turret show what less money, less advanced technology, and much better design can achieve.

Obviously, the Army too has its systems-command syndrome, in a most acute form. In fact, it is downright frivolous to complain of the Army's failure to innovate in tank design, when its abundantly staffed research-and-development commands did not even develop the Army's most basic kit of weapons: the standard rifle (still the wretched M-16, a private design and a poor one), squad machine gun (Belgian), light mortar (British), and antitank rocket (Swedish). One wonders what the Army's Armament Research and Development Command really does with its thousands of civilians and hundreds of officers and men. A 1982 brochure[31] does mention, among other things, "Sadarm," a typical merry-go-round project that "may resolve the Army's 25-year search for the ultimate anti-tank weapon," with "may" and "ultimate" being the key words. Meanwhile the American infantry remains with a disgraceful little rocket for antitank defense, and will soon have an imported design.

Altogether more questionable than the new tank is the other major combat vehicle of the Army, the M-2/M-3 *Bradley* combat carrier for the infantry, which comes in at just over $1 billion for 710 in 1985, or $1.49 million each, *without* the built-in weapons, which are billed separately.[32] The *Bradley* actually combines two vehicles in one—a troop carrier and a weapons carrier, with a turret fitted with both an automatic cannon (25mm) and TOW missile launchers. Any mechanical defects the *Bradley* may have are beside the point, for it is wrong in concept, the product of a development program unguided by any sound concept of tactical use.

To cross the zone beaten by the enemy's artillery, which may extend for 20 or more kilometers behind the front, the infantry does need an armored truck to move about in, until the men dismount to fight on foot; to travel across country, in order to avoid congested and vulnerable roads, that vehicle should have tracks rather than wheels. The result is a tracked armored carrier such as the M-113, which is in standard issue and has been for more than twenty years; it was last purchased in 1984 at $183,000 each.[33] Though good enough to protect the troops inside from artillery fire, the M-113 is so poorly armored that it can be penetrated by plain machine guns and even the least accomplished of anti-tank weapons (the hand-held Soviet RPG-7, which is very accomplished indeed, blows it away); and to make matters worse, its aluminum hull burns very quickly. Nevertheless, its notorious weakness was tactically acceptable, because the M-113 was not regarded as a fighting vehicle: once it reached the zone of close combat, the infantry was to leave it in order to fight on foot. Still, it made sense to research and develop a vehicle with more protection. Had money been short and the need urgent, the M-113 would have been followed by another M-113 made of steel instead of aluminum, and protected not with plain armor that is too heavy for a 10-ton chassis but rather new materials and new techniques.*

The Army's Tank-Automotive Command, however, did not have the discipline of tight budgets nor any sense of urgency. It therefore set out to design a totally new armored carrier, much larger than the M-113 and twice as heavy. Instead of a mere "battle taxi," the new carrier would be made for combat; in fact, it was originally known as the "mechanized infantry combat vehicle." Because the carrier was already so large and costly, it seemed logical to arm it with a 25mm cannon instead of the mere machine guns employed by the M-113; because so powerful a weapon was provided, it then made sense to mount it in a $200,000+ stabilized turret. Because the turret was there, it was then "cost-effective" to equip it with the fancier kind of night-vision sights (thermal) and more trimmings of that ilk; because such elaborate weapon controls were already in place, it then became economical to add TOW missile launchers to the turret, which then became very large.

Thus the plain troop carrier that would nowadays cost perhaps $400,000 became the $1.5-million *Bradley*. Only in one aspect was the new machine scarcely better than the old M-113: its protection—which had increased, but not by much, and certainly not by enough to shield it from many commonplace battlefield weapons.

Unfortunately, while the *Bradley* was slowly being developed, be-

---

* Lightweight fiber armors and novel forms of protection against hollow-charge effects are now available.

coming more and more elaborate in the process, the antitank revolution was under way. The modern rockets, less modern guns and recoilless weapons, and the many kinds of antitank missiles that now saturate the battlefield are not really very effective against the latest 50–60-ton battle tanks. But they are devastating against all tank-sized targets that do not have tank-like levels of protection. With its thin armor, the 20-ton *Bradley* cannot survive on the battlefield—i.e., within the inner zone of close combat—any better than the one-tenth-the-price M-113 could. But if the *Bradley* is employed as a mere troop carrier, to be left behind by the infantry before it enters a fight, then its million-plus dollars' worth of weapons will be wasted.

Engineers see merit in improving armor or anything else degree by degree; but war is dominated by abrupt discontinuities. Engineers see graphs in their minds showing costs increasing gradually as armor weight increases, and they will limit their ambitions to fit some cost ceiling imposed from above. But war nowadays allows only two levels of protection—either the heavy tank or nothing at all. (In the 1982 Lebanon war, the Israelis advanced to Beirut in their extra-protected tanks and also on foot; the M-113s were kept well to the rear, and used as mere trucks.) Engineers are necessary to develop all weapons of war; but no weapon should be developed by engineers alone—including Army officers too well educated in engineering to remember that tactics, operations, and war itself also exist.

To conclude, it is interesting to look at the cost of the cheapest weapons, the small arms of the infantry. When last purchased in 1984, the common M-16 rifle of the Army and Marines was priced at $489—very cheap indeed: the sturdier, heavier, and better-equipped rifles of our allies cost twice as much. The standard machine gun, the M-60, was far more expensive at $2,989, and the reason is clear: none was purchased for some years, and then production was restarted in 1984 for a mere 368. A total sale of $1.1 million is scant reward for a defense contractor who must fill in acres of forms, satisfy all manner of special requirements, accept a variety of inspections, and retain costly lawyers merely to negotiate the very complicated contract.

Finally, consider the humblest weapon of all (actually only an intended purchase, since the weapon itself has not yet been selected): the "9mm Personal Defense Weapon"—i.e., the plain pistol. None was in fact bought, as we noted earlier, because the leading candidate, the Beretta, and other trusty killers were rejected by the Army's inspectors.* But the money set aside in 1984 for the initial purchase worked out to $339 per pistol—not more than one's friendly neighborhood gun merchant would charge. This is an example of what happens when there is real competition: only one shipyard makes aircraft carriers; dozens of companies make 9mm pistols.[34]

* The 9mm Beretta has since been purchased.

CHAPTER NINE

☆

The Great Budget Game and the Lessons of History

The same budget can be examined in a different way: the numbers presented to Congress under the traditional headings can also be divided among the "major force programs"—bureaucratic language for a set of very broad categories which do, however, have some strategic meaning.

☆

Devised in the era of McNamara, when business-school clarity prevailed, the breakdown by force "programs" has not been changed since then. The categories are as follows:

—Strategic Forces, where "strategic" means long-range and nuclear, including the Navy's ballistic-missile submarines, the intercontinental ballistic missiles and long-range bombers of the Air Force; sundry communications and warning systems; and also the few fighter squadrons kept for the defense of the continental United States, Alaska, and Hawaii.*

—"General Purpose" Forces, Pentagon jargon for the ordinary combat forces of the Army, Navy, Marine Corps, and Air Force. Although they do include the "tactical" nuclear weapons belonging to those forces (artillery shells, bombs, depth charges, etc.), these are very largely nonnuclear "theater" forces, as opposed to the strategic nuclear forces, which are inherently of global effect.

* The nuclear devices built into the bombs, missile warheads, depth charges, and so on are funded separately under the Department of Energy budget.

228

—Intelligence and Communications, which include all intelligence and communications not built into the combat forces themselves.

—Airlift and Sealift, which pays for the large and medium transports of the Air Force and the tankers and cargo ships of the Navy, including chartered vessels.

—Guard and Reserve Forces, a rather small category that pays for rather large forces, since their "readiness" costs are quite low.

—Research and Development, more narrowly defined than in the breakdown by appropriation titles.

And then there is the pure overhead, under three headings:

—Central Supply and Maintenance, mainly business handled by defense agencies for all the services;

—Training, Medical, Other General Personnel Activities;

—Administration & Associated Activities;

—Support of Other Nations, which covers training schemes as well as gifts of equipment. Once very large, this category is now quite small ($741 million in 1984), because most weapons supplied to other countries are nowadays sold, not given.

Strategic Forces

One interesting fact that can be learned from these very rough categories is that the strategic nuclear forces—all those "controversial" bombers and missiles that we endlessly debate and try to limit, control, and freeze—at least have the virtue of being relatively cheap:

Defense Budget by "Major Force Programs"
(in billions of dollars) *[1]

	1980	1982	1983	1984	1985 [request]
Strategic Nuclear Forces	11.1	15.3	19.6	26.1	31.4
Total Budget	142.1	211.3	238.7	259.1	305.7
Percentage for strategic forces	7%	7%	9%	10%	10%

* Total Obligational Authority, which includes moneys for future-year payment, for future-year deliveries.

One can therefore see that much of the media coverage of the Reagan buildup was profoundly misleading in constantly insinuating that the large budget increases of 1981–1983 were caused by increased spending on the strategic nuclear forces. The figures show that the rebirth of the B-1B bomber and the first lots of the 100 MX missiles placed in production have indeed increased the "strategic" share of the total budget—but not by much: from 7 percent under Carter, the arms-controller, to 10 percent (or more exactly, 10.28 percent) under Reagan, the great advocate of nuclear strength. A more refined calculation, by which Intelligence and Communications money and other overhead costs are distributed between the strategic and other forces, would show a higher percentage for the strategic forces, but not by much.

Actually, the strategic nuclear forces are now cheaper in absolute terms than they were throughout the Eisenhower–Kennedy years. With all amounts stated in constant 1985 dollars to remove the distortion of inflation, the $31.4 billion requested for 1985 and the $27.5 billion actually granted by Congress in 1984 may be compared with the $38.7 billion spent in 1951, the $57.8 billion of the all-time peak of strategic spending in 1952, and the annual average of $43.1 billion spent during all the years that followed, until 1964.[2]

It was the expenditure of those years that gave the United States a distinct superiority in strategic nuclear forces which lasted until the mid-1970s. We lived off the abundant inheritance accumulated from 1951 to 1964 without being able to preserve it, let alone increase it during the troubled years that followed. It was the stock of strategic nuclear weapons built up by 1964 that sustained the overall military balance, nuclear and nonnuclear, by offsetting the Soviet advantage in conventional warmaking. Until the Reagan buildup, the United States was relentlessly sliding into inferiority; now, at best, there is a modest recoupment, but the somewhat higher strategic spending of today would have to be kept up for a full decade and more to rebuild the inheritance dissipated after 1964.

It was not just that the money spent then was truly big money, but also that it was spent so economically, because the overhead was distributed over large numbers of weapons. The current production of 100 B-1Bs may be compared with the 2,048 B-47s (the first pure-jet bomber) built between 1951 and 1957, or the 744 B-52s built between 1955 and 1962.[3] The 241 B-52s still in service are one of the last remnants of the pre-1964 inheritance: now much modified, they are still a very important part of the current strategic forces; indeed, it is only their large payload that offsets in some small degree the great Soviet advantage in missile capacity at intercontinental range. Similarly, the 100 MX missiles now being produced over a span of several years after delays, cuts, modifications, and restarts may be compared with the 200 + -per-year production rate of the *Minuteman* missile during the early 1960s. Mass production reduced unit costs; not only was more money spent, but each dollar also bought a lot more.

At first, the post-1964 decline in spending was a rational response to the plain facts of the situation. Soviet leaders had talked big after the *Sputnik* success, but they could not yet build practical ballistic missiles, so the United States—with very large superiorities in both land-based and sea-based missiles and even more in bombers—had little reason to keep spending for even more offensive power. On the other hand, there were no antimissile weapons yet worth building, and the Soviet bomber force was still feeble, so there was no incentive to spend much on defensive weapons either.

It was fully understood that the amount of real diplomatic leverage that could be obtained from weapons so catastrophic could not increase without limit, and certainly not in proportion to their number or destructive capacity. And by 1965 it was plain that the outer limits of diplomatic utility were about to be reached. Whatever advantage the United States could obtain from its strategic superiority was already being obtained— as shown by the surrender of Soviet pretensions over West Berlin, by the outcome of the Cuban missile crisis, and later by the prudent Soviet stance in the 1967 Arab–Israeli war—in sharp contrast to the Soviet threats that punctuated the next war of 1973, which erupted at a time when the United States no longer had any definite strategic superiority.

And of course by 1965, any possible requirement for self-protection by deterrence had long been abundantly met. It was therefore not because of any unstrategical urge, or any failure of nerve, that spending on the strategic forces declined to $24.3 billion in 1965, and declined again in 1966, to $22.1 billion (still in 1985 dollars).[4]

By 1967 the dimensions of the Soviet effort to build strategic weapons were becoming apparent, but the Vietnam war was then going full blast, and money for everything else was in short supply. Just as important, however, was the psychological effect of the war, or more precisely the erosion of will induced by its follies and tragedies. It was not the public at large that was affected, or Congress—as always its faithful mirror—but rather our peculiarly insecure elite of government-minded academics and academic-minded government officials, including the very authors of the Kennedy buildup, notably Robert S. McNamara. Under the impact of Vietnam, that elite began to lose faith in the utility of military power in all its forms, undergoing a gradual intellectual decline that would eventually make wishful disarmers out of the great architects of American strategic power.

The first symptom of this failure of nerve, clearly manifest by 1967, was the refusal to believe the steadily accumulating evidence which showed that the Soviet Union had launched a force-building effort of unprecedented dimensions—and not with the intention of reaching any sort of parity. Satellite photographs were bringing back pictures showing that more and more missile silos were under construction; that some of those missiles were much larger than needed for strike-back deterrence (against cities), and were instead of the kind needed to attack *Minuteman* silos; and that Soviet submarine yards were being enlarged to accommodate more and more new hulls at one time. But the politics of strategic policy dominated the process of intelligence analysis.[5] Crisp photographs could not be denied, but their meaning could be and was; each year, the output of Soviet strategic nuclear weapons was greatly underestimated in the preparation of projections for the future; the following year, the listings of weapons actually in place would duly be revised to reflect the new totals, but the output projections were not, thus leading to another underestimate for the following year.[6] At each remove, the claim was made that the upsurge in weapons just recorded was exceptional, and that the Soviet Union would soon stop adding weapons, as the United States had done unilaterally from 1967. (In that year strategic spending declined again, to $21.7 billion, less than half of the post-Korean average till 1964.[7])

The second symptom of the failure of nerve was the corruption of the perfectly worthy aim of negotiating arms limits with the Soviet Union into a pure-faith ideology of arms control. Since the United States has a clear technological advantage, manifest in its greater ability to design and build innovative strategic weapons, while the Soviet Union has the advantage in mustering large armies, an arms-control policy guided by strategy would require parallel progress in limiting high-technology nuclear weapons *and* the land forces that American nuclear weapons must help to deter. But for the believers, the great criterion of arms-control proposals has been their "negotiability." Parallel negotiations would be exceedingly complicated at best, and the Soviet interest in arms limitation is understandably confined to nuclear forces alone. On the spurious ground that "nuclear weapons alone can destroy the world"—as if the occasion of their use would not be created by a conventional imbalance leading to conventional war and then escalation—the ideological arms-controllers persuaded the entire nation that one-sided limitations on strategic forces alone were not merely tolerable but positively desirable.

Actually, the Kremlin leaders reacted to the illogical American enthusiasm for controls on nuclear weapons alone with a mixture of satisfaction and suspicion: satisfaction, because the combination of strategic "parity" with its growing land-power superiority would leave the Soviet Union clearly superior in total military power overall; suspicion, because the technicians of power who rule the Soviet Union could not quite bring themselves to believe that the United States would deliberately set out to nullify its development advantage in strategic forces while doing nothing to limit the Soviet advantage in raising large land forces. Deep down they always believed that it was all, somehow, a deceitful maneuver.

Strategy rewards pessimists more often than not, and the Soviet leaders were right in substance, even though there was no deceitful intent. It was the technological innovation of a free society that outmaneuvered the Soviet Union, the arms-controllers, and the process of arms control itself. As soon as restraints were placed on ballistic missiles of high parabolic trajectory, the flat-flying cruise missile emerged, the fruit of just-achieved advances in computers and lightweight jet engines; as soon as all missiles were placed under restraint, the bomber obtained a new lease on life in its new "stealthy" form.

But though the ideological arms-controllers were destined not to achieve their declared goal of reducing armaments on both sides, by the end of the 1960s they had a broad and powerful influence that reinforced the national disenchantment with all things military which then prevailed. Though still vastly superior in strategic arms, the United States was rapidly losing its advantage, but there was no inclination on the part of Congress to pay for a strategic policy that would maintain superiority. Thus when President Nixon took office in 1969, he could not implement a Nixonian strategic policy. Spending on the strategic forces continued to decline—from $26.6 billion in the last Johnson year of 1969, to $20.5 billion in 1970, and down again each year after that, reaching $14 billion by 1976.[8]

Unable to build weapons, the Nixon Administration did the next-best thing: it started developing the *Trident* submarine and missile and the B-1 bomber, and began funding the engineering of the spontaneously emerging cruise missile. Instead of resisting the tidal pressure for arms control, Nixon made it his own policy, with Henry Kissinger as his formidable executive and then coequal, if not more. Out of their efforts came the 1972 SALT I agreements, which set limits on both land-based and sea-based ballistic missiles, which virtually banned antimissile defenses by treaty, and which explicitly recognized the advent of strategic-nuclear "parity."

By the time Jimmy Carter became President in 1977, the enthusiasm of the public and Congress for détente had greatly diminished. Having so strongly supported the arms-control agreements that officially registered strategic "parity" with the Soviet Union, the public and Congress logically should have been willing to accept a great increase in Soviet action on the international scene. But they reacted most unfavorably when the Soviet Union naturally enough started to behave as the world's first military power, equal in strategic nuclear strength and superior in land power. The Soviet role in the 1973 Arab–Israeli war—its concealment of Egyptian and Syrian offensive intentions, its call to other Arab countries to join in, its airlift of weapons (which eventually prompted the American airlift to Israel), and its threatening posture when its clients were facing defeat—was ill received in America, as was the 1975 takeover of Angola by the Soviet Union's Cubans, and later its intervention in Ethiopia.

Suppressed by ignorance or ideology, strategy asserts itself nonetheless. Having been handed superiority, Soviet leaders behaved as should have been expected—and actually with restraint, given their enhanced position in the world. But American opinion reacted as if "parity" in strategic arms did not mean what it must mean in a world where there is no parity in land power.

President Carter was therefore given the opportunity to rebuild American strategic strength: both the B-1 and various cruise missiles were ready for production, the MX missile was not far behind, and in the new post-détente atmosphere, both public and Congress were willing to grant the necessary moneys. The Carter Administration, however, had quite different priorities: its goal was not to build weapons but to reduce their number very substantially, by more negotiations with the Soviet Union. The new administration criticized its predecessors for only trying to set limits on further growth instead of seeking outright reductions and large ones; it took for granted that the Soviet Union would share its lofty aim. But though they are always interested in arms control, as long as it limits nuclear forces alone, the Kremlin leaders were unalterably opposed to any actual reductions. In their view, the proper business of superpowers is to become even more powerful—not to reduce the gap between themselves and the next lot of great powers with nuclear weapons. Moreover, those other nuclear-armed powers, Britain, China, and France, all consider themselves threatened by the Kremlin and are therefore aligned against the Soviet Union.

Unable to achieve the longed-for reductions, and eventually denied the second-best of a SALT II treaty (duly negotiated in 1979, but too late—for the Senate would not ratify it in the wake of the Soviet invasion of Afghanistan), the Carter Administration could at least contain the growing public pressure for some substantial response to the Soviet strategic buildup. The B-1 was cancelled in favor of the rather leisurely development of the "Stealth" bomber, and the MX missile was delayed. Thus the absolute low point in strategic spending (post-1950) was reached in 1979, when a mere $12.7 billion in 1985 dollars ($8.3 billion at the time) was provided for the strategic forces.[9]

The invasion of Afghanistan, the agony of the Iran hostage crisis, and the approach of the Presidential elections all served to induce a greater realism in Mr. Carter's White House, and for Fiscal 1981 strategic spending was raised to $15.1 billion in 1985 dollars ($12.4 billion at the time).[10] Given that very low starting point, it was easy to misperceive the strategic expenditures that followed in the Reagan years as exceptional and inordinately high. But in the context of the last thirty years they should be recognized as no more than a belated return to normality—even when one does not take into account the great upsurge of Soviet strategic-nuclear strength that took place during the 1970s. As it is, the Reagan strategic budgets are positively modest.

The 10.28 percent of the defense budget that now goes to the strategic forces (15 percent or so including various overheads) is paying for the upkeep of 1,000 Minuteman intercontinental ballistic missiles based on land (and also the last of the Titan IIs, now being phased out) and the building of the new MX missiles; the upkeep of 56 FB-111 medium bombers, 241 B-52G and H heavy bombers (and their conversion to carry air-launched cruise missiles); the building of the new B-1B bombers and the operation of some 500 tanker aircraft that refuel the bombers; the upkeep of 31 Poseidon submarines (and their conversion to carry the new Trident I missiles) as well as the first 4 *Ohio*-class submarines already at sea (and the building of more); the building of an entire variety of warning, detection, and communication systems (some airborne) at home, abroad, and in space; and also a token force of five squadrons of fighter-interceptors. That is a lot for relatively little, at least by the standards of the Pentagon.

The secret of the cheapness of the strategic forces is that they mostly consist of weapons and not people: they are "capital intensive," in the language of the economists. Although the bombers, missile submarines, and the rest are even more expensive pound for pound than other weapons, their use of manpower is by contrast very frugal—some 94,100 active-duty people, out of a total of more than 2 million at last count.[11]

Intelligence and Communications

Intelligence and communications are present in some form within every combat force—down to the 10-man infantry squad with its eyes and radios—and their role in warfare continues to grow. In fact, the entire evolution of warfare from its earliest recorded days may be charted far better by the progress of intelligence and communications than by advances in weaponry. Throughout history, forces better able to gather intelligence and to communicate the orders inspired by that knowledge have been able to outclass enemies just as well armed; that was the great strength of the Romans, whose signal towers still stand in many places and whose eagle standards were by no means only decorative.

The military are routinely accused of refusing to learn the lessons of history, but in this case the lesson has been not merely learned but probably overlearned. One aspect of the Vietnam war was the frantic overcommunication whereby senior officers in overstaffed headquarters intruded in the pettiest tactical decisions of units in the field. Another was the sheer mass of intelligence that was collected, which greatly exceeded the capacity of interpreters and analysts, to the point where much of the stuff was not even screened till weeks had passed.* At present, similarly, there are actually more signalmen than riflemen among the 220,000 Army troops in Europe.[12]

This too is a hidden cost of keeping military forces with too many senior officers. With not enough to do, they interfere downward and

---

* Long after the complete surprise of the Viet Cong's all-out Tet offensive in 1968, all sorts of warnings were uncovered in the intelligence that no one had yet been able to look at.

demand the instant supply of very detailed information, which they need to intrude all the better into decisions that should be left to their juniors. The overcentralization that usually delays action in wartime—as decisions are reserved for senior officers far away, often resulting in orders from the top that are removed from reality, and always undercutting the officers in between—is quite impossible without overcommunication. It is interesting to contrast the great stress on "initiative" in the official teachings of the U.S. military with the unprecedented volume and highly detailed content of their communications, in both exercises and real combat.

But the Intelligence and Communications that are a "major program" in the function-by-function breakdown of the budget are not built into the forces themselves. They are instead the *central* intelligence and communications operated by the "Security,"* Communications, and Intelligence branches of each service, under the coordination of the National Security Agency, Defense Intelligence Agency, and Defense Communications Agency. They collect signal intelligence for the National Security Agency (whose task is to hear everything that others want to keep secret), obtain photographic and other intelligence for the Defense Intelligence Agency, as well as the CIA and the Intelligence headquarters of each service, and provide higher-echelon communications in worldwide networks whose administrative focal points are the major headquarters of each service, and whose operational focal points are the "unified" and "specified" joint commands, and above them, the ground and airborne "war rooms" of the Pentagon and White House.

At last count, in mid-1983, 33,400 active-duty personnel were employed in Intelligence, a good many of them in the service outfits (Army Security Agency and its Navy and Air Force counterparts) that operate the listening posts of the National Security Agency; another 33,600 were in centrally managed communications, coordinated by the Defense Communications Agency.[13] The combined total reached the respectable proportion of 3 percent of all people on active duty.

But that is not enough, it seems. One lesson that the Napoleons who conquered Grenada learned, they said, was that there was not enough Intelligence and Communications for the Atlantic Command. Apparently the admirals in charge did not think of merely sending some junior officers on tourist leave to Grenada with radios in their luggage to relay

---

* When used as a unit designator, "security" is in fact a cover title for units whose tasks are electronics, intelligence, cryptology, and the safeguarding of emissions and communications.

back intelligence. (Americans did not even need visas to enter the island.) Neither did the good admirals reflect on the implications of their need for more communications: flawed plans can easily make totally unnecessary demands for close coordination. (In war, only the simple works, and if plans are kept simple and initiative is given ample scope, not much communication is needed.) Even before Grenada, there were plans to increase the number of personnel in the Intelligence and Communications functions to reach 73,000 by 1984—an increase of more than 10,000 since 1981, or one-sixth of the modest growth in the forces during those years. This too is one of those ancillaries that can quietly increase to absorb the entire active-duty force over the fullness of time.

Expenditure on Intelligence and Communications has greatly increased under Reagan, but not because of any special Reaganite propensities. Long before the new administration assumed office, hawks and doves agreed that the existing central communication systems—linking all military bases and forces worldwide with the main headquarters and command posts by voice channels, open and secure, and by teleprinter and data link (i.e., computer-to-computer)—were in need of fundamental overhaul. Having grown bit by bit over the years, as new links and new techniques of transmission were gradually added, the networks were plagued by breakdowns and errors, both human and mechanical, and also consumed much manpower, sometimes to operate manual switchboards of antique design. More patches and add-ons could no longer do the job, and the huge task of reconstruction could no longer be delayed.

Moreover, hawks and doves were in full agreement over the need to reduce the vulnerability of higher-echelon communications to nuclear attack. Quite aside from physical destruction of the familiar kind (even in the totally unfamiliar magnitude that would result from nuclear explosions), telecommunications are also in danger from the invisible effects of electromagnetic pulse, which can destroy electrical circuits even when they are safe from blast or heat damage.

Whether to pursue rational strategic aims in the middle stages of a nuclear war (to end the conflict with minimum damage) or merely to prevent an uncontrolled nuclear escalation by default, the President and the higher commands must have working and secure lines of communication with at least the "launch-control centers" of the *Minuteman* missiles, the strategic air bases and in-flight bombers of the Air Force, and the remote and submerged missile submarines of the Navy. And in order to know what to tell them, the national command authorities must also remain in touch with the people who monitor the ground radars and warning satellites that observe the Soviet nuclear forces, and with the nuclear-detonation reporting net and satellites that would reveal the scope of a nuclear attack. In practice, however, many more forces must be linked by secure communications to enable the authorities to retain even a minimum of control over a conflict, notably the ground, air, and naval forces overseas that have nuclear weapons with them—that is, *all* major units.

Every medium of telecommunication, from leased commercial telephone lines to satellite-relayed microwave and radio in many forms, is employed in an attempt to obtain maximum redundancy, and therefore survivability. The systems that are specifically related to the strategic-nuclear forces, such as the converted transport aircraft that communicate with submarines by trailing the long wires of low-frequency antennas (the lower the frequency, the longer the wave, and the better it penetrates water) come under the "strategic" heading of the budget, but expenditures for intelligence and communications as such cover all other central communications ("common-user communications"). These include the worldwide telephone system of the Defense Department, the Autovon network familiar to all servicemen (now being replaced by a new Defense Switched Network); a computer-to-computer system, the Defense Data Network, which is also being remade; a secure voice telephone system (the phones are red, and their possession a bully status symbol), also being improved; and the Pentagon's equivalent of Western Union, the Automatic Digital Network, which teleprints the bulk of intelligence that comes in and orders that go out, a twenty-year-old system also being drastically modernized.

Only technical experts understand this room of the house of defense, yet the Congressional review of these expenditures is unusually well informed: tactical knowledge and strategic insight are nowhere to be found in civilian society, but there is much civilian expertise in telecommunications, and it seems to find its way into the committee rooms of Congress.

The ostensible growth in these expenditures from the level of 1980 to the requested level for 1985, in current dollars magnified by inflation, would be a spectacular 286 percent (total budget growth through the same distorting lens was 215 percent). But if we compare the real growth in constant 1985 dollars, from $12.1 billion in 1980 to $26 billion requested for 1985 (actually $25,968 million), the increase is still a very respectable 215 percent.[14] So long as they are not misused for micro-

Expenditures for Intelligence and Communications,
Selected Fiscal Years (in billions of dollars) * [15]

	1980	1982	1983	1984	1985†
Intelligence & Communications	9.1	13.9	17.4	20.0	26.0
Total Budget	142.1	211.3	238.7	259.1	305.7
Percentage for I & C	6%	7%	7%	8%	8.5%

   * Total Obligational Authority, which includes moneys for future-year payment, for future-year deliveries.
   † Request.

tactical interference in minor affrays greatly removed from nuclear dangers (and thus best left to the commanders on the spot), these are expenditures that no one should begrudge.

Airlift and Sealift

Airlift and Sealift are far more tangible commodities than Intelligence and Communications; the end point of the expenditures that come under this heading are the transport aircraft operated by the Air Force for all services and the civilian-manned tankers and cargo ships operated by the Navy's Military Sealift Command, owned by the government or under charter. In peacetime, these aircraft and ships provide for the normal supply of bases and forces overseas, and for the movements of individuals and units to and fro (commercial airlines and air charters are also used). In wartime, the value of all ground and tactical air forces kept within the United States would depend strictly on the airlift and sealift that are available to carry them to war zones overseas.

The essential strategic predicament of the United States, which has most of its ground and air forces on the wrong side of the ocean, removed from all possible theaters of major war so far imagined, emerges in physical form, and in dollars and cents, under this heading of the budget. Maintaining forces overseas is costly and is also likely to mean that we are keeping them in the wrong place—because the maneuvering enemy will tend to attack where our forces are not, especially in the age of nuclear weapons. Thus any place where strong forces are sent automatically becomes the "wrong" place—in the sense that conflict successfully deterred in one theater is likely to emerge in another. But of course if the first theater is rightly chosen as the most worthy of protection, the displacement is still a gain.

Keeping the people at home while "prepositioning" complete unit sets of heavy equipment in storage overseas cuts down drastically on the air transport needed for quick deployment. But this practice suffers from both the defects mentioned above and one more: the enemy has a huge incentive to disrupt the mating of the men flown in with the heavy weapons and equipment waiting for them. Warehouses, supply dumps, and airfields crowded with incoming transports are much more vulnerable to attack than forces duly armed with the prepositioned equipment, and spread out over the countryside. If the balance of military forces in the theater is very different before and after (as it would be in Europe, where American ground forces would be doubled), the temptation to prevent the rendezvous is apt to be overwhelming.

If a war is already in progress but is still being fought in a highly controlled fashion, perhaps only with frontal engagements and no deep air attacks, let alone nuclear, the enemy might abruptly escalate to prevent the mating by air strikes against the deep rear (where the equipment is stored). If there is no fighting yet, but there is a crisis serious enough to have provoked a troop airlift, its impending arrival might cause the outbreak of war. Knowing this, the governments of our allies in Europe would quite likely ask for a delay in such an airlift, thus utterly disrupting the reinforcement process on which the deterrence of an actual conflict in a deep crisis is thought to depend. The war plans of American forces and their security in the theater depend on the successful arrival of reinforcements; if these are denied, the tensions within the Alliance could become explosive.

The economies of prepositioning look much less attractive when its alliance-breaking potential is duly recognized. But the Pentagon and Congress have evidently accepted this risk, since a plan to preposition six divisional equipment sets is proceeding apace. The alternative of permanently stationing yet more American forces in Europe is theoretically open, and so is a greater reliance on European reserve forces, manned by trained ex-conscripts organized for recall, refresher-trained and with their equipment ready. Both choices are politically unlikely; both are strategically far more desirable than the built-in escalation trigger of prepositioning.

There is finally the situation for which the "rapid-deployment" idea was born: the urgent theater of war in which there are neither forces in place nor any prepositioned equipment. This poses very difficult problems if armored forces are needed in a hurry, because even the huge C-5s, our largest transport aircraft, can deliver only a single tank at a time.

Until recently there was no middle option between sending armored forces that could arrive only slowly (several weeks per division, using all airlift capacity) and sending plain infantry that might arrive sooner, only to be defeated once it reached its destination. Now the Army is experimenting with the first of several planned light-infantry divisions that are to be trained and officered to do all the things that the firepower-rich American Army has not done in any recent war: to work their troops into the terrain and really use it, as guerrillas might, but on a much larger scale. They are to be agile in tactics, to evade the enemy's strengths and seek out his weaknesses, instead of relying on ponderous advance or stolid defense; they are to fight at night by deliberate choice and cope during the day, instead of the other way around, as firepower-rich forces naturally do; they are to accept and even favor fluid operations with no front line, instead of reaching out left and right, unit by unit, to make the solid front favored by firepower-rich forces (which need a firm front to compel the enemy to gather for its assaults, thus forming conveniently targetable concentrations).

If these sharp breaks with the American military culture are indeed achieved, the strategic mobility/tactical-effectiveness dilemma might yet be overcome. (The easier it is to transport, the less a force can do —if the doing is all done by sheer material superiority, the dumb-rich style of war.)

Because of the rapid-deployment requirement, there is now a large deficit in airlift, even though the current capacity is very large by any other standards than the scale of American needs. The longer-ranged "intertheater" aircraft of the Air Force now include 70 of the huge C-5s (and 50 more are being purchased), 234 of the merely large C-141s, and 35 of the convertible KC-10A tanker/transports (modified civilian DC-10s), which are being bought at the rate of 8 per year. The one transport that falls into the (relatively) shorter-range "intratheater" category is the 25-year-old and always new C-130, the sturdy four-engined turboprop that can always take off, no matter how short the field, and always comes home, no matter now many bullets it stops. This classic aircraft, the true *Dakota* of our era, also comes in battle dress as a gunship for the Special Operations squadrons of the Air Force, as a low-altitude clandestine intruder (Combat Talon MC-130) operated by the same squadrons, as a tanker employed by the Marines, as an intelligence retriever fitted out with nets to catch falling film cassettes from satellites overhead, ski-equipped to supply Antarctic base camps, and in more variants besides. But the 216 paid for under this heading are the plain transports of the Air Force.* (Among the 38 Navy and Marine Corps "tactical support" aircraft there are more C-130s, as well as smaller transports.)

Sealift for the forces and bases overseas could be augmented in war or crisis by the 214 ships of the National Defense Reserve Fleet. But the ships currently in use include 38 tankers (12 chartered) and 54 dry-cargo ships (40 chartered).[17] One of the great nonproblems of our national defense is the decline of the U.S.-flag merchant fleet, caused by very high labor costs. More than one-third of all private U.S.-flag ships are subsidized by the Federal Government in a neat arrangement that requires the use of American-citizen (that is, union) crews, but the decline still continues. (In 1982 more than 38 percent of U.S.-flag ships were in excess of twenty years old.)[18] This is one industry that has no need of Japan's wisdom: shipowners and their all-union crews already cooperate fully in demanding more subsidies for the merchant fleet, arguing that in war, all the shipping would be urgently needed (true) and that it could not be provided by chartering Liberian or Panamanian ships (untrue). The claim is that foreign sailors would not be willing to man their ships in dangerous waters, but the experience of two world wars and of Korea and Indochina shows otherwise. Foreign sailors were willing to brave German U-boats to bring supplies to American forces overseas, even in the most sinister days of the Battle of the Atlantic, when each night saw the sinking of a dozen ships. And foreign sailors were willing to risk not only all the ports of Vietnam during the war, but also the really dangerous passage up the Mekong, to supply Cambodia in its final agony. Modest "danger money" is quite sufficient to obtain the services of men who usually respect the sea far more than any weapons that might attack them.†

---

* *Active* Air Force, that is: another 302 C-130s are operated by the reserve forces, in one of their most important roles.[16]

† As of this writing, it is reported that some tanker crews are refusing to steam up the Persian Gulf in the face of Iranian and Iraqi air attacks—because the owners will not pay them danger money, not because of the odd missile or bomb.

Largely because of the purchase of the C-5Bs, the Airlift and Sealift expenditures have increased substantially of late, while still claiming only a modest proportion of the budget:

Expenditures for Airlift and Sealift, Selected Fiscal Years (in billions of dollars)* [19]

	1980	1982	1983	1984	1985†
Air and Sealift	2.1	3.9	4.3	5.6	7.3
Total Budget	142.1	211.3	238.7	259.1	305.7
Percentage for A & S	1.4%	2%	2%	2%	2%

* Total Obligational Authority, which includes moneys for future-year payment, for future-year deliveries.
† Request.

Guard and Reserve Forces

Guard and Reserve Forces provide very substantial forces for very little money. At last count, a total of just over a million men and women were serving in the Army National Guard (433,000), Army Reserve (278,000), Naval Reserve (122,000), Marine Corps Reserve (44,000), Air National Guard (104,000), and Air Force Reserve (70,000).*

Aside from individual reservists with assigned mobilization slots, a variety of filler units of one kind or another, and a whole host of specialized units (from mobile hospitals to tanker aircraft for the Strategic Air Command), the Guard and Reserve operate an impressive array of major formations:

Ground Forces
Army National Guard/Army Reserve:
    2 armored divisions
    5 infantry divisions

* All figures for the Selected Reserves only, whose members train regularly within organized and equipped units; there are in addition 396,461 Individual Ready Reservists and Inactive National Guard members who do not usually participate in organized training; this group includes individuals retired from the active forces who still have mobilization assignments.[20]

1 mechanized division
4 armored brigades
9 mechanized brigades
12 infantry brigades
4 armored-cavalry regiments
Marine Corps Reserve:
1 division

Sea Forces

Navy Reserve:
14 reserve warships in the deployable battle forces
18 support ships

Air Forces

43 Air National Guard and Air Force Reserve fighter/attack squadrons with a total of 852 combat aircraft
11 Air National Guard fighter-interceptor squadrons with a total of 180 combat aircraft
10 Navy Reserve (carrier-qualified) fighter/attack squadrons with a total of 120 combat aircraft
7 Marine Reserve fighter/attack squadrons with a total of 84 combat aircraft
38 Air Force Reserve and National Guard transport squadrons with a total of 302 C-130s.
33 Navy Reserve and Marine Corps Reserve transport aircraft.[21]

At present, the quality of the reserve forces is uneven. Some Army National Guard forces are so poorly trained that they would need months, in effect complete retraining, to become fit for combat. And they would also need much new equipment, and many new officers of higher caliber. Such units are little more than hollow frameworks filled with unmotivated soldiers who serve strictly for the money, and officers who are amateurs. Other National Guard combat forces, however, have officers and men who would need only the briefest of refreshers to go into combat, in fighting trim, and some are so well equipped that they have received brand-new M-1 tanks many years ahead of active-Army forces.

The Air National Guard and Air Force Reserve are notoriously well provided with pilots and ground crews of high skill and long experience. For years, excellent manpower was wasted on a variegated collection of older aircraft, some old enough to be outclassed by Soviet fighters and others that were hard just to keep flying. More recently, however, Guard and Reserve air units have been receiving increasing numbers of new aircraft (if only the subsonic A-10 tank-buster, despised by true fighter jocks) and early versions of first-line F-16 fighters; even some F-15As are to be delivered soon. More important, the bulk of the hand-me-downs now in service are still very effective machines, such as the C-130s of the airlift squadrons and the F-4 Phantom fighter-bombers. With its two-man crew and powerful radar, the old F-4 can be more useful than a brand-new F-16, especially in bad weather, and especially if flown by veteran pilots.

The active-duty Navy has been much less generous with its reserves than either the Army or the Air Force. While a token number of new aircraft are being provided to the reserve air squadrons, there is no fleet of warships for the reserves comparable to the array of Air Force reserve aircraft or, for that matter, the tanks and guns that the Army has given to its reserve forces.*

The Marines, finally, treat their reserve division as a real fighting force, somewhat less ready than its active counterparts, but otherwise comparable.

Any scheme that one might suggest to improve the Pentagon exchange rate between the money that goes in and the forces that come out must include a greater emphasis on the reserves, because they are so cheap. But that is not the preference of the Reagan Administration:

Expenditures for Guard and Reserve Forces, Selected
Fiscal Years (in billions of dollars)* [22]

	1980	1982	1983	1984	1985†
Guard and Reserve Forces	7.9	10.3	11.7	12.6	16.5
Total Budget	142.1	211.3	238.7	259.1	305.7
Percentage for Reserves	6%	5%	5%	5%	5%

* Total Obligational Authority, which includes moneys for future-year payment, for future-year deliveries.
† Request.

As we shall see, the small decline in the share of the budget for the reserve forces—and more significant, the absence of the substantial growth one might have expected—is explained by the great, indeed

* Naval Secretary Lehman, himself a reserve officer, has tried to remedy the imbalance: under current plans, the reserves are to receive 18 FFG-7 and eight FF-1052 frigates by 1989.

unprecedented, emphasis that the Reagan Administration has placed on the Navy. Because the Navy makes so little of its own reserves, the more it receives the less there is for the reserve forces as a whole.

The great problem with the use of reserve forces in American strategy is yet another manifestation of our geographic predicament. In conditions of nuclear parity, a Soviet nonnuclear aggression must be matched by nonnuclear means, if the United States is to avoid the onus and catastrophe of the ultimate escalation; because the instrument of any large aggression must be the Soviet Army, the most reliable answer is to match its strength in ground forces with American ground forces; because the Soviet Army relies on mobilized reserve forces for two-thirds of its divisions, so should the United States, if it is to meet the need at tolerable cost. But the Soviet Union can convey its reserve divisions to combat by road and rail across manageable distances, while the United States would have to choose between straight airlift, costly and vulnerable, and the cheaper but altogether more vulnerable mix of troop airlift and prepositioned heavy equipment. The lack of any plausible and quick way of sending reserve ground forces overseas undercuts their strategic value.

If one accepts the present defense priorities, and considers the reserves alone, there is simply no way of overcoming the problem of rapid deployment. But a solution would readily emerge if we could restructure the *total* forces, both active and reserve, in two steps. First, shift funds from the active Navy and Air Force to the *active* Army, in order to increase its size while keeping up quality; second, transfer more funds from the same sources to the naval and Air Force *reserves*.

The logic is simple: air squadrons and warships can cross the oceans (with refueling in some cases) on their own—in other words, they can rapidly deploy themselves. The ground forces cannot. To be really useful, they should be stationed overseas from the start. But this is impossible for reserve forces. Hence it is the active Army that should be built up, and we can find the means to do so by handing over air and naval units to the much cheaper reserves. The result of the reshuffle would be to increase the *overall* deployability of American military power, and thus its true strategic worth.

One obvious counterargument is that the Navy—if not the Air Force —is not merely active in status but actively used, and warships manned by reservists would not be available to spend 100 + days at sea in the Indian Ocean every time there is an Iran crisis. Nor could they provide the year-round fleet presence of the carrier battle groups in both the

Mediterranean and Pacific whose upkeep, as it is, strains the entire active fleet. The weight given to this objection depends on one's opinion of the true strategic and diplomatic value of those naval deployments. This writer, for one, thinks that it is greatly overstated: precisely because the presence of our fleets is a matter of routine, few people other than our own admirals pay much attention to them. And nowadays the 34 attack aircraft on each deck would count for so little in any major combat that their services could be comfortably awaited during the extra days that a part-reserve force would take to reach the scene.

Research and Development—and the Overhead

Research and Development, R & D in the familiar initials, is a category of expenditure that we would have expected to see greatly increased under the Reagan Administration, which has been such a great promoter of technological advancement. But the numbers tell a different story:

Expenditures for Research and Development, Selected Fiscal Years (in billions of dollars) [23]

	1980	1982	1983	1984	1985†
Research and Development	11.8	16.9	18.7	21.4	26.7
Total Budget	142.1	211.3	238.7	259.1	305.7
Percentage for R & D	8%	8%	8%	8%	9%

* Total Obligational Authority, which includes moneys for future-year payment, for future-year deliveries.
† Request.

There has therefore been no relative increase, with the dubious exception of the increase for 1985—which is not an actual number but merely a request.

The answer to this mystery is in three parts. First, the Reagan Administration assumed office after a very long period in which the actual purchase of weapons had been more starved for funds than research and development. For a full decade after the American withdrawal from Indochina, the defense budget was squeezed by actual cuts and also by inflation. Because the forces were not reduced in proportion, manpower costs took up an increasing share of the total budget, leaving less for everything else. In 1975, for example, total pay and benefits (military and civilian) accounted for 54 percent of the total outlays. (The 1984 percentage was, by contrast, only 36 percent.)[24] With only 46 percent of the 1975 budget left for Operation & Maintenance, construction, procurement, and R & D, there was simply not enough to go around, and a choice had to be made. Prudently enough, as it turns out—because there was no major combat in between—the Johnson, Nixon, Ford, and Carter Administrations all chose to sacrifice the present for the sake of the future, keeping up a strong R & D effort while buying few weapons. Thus by the time the Reagan Administration took office, there was a large backlog of weapons fully developed but not produced, or produced only in small numbers. Rather than adding to the backlog, the emphasis —as we have seen—was shifted to procurement.

The second reason is that some of the most highly advertised new R & D initiatives of the Reagan Administration—such as the Midgetman missile and, above all, strategic defense by space-based energy beams (ridiculed as "star wars")—are mostly "R" with not much "D"; they are not actually being engineered, but remain at the research stage. Studies, experiments, and analyses conducted in university laboratories and think tanks all over the country, even with the most generous funding, cannot consume more than a few hundred million dollars (i.e., an amount easily spent in the engineering development of a fairly trivial weapon).

Engineers are not more costly than scientists, but there are so many more of them, and they work for profit-making contractors rather than academic establishments and other nonprofit institutions.

The third reason for the discrepancy between all the high-technology talk and the reality of the budget is, yet again, that the Navy and the tactical slice of the Air Force claim such a large share of the total expenditure. The great goals are the "600-ship Navy" and "40-wing Air Force" new-technology forces; for these metal must be cut and hulls laid down without waiting for novel designs or more R & D. For the "strategic" Air Force, on the other hand, the backlog phenomenon was present in acute form, with both the B-1 bomber and MX missile ready for production, but unfunded.

The Overhead

The two "major programs" that are part of the overhead—Training, Medical and Other Personnel Activities, and Administration & Associated Activities—have claimed a diminishing share of increasing budgets:

Expenditures for Remaining "Major Force Programs,"
Selected Fiscal Years (in billions of dollars) * [25]

	1980	1982	1983	1984	1985†
Training, Medical, etc.	29.3	39.8	42.3	44.0	35.0
Administration & Assoc.	2.5	3.7	4.1	4.9	5.8
Total Budget	142.1	211.3	238.7	259.1	305.7
Combined total as percentage of budget	22%	21%	19.4%	19%	13%
Central Supply & Maintenance	15.3	18.8	20.8	23.2	27.0

  * Total Obligational Authority, which includes moneys for future-year payment, for future-year deliveries.
  † Request.

The gratifyingly low 13 percent for 1985 should not be taken too seriously, because when Congress has finished cutting that year's budget (reducing activities and purchasing rather than overhead), the final percentage is likely to revert to the 1984 level. Central Supply & Maintenance provides for all services, in part under the coordination of the Defense Logistic Agency. The feeble proportion of these expenditures in the Pentagon's total purchases* of more than $131 billion in 1984 tells us roughly how much defense unification has been achieved, as far as joint purchasing is concerned. Air Force, Navy, and Marines each still insist that they must buy separately the fighters they all fly, usually choosing different designs from different manufacturers; Air Force, Army, Marine Corps, and Navy (and the Coast Guard, too) each have their distinct preferences when it comes to helicopters as well. But the

  * I.e., operation and maintenance (less pay) plus procurement.[26]

services long ago gave up their right to buy separately such things as paper clips and diesel fuel. Having conceded the principle during the evil days of Robert McNamara, each service now finds itself forced to share all sorts of purchases with other services uncaring of its special needs. Naturally this plot against the procurement, contracting, auditing, and inspection bureaucracies of each service has not yet advanced to the point at which weapons are centrally purchased, except in very rare cases. But the threat looms.

The large question that arises in regard to Training, Medical and Other General Personnel Activities is simply the large cost. As regards the training part, which pays for all the military academies, staff colleges, war colleges, training bases, and special-skill schools, one must ask why a supposedly professional, long-service force needs quite so much training. One answer is that the "all-volunteer force" is only in part made up of *life*-career professionals, as the only other comparable armed force, the British, is.

Reenlistment rates go up and down mainly according to the state of the civilian economy (a good indicator of the true motivation of many of those who serve in uniform), and turbulence remains high: during 1983, for example, the forces took in 330,700 recruits, while increasing by only 13,000 for Fiscal 1984.[27] All but a fraction of those recruits were needed to replace enlisted men who had retired. The result was that the cost of training the new 330,700 recruits had to be paid through the costly upkeep of fourteen large basic-training establishments (one Air Force, two Marine Corps, three Navy, and eight Army "boot" camps). In fact, in 1983, of the grand total of 2.1 million man-years provided by all personnel on active duty, almost 18 percent* were expended on giving or receiving training. In other words, 18 out of every 100 on active duty were not contributing to the combat forces in being.

* A total of 326,900 trainers, trainees, and cadets, plus half of the 75,800 transients assumed to be going to and from training.[28]

☆

CHAPTER TEN

The Great Budget Game and the Neglect of Strategy

It would take many acres of computer printouts to investigate the merits of each opaque category of the defense budget. But the largest questions are raised by the expenditures on the so-called "general-purpose," or theater, forces, which include all the combat forces of the Army except for ballistic-missile defense, the entire Marine Corps, the Tactical Air Command of the Air Force, and above all the Navy, minus the ballistic-missile submarines and what goes with them. And an examination of our expenditures on all these forces reveals a fundamental imbalance in American strategy.

☆

Because expenditure on the strategic nuclear forces did not, after all, increase by much, and because most other categories did not grow in proportion either, the Reagan budget increases have provided much more money for the largely nonnuclear theater forces:

Expenditures for "General-Purpose" Forces, Selected Fiscal Years (in billions of dollars) * [1]

	1980	1982	1983	1984	1985†
General-Purpose forces	52.4	87.8	99.2	100.1	129.2
Total Budget	142.2	211.4	240.5	259.1	305.7
Percentage for general-purpose forces	37%	42%	41%	39%	42%

* Total Obligational Authority, which includes moneys for future-year payment, for future-year deliveries.
† Request.

Having compared current strategic spending with that of previous years —only to find that in real, constant, money we are spending less money on long-range nuclear weapons than in the 1950s and early 1960s—it is very enlightening to make the same comparison in constant 1985 dollars for the theater forces. The results are very different.

For the strategic forces, the 1984 expenditure of $27.5 billion, though higher than in recent years, was still much below the pre-Vietnam average. But in the case of the theater forces, we are now spending much more than in the past. In fact, one has to go all the way back to 1952, the highest point of the Korean buildup, to encounter a higher level of expenditure than in the Reagan years. In that year, when $135.4 billion (1985 dollars, that is) was spent on the theater forces, there was not only a real and fair-sized war under way but also a very considerable mobilization to strengthen American military forces worldwide. And 1952 was very much the peak: the 1951 level of spending on the theater forces had been $107.9 billion; in 1953 it declined to $95.5 billion.[2]

We are now spending *much* more on the theater forces than during the 1970s—roughly 70 percent more on average. What is remarkable is that we are outspending even the peak years of the Vietnam war: the Reagan 1982–1984 average was $105.4 billion in constant 1985 dollars; in 1967–1968, when the United States was attempting to become the world's largest Southeast Asian power, with more than half a million servicemen in Vietnam, annual expenditure on the theater forces at war was $102.7 billion on average. And after that there was a rapid decline, with expenditures going down to a low point of $58.1 billion in fiscal 1975, before slowly drifting up again to the $70-billion level during the Carter years.[3]

Because the middle 1970s were the years of American military decline, it is not surprising that we then spent some $40 billion less on average than in the Reagan years. But when we look at the pre-Vietnam period—when strategic spending, as we have seen, was distinctly higher than now—we discover that expenditure for the theater forces was much lower: an annual average of $65 billion during 1954–1961, the years between the Korean war and the Berlin crisis, and an average of $70 billion during the Kennedy years, until 1964. And those were the years when we were supposed to be striving for more conventional strength under the "flexible response" strategy, whose goal was to reduce Western reliance on early nuclear escalation.

A table of comparisons (in constant dollars) reveals the full dimensions of the Reagan spending increases for the theater forces:

Expenditure on "General-Purpose Forces"
(in billions of constant 1985 dollars) *[4]

Fiscal Year 1945	
War; 12 million on active duty	313.1
Fiscal Year 1950	
Pre-Korea low; 1.4 million in uniform	30.7
Fiscal Year 1952	
Korean war at peak; general buildup	135.5
Fiscal Year 1960	
Massive retaliation; Berlin crisis I	58.2
Fiscal Year 1962	
The Kennedy buildup; Berlin crisis II	72.4
Fiscal Year 1965	
Last pre-Vietnam budget	70.8
Fiscal Year 1967	
Peak year of Vietnam expenditures	104.7
Fiscal Year 1975	
Post-Vietnam low point	58.1
Fiscal Year 1983	
Peak Reagan year so far for theater forces	109.2

* TOA: Total Obligational Authority—i.e., money authorized, not necessarily for actual payouts during the same fiscal year; TOA for major weapons systems is usually expended over several years.

A sharper comparison, focused on the most recent past, reveals very clearly the magnitude of the Reagan increase in expenditure on the theater forces. When a new President is inaugurated, he must govern on the budget obtained from Congress by the previous administration until the following October, although he does have the opportunity of presenting supplementary requests. He also finds the budget for the following fiscal year ready and presented Congress. Substantial changes are possible, but they must be engineered through the committees and obviously depend on the degree of political backing that the new President enjoys in Congress. In practice, a few really important changes are made, along with some symbolic ones, but the great mass of the detailed requests remains unchanged. With these reservations in mind, we may compare the amounts obtained from Congress for the theater forces during the first three years of the Carter and Reagan Administrations:

Expenditure* on "General-Purpose Forces"
(in billions of constant 1985 dollars)

The Carter Level, Fiscal 1978–1980
First three fiscal years, average   71.2

The Reagan Level, Fiscal 1982–1984
First three fiscal years, average   105.4

* Total Obligational Authority.

At first sight, there seems to be a very simple justification for the great increase in spending: the Soviet military buildup under way since the mid-1960s has been largely devoted to the theater forces. The Soviet Air Force and Navy have both greatly increased in capacity, but the growth of the Soviet Army has been even more substantial: over the period 1971 to 1984, the number of Soviet divisions has increased from 160 to 194, and many of the divisions have also become significantly larger, with much equipment added, and also manpower; first-line armored divisions increased from 8,400 men to 11,000 each, while the more abundant mechanized divisions went from 10,500 to 14,000 each.[5] Taking both numbers and content into account, the Soviet army is now some 40 percent larger than it was at the beginning of the 1970s.

Much more than the Soviet Air Force, which is only its ancillary arm, and certainly far more than the navy, which would play only a lesser role in any serious conflict, it is the expansion of the Soviet Army that weighs on the overall balance of military power. It is the army, not the good-looking ships of the Soviet Navy, that imposes a strategy of nuclear escalation on the Western alliance in Europe. It is the Soviet Army and not the navy that has made the Persian Gulf a zone of danger where the United States cannot lightly intervene, even to protect tangible interests of great value, for behind the ayatollahs and the terrorists stand 25 Soviet divisions. And it is the army that presses upon China and Korea, keeping the former under a threat that limits cooperation with the United States, and the latter in permanent danger, even if a North Korean invasion can be defeated.

So long as the United States retained its superiority in strategic-nuclear forces, the threatening potential of the Soviet Army was largely neutralized. As we have seen, however, that is no longer so: in a state of strategic "parity," the Soviet Army must be countered on an equal footing, and now there is so much more of it to be countered.

If the Reagan increases were therefore paying for a responsive expansion in the theater forces, with a stress on land power, there would be nothing remarkable about the current spending levels. On the contrary, a 20–30-percent growth in the theater forces would be only a belated and incomplete response to the Soviet buildup. But what is extraordinary about the Reagan upsurge is that it has *not* been accompanied by any significant numerical increase of the armed forces, except for the Navy—whose forces are the least useful in countering the strongest part of Soviet military power.

Hence the truly unprecedented character of present spending increases: during the two previous upsurges, which peaked in 1952 and again 1967, the great increase in expenditure was linked to equally dramatic growth in the size of the armed forces. In 1952, during the Korean war, there were 3.64 million on active duty in all services—a very sharp rise over the 1.46 million of 1950; and in 1967, with Vietnam at its peak, the number on active duty was 3.38 million—a considerable increase over the 2.66 million of 1965. But no such expansion has taken place under Reagan: the average number on active duty during Carter's first three fiscal years (1978–1980) was 2.05 million; the average in the Reagan years of 1982–1984 was only very slightly higher, at 2.16 million.[6] In other words, a very sharp increase in expenditure on the theater forces—more than 48 percent on average over the first three years of the Carter Presidency—was accompanied by a mere 5-percent increase in the numerical size of the armed forces on active duty.

Surveying the structure of forces, we find that the number of Army divisions did not increase at all: it was 16 in Fiscal Year 1981, when Reagan took over, and it remained 16 in 1984. Although a new "light" division is to be formed by the end of 1985, this important addition to the Army's forces does not result from any budget or manpower increase. In fact, the numbers on active duty in the Army increased only fractionally, from 776,000 in 1980 to 780,000 in 1984.[7] In a most commendable initiative, the manpower slots needed for the new division (10,000+) are being taken from the overhead, while the equipment cost is quite small, because the new division will be an elite force of truly light infantry without costly heavy weapons.

Similarly, there has been no increase in the number of active-duty Marine divisions, which remains unchanged at three. As for the fighter and attack squadrons of the Marines, their number actually declined between 1980 and 1985, from 25 to 24, even though the actual number of aircraft is supposed to revert to the 1980 level of 422 after a dip to 401 in 1983–1984.* Thus the Marine force structure has not increased at all, though the number of active-duty Marines did increase somewhat, from 188,000 in 1980 to 197,000 in 1984.[9]

There has been no growth either in the number of Air Force fighter and attack squadrons, which reverted to 79 in Fiscal Year 1985, after a dip to 78 during the intervening years. When we look at the actual number of aircraft, we can detect an increase, but a small one: from 1,680 in 1980 to 1,782 in 1985, an increase of only 6 percent.[10] There is some growth to come from aircraft funded during the period but not yet delivered, but this is only marginal. Air Force personnel did grow in number by 6 percent or so, from 558,000 in 1980 to 594,000 in 1984, but only a fraction of this increase was in the theater forces.[11]

Only the Navy has significantly expanded its forces (*but of course with pre-Reagan ships*) in the number of vessels and even more in substance, since there is more ship in the average 1985 ship. Between 1981 and 1985 the number of deployable carriers (one more is always in overhaul) increased by only one, to 13, but that one was the nuclear-powered 96,000-ton *Carl Vinson*. The number of battleships increased from 0 to 2 (taken out of mothballs), and the decline in the number of deployable cruisers and destroyers, from 107 in 1980 to 99 in 1985, was offset by the sharp increase in the number of the smaller warships classified as "frigates," from 71 to 110. Most spectacular was the growth in the number of nuclear-attack submarines, from 74 in 1980 to 96 in 1985. Amphibious ships to convey the Marines to their landing beaches declined in number, from 66 to 61, but not in tonnage, because much larger units replaced old ships that were retired, and the rest of the "deployable battle forces"—that is, the handful of missile boats as well as mine-warfare, logistic, and support ships (fleet oilers, etc.)—increased significantly, from 95 in 1980 to 117. Excluding the "strategic" ships (missile submarines and their tenders) and the few reserve ships, the "deployable battle forces" total increased from 428 in fiscal 1981 to 489 in 1985.†

When we examine naval aviation, we note an increase equally significant, from 60 squadrons in 1980, with 894 aircraft, to 65 squadrons and

---

* There are 12 *operational* (unit equipment) fighter aircraft in a Marine squadron, with several more *authorized* as a "maintenance float." The figures here cover the total, or "primary authorized aircraft."[8]

† This number does not include 43 auxiliary and sealift ships, nor warships in overhaul.[12]

967 aircraft in 1985. (There are 12 operational aircraft in each squadron, but these are the "authorized" totals, which include a maintenance float.) And the number of Navy active-duty personnel grew in step, and therefore more than the other services, from 527,000 in 1980 to 565,000 in 1984—an increase of 7 percent.[13]

Of course, only a small part of the increase in the ship numbers can be attributed to the Reagan increases in expenditure from Fiscal 1982 onward. The two reactivated battleships were taken out of mothballs with Reagan money at the initiative of his Secretary of the Navy, that great navalist John Lehman. But only a handful of other warships could actually be added to the fleet by 1985 from the new construction started in the first year of the Reagan Administration. Ship construction is nowadays so slow a process that on average less than 5 percent of the shipbuilding money authorized in a given year is actually spent before its end, and by the end of the second year, the cumulative percentage remains below 20 percent. The two carriers authorized in 1982 will not be in service in this decade.[14] But for the Navy, at least, there has been at least some force expansion, and there is much more to come with the added shipbuilding money authorized since 1981.

This, then, is the meaning of the great Reagan increases in expenditure for the theater forces: first, the Navy has received the lion's share;[15] second, all the services except the Navy, rather than expanding their forces, have used the money to add weapons and supplies, and also to "enrich" their rank structure instead of increasing their numbers. In just the twelve months between March 31, 1982, and March 31, 1983, the number of officers in all services increased from 286,617 to 293,026—i.e., by 2.2 percent—while the number of enlisted men hardly increased at all, from 1,807,388 to 1,821,315—i.e., less than 0.1 percent.[16] And within that enlisted total there has also been grade "enrichment": the number of E-9s, the most senior of all noncommissioned officers, increased from 13,338 to 13,587—i.e., almost 2 percent—and the E-8s increased from 35,057 to 36,139—i.e., by 3 percent.[17]

But there was more to it than that: the Reagan administration also had to pay the bill for past neglect. During the 1970s, as each budget voted by Congress was overtaken by inflation in the course of its year, a miracle of loaves and fishes was seemingly accomplished by the Pentagon—the forces were not reduced in size, people were not sent away, nor were purchases of the major weapons cut off. There was no miracle, however, only subterfuge: most of the budget-wide loss of purchasing power caused by each year's unexpected inflation was made up by drastic cuts in the unglamorous invisibles that go into the operation and maintenance accounts. The initial stocks of spare parts that come with new weapons were reduced, so we had the shiny new weapons but not the spares needed to keep them going; not enough replenishment spares were bought to keep older equipment in running order; depot-level work was cut back, so it took longer and longer to repair things or modify them as needed; fuel and ammunition for the ships and aircraft to train with and the stocks of ordnance needed for combat were all reduced, as was the purchase of "secondary items," the 3 million or more diverse bits and pieces, from boots to paper clips. All the forces were affected, but the theater forces especially so. Certainly liberties were not so lightly taken with the strategic-nuclear forces, whose upkeep remained at a very high standard.

Thus a good part of the increased spending on the theater forces, especially during the first two Reagan years, is easily explained. Having inherited forces that were greatly dilapidated behind their undiminished facade, the new administration had a problem on its hands that plain money could remedy. No strategic decision was called for to pay for overdue maintenance and spare parts in short supply, more training fuel and ammunition, and larger stocks for combat. Some problems *can* be solved by throwing money at them.

Although other forces were also the beneficiaries, it was mainly the theater forces that accounted for the increased spending on initial spares, from $2.5 billion in fiscal 1982 (largely a Carter budget) to $3.7 billion in 1984, and on replenishment spares, from $3.7 billion in 1982 to $4.8 billion in 1984.[18] Spare parts are the classic invisible, easily reduced by Congressional aides in a hurry to find cuts for the usual last-minute budget compromise. And they are a fertile field for overcharging by contractors, simply because their purchase is not nearly as closely scrutinized as that of the weapons themselves. (Even the smallest weapons are the subject of a separate line item, whereas spares of far greater *total* cost are lumped together under opaque titles.)

Expenditure on ordnance, ammunition, bombs, and tactical missiles, largely for the theater forces, also grew greatly under Reagan, and because of shorter lead times, some of the extra purchasing was done in the very first year of the new administration. We therefore may compare the $4.8 billion spent in fiscal 1981 with the $10.3 billion spent in 1984, a remarkable 215-percent growth. And the Army received a proper share of this bounty at least: its munitions procurement increased from $2.4 billion in fiscal 1981 to $4.6 billion in 1984, thus replenishing stocks long scandalously depleted.[19]

All this worthy spending, however, only explains a small part of the spectacular growth of expenditure on the theater forces—an additional $30 billion on average during the first three Reagan years, as compared with the three previous years. It was procurement rather than operation and maintenance that did it, and chiefly the Navy's purchases of ships and aircraft. In fact, the Navy has claimed the greatest share of procurement for the theater forces, the largest item of the entire Reagan buildup. When we look at the separate categories that come under the procurement heading, we see that between 1982 and 1984 the total amount authorized for shipbuilding and conversions (in actual then-current dollars) must have impressed even the most jaded Pentagon-watcher: $40 billion.[20] And during those same three years, another $32.8 billion was spent on Navy aircraft (almost all for the theater forces).

In other words, in the span of three years, a total of more than $70 billion was invested in the future ships and aircraft of the Navy.[21] In 1983, the year of the two carriers, the $37.2 billion claimed by total Navy procurement (in 1985 dollars) may be compared with the total of $109.2 billion spent on all the needs of the theater forces of all services; shaving off $3 billion for "strategic" and "mobility" procurement, the proportion is 31 percent, leaving just over $74 billion for the theater-force procurement of the other services as well as the operation and maintenance of all theater forces, Navy included.[22]

A broader comparison of service budgets as a whole confirms these results. Of the $130.2 billion (1985 dollars) added to the defense budget by the Reagan buildup over and above the 1981 ("baseline") level during the three fiscal years 1982–1984, the Army's share of the increase was $28.5 billion, while the Navy did very much better with $43.8 billion.*

If we stand back from the details and all these rough calculations, we can recognize their larger meaning: at a time when the United States no longer has the shield of strategic-nuclear superiority to suppress the invasion potential of the Soviet Army in Central Europe, Western Asia, and Korea, it is the land forces (ground and tactical air) that should have

* The Air Force share of the increase was larger still, but in its case much of the money went to the strategic and "mobility" forces.[23]

been strengthened to maintain the balance of deterrence that keeps the peace; yet in the Reagan buildup, the major effort has been to strengthen the naval forces. Instead of seeking to establish land-power parity, which is the required counterpart to strategic-nuclear parity, the declared goal is to build a "600-ship Navy," the number said to be necessary to restore American naval supremacy.

To be sure, superior naval power can be highly effective even against a continental land power, by blockade. Though naval forces (sea-based airpower included) can do little to defeat the enemy's land forces in the field, they can weaken or even strangle the economy that sustains them, by cutting off supplies of essential raw materials imported by sea. The method is slow and indirect, but given time, it can be just as powerful as any force mustered to fight on land. The complete interruption of its ocean commerce greatly weakened Germany in both World Wars, and when finally achieved in 1944, it strangled the Japanese war economy, to the point at which Japanese resistance persisted only by the most desperate improvisations. But a blockade would be totally ineffective against the Soviet Union. Even today, the Soviet economy does not depend on oceangoing commerce for any essential need. (The much-imported grains are to feed cattle, not people—and in war, the meat ration is soon cut.)

To be sure, superior naval forces need not be impotent against land-based airpower and ground forces. First, even a continental land power may seek to stage amphibious landings or to employ sea-based gunfire and air strikes, at least as ancillaries to its major actions conducted on land; in conditions of absolute naval inferiority, such operations would be impossible. Second, superior naval forces can stage their own amphibious landings to outmaneuver enemy forces on land, they can dominate coastal zones by gunfire, and they can attack much deeper with carrier-based aircraft.

But naval operations would be largely irrelevant for Soviet military action in the major continental theaters of war—Central Europe, Western Asia, and the Russo-Chinese border zones. Even in the context of an invasion aimed at the Persian Gulf, the strategy of the Soviet Union would rely on the overland advance of its ground forces across Iran. Thus even the total defeat of the Soviet Navy would not seriously impair the Soviet Union's capacity for invasion.

On the other hand geography alone would rule out American amphibious landings and naval gunfire intended to outmaneuver or directly oppose Soviet invasions in Central Europe and the Russo-Chinese border zones. And the bombers of the Soviet naval air force would make such actions impossibly hazardous in the Persian Gulf and Korea.

The Navy does, of course, have defenses against air attack, and as we have seen, they are highly developed. But to have a fighting chance, the carrier task forces must stay well away from hostile land, in order to obtain adequate warning and to have room to defend in depth. Both are impossible if the mission is to stage amphibious landings or cannonade the shore. To operate in the Persian Gulf or off Korea, so near to Soviet or Soviet-controlled territory (Afghanistan), the United States would first have to attack and put out of action all the air bases in the region that could be used by Soviet strike aircraft. That would be very hard to do, since long-range aircraft of the *Backfire* type could intervene effectively even from bases in the deep interior of the Soviet Union.

Far more important, such attacks on Soviet soil would probably mean that the United States would be drastically escalating a conflict that till then had not spread to the homeland of either the Soviet Union or the United States. It is hard to imagine that an American President would authorize such very dangerous action merely to obtain the military benefits of amphibious landings and naval gunfire.

As for the Navy's own carrier-based air power, which can be utilized without bringing the fleet so close to land, the defect of its counterinvasion potential is in the numbers: As we have seen, even the largest carriers have only 34 attack aircraft, which can only fly a maximum of 70–80 medium-range sorties every twenty-four hours. If the range from the target is kept longer for the sake of the carriers' safety, the number of sorties per day must decline. For example, if carrier-based air power were employed to resist a Soviet invasion across Iran, the carriers would certainly be kept in fleet stations outside the Gulf; each carrier then could generate no more than one sortie per attack aircraft per day, even making the fullest use of air refueling, presumably from land-based tankers (only four tanker versions of the A-6 are normally included in each carrier air wing).

In other words, all thirteen operational aircraft carriers of the Navy would have to be in one place to make possible the 400–500 attack sorties per day necessary to have a serious impact on a Soviet invasion across Iran. This would in turn require a constant shuttle of support ships to keep the carriers supplied with jet fuel and ordnance. It would therefore require the gathering of all the fleets from their usual stations worldwide, to provide the carriers and their escorts, as well as to protect the supply ships in transit to the operational zone. It would take time to concentrate the entire Navy in this manner, and it would entail the first-class strategic risk of its being in the wrong place—and all that in order to obtain as much air strength as any middling regional power has at its command. Thus the role of the Navy in resisting any major Soviet action in any major theater of war is likely to be marginal, unless really heroic assumptions are made.

To be sure, it is not only by the test of a hypothetical major war that we measure the worth of any particular form of military power. Moreover, it would be foolish to treat the Soviet Union as the only possible antagonist. The usefulness of a force in lesser combat must also be taken into account, and so must its combat potential against other enemies than the Soviet Union. It is also important to assay the psychological impact, and thus the diplomatic value, of naval power, even in the absence of any combat. Certainly all nations maintain some forms of military power—commando or gendarmerie units, for example—that are primarily useful in minor combat, and find them well worth their keep even if they would be insignificant in an all-out war. Similarly, all nations maintain some kind of demonstration forces (royal guards are the classic case) for reasons other than their combat utility.

Broadening our view to take these other dimensions of usefulness into account, we find that:

—The strategic worth of the Navy, especially its core of aircraft carriers and their escorts, increases as conflict intensity diminishes. At one extreme, the carriers would be almost entirely useless in an all-out nuclear war. At the other extreme, they are the best of all military instruments for noncombat "showing the flag" visitations.

—The impact of the Navy, and especially its carrier task forces, on the outcome of conflict increases to the degree that the antagonist is less powerful and more accessible from the sea. At one extreme, the carriers would be of slight effect in fighting the forces of the Soviet Union in its own or adjacent territory. At the other extreme, they can easily be decisive in fighting a small and weak island state.

The Navy's carriers, surface warships, amphibious shipping, and attack submarines are therefore useful in a wide variety of situations, including armed interventions of the Grenada type. They are equally useful in deterring Soviet interventions in distant areas. Moreover, it is self-evident that to operate overseas with its ground and land-based air forces, the United States must be able to protect supply ships from submarine, surface-ship, and air attacks (the "sea control" mission). But that, of course, is a *supporting* function, whose strategic value strictly depends on how much ground and tactical air power there is to send and supply overseas. And that in turn depends on what is left of the budget after the Navy has taken its share.

While granting all due importance to the secondary and supporting functions of the Navy, we can now recognize that a classic strategic error has been made in devoting so much money to the aircraft carriers and all that goes with them. At a time when the extraordinary magnitude of the Soviet military buildup compels the United States to focus its military resources more than ever on deterrence and defense in the major continental theaters, the single largest American force-building effort is devoted to a form of military power whose usefulness is least precisely when used to oppose the Soviet Union in those same theaters. At the level of grand strategy this is the equivalent of outmaneuvering oneself: the United States is giving its highest budget priority to naval forces, which in a major conflict with the Soviet Union would be the least useful, except to oppose the Soviet Navy, *to which the Soviet Union gives the lowest budget priority*—after the army, tactical air-power, the strategic-nuclear forces, and homeland air defenses.

Naturally the United States needs a powerful navy; indeed, it requires "ocean supremacy" across all major transatlantic and transpacific sea-lanes and their junction in the Indian Ocean. The Navy therefore needs its present forces of attack submarines and land-based patrol aircraft to fight both Soviet submarines and surface warships. To provide close-in protection for convoys, the Navy needs its escorts ("frigates") just as much, and the Marines still need amphibious shipping to intervene over the beach—though not necessarily on the present scale, which is sized for very large landings in a world where only small ones can actually happen. And the Navy needs sea-based air power in order to protect all other ships from the enemy's air power, and also to carry out whatever small attacks against lesser land targets that 34 attack aircraft per deck will allow.

The Reagan Administration was fortunate to have a powerful carrier fleet in hand when it assumed office; and it would have made sense, even under the stress of strategic parity, to ensure the future of the carrier force by starting work on new medium carriers large enough to carry a couple of squadrons of fighters. But to have added two more large-deck carriers of the most costly nuclear type, with their full ration of billion-dollar cruisers and scarcely less costly destroyers, was down-right frivolous, given the magnitude of the land-power deficit caused by the advent of strategic parity.[24]

The choice that the Reagan Administration appears to have made is therefore strategically unsound—but in truth, no choice was made at all. The President strove mightily to secure funding from Congress for a much-needed rearmament, but allowed the Secretary of Defense full discretion in running the Pentagon; and the latter simply absented himself from the making of national military strategy, in order to attend to a variety of other business that he deemed more important. (He has offered lively competition to two Secretaries of State in the making of foreign policy.) While a highly dynamic Secretary of the Navy imposed his own priorities on the entire defense budget, his nominal superior, the Secretary of Defense, applied his own energies mainly to administrative matters, chiefly the reduction of waste, fraud, abuse, and mismanagement in the defense establishment—with a definite emphasis on fraud and abuse (i.e., overcharging), if only because of the famous spare-parts scandals of 1983–1984. After great efforts, splendid results were seemingly achieved and proudly presented to Congress in the January 1984 Annual Report. Among a variety of audit reports involving larger sums recovered and savings achieved, we find the following:

Activities to Curb Waste, Fraud and Abuse (FY 1983)[25]

Heading: Investigative Cases

16,357 Cases Closed
8,023 Cases Referred for Prosecution or Administrative Action
657 Convictions
Fines, Penalties, Restitutions and Recoveries
Collected from Referrals to:
Justice Department: $5.2 million
Military Departments: $9.6 million

Money-making by others easily inspires resentment, and when fraud is involved, so must be the law. But to neglect the consideration of strategy to the point where tens of billions are misused, while celebrating the recapture of $14.8 million (0.00006 percent of the budget)* is not the order of priorities that best serves the nation.

---

* The maximum total of actual and potential savings under all headings claimed does not exceed 1.5 percent of the budget.

CHAPTER ELEVEN

─────────────── ☆ ───────────────

Toward Reform

☆

"Although most history books glorify our military accomplishments, a closer examination reveals a disconcerting pattern: unprepared-ness at the start of a war; initial failures; reorganizing while fighting; cranking up our industrial base; and ultimately prevailing by wearing down the enemy—by being bigger, not smarter."
GENERAL DAVID C. JONES
Chairman of the Joint Chiefs of Staff,
1978–1982[1]

☆

This honest appraisal, seemingly so harsh, is actually overoptimistic in leaving us with the prospect of ultimate victory, if achieved only slowly and by sheer material superiority. But that method can work only in a conventional war against regular, front-holding forces that we can out-gun. It will not defeat a guerrilla enemy, for example: when confronted by superior firepower, guerrillas will simply refuse to assemble in con-veniently targetable formations, and the futility of mass-producing fire-power against a greatly dispersed enemy was amply demonstrated in Vietnam. Nor can the method contend with the lesser combat that ter-rorism and lawless states send our way: the sequence of initial failure, hurried reorganization, and brute-force attack becomes absurd when the task is a swift commando raid or a one-night *coup de main,* such as the seizure of Grenada should have been.

But in fact, the reorganize-and-outproduce method will not work even

266

for a large war against regular forces—if they happen to be Soviet. It did defeat Germans already worn down by others before American forces ever had to fight them in earnest, and it was even more successful against the Japanese, brave and skilled but poor in industry and poorer still in raw materials. The Soviet Union is another matter altogether; it is not so easily outproduced, it is impervious to blockade, and it has nuclear weapons to cut short any belated wartime reconstruction of American military power.

Our goal, of course, is to avoid a Soviet–American war rather than to fight it well. But it is precisely by operational competence and sufficient strength that we can extinguish the fatal optimism necessary for aggression—and with the present unreformed system, our competence must remain in doubt, while the upkeep of sufficient strength is altogether more costly than it should be.

In the Second World War, early defeats were eventually overtaken by large victories. But today, we would be tempted to redeem initial defeats by nuclear escalation, while the Soviet Union in turn would use nuclear weapons to interrupt our slow sequence of military reorganization and industrial mobilization. In films, TV spectaculars, and novels, and in the speech of the devotees and propagandists of arms control, nuclear war is usually depicted as the outcome of computer breakdowns, radar misreadings, or other such fatal technical errors in the tense circumstances of a diplomatic crisis. But as soon as one begins to examine the actual procedures for the control of the bomber forces and ballistic missiles, one discovers that technical breakdowns will quite likely prevent fully intended nuclear attacks, not cause accidental ones.

Contrary to the standard dramatic scenario, there are no automatic attack procedures that have to be called off in time while the doomsday clock ticks away. On the contrary, if duly authorized orders, repeated and confirmed, do not get through, no weapons are released at all, and the attack sequence simply stops: the entire "fail-safe" imagery is the exact opposite of the truth. The great danger is not a melodramatic leap from peace to nuclear war by mere accident, but rather the deliberate use of nuclear weapons in desperate reaction to nonnuclear warfare gone wrong. The United States could not avenge Pearl Harbor on the next day by nuclear strikes against the Japanese fleet steaming back across the Pacific, nor could it punish Rommel's army with nuclear weapons for its victory at the Kasserine Pass, where the new American forces lost their first battle against the Germans. Today, however, delusions of adequacy might propel us into a major debacle, some "Desert

One" on a large scale, and then the shock of defeat and the fear of its results might tempt us to redeem failure by resorting to nuclear weapons. Thus the reluctance of Congress, the White House, and defense politicians to break the amiable conspiracy that so easily forgives our combat failures and tolerates the strategic vacuum at the core of our military policy not only harms our military reputation and misuses our wealth, but also leaves us open to nuclear danger—by our own doing.

As we have seen, the fundamental problems are all structural: it is the organization that must be changed, not the culture; there is nothing in our political system that precludes sound strategy, as there is nothing in the spirit of young Americans that prohibits military success. In the most obscure fighting of Vietnam—the mere routine that remained unreported alongside the drug scandals and the "fragging" incidents—American soldiers set out on patrol day after day, through jungle and high grass made for ambushes and man-traps, across swamps infested with blood-sucking leeches, with water up to their chests and soft mud under their feet. Meanwhile the airmen flew their sorties, sometimes twice a day, risking death or foul imprisonment each time, and the sailors aboard ship carried out a routine of backbreaking labor, interrupted only by sleep and numbing boredom. It was not the fault of those young men but of the command structure above them that the patrols and the sweeps, the air strikes and the warships served ritualistic tactics, vacuous operational methods, and strategies of defeat.

And in the small combat on Grenada, we saw how the Rangers fought hard and did not lack brave officers to lead them—when totally inexcusable planning had them parachute directly in front of some of the very few antiaircraft guns on the island, as part of an operation that was fundamentally wrong in concept. We do not face the impossible task of remaking cowards and time-servers into effective fighting men. The challenge is rather to redeem abundant valor and dedication by reorganizing our military establishment.

Absolutely the first priority is to provide a central military staff that can present the true choices of national military strategy for the policy decisions of the President and Secretary of Defense: how much to spend on nuclear weapons and which ones, according to the expressed purposes of the civilian authority; how much to spend on "readiness" as opposed to the building up of the forces, according to the best estimates of the risk of *imminent* conflict; which forces to increase and which to reduce among aircraft carriers and armored divisions, fighter squadrons and submarines, according to the most prudent assessment of what threats will need to be averted or defeated. At present, by an omission that is so huge and amazing that it remains unsuspected by the citizenry at large, there is no such source of *national* military advice.

The organization of the Joint Chiefs of Staff, which is supposed to provide the brain for the military body, certainly plays no such role. And how could it? Only the Chairman and his personal secretary have a national responsibility. Everyone else, from the chiefs of staff of each service who come in for their weekly meetings down to every officer serving with the Joint Staff, can only represent the interests of his own service. Every attempt to obtain strategic advice from the Joint Chiefs yields only all-service demands for more money for everything, with no order of priorities and no real choices offered. Each new Secretary of Defense soon learns that it is futile to expect any considered strategic judgment from the Joint Chiefs and their Joint Staff; no matter what the question, the answer is always the same: the lowest common denominator on which all the services can agree.

In the absence of expert advice, we have seen each successive administration fail in the business of strategy—yielding a United States twice as rich as the Soviet Union but much less strong. Only the manner of the failure has changed. In the 1960s, under Robert S. McNamara, we witnessed the wholesale substitution of civilian mathematical analysis for military expertise. The new breed of the "systems analysts" introduced new standards of intellectual discipline and greatly improved bookkeeping methods, but also a trained incapacity to understand the most important aspects of military power, which happen to be nonmeasurable. Because morale is nonmeasurable it was ignored, in large and small ways, with disastrous effects. We have seen how the pursuit of business-type efficiency in the placement of each soldier destroys the cohesion that makes fighting units effective; we may recall how the *Pueblo* was left virtually disarmed when it encountered the North Koreans.* Because tactics, the operational art of war, and strategy itself are not reducible to precise numbers, money was allocated to forces and single weapons according to "firepower" scores, computer simulations, and mathematical studies—all of which maximized efficiency, but often at the expense of combat effectiveness.

An even greater defect of the McNamara approach to military decisions was its businesslike "linear" logic, which is right for commerce or engineering but almost always fails in the realm of strategy. Because

* Strong armament was judged as not "cost-effective" for ships of that kind.

its essence is the clash of antagonistic and outmaneuvering wills, strategy usually proceeds by paradox rather than conventional "linear" logic. That much is clear even from the most shopworn of Latin tags: *si vis pacem, para bellum* (if you want peace, prepare for war), whose business equivalent would be on the orders of "if you want sales, add to your purchasing staff," or some other, equally absurd advice. Where paradox rules, straightforward linear logic is self-defeating, sometimes quite literally. Let a general choose the best path for his advance, the shortest and best-roaded, and it then becomes the worst of all paths, because the enemy will await him there in greatest strength. Let us build ships to match the Soviet Navy and we will be caught in a losing game, because it takes an entire task force to cope with a few submarines; but if we build advanced "stealth" bombers instead, thus forcing the Soviet Union to re-equip its air defenses, we would then see the naval balance shifting in our favor, as the low-priority Soviet navy is increasingly starved of funds for the high-priority air-defense forces. Let us place most of our forces to defend the most valuable central perimeter, and we will see them become the least employed, as the adversary maneuvers to circumvent them left and right. Let us choose carefully the case in which we might intervene, doing so only when "really vital" interests are at stake, and then we will find that the contending forces will strike instead at all the other interests that individually do not quite deserve our protection—and then over time, after many abandonments, each of them seemingly prudent, we will discover that the loss of many less-than-vital interests here and there, large and small, has made it impossible, or quite pointless, to defend that which had previously been deemed worthy of protection.

Linear logic is all very well in commerce or engineering, where there is lively opposition, to be sure, but no open-ended scope for maneuver: a competitor beaten in the marketplace will not bomb our factory instead, and the river duly bridged will not deliberately carve out a new course. But such reactions are merely normal in strategy. Military men are not trained in paradoxical thinking, but they do not have to be. Unlike the business-school expert, who searches for optimal solutions in the abstract and then presents them with all the authority of charts and computer printouts, even the most ordinary military mind can recall the existence of a maneuvering antagonist now and then, and will therefore seek robust solutions rather than "best" solutions—those, in other words, which are *not* optimal but can remain adequate even when the enemy reacts to outmaneuver the first approach.

Under McNamara and those of his successors who chose his path, the substitute for military expertise absent at the top was thus error made systematic—error that still lives on in the "optimized" designs of some weapons that remain in service, each very efficient and thus vulnerable. Nowadays, by contrast, with Caspar Weinberger as the Secretary of Defense, the interference of civilians in military decisions has greatly diminished, but nothing has been put in its place, leaving a vacuum where strategy is supposed to be. Aside from the great upsurge in the naval forces (which reflects no strategy at all but only the odd politics that yields a consensus on naval unilateralism out of the clash of budget-cutting isolationists and Alliance-minded activists), we see the loot shared out according to inherited priorities, with scant regard to all the vast changes that have so greatly diminished the value of some forces, while increasing the value of others.

So far we have addressed strategy as meaning *national* military strategy, which is supposed to guide our spending decisions to build the future forces required by policy, as well as to maintain the forces we choose to keep. At that level, the present absence of meaningful military advice results in the waste of our resources—not the petty waste of carelessness, but the huge and systematic waste inevitable when powerful service fiefdoms share out the money without any coherent overall design set at the national level.

The same fatal defect, however, is just as manifest at the lower levels of strategy, which are supposed to guide the geographic deployment of the forces we actually have, and their planned use in combat, large and small. As we have seen, the Iran rescue attempt exemplified in pure form what we can expect when the "joint" system goes to war: i.e., the willful disregard of the most basic principles of war for the sake of bureaucratic harmony among competing services. The two "unified" commands in charge of Vietnam—the Pacific Command in Honolulu and Saigon's MACV below it—manifested the same disease in much more varied form over a period of years, and so did the Atlantic Command in planning the seizure of Grenada. No better result can be expected when plans are made and forces are commanded by a committee of bureaucracies with a shifting cast of characters who happen to be serving their joint-command "tour" at that time and in that place—each wholly dependent on his own service alone for his own career advancement.

Therefore it is not enough to obtain budgetary advice from some selected group of superofficers, somehow freed of any service bias.

There really is no substitute for a new cadre of "national defense officers" able to carry out three essential functions now left to ineffectual gatherings of service representatives:

—The planning of large and small combat operations, immediate and contingent, when more than one service is involved—i.e., virtually all military planning, from a commando raid tomorrow, to plans for the defense of Europe that we hope will never be tested;

—The higher command of the forces of diverse services that must cooperate in any theater or expeditionary setting, to replace the present "unified" and "specified" commands with the genuine article: unitary commands, headed by officers who share the same all-service training and the same higher loyalty;

—The supply of professional military advice to assist the Secretary of Defense and the President in their policy and budget decisions on the distribution of the forces in different regions of the world and for different purposes; the distribution of the money among different kinds of forces—nuclear and not, naval and land, ground and air, and so on—in much finer detail; and, finally, the distribution of spending over time, between immediate "readiness" (and for which forces), force-building for the next five to ten years (it takes that long to build ships, aircraft, and even tanks), and research-and-development for entirely new forces.

Where are such national-minded officers to be found? Obviously we do not have them now, either by background or by training. (Officers sent to the Joint Staff or to one of the "unified" commands do not even receive a "joint" course before taking up their duties.) And it is just as obvious that we cannot possibly create "national-defense officers" from scratch, in a new superservice without any forces of its own, which would take in young cadets and make fairly senior officers out of them through a sequence of school courses and office jobs. To place such rarefied souls above regular officers who have served in the forces and risen to command them, perhaps with some actual combat experience, would be an invitation to mutiny in a real crisis, and would certainly produce useless advice, and worse plans.

Only one other solution remains, and that is to recruit the new body of national-defense officers from the services themselves. Army, Navy, Marine Corps, and Air Force officers of middle-high rank (say colonel/ Navy captain) who have already filled staff and command positions and who have been selected for early promotion by their own service would be given the opportunity to start a new career as national-defense officers—if they pass stiff entrance examinations and survive demanding interviews.

Once selected for the new cadre and formally discharged from their original service, these national-defense officers would familiarize themselves with the forces, tactics, doctrine, jargon, and procedures of every other service before attending a national-defense training school. There they would receive a standard "staff-and-command" education in the new format of national rather than one-service operations. Staff assignments would follow, and then command positions at a higher and higher level, over larger and larger groups of multiservice forces. In between, national-defense officers would have working tours with all services other than the one they came from, and before selection for the very highest ranks, another educational interval might be appropriate, in a suitably broad-gauged higher-defense college. Thus young colonels/ Navy captains might have a second career before retirement, mainly as flag-rank officers.

The obvious attraction of the new career would be its monopoly over the higher direction of our national defense. The geographic commands for Europe, the Pacific, the Atlantic, Latin America (Southern Command), and the so-called Central Command—whose envisaged operational area is the Persian Gulf—as well as the "specified" strategic-nuclear commands, both offensive and defensive, would all be headed by senior "national-defense officers," with their more junior counterparts in charge of the usual staff departments of each command.

Even more senior national-defense officers would be in charge of the main departments of a new National Defense Staff, at the apex of the entire military structure, whose task would be to provide professional military advice to the Secretary of Defense and the President, as the Joint Chiefs organization is now supposed to do.

The head of the National Defense Staff would be the nation's chief military officer: not a commander-in-chief, of course, but rather a chief adviser, as the Chairman of the Joint Chiefs now is—except that instead of quite suddenly having to think in multiservice terms after a lifetime devoted to one service, that chief adviser will have had many years of experience as a national-defense officer.* Under its Director or chief officer (whose status might be recognized by a unique five-star rank),

---

* If the entire radical reform is carried out, it may also be possible to rename the post: "chairman" has weak, commercial connotations; the British, who are good at that sort of thing, have a "Director" in charge of their central defense staff.

the National Defense Staff would be managed by three-star department chiefs, with less senior national-defense officers to provide the working staff. One-service officers would also be present, but in the capacity of professional experts rather than representatives of service interests. (This distinction would have to be actively preserved.)

Having commanded battalions and brigades, warships and air squadrons before they ever started their new career, and having shouldered higher staff and command responsibilities ever since, the new officers should not be lacking in prestige. Indeed, they should gain added respect because of their freedom from the bureaucratic interests of any one service. A residual loyalty to their service of origin is only human and decent, and fully to be expected among the new officers; but such ties would be merely sentimental, because all promotion would be exclusively within the national-defense cadre itself. No longer would we witness the sorry spectacle of officers on "joint" duty torn between the career imperative of asserting narrow service interests and their own personal sense of what is best for the nation.

In the two-track system here envisaged, officers who choose to remain within their own service could still have a fully satisfying career reaching up to the highest ranks—except that if they remained one-service officers, they could not aspire to the higher direction of the armed forces, in which they now share if they serve tours in one of the unified or specified commands, or in the Joint Chiefs of Staff organization. As it is, the four-star chief officer of each service—i.e., the Chiefs of Staff of the Army and Air Force, the Chief of Naval Operations, and the Commandant of the Marine Corps—have no operational responsibilities. They are *not* in the present chain of command which runs from the Secretary of Defense to the appropriate unified or specified commands. The most senior officers of each service are therefore administrators, inspectors, and moral leaders—not war planners or commanders. Moreover, their force-building decisions and budget priorities are already supposed to be guided by national priorities set by the Secretary of Defense.

Under the proposed reform, the distinction already in place between operational and administrative responsibilities would be extended just a little; one-service officers in command positions would continue to have both operational and administrative powers (both are, of course, essential to leadership), but not beyond the level where specific military expertise dominates. It goes without saying that warships should be commanded by sailors, divisions by soldiers, and air wings by airmen rather than by national-defense officers who may or may not have originated in the relevant service. It is just as clear, however, that the operational commanders of the forces in an entire theater—even if of only one service; for example, the naval forces in the Mediterranean or the air forces in the Pacific—need expertise in dealing with other services, and indeed other countries, even more than they need one-service expertise, of which they should have a great deal anyway in their staffs.

It therefore seems reasonable to establish a cut-off point at the three-star level: one-service officers would still control substantial forces, up to the divisions and corps of the Army, the numbered fleets of the Navy, and the numbered "air forces" of the Air Force; above that level, however, command positions would be reserved for the new cadre of national-defense officers. The one-service officers in charge of the Pacific Fleet or the U.S. Army, Europe, would remain in place as administrators and moral leaders, but the forces contained within those frameworks would be controlled by the appropriate regional commands, staffed and headed by national-defense officers.

The geographic commands that are now "unified"—for Europe, the Pacific, the Atlantic, Latin America (Southern Command), the home forces (Readiness Command), and the Middle East (Central Command) —might be rationalized, once they are taken over by national-defense officers with no service prerogatives to protect. But no change is immediately required by the reform. However, for operations of war smaller than the imaginary all-out, worldwide conflict for which the present "unified" commands are scaled—that is, for the fighting that actually happens, ranging all the way from Vietnam to Grenada—the appropriate geographic command would form a separate headquarters sized for the job, staffed and led by national-defense officers. Thus a craft approach to war could be restored, with operational coherence and a sharp sense of the milieu, terrain, and enemy no longer hopelessly dissipated in overlarge headquarters colonized by competing services.

The military profession is conservative by nature, and officers are entitled to be cautious in the face of a reform that would impose drastic changes in their chosen careers. But over time, officers would get used to the idea that the military profession can offer two alternative paths of equal merit. One would offer all the rewards of the kinship of men in the day-to-day life of the services; the other would offer the satisfaction of working within the stream of national policy. One would attract the "regimental" type of officer and the other his "staff officer" counter-part; one would be able to claim all the traditions of military service, while the other would offer the challenge of the new. One thing above all would facilitate the reform: whatever they may now say in public, while still being inmates in their one-service prisons of ideas, most officers of reflective disposition know that the present system is funda-mentally defective. If nothing else, the deep-felt patriotism common in the officer corps should prevail over the narrower loyalty evoked by the services.

Actually, we already have quite a few self-made "national-defense officers." They still wear one-service uniforms and are not officially recognized as such, but everyone knows who they are. Having freed themselves from service parochialism and acquired wider interests, these officers strive to bridge the gap between the services, taking much more than their share of the "joint" assignments—even though their promotion suffers in the process. One does not know whether such men deserve praise or blame: if it were not for them, the present system might have been given up long ago as totally unworkable. The creation of the national-defense career would recognize and legitimize their professional orientation, and also extend its scope.

Thus the reform here envisaged would change the human substance, instead of merely rearranging the organizational boxes. The belief that the true workings of complicated institutions can be seriously improved by tinkering with their formal structure is one more symptom of the "administrator's delusion"; but after a great many new letterheads have been reprinted and many new signs provided for office doors, one usu-ally discovers that the real problems persist. In this case the real prob-lem is that the rival service fiefdoms dominate the weak and sterile "joint" structures that are supposed to provide them with coherent direction at the national level; and the real solution is to subordinate the services to a selection of their best men, formed into a cohesive cadre.

Chart 8 illustrates the present organization of the Defense Depart-ment. Because of its substantive content, the proposed reform, as shown in Chart 9, would leave the formal organization of the Defense Department largely unchanged. There would be no drastic changes in structure, except for the long-overdue consolidation of some functional commands of the Navy and Air Force, which are now separated purely because there are no "transservice" military officers available to pro-vide the higher command of both. The job of delivering people and

CHART 8

The Present Organization of the Department of Defense

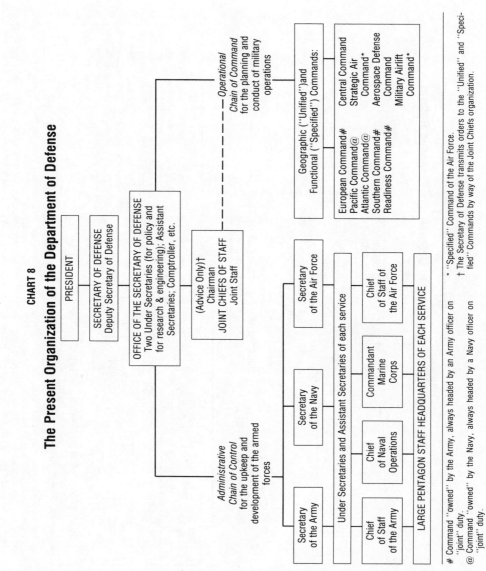

PRESIDENT

SECRETARY OF DEFENSE
Deputy Secretary of Defense

OFFICE OF THE SECRETARY OF DEFENSE
Two Under Secretaries (for policy and for research & engineering); Assistant Secretaries; Comptroller, etc.

(Advice Only)†
Chairman
JOINT CHIEFS OF STAFF
Joint Staff

Administrative Chain of Control for the upkeep and development of the armed forces

Operational Chain of Command for the planning and conduct of military operations

Secretary of the Army

Secretary of the Navy

Secretary of the Air Force

Under Secretaries and Assistant Secretaries of each service

Chief of Staff of the Army

Chief of Naval Operations

Commandant Marine Corps

Chief of Staff of the Air Force

LARGE PENTAGON STAFF HEADQUARTERS OF EACH SERVICE

Geographic ("Unified") and Functional ("Specified") Commands:

European Command#
Pacific Command@
Atlantic Command@
Southern Command#
Readiness Command#

Central Command
Strategic Air Command*
Aerospace Defense Command
Military Airlift Command*

\# Command "owned" by the Army, always headed by an Army officer on "joint" duty.

@ Command "owned" by the Navy, always headed by a Navy officer on "joint" duty.

* "Specified" Command of the Air Force.

† The Secretary of Defense transmits orders to the "Unified" and "Specified" Commands by way of the Joint Chiefs organization.

277

CHART 9

The Organization of the Department of Defense: the Proposed Reform

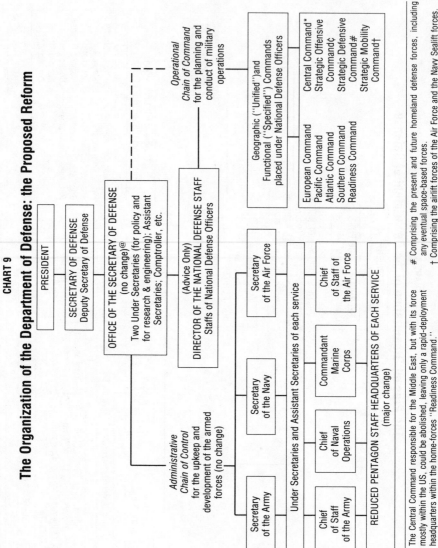

PRESIDENT

SECRETARY OF DEFENSE
Deputy Secretary of Defense

OFFICE OF THE SECRETARY OF DEFENSE
(no change)@
Two Under Secretaries (for policy and for research & engineering); Assistant Secretaries; Comptroller, etc.

Administrative Chain of Control for the upkeep and development of the armed forces (no change)

(Advice Only)
DIRECTOR OF THE NATIONAL DEFENSE STAFF
Staffs of National Defense Officers

Operational Chain of Command for the planning and conduct of military operations

Secretary of the Army

Secretary of the Navy

Secretary of the Air Force

Under Secretaries and Assistant Secretaries of each service

Chief of Staff of the Army

Chief of Naval Operations

Commandant Marine Corps

Chief of Staff of the Air Force

REDUCED PENTAGON STAFF HEADQUARTERS OF EACH SERVICE
(major change)

Geographic ("Unified") and Functional ("Specified") Commands placed under National Defense Officers

European Command
Pacific Command
Atlantic Command
Southern Command
Readiness Command

Central Command*
Strategic Offensive Command¢
Strategic Defensive Command#
Strategic Mobility Command†

---

* The Central Command responsible for the Middle East, but with its force mostly within the US, could be abolished, leaving only a rapid-deployment headquarters within the home-forces' "Readiness Command."

¢ Comprising the present Strategic Air Command of the Air Force and the strategic-missile forces of the Navy.

\# Comprising the present and future homeland defense forces, including any eventual space-based forces.

† Comprising the airlift forces of the Air Force and the Navy Sealift forces.

@ The Secretary of Defense retains the option of direct communication.

goods overseas, presently divided between the Military Airlift Command of the Air Force and the Navy's Military Sealift Command, with the former a nominally joint "specified" command and the latter not, is clearly irrational. (Only the operational control of the forces would be affected; the services would remain responsible for the upkeep, development, and direct command of the ships and aircraft themselves.) Similarly, the divided command of long-range nuclear weapons—between the bombers and ballistic missiles which come under the "specified" Strategic Air Command of the Air Force and the sea-based missiles which the Navy keeps under its geographic Fleet commands—is also irrational: all those forces are aimed at the same targets. The fact that service boundaries cut across the strategic-nuclear forces of the nation is a source of needless complications. Even these minor changes are not actually required by the reform here envisaged; but once the new cadre of national-defense officers is in place, the long-overdue consolidation will no doubt follow.

More important, the constitutional relationship and real-life divisions of power and responsibility between the civilian authority and military officers would not be changed in any way. The Secretary of Defense remains the executive official of the President, to assert civilian control over the entire military structure by two complementary lines of authority—the operational chain of command, direct to the geographic and functional commanders, and the administrative chain of control, which reaches into each service by way of its civilian Secretary and chief military officer.

Only time will tell how successful the new cadre of national-defense officers will be in making plans for the file cabinets of contingency planning and for immediate use. One may reasonably hope, however, that the principle of simplicity will be restored to our operations of war, once it is no longer necessary to satisfy the claims of every service. Only the experience of actual combat will show how well national-defense officers can command multiservice forces in groupings large and small, but at least the principle of the unity of command will no longer be systematically violated for the sake of bureaucratic harmony, with the atrocity of multiple commanders in one spot and jurisdictions split arbitrarily along service lines.

One thing is certain: national-defense officers will be much better equipped from the start to provide useful advice to the Secretary of Defense and his civilian officials—not to impose policy, of course, but rather to offer clear-cut options for civilian decisions, in place of the diluted compromises of today, which are often unrealistic and which always violate the essential nature of strategy. Only rarely will a compromise coincide with one of the discrete options that are valid in strategy. In war, one may win by attacking to the left or the right—but never by diluting one's strength across the front. And in peacetime also, choices just as clear must be made.

When the Secretary of Defense begins to receive coherent proposals and genuine choices from the military professionals of the National Defense Staff, he will have less need to rely on "systems analysts" and assorted civilian experts for military advice. And once a National Defense Staff can subject the services to the discipline of a coherent strategy, the Secretary of Defense will also have less need to rely on civilian officials in order to monitor and review service decisions. In due course, this should result in a gradual decline in the size of the Office of the Secretary of Defense, which now employs almost 2,000 officials, and whose growth over the years was largely caused by the failure of the Joint Staff to do its job.[2] That in turn will help to reduce the "layering" of management, which is the recognized source of the near-paralysis of the Defense Department.

An even more powerful effect will be manifest in the Washington headquarters staffs of the Army, Navy, Marine Corps, and Air Force. At present, they employ almost 9,000 people in uniform (mostly officers, and many of them of middle rank)—far more than in the Office of the Secretary, the Joint Staff (1,300) and the civilian-run secretariats of the Army, Navy, and Air Force combined (1,600).[3] These numbers reveal the true balance of power: although the official table of organization puts them at the bottom—below the civilian secretariats, who are in turn below the Secretary of Defense and his Office—it is in fact the service headquarters that have the greatest power. Their huge size is only partly explained by their supervisory role over their own services (which is already the second layer of supervision, the first being provided by the management and force commands outside the Pentagon). In fact, the size of the Washington headquarters of each service also reflects their undeclared function, which is to manipulate the Joint Staff and even more to outmaneuver the Office of the Secretary of Defense. When a civilian official in that office produces a ten-page paper to argue for some decision or other that is uncongenial to a service, its Washington staff can reply with a one-hundred-page refutation; when three civilian officials probe a questionable service proposal, its staff can assign ten officers to defend the service point of view. By controlling the information on detailed matters within the service domain, and by sheer numbers, the headquarters of each service thus systematically resist central direction. If only because of the lively possibility of a hostile Congressional reaction, stimulated by the friends of each service on Capitol Hill, Secretaries of Defense are usually reluctant to overrule professional military advice—which now comes from the service head-quarters alone; and to seek alternative options from the Joint Chiefs and the Joint Staff is futile.

Once a National Defense Staff breaks the one-service monopoly over professional military advice, the Secretary of Defense will no longer have to choose between the bureaucratically biased but professional advice of the service headquarters and the alternatives offered by his civilian officials, whose competence in strictly military matters must remain in doubt. If the National Defense Staff is successful in consoli-dating its authority, the role of the service headquarters must gradually diminish. Eventually, this should also result in their numerical decline. Officers now employed in upholding service interests in the highly com-plicated free-for-all politics of the present, rudderless, Pentagon will have much less to do, once the National Defense Staff enables the Secretary of Defense to issue clear-cut directives instead of today's tentative guidelines, which offer much room for argument and counter-argument on every question, large and small. As the actual work of the service headquarters begins to resemble the official scope of their duties —i.e., the supervision of one-service affairs—there will be a great many empty In trays and visibly underemployed officers. In due course, one may hope, decency will prevail, and the number of positions on the service staffs will be reduced.

In this way, there is a real prospect of reversing the dynamics of bureaucratic expansion, whereby the need to reply to memos and phone calls, represent office views in decision meetings, prepare policy-driving "studies" and counterstudies, and review other people's documents has stimulated the responsive growth of the Office of the Secretary of De-fense and the Washington headquarters staffs, which then in turn stim-ulate the growth of the different management headquarters of each service, and notably the huge matériel and systems commands.

Moreover, as the authority of the National Defense Staff increases, it will be easier to overcome service resistance to the expansion of the centralized "defense agencies" that now provide common services to the Army, Navy, Marine Corps, and Air Force. Some of these agencies, such as the Defense Intelligence Agency, have already absorbed most of the work that used to be done on a triplicate basis by each one of the services. Others, such as the Defense Logistics Agency, have only scratched the surface: nuts and bolts, hammers and radios, blankets and ammunition identical in every way continue to be purchased separately, stored separately, and transported separately—often to the same destinations.

A glance at the budget figures shows that there is much room for centralization: in Fiscal Year 1984, for example, out of $258.2 billion of total budget authority obtained, the thirteen "defense agencies" accounted for less than $11 billion, with the rest in the hands of the separate services.[4] Without imposing an excess of uniformity that would violate meaningful differences in their style of combat and preferred tactics, it should be possible to reduce the triplication that now goes on, not in such things as the development of combat aircraft (where competition is of real value), but certainly in the research, development, production, storage, and distribution of the great mass of prosaic supplies and standard components. At present, however, the power of the service fiefdoms is felt at its strongest in resisting precisely this sort of centralization, which they view as the thin end of a wedge whose broad end is the great and chimerical specter of out-and-out unification. So long as all the services resist centralization—for once in full solidarity —a great deal of triplication will endure, because only a brave or foolhardy Secretary of Defense will overrule military judgment in this matter.

The real reward of a centralization of logistics is not so much in the money that could be saved but rather the resulting debureaucratization of the armed forces. While the direct impact of the National Defense Staff would be felt from above, in reducing the number of officers kept in Pentagon office jobs to safeguard service interests, its indirect effect would be felt from below, in reducing the great number of soldier-clerks and their officer-managers.

In order to do its job, the proposed National Defense Staff would need at least seven major departments:

—"Plans," to prepare war-contingency plans at the level of national strategy, in response to the policy directives of the Secretary of Defense, and to assist him in reviewing and coordinating the contingency plans of each geographic command and the three functional commands. This department should also include a small and stable team specialized in the planning of "special"—i.e., commando—operations. In order to avoid dissipating scarce expertise, this task should not be left to the geographic commands.*

—"Operations," to monitor and evaluate the ongoing activities of the armed forces worldwide—i.e., their day-to-day routine, exercises, maneuvers, fleet movements, etc., in peacetime as well as in combat operations as they occur—in order to keep the Secretary of Defense informed of what is going on, and to advise him on all aspects of such operations, including their coordination at the national level. Naturally, the Secretary of Defense will also continue to receive information directly from the geographic and functional commands (the latter are in the chain of command, unlike the National Defense Staff). This department should be expanded in the event of large-scale combat, rather than kept overstaffed and underemployed on a permanent basis. The various "war rooms" in the Pentagon and White House and their evacuation alternatives, including the airborne command posts, should be supervised by this department.

—"Logistics," to advise the Secretary of Defense on the distribution of current operating and maintenance funds, to help him set priorities in "readiness" for the different forces of the different services. This, of course, implies a prior set of broader decisions on how the total defense funds should be distributed over time—i.e., between the immediate "readiness" of the forces, force-building for the next five to ten years, and research-and-development for future weapons. Advice on those key decisions of national military strategy should come from the Director of the National Defense Staff, in consultation with his department heads and the chief officers of the separate services.†

—"Force Planning," to advise the Secretary of Defense on the distribution of force-building funds, notably weapon purchases, among the diverse forces of the different services. This too implies a prior set of

---

* Officers of the various special-operations forces (Rangers, SEALs, etc.), even if quite junior, must also participate in the planning, for only they know what their forces can and cannot do.

† As soon as "readiness" priorities are set at the national level, it is quite likely that the Navy's habit of keeping the maximum feasible number of its ships and submarines operating at sea will begin to be questioned. Both the Soviet Navy and the Royal Navy retain their professional competence and keep up a sufficient diplomatic visibility without the frantic activity typical of the U.S. Navy. Our admirals claim to be impressed by the sheer size of the Soviet fleet, while simultaneously criticizing its practice of keeping its ships tied up at dockside for much of the time. But of course one way of having many ships is precisely to spend less money on operating them nonstop.

broader decisions on the "time distribution" of defense funds. Under the present system, a Secretary of Defense who takes his job seriously must choose between buying tanks and aircraft, building ships and missiles, without being helped by professional military advice—because the Joint Staff is incapable of setting strategic priorities that cut across service preference, and will unfailingly suggest the sharing out of raises and cuts among all the services. It may safely be anticipated that this department of the National Defense Staff will make the most immediate contribution to the quality of American defense policy.

—"Research and Development," to advise the Secretary of Defense on the distribution of R & D funds among the different forces. Obviously, national-defense officers cannot have the scientific and technical expertise needed to choose between different technological paths to each military goal. And it is also true that those goals must be continuously reevaluated, in step with evolving scientific and technical feasibility, another task that requires scientific and technical expertise. But at budget time, choices between diverse R & D projects must somehow be made, and this department of the National Defense Staff will at least help the Secretary of Defense avoid the distortions caused by one-service decisions. The propensity to fund most generously R & D that reinforces each service's role, while neglecting other projects, is by now notorious: the Air Force easily spends billions to develop new manned aircraft, but pilot-displacing remotely piloted aircraft remain unfunded; the Navy is similarly reluctant to grant money for the development of mine warfare, while spending vast sums on every aspect of ship development; and the Army neglects R & D for small arms, mortars, engineer equipment and other such things, while funding most generously tank and helicopter development.

—"Organization," to propose structural reforms to the Secretary of Defense, thus creating a center of professional military advocacy for the innovation of the armed forces and their command system. This department is meant to serve as a counterweight to the natural inertia of large institutions and the conservatism of military men. Almost inevitably, this department would soon find itself addressing the diverse aspects of the officer surplus and the resulting bureaucratization of the services.

—"Inspectorate," to advise the Secretary of Defense on the performance of the armed forces and all their support structures, to set evaluation criteria for "readiness" and other measures of effectiveness, and in general to bring errors, malpractices, and specific problems to his attention.

To act as here advertised, the National Defense Staff will of course need highly capable officers, but its formal powers need not be greater than those of the Joint Chiefs organization. With the one minor exception of commando-planning, the new Staff is a purely advisory body charged with the duties that the Joint Chiefs and their Joint Staff are already supposed to perform. Of course, over time, as successive Secretaries of Defense come to rely increasingly on its professional yet disinterested advice, the real influence of the National Defense Staff—and thus its ability to spread reform throughout the military establishment—should steadily increase.

In spite of its larger role and far greater potential, the National Defense Staff should not require more officers than the present Joint Staff, whose members now spend much of their time in watching one another in order to safeguard service interests. Besides, the National Defense Staff will be all the more effective if it is somewhat understaffed, so that its members are compelled to focus on the truly important things.

Once the need for fundamental military reform is accepted, there is a choice to be made: either to seek a great variety of remedies to deal with each separate problem, or else to take the bull by the horns and create a new body of military officers able to deal with those same problems. It is not always a good idea to take bulls by their horns, and there is much to be said for the case-by-case remedial approach. Congress already imposes many detailed decisions on the Pentagon, and it could impose some more, perhaps at the initiative of the "Military Reform Caucus" that has been in existence for some years. Similarly, the powers of the civilian staffs serving the Secretary of Defense could be further increased, to intrude even more in purely military matters, in order to seek out problems and devise solutions. The remedial approach fits very well with the national preference for one-thing-at-a-time pragmatism; it certainly has the virtue of continuity. That, however, is also its greatest defect: we have been trying the remedial approach for many years without success.

It cannot be denied that the great reform proposed here, which is intended to accomplish all the others, would itself be very hard to achieve. For one thing, it would require a major change in the National Security Act, which Congress is unlikely to enact without much Presidential persuasion. The new cadre of nonservice officers will immediately evoke the dread prospect of all-service unification, arousing much Congressional opposition for all sorts of reasons, from the plain sentimentality of some veterans, to antique fears of military usurpation by armed forces that are no longer divided. Other Congressmen will decry the "elitism" of the reform, which would reserve the higher command of the forces and the national advisory role to a small body of selected officers. The same Congressman who would never dream of going to a nonelite and quite inexperienced surgeon for a minor operation might insist without any sense of incongruity that the safety of the nation is best left in the hands of nonelite officers, not specially trained in the art of multiservice staff and command.

And when the time comes for the preliminary hearings at which expert witnesses will be asked to testify, no help can be expected from military officers on active duty. Any number of retired generals and admirals will readily join General David Jones in denouncing the present system, but it is idle to expect confirmation from the inmates of the present service-dominated structure. With their careers at stake, on the ground of service loyalty, they cannot criticize the system unless they are totally certain that it will be changed, and very soon.

Because of these obstacles and more, the one great reform here proposed is therefore most difficult to achieve. But there really is no other choice. To select the best military officers, to liberate them from the one-service prisons in which they must now operate, and to let them get on with the job of running the show, while carefully initiating more detailed reforms, is the only remedy that can really work. If this reform is rejected, if the present system is allowed to endure, it will continue to absorb much treasure and give us inadequate military power. And it will continue to yield failure in combat, in spite of the true patriotic dedication, high skill, and fighting courage that are so abundant in our armed forces.

APPENDIX

Officers on Active Duty by Grade and Service
30 June 1945

	Total Dept. of Defense	Total War Dept.	Army and Air Force		Navy (Excluding Coast Guard)	Marine Corps
			Army Commands	Air Force Commands		
TOTAL OFFICERS and ENLISTED	12,123,455	8,267,958	5,985,699	2,282,259	3,380,817	474,680
OFFICERS—Total	1,260,109	891,663	510,209	381,454	331,379	37,067
Gen of Army/Fleet Adm	7	4			3	—
General/Admiral	31	13			17	1
Lt. General/Vice Adm	101	50			49	2
Maj Gen } Rear Adm[a]	1,929	392	1,221	298	401[a]	28
Brig Gen		1,060				48
Colonel/Captain	14,989	10,721	8,145	2,576	3,877	391
Lt. Colonel/Commander	36,967	29,077	21,852	7,225	6,861	1,029
Major/Lt. Cmdr	91,602	70,086	46,686	23,400	19,356	2,160
Captain/Lieut	300,610	197,591	125,885	71,706	96,784	6,235
1st Lieut/Lieut (JG)	436,792	328,245	193,328	134,917	94,278	14,269
2nd Lieut/Ensign	294,121	198,164	96,229	101,935	86,316	9,641
Chief or Comm Warrant } Warrant JG or Warrant Flight Officers	82,960	56,260	16,863	39,397	23,437	3,263
ENLISTED—Total	10,795,775	7,374,710	5,473,905	1,900,805	2,988,207	432,858

[a] Includes 140 Commodores.

Source: Progress Reports and Statistics, Office of Secretary of Defense, 5 August 1958

Officers on Active Duty by Grade and Service
30 June 1946

	Total Dept. of Defense	Army and Air Force			Navy (Excluding Coast Guard)	Marine Corps
		Total War Dept.	Army Commands	Air Force Commands		
TOTAL OFFICERS and ENLISTED	3,030,088	1,891,011	1,435,496	455,515	983,398	155,679
OFFICERS—Total	422,513	267,144	185,411	81,733	141,161	14,208
Gen of Army/Fleet Adm	7	3			4	
General/Admiral	25	11			13	1
Lt. General/Vice Adm	78	37	689	174	38	3
Maj Gen ⎫ Rear Adm[a]	1,286	254			412[a]	26
Brig Gen ⎭		558				36
Colonel/Captain	13,384	8,679	6,864	1,815	4,340	365
Lt. Colonel/Commander	24,716	16,369	13,156	3,213	7,447	900
Major/Lt. Cmdr	44,676	27,603	19,954	7,649	15,932	1,141
Captain/Lieut	96,466	69,815	49,970	19,845	24,146	2,505
1st Lieut/Lieut (JG)	134,263	93,499	60,668	32,831	36,443	4,321
2nd Lieut/Ensign	82,417	40,472	28,080	12,392	39,253	2,692
Warrant & Flight Officers	25,195	9,844	6,030	3,814	13,133	2,218
ENLISTED—Total	2,598,739	1,622,546	1,248,764	373,782	834,722	141,471

[a] Includes 103 Commodores.

Source: Statistical Service Center, Office of Secretary of Defense, 26 February 1959

Officers on Active Duty by Grade and Service
30 June 1949

	Total Dept. Def.	Army Commands	Navy	Marine Corps	Air Force Commands
TOTAL OFFICERS and ENLISTED	1,615,360	660,473	449,575	85,965	419,347
OFFICERS—Total	190,348	77,272	47,975	7,250	57,851
Gen of Army/Fleet Adm	6	3	3	—	
General/Admiral	15	5	5	1	4
Lt. General/Vice Adm	56	20	22	2	12
Maj Gen } Rear Adm[a]	787	143	235[a]	15	84
Brig Gen	177	177		26	107
Colonel/Captain	7,816	3,100	2,565	257	1,894
Lt. Colonel/Commander	17,392	8,362	4,592	678	3,760
Major/Lt. Cmdr	25,955	11,349	6,589	963	7,054
Captain/Lieut	52,112	21,564	10,118	1,530	18,900
1st Lieut/Lieut (JG)	59,523	22,704	13,807	1,962	21,050
2nd Lieut/Ensign	15,987	6,033	6,142	904	2,908
Chief or Comm Warrant	5,960	1,726	3,066	445	723
Warrant JG or Warrant	4,739	2,086	831	467	1,355
ENLISTED—Total	1,416,015	581,422	396,242	78,715	359,636
OFFICER CANDIDATES—Total	8,997	1,779	5,358		1,860
Cadets USMA	1,779	1,779			
Navy Officer Candidates	5,358		5,358		
Aviation Cadets	1,860				1,860

Source: Progress Reports and Statistics, Office of Secretary of Defense, 27 October 1952

[a] Includes 4 Commodores.

Officers on Active Duty by Grade and Service
30 June 1950

	Total Dept. Def.	Army Commands	Navy	Marine Corps	Air Force Commands
TOTAL OFFICERS and ENLISTED	1,460,261	593,167	381,538	74,279	411,277
OFFICERS—Total	181,467	72,566	44,641	7,254	57,006
Gen of Army/Fleet Adm	6	3	3	—	—
General/Admiral	13	5	4	1	3
Lt. General/Vice Adm	61	22	23	2	14
Maj Gen ⎱ Rear Adm[a]	801	143	237[a]	15	93
Brig Gen ⎰		170		26	117
Colonel/Captain	7,752	3,090	2,512	303	1,847
Lt. Colonel/Commander	17,084	7,650	4,852	695	3,887
Major/Lt. Cmdr	26,405	10,480	7,302	1,022	7,601
Captain/Lieut	49,576	19,739	10,471	1,845	17,521
1st Lieut/Lieut (JG)	50,869	19,934	10,088	1,580	19,267
2nd Lieut/Ensign	17,483	6,548	5,500	871	4,564
Chief or Comm Warrant	5,850	1,588	2,876	681	705
Warrant JG or Warrant	5,567	3,194	773	213	1,387
ENLISTED—Total	1,269,891	518,921	331,860	67,025	352,085
OFFICER CANDIDATES—Total	8,903	1,680	5,037		2,186
Cadets USMA	1,680	1,680			
Navy Officer Candidates	5,037		5,037		
Aviation Cadets	2,186				2,186

Source: Progress Reports and Statistics, Office of Secretary of Defense, 27 October 1952

a Includes 5 Commodores.

292

Officers on Active Duty by Grade and Service
30 June 1951

	Total Dept. Def.	Army Commands	Navy	Marine Corps	Air Force Commands
TOTAL OFFICERS and ENLISTED	3,249,455	1,531,774	736,680	192,620	788,381
OFFICERS—Total	323,302	130,540	70,513	15,150	107,099
Gen of Army/Fleet Adm	7	4	3	—	—
General/Admiral	15	5	5	1	4
Lt. General/Vice Adm	73	27	25	4	17
Maj Gen ⎱ Rear Adm[a]	952	167	243[a]	15	105
Brig Gen ⎰		233		30	159
Colonel/Captain	10,794	4,636	2,800	422	2,936
Lt. Colonel/Commander	25,074	11,594	5,760	868	6,852
Major/Lt. Cmdr	39,272	14,825	8,851	1,627	13,969
Captain/Lieut	93,604	36,784	16,895	2,883	37,042
1st Lieut/Lieut (JG)	90,874	35,509	21,332	5,133	28,900
2nd Lieut/Ensign	44,021	16,901	9,540	3,121	14,459
Chief or Comm Warrant W-4	309	199	19	16	75
Chief or Comm Warrant W-3	856	455	131	106	164
Chief or Comm Warrant W-2	6,827	1,921	3,301	806	799
Jr Warrant or Warrant W-1	10,624	7,280	1,608	118	1,618
ENLISTED—Total	2,917,277	1,399,362	661,639	177,470	678,806
OFFICER CANDIDATES—Total	8,876	1,872	4,528		2,476
Cadets USMA	1,872	1,872			
Navy Officer Candidates	4,528		4,528		
Aviation Cadets	2,476				2,476

Source: Progress Reports and Statistics, Office of Secretary of Defense, 27 October 1952

[a] Includes 3 Commodores.

Officers on Active Duty by Grade and Service
30 June 1952

	Total Dept. Def.	Army Commands	Navy	Marine Corps	Air Force Commands
TOTAL OFFICERS and ENLISTED	3,635,912	1,596,419	824,265	231,967	983,261[b]
OFFICERS—Total	375,829	148,427	82,247	16,413	128,742
Gen of Army/Fleet Adm	6	3	3	—	—
General/Admiral	19	8	5	1	5
Lt. General/Vice Adm	65	22	25	4	14
Maj Gen } Rear Adm[a]	1,052	165	256[a]	18	120
Brig Gen		281		31	181
Colonel/Captain	12,490	4,869	2,983	516	4,122
Lt. Colonel/Commander	28,927	12,830	6,632	1,011	8,454
Major/Lt. Cmdr	53,008	17,249	12,222	2,848	20,689
Captain/Lieut	107,412	36,988	24,958	5,549	39,917
1st Lieut/Lieut (JG)	81,556	36,595	15,004	647	29,310
2nd Lieut/Ensign	65,937	24,922	14,356	4,932	21,727
Chief or Comm Warrant W-4	447	281	15	20	131
Chief or Comm Warrant W-3	2,507	853	1,011	358	285
Chief or Comm Warrant W-2	6,706	2,243	2,974	459	1,030
Jr Warrant or Warrant W-1	15,697	11,118	1,803	19	2,757
ENLISTED—Total	3,245,310	1,446,266	735,753	215,554	847,737
OFFICER CANDIDATES—Total	14,773	1,726	6,265		6,782
Cadets USMA	1,726	1,726			
Navy Officer Candidates	6,265		6,265		
Aviation Cadets	6,782				6,782

[a] Includes 4 Commodores.
[b] Includes 9,787 Army personnel in training for special duty.

Source: Progress Reports and Statistics, Office of Secretary of Defense, 27 October 1952

Officers on Active Duty by Grade and Service
30 June 1953

	Total Dept. Def.	Army Commands	Navy	Marine Corps	Air Force Commands
TOTAL OFFICERS and ENLISTED	3,555,067	1,533,815	794,440	249,219	977,593
OFFICERS—Total	376,864	145,633	81,731	18,731	130,769
Gen of Army/Fleet Adm	6	3	3	—	—
General/Admiral	20	7	5	1	7
Lt. General/Vice Adm	73	26	25	4	18
Maj Gen } Rear Adm[a]	1,098	156	244[a]	21	134
Brig Gen }		287		33	223
Colonel/Captain	12,782	5,142	2,818	508	4,314
Lt. Colonel/Commander	29,440	13,046	6,887	1,183	8,324
Major/Lt. Cmdr	52,183	18,151	10,792	2,435	20,805
Captain/Lieut	98,239	33,092	24,309	4,189	36,649
1st Lieut/Lieut (JG)	83,723	31,605	16,894	3,134	32,090
2nd Lieut/Ensign	74,870	30,851	13,730	6,084	24,205
Chief or Comm Warrant W-4	611	430	14	28	139
Chief or Comm Warrant W-3	3,507	1,407	1,387	316	397
Chief or Comm Warrant W-2	8,029	3,469	2,818	467	1,275
Jr Warrant or Warrant W-1	12,283	7,961	1,805	328	2,189
ENLISTED—Total	3,161,030	1,386,500	706,375	230,488	837,667
OFFICER CANDIDATES—Total	17,173	1,682	6,334		9,157
Cadets USMA	1,682	1,682			
Midshipmen USNA	3,455		3,455		
Naval Aviation Cadets	2,879		2,879		
Aviation Cadets	9,157				9,157

[a] Includes 1 Commodore.

Source: Progress Reports and Statistics, Office of Secretary of Defense, 13 January 1954

Officers on Active Duty by Grade and Service
30 June 1961

	Total Dept. Def.	Army	Navy	Marine Corps	Air Force
TOTAL OFFICERS and ENLISTED	2,483,771	858,622	627,089	176,909	821,151
OFFICERS—Total	314,827	99,921	69,981	16,132	128,793
Gen of Army/Fleet Adm	4	3	1	—	—
General/Admiral	29	10	8	1	10
Lt. General/Vice Adm	101	35	33	6	27
Maj Gen ⎫ Rear Adm[a]	1,120	187	251	20	170
Brig Gen ⎭		240		33	219
Colonel/Captain	14,488	4,850	4,017	602	5,019
Lt. Colonel/Commander	31,445	11,324	8,191	1,406	10,524
Major/Lt. Cmdr	55,604	15,490	11,954	2,224	25,936
Captain/Lieut	96,739	29,412	17,838	4,265	45,224
1st Lieut/Lieut (JG)	60,731	15,404	13,119	4,207	28,001
2nd Lieut/Ensign	36,724	13,111	11,345	2,390	9,878
Chief Warrant Officer W-4	2,423	1,098	853	87	385
Chief Warrant Officer W-3	4,795	2,478	906	174	1,237
Chief Warrant Officer W-2	8,767	5,291	1,108	206	2,162
Warrant Officer W-1	1,857	988	357	511	1
ENLISTED—Total	2,158,530	756,932	551,603	160,438	689,557
OFFICER CANDIDATES—Total	10,414	1,769	5,505	339	2,801
Cadets USMA	1,769	1,769			
Midshipmen USNA	3,980		3,980		
Cadets USAFA	2,267				2,267
Naval Aviation Cadets	659		659		
Naval Enlisted Off. Cand.	866		866		
Marine Aviation Cadets	339			339	
Aviation Cadets	534				534[a]

[a] Excludes 1 E-5 Enlisted Aviation Student shown as enlisted.

Source: Directorate for Statistical Services, Office of Secretary of Defense, 31 August 1961

Officers on Active Duty by Grade and Service
30 June 1962

	Total Dept. Def.	Army	Navy	Marine Corps	Air Force
TOTAL OFFICERS and ENLISTED	2,807,819	1,066,404	666,428	190,962	884,025
OFFICERS—Total	343,121	116,050	75,302	16,861	134,908
Gen of Army/Fleet Adm	4	3	1		
General/Admiral	34	13	9	1	11
Lt. General/Vice Adm	110	37	35	6	32
Maj Gen ⎫ Rear Adm[a]	1,155	207	252	21	174
Brig Gen ⎭		252		33	216
Colonel/Captain	14,997	5,213	4,077	597	5,110
Lt. Colonel/Commander	37,448	12,786	8,366	1,406	14,890
Major/Lt. Cmdr	56,682	17,856	12,390	2,351	24,085
Captain/Lieut	105,507	31,127	20,357	4,262	49,761
1st Lieut/Lieut (JG)	63,731	18,473	14,994	4,114	26,150
2nd Lieut/Ensign	45,035	19,258	12,090	2,833	10,854
Chief Warrant Officer W-4	2,699	1,226	821	97	555
Chief Warrant Officer W-3	5,100	2,799	690	151	1,460
Chief Warrant Officer W-2	8,089	5,042	1,215	226	1,606
Warrant Officer W-1	2,530	1,758	5	763	4
ENLISTED—Total	2,452,468	948,597	584,071	173,615	746,185
OFFICER CANDIDATES—Total	12,230	1,757	7,055	486	2,932
Cadets USMA	1,757	1,757			
Midshipmen USNA	4,137		4,137		
Cadets USAFA	2,520				2,520
Naval Aviation Cadets	702		702		
Naval Enlisted Off. Cand.	2,216		2,216		
Marine Aviation Cadets	486			486	
Aviation Cadets	412				412[a]

[a] Excludes 2 E-5 Enlisted Aviation Students shown as enlisted.

Source: Directorate for Statistical Services, Office of Secretary of Defense, 21 August 1962

Officers on Active Duty by Grade and Service
30 June 1963

	Total Dept. Def.	Army	Navy	Marine Corps	Air Force
TOTAL OFFICERS and ENLISTED	2,699,677	975,916	664,647	189,683	869,431
OFFICERS—Total	334,351	108,302	75,549	16,737	133,763
Gen of Army/Fleet Adm	4	3	1	—	—
General/Admiral	37	13	9	1	14
Lt. General/Vice Adm	108	38	32	5	33
Maj Gen } Rear Adm	1,143	200	256	23	167
Brig Gen }		252		32	213
Colonel/Captain	15,183	5,127	4,169	568	5,319
Lt. Colonel/Commander	36,613	12,371	8,111	1,354	14,777
Major/Lt. Cmdr	35,846	17,111	12,457	2,365	23,913
Captain/Lieut	104,649	29,483	20,068	3,997	51,101
1st Lieut/Lieut (JG)	55,350	15,560	14,635	4,185	20,970
2nd Lieut/Ensign	49,070	18,464	13,700	2,752	14,154
Chief Warrant Officer W-4	2,644	1,153	733	89	669
Chief Warrant Officer W-3	5,219	2,672	636	132	1,779
Chief Warrant Officer W-2	6,184	4,349	741	440	654
Warrant Officer W-1	2,301	1,506	1	794	—
ENLISTED—Total	2,354,531	865,768	583,596	172,541	732,626
OFFICER CANDIDATES—Total	10,795	1,846	5,502	405	3,042
Cadets USMA	1,846	1,846			
Midshipmen USNA	4,113		4,113		
Cadets USAFA	2,660				2,660
Naval Aviation Cadets	639		639		
Naval Enlisted Off. Cand.	750		750		
Marine Aviation Cadets	405			405	
Aviation Cadets	382				382

Source: Directorate for Statistical Services, Office of Secretary of Defense, 21 August 1963

Officers on Active Duty by Grade and Service
30 June 1964

	Total Dept. Def.	Army	Navy	Marine Corps	Air Force (Prelim)
TOTAL OFFICERS and ENLISTED	2,687,409	973,238	667,596	189,777	856,798
OFFICERS—Total	337,502	110,870	76,400	16,843	133,389
Gen of Army/Fleet Adm	3	2	1		
General/Admiral	38	14	9	1	14
Lt. General/Vice Adm	115	41	32	5	37
Maj Gen } Rear Adm	1,138	201	250	23	163
Brig Gen		249		31	221
Colonel/Captain	15,323	5,168	4,197	606	5,352
Lt. Colonel/Commander	36,347	12,386	8,022	1,402	14,537
Major/Lt. Cmdr	55,081	17,122	12,054	2,434	23,471
Captain/Lieut	105,884	30,063	21,370	3,766	50,685
1st Lieut/Lieut (JG)	59,337	15,935	16,726	4,939	21,737
2nd Lieut/Ensign	47,864	19,459	11,902	2,102	14,401
Chief Warrant Officer W-4	2,879	1,152	791	83	853
Chief Warrant Officer W-3	5,269	2,703	574	113	1,879
Chief Warrant Officer W-2	5,418	4,265	472	642	39
Warrant Officer W-1	2,806	2,110		696	
ENLISTED—Total	2,338,153	860,514	584,700	172,567	720,372
OFFICER CANDIDATES—Total	11,754	1,854	6,496	367	3,037
Cadets USMA	1,854	1,854			
Midshipmen USNA	4,150		4,150		
Cadets USAFA	2,838				2,838
Naval Aviation Cadets	719		719		
Naval Enlisted Off. Cand.	1,627		1,627		
Marine Aviation Cadets	367			367	
Aviation Cadets	199				199

Source: Directorate for Statistical Services, Office of Secretary of Defense, 20 August 1964

Officers on Active Duty by Grade and Service
31 December 1968

	Total Dept. Def.	Army	Navy	Marine Corps	Air Force
TOTAL OFFICERS and ENLISTED	3,408,230	1,462,960	745,320	313,030	886,920
OFFICERS—Total	417,726	170,131	85,409	24,976	137,210
Gen of Army/Fleet Adm	2	2			
General/Admiral	38	17	8	1	12
Lt. General/Vice Adm	138	44	43	8	43
Maj Gen ⎫ Rear Adm	1,176	200	263	28	160
Brig Gen ⎭		257		40	228
Colonel/Captain	17,967	6,357	4,235	756	6,619
Lt. Colonel/Commander	44,281	16,540	9,185	2,113	16,443
Major/Lt. Cmdr	70,998	23,749	13,680	3,957	29,612
Captain/Lieut	113,355	35,770	26,135	5,274	46,176
1st Lieut/Lieut (JG)	82,687	39,082	17,955	7,116	18,534
2nd Lieut/Ensign	58,415	26,376	9,394	4,394	18,251
Chief Warrant Officer W-4	3,579	1,755	632	77	1,115
Chief Warrant Officer W-3	3,476	3,145	163	151	17
Chief Warrant Officer W-2	12,339	10,707	1,214	418	—
Warrant Officer W-1	9,275	6,130	2,502	643	—
ENLISTED—Total	2,977,093	1,289,349	653,422	288,054	746,268
OFFICER CANDIDATES—Total	13,411	3,480	6,489	—	3,442
Cadets USMA	3,480	3,480			
Midshipmen USNA	4,129		4,129		
Cadets USAFA	3,442				3,442
Naval Enlisted Off. Cand.	2,360		2,360		

Source: Directorate for Statistical Services, Office of Secretary of Defense, 28 March 1969

Officers on Active Duty by Grade and Service
31 December 1969

	Total Dept. Def.	Army	Navy	Marine Corps	Air Force
TOTAL OFFICERS and ENLISTED	3,297,888	1,431,839	721,707	301,675*	842,667
OFFICERS—Total	407,952	167,556	81,183	25,217	133,996
Gen of Army/Fleet Adm	1	1	—	—	—
General/Admiral	40	17	8	2	13
Lt. General/Vice Adm	142	47	42	9	44
Maj Gen ⎫ Rear Adm	1,156	195	261	28	156
Brig Gen ⎭		253		39	224
Colonel/Captain	18,181	6,319	4,455	717	6,690
Lt. Colonel/Commander	43,993	16,469	9,098	2,008	16,418
Major/Lt. Cmdr	69,987	24,220	13,740	3,873	28,154
Captain/Lieut	116,859	42,669	22,232	6,645	45,313
1st Lieut/Lieut (JG)	67,917	22,589	17,875	6,469	20,984
2nd Lieut/Ensign	58,893	30,637	8,889	4,174	15,193
Chief Warrant Officer W-4	3,182	1,755	531	91	805
Chief Warrant Officer W-3	3,428	3,236	50	140	2
Chief Warrant Officer W-2	14,626	11,674	2,196	756	—
Warrant Officer W-1	9,547	7,475	1,806	266	—
ENLISTED—Total	2,876,679	1,260,528	634,772	276,458	704,921
OFFICER CANDIDATES—Total	13,257	3,755	5,572	—	3,750
Cadets USMA	3,755	3,755			
Midshipmen USNA	4,148		4,148		
Cadets USAFA	3,750				3,750
Naval Enlisted Off. Cand.	1,604		1,604		

Source: Directorate for Information Operations, Office of Secretary of Defense, 18 March 1970

* Revised.

Officers on Active Duty by Grade and Service
31 December 1972

	Total Dept. Def.	Army	Navy	Marine Corps	Air Force
TOTAL OFFICERS and ENLISTED	2,347,890	862,262	581,874	196,722	707,032
OFFICERS—Total	328,761	119,387	71,398	19,268	118,708
Gen of Army/Fleet Adm	1	1	—		—
General/Admiral	38	13	9	2	14
Lt. General/Vice Adm	142	49	45	8	40
Maj Gen/Rear Adm (U)	477	195	104	24	154
Brig Gen/Rear Adm (L)	654	250	154	37	213
Colonel/Captain	16,540	5,595	4,119	695	6,131
Lt. Colonel/Commander	36,683	12,324	8,445	1,532	14,382
Major/Lt. Cmdr	61,028	20,004	15,326	3,100	22,598
Captain/Lieut	112,186	38,894	18,943	5,407	48,942
1st Lieut/Lieut (JG)	44,251	15,305	11,253	4,492	13,201
2nd Lieut/Ensign	35,199	11,274	8,609	2,459	12,857
Chief Warrant Officer W-4	1,893	1,453	101	163	176
Chief Warrant Officer W-3	4,738	3,297	705	736	—
Chief Warrant Officer W-2	12,246	9,166	2,574	506	—
Warrant Officer W-1	2,685	1,567	1,011	107	—
ENLISTED—Total	2,005,753	738,954	504,953	177,454	584,392
OFFICER CANDIDATES—Total	13,376	3,921	5,523	—	3,932
Cadets USMA	3,921	3,921			
Midshipmen USNA	4,219		4,219		
Cadets USAFA	3,932				3,932
Naval Enlisted Off. Cand.	1,304		1,304		

Source: Department of Defense, OASD (Comptroller), Directorate for Information Operations, 26 March 1973

Officers on Active Duty by Grade and Service
30 April 1973

	Total Dept. Def.	Army	Navy	Marine Corps	Air Force
TOTAL OFFICERS and ENLISTED	2,273,866	820,569	563,671	196,931	692,695
OFFICERS—Total	324,049	117,661	70,619	19,199	116,570
Gen of Army/Fleet Adm	1	1	—		
General/Admiral	36	11	9	2	14
Lt. General/Vice Adm	138	48	45	7	38
Maj Gen/Rear Adm (U)	478	196	102	26	154
Brig Gen/Rear Adm (L)	636	245	144	36	211
Colonel/Captain	16,137	5,406	3,981	665	6,085
Lt. Colonel/Commander	36,359	12,120	8,346	1,510	14,383
Major/Lt. Cmdr	59,794	19,593	15,108	3,044	22,049
Captain/Lieut	109,337	38,193	18,193	5,296	47,655
1st Lieut/Lieut (JG)	45,939	14,818	11,324	4,480	15,317
2nd Lieut/Ensign	34,061	11,840	9,068	2,624	10,529
Chief Warrant Officer W-4	1,847	1,439	76	197	135
Chief Warrant Officer W-3	4,643	3,290	687	666	—
Chief Warrant Officer W-2	11,713	8,726	2,523	464	—
Warrant Officer W-1	2,930	1,735	1,013	182	—
ENLISTED—Total	1,937,100	699,097	487,907	177,732	572,364
OFFICER CANDIDATES—Total	12,717	3,811	5,145	—	3,761
Cadets USMA	3,811	3,811			
Midshipmen USNA	4,027		4,027		
Cadets USAFA	3,761				3,761
Naval Enlisted Off. Cand.	1,118		1,118		

Source: Department of Defense, OASD (Comptroller), Directorate for Information Operations, 12 July 1973

Military Personnel on Active Duty by Grade and Service (31 March 1982)

OFFICERS

Rank/Grade	Army	Navy	Marine Corps	Air Force	Total DoD
General/Admiral	9	9	2	13	33
Lt. General/Vice Admiral	43	30	7	34	114
Major General/Rear Admiral (U)	147	79	23	121	370
Brig General/Rear Admiral (L), Commodore	198	134	33	169	534
Colonel/Captain	4,677	3,779	581	5,291	14,328
Lt. Colonel/Commander	10,962	7,724	1,521	12,633	32,840
Major/Lt. Commander	16,100	12,495	2,999	18,187	49,781
Captain/Lieutenant	32,418	18,127	4,829	35,106	90,480
1st Lieutenant/Lieutenant (JG)	13,405	9,909	4,182	15,072	42,568
2nd Lieutenant/Ensign	9,461	10,643	2,837	14,088	37,029
Chief Warrant Officer W-4	1,524	512	151	—	2,187
Chief Warrant Officer W-3	4,157	986	154	—	5,297
Chief Warrant Officer W-2	4,963	1,378	687	—	7,028
Warrant Officer W-1	3,532	—	496	—	4,028
Total	101,596	65,805	18,502	100,714	286,617

ENLISTED

Rank/Grade	Army	Navy	Marine Corps	Air Force	Total DoD
E-9	3,888	3,466	1,236	4,748	13,338
E-8	13,517	8,626	3,402	9,512	35,057
E-7	46,848	30,821	8,730	34,495	120,894
E-6	79,257	67,395	12,909	53,509	213,070
E-5	121,503	87,274	27,461	102,626	338,864
E-4	192,996	88,117	31,711	106,769	419,593
E-3	105,906	99,914	42,817	106,069	354,706
E-2	55,688	53,042	28,270	32,120	169,120
E-1	66,345	34,706	16,919	24,776	142,746
Total	685,948	473,361	173,455	474,624	1,807,388

Source: *Defense* (September 1982), pp. 27–28).

Military Personnel on Active Duty by Grade and Service (31 March 1983)

OFFICERS

Rank/Grade	Army	Navy	Marine Corps	Air Force	Total DoD
General/Admiral	12	8	2	12	34
Lt. General/Vice Admiral	45	32	6	35	118
Major General/Rear Admiral (U)	140	78	24	120	362
Brig General/Rear Admiral (L), Commodore	198	131	33	170	532
Colonel/Captain	4,645	3,738	585	5,431	14,399
Lt. Colonel/Commander	10,809	7,328	1,594	12,659	32,390
Major/Lt. Commander	16,372	12,806	3,051	18,621	50,850
Captain/Lieutenant	31,564	18,848	5,329	36,303	92,044
1st Lieutenant/Lieutenant (JG)	16,425	10,538	3,956	16,438	47,357
2nd Lieutenant/Ensign	8,424	10,623	3,245	13,475	35,767
Chief Warrant Officer W-4	1,520	479	141	—	2,140
Chief Warrant Officer W-3	4,302	1,204	186	—	5,692
Chief Warrant Officer W-2	5,622	1,249	705	—	7,576
Warrant Officer W-1	3,218	—	547	—	3,765
Total	103,296	67,062	19,404	103,264	293,026

ENLISTED

Rank/Grade	Army	Navy	Marine Corps	Air Force	Total DoD
E-9	4,056	3,443	1,237	4,851	13,587
E-8	14,969	7,910	3,610	9,650	36,139
E-7	48,052	29,210	8,998	35,179	121,439
E-6	82,362	66,761	14,567	54,614	218,304
E-5	118,498	91,887	27,987	105,155	343,527
E-4	180,520	93,610	34,081	107,546	415,757
E-3	115,747	105,923	45,797	121,099	388,566
E-2	48,124	45,943	26,841	24,579	145,487
E-1	61,700	38,993	16,052	21,764	138,509
Total	674,028	483,680	179,170	484,437	1,821,315

Source: *Defense* (September 1983), pp. 27–28.

NOTES

CHAPTER 1

1. Compare Guenter Lewy's *America in Vietnam* (1978) with Stanley Karnow's *Vietnam: A History* (1984). See also Norman Podhoretz, *Why We Were in Vietnam* (1983), pp. 207–9.
2. Richard A. Gabriel and Paul L. Savage, *Crisis in Command: Mismanagement in the Army* (1978), p. 11.
3. Shelby L. Stanton, *Vietnam Order of Battle* (1981), p. 333. Appendix A, Summary table.
4. George S. Eckhardt, *Command and Control 1950–1969*, U.S. Army Vietnam Studies (1974), p. 42.
5. General William W. Momyer, *Airpower in Three Wars (WW II, Korea, Vietnam)* (Washington: Department of the Air Force, 1978), p. 70.
6. Stanton, *op. cit.,* p. 59.
7. Momyer, *op. cit.,* p. 70.
8. Gabriel and Savage, *op. cit.,* pp. 9–10.
9. General Bruce Palmer, Jr., *The 25-Year War: America's Military Role in Vietnam* (New York, 1984), p. 63.
10. Stanton, *op. cit.,* pp. 71 and 74, and 66–67 for the corps echelons; for the 1945 number see Martin Van Creveld, *Fighting Power* (1982), p. 52.
11. LTG Julian J. Ewell and MG Ira A. Hunt Jr., *Sharpening the Combat Edge: The Use of Analysis to Reinforce Military Judgment,* Department of the Army (1974), Vietnam Studies series.
12. Stanton, *op. cit.,* Appendix A, p. 333 (both tables).
13. William L. Hauser, *America's Army in Crisis* (1973), p. 175 (for medal totals); Edward L. King, *The Death of the Army* (1972), pp. 103, 210–11 (for generals); both as cited in Gabriel and Savage, *op. cit.,* note 14, p. 205. For battle deaths, *ibid.,* Table 7, n.p. For Grenada medals, *Washington Post* (March 30, 1984), p. A17, "Army Awards 8,612 Medals for Grenada."
14. A total of 11,260,000 served in the Army during the Second World War

versus 4,368,000 in Vietnam. Moreover, the exposure to combat was much smaller in Vietnam owing to the one-year tour of duty; during the Second World War all served for the duration. The 294 Army Medal of Honor winners of 1941–46 may be compared with the 234,874 killed in action, a ratio of 1:799; the 155 Army recipients of Vietnam may be compared with the 30,867 Army men killed between August 4, 1964, and January 27, 1973, a ratio of 1:199. For Vietnam, see Stanton, *op. cit.*, p. 352. For troop levels and battle deaths, see *Defense* (September 1983, Almanac Issue), p. 46.

15. Stanton, *op. cit.*, p. 301, item 6.
16. Gabriel and Savage, *op. cit.*, p. 71.
17. Palmer, *op. cit.*, p. 53.
18. *Ibid.*
19. Gabriel and Savage, Table 1, n.p., after p. 179.
20. In 554 of the cases the intent to kill, wound, or intimidate was considered proved; in 413 cases the intended victim was an officer or NCO; total deaths numbered 86, and 714 were wounded. Gabriel and Savage, *op. cit.*, Table 3, after p. 179.
21. As documented, for the ground forces, in Shelby L. Stanton's excellent *The Rise and Fall of an American Army: U.S. Ground Forces in Vietnam, 1965–1973* (Novato, Cal., 1985).
22. Gabriel and Savage, *op. cit.*, Table 7.
23. See the vivid account in Joseph C. Goulden, *Korea: The Untold Story of the War* (1982), pp. 220–23.
24. Gen. William W. Momyer, *Air Power in Three Wars*, p. 279.
25. *Ibid.*, p. 280.
26. Stanton, *op. cit.*, table on p. 347.

CHAPTER 2

1. No official document spells out this well-known practice, but see Paul R. Ignatius, *Department of Defense Reorganization Study Project, Department Headquarters Study*, A Report to the Secretary of Defense (June 1, 1978), pp. 50–51.
2. The full story is still locked in the classified version of the *Holloway Report*, whose published unclassified version was remarkably polite to a collection of officers who richly deserved to be cashiered. For a well-documented critical account, see Maj. Robert L. Earl, USMC, "A Matter of Principle," *U.S. Naval Institute Proceedings* (February 1983), pp. 29–36. The ground-force commander, Col. Charles A. Beckwith (Ret.), has published an inadvertently revealing apologia whose main value is in exposing the short-comings of the higher-ranking officers who chose a man of his own low caliber to raise, train, and command the nation's elite commando force. See Col. Charlie *[sic]* A. Beckwith USA (Ret.) and Donald Knox, *Delta Force: the U.S. Counter-Terrorist Unit and the Iran Hostage Rescue Mission* (San Diego, 1983).

3. Beckwith and Knox, *op. cit.,* p. 278.
4. See the comment and chain-of-command diagram in Earl, *op. cit.,* p. 35.
5. Beckwith and Knox, *op cit.,* p. 277.
6. Richard Halloran, *New York Times* (August 3, 1983), p. A7.
7. *The Washington Post* (August 24, 1983), p. A22.
8. Based on personal observation with the Atlacatl battalion in northern Morazán, El Salvador, May 1983.
9. The quality of many of the trainers is nevertheless high. But some of the men sent to El Salvador can hardly speak Spanish, and others are native Spanish-speakers who can claim no other virtue. Personal information.
10. "Report of the Department of Defense Commission on Beirut International Airport Terrorist Act, October 23, 1983." Issued by the Department of Defense, Washington, D.C. (December 20, 1983), hereinafter Long Commission, para. A. (1), p. 9.
11. Long Commission, p. 52.
12. Long Commission, Para. 3, p. 4, heading: "Security following the October 23 Attack."
13. The 22nd Marine Amphibious Unit (MAUs include a battalion of infantry with small artillery and tank support detachments as well as an air group), and the 1st and 2nd Ranger Battalions of the 75th Infantry Brigade.
14. Only 45 Grenadian soldiers were killed in action, along with 24 Cubans. Christopher C. Wright, "U.S. Naval Operations in 1983," U.S. Naval Institute *Proceedings,* May 1984, Vol 110/5/975, p. 67.
15. LTC Michael J. Byron, USMC, "Fury from the sea: Marines in Grenada," U.S. Naval Institute *Proceedings,* Vol. 110/5/975, p. 123, and Richard Halloran, *New York Times* (October 31, 1983), p. 1, "U.S. Won't Dispute Havana on Tally."
16. Rich Jaroslovsky, *Wall Street Journal* (October 27, 1983), p. 3, "U.S. Sees Military Victory Despite Stiff Resistance from Cubans."
17. Byron, *op. cit.,* p. 128; see also the dramatic if not very accurate account in *Newsweek* (November 7, 1983), pp. 69 and 72.
18. John J. Fialka, *Wall Street Journal* (November 15, 1983), p. 1, "In Battle for Grenada Commando Missions Didn't Go as Planned."
19. Byron, *op. cit.,* p. 128. That was Company G.
20. *Ibid.* That was Company F.
21. Fialka, *op. cit.,* and *Newsweek* (November 7, 1983), p. 75.
22. Byron, *op. cit.,* p. 126.
23. Fred Hiatt, *Washington Post* (November 1, 1983), "Accidents, 'Friendly Fire' Blamed for Many U.S. Casualties in Grenada."
24. *Newsweek* (November 7, 1983), p. 76.
25. Doyle McManus, *Los Angeles Times* (October 29, 1983), p. 1, " 'Lacked Intelligence Data on Cubans' U.S. Admiral Says."
26. Halloran, *New York Times* (October 31, 1983), as cited.
27. W. V. Kennedy, *Philadelphia Inquirer* (November 15, 1983), p. 15, "Army and Navy Have Their Own Fiefdoms."
28. Wright, *op. cit.,* pp. 59–60.
29. *Aviation Week & Space Technology* (December 12, 1983), letter on p. 25.

30. Kip Cooper, "Admiral Blames Washington for Loss of 2 Planes Over Syria *[sic]*," *San Diego Union* (May 12, 1984), pp. A4–A5.
31. General Jones testified repeatedly before Congress in order to spell out his criticisms. For a concise summary of his views, see his Introduction to Archie D. Barrett, *Reappraising Defense Organization*, National Defense University (Washington, DC, 1983), pp. xxiii–xxv.
32. Barrett, *op. cit.*, p. xxv.
33. Elmo R. Zumwalt Jr., *On Watch* (New York, 1976); see especially pp. 63–64.

CHAPTER 3

1. Personnel figures as of March, 1983. The handiest source is the "almanac" issue of *Defense*, published in September of each year by the American Forces Information Service and distributed by the GPO. For the numbers stated, see the September 1983 issue (hereinafter cited as *Defense*), p. 24.
2. *Defense*, p. 24. In that source, the Guard and reserve total is 1,421,902; the lower figure given in the text describes the "selected reserve." See *Annual Report to the Congress: On the Fiscal Year 1985 Budget, Fiscal Year 1986 Authorization Request and Fiscal Year 1985–89 Defense Programs* (hereinafter cited as *Annual Report*), Table 3, p. 284.
3. *Ibid.*
4. *Defense*, pp. 50–51.
5. See *Annual Report*, pp. 185–202; *Defense*, pp. 40–41.
6. *Ibid.*, also IISS, *Military Balance*, 1983–84.
7. *Annual Report*, pp. 113–31 and p. 287; see also the *Annual Report of the Secretary of the Army and Chief of Staff of the Army*, Office of the Secretary of the Army, Washington, D.C.
8. *Annual Report*, pp. 157–71; see also the *Annual Report of the Secretary of the Air Force and Chief of Staff of the Air Force*, Office of the Secretary of the Air Force, Washington, D.C.
9. *Annual Report*, pp. 133–55; see also the *Annual Report of the Secretary of the Navy and Chief of Naval Operations*, Office of the Secretary of the Navy, Washington, D.C.
10. *Defense*, p. 41.
11. *Annual Report*, Table III.B.1, pp. 136 and 287.
12. For the geographic distribution of personnel overseas in complete detail service by service and country by country, as of March 31, 1983, see *Defense*, pp. 26–27.
13. For the worldwide distribution of the deployed combat forces in a convenient summary form, see the maps in *Defense*, pp. 42–43.
14. *Ibid.*
15. *Ibid.*
16. *Defense*, p. 26.
17. *Defense*, p. 42.
18. *Defense*, p. 43.

19. See Edward N. Luttwak, *Political Uses of Sea Power* (Baltimore, 1976), pp. 31–32, with citations.
20. *Defense,* pp. 26–27 (out of a total of 2,127,422 in uniform, on March 31, 1983).
21. *Ibid.*
22. See the functional breakdown in *Defense,* p. 25.
23. For a critical appraisal of the system see Archie D. Barrett, *Reappraising Defense Organization: An Analysis Based on the Defense Organization Study 1977–80,* National Defense University (Washington, D.C., 1983), pp. 89–145.
24. It is said that the hospitality of the Egyptian Government was unsuccessfully solicited; the staff at Central Command has rejected the politically easy but supremely uncomfortable option of a floating command post in the Indian Ocean.
25. *Defense,* p. 25.
26. Howard Finley, "Comment on aircraft maintenance and the paper chase," U.S. Naval Institute *Proceedings,* Vol. 110/4/974 (April 1984), p. 96.
27. As of December 31, 1982; *Defense,* pp. 24–25.
28. *Ibid.*
29. *Ibid.*
30. *Ibid.*
31. *Ibid.*
32. *Ibid.*
33. *Annual Report,* table on page 163, based on the 1985 request—i.e., $4.145 billion for 150 aircraft.
34. Oral information from Systems Command official.

CHAPTER 4

1. See the table in *The Washington Post* (June 28, 1983), p. 13.
2. Abraham Becker is the acknowledged expert on the "index number" problem and Soviet defense expenditure in general. See, e.g., his "overview" in 97th Congress, 2nd Session, Joint Economic Committee, *Soviet Economy in the 1980's: Problems and Prospects,* Part I (GPO, 1983), pp. 287–96.
3. Between 1968 and 1982 the published figure for the Soviet military budget remained constant at roughly 17 billion rubles, or less than 3 percent of the gross national product. See the discussion in Herbert Block in Appendix I: "The Economic Basis of Soviet Power," in Edward N. Luttwak, *The Grand Strategy of the Soviet Union* (London, New York, 1983, 1984).
4. *Report of the Secretary of Defense to the Congress on the FY 1985 Budget, FY 1986 Authorization Request and FY 1985–89 Defense Programs* (hereinafter *Annual Report*), Washington, D.C. (February 1, 1984), Chart I.A.2, p. 201. See also the previous *Annual Report for FY 1984,* pp. 22–23.
5. *Ibid.*
6. See *Annual Report for FY 1984,* Chart I.B.3, p. 23.
7. *Ibid.*

8. *Annual Report* (for FY 1985), Chart I.A.4., p. 23.

9. *Ibid.,* and for the Bradley combat carriers, see p. 120 of the *Annual Report.*

10. *Annual Report,* p. 160.

11. See Brooke Nihart, *Armed Forces Journal* (July 1972), pp. 32–35 (the good news) and the revealing exchange of letters in *Aviation Week & Space Technology* by Capt. Donald D. Carson USAF (October 29, 1973) and Lt. Cdr. Pete Pettigrew (December 3, 1973). The actual numbers quoted are from an unpublished study by Richard Polowsky.

12. *Ibid.*

13. See the important article by Major Barry Watts USAF in *Topgun Journal* (Navy Fighter School), Vol. 2. No. 2 (Winter 1979/80), "Fire, Movement and Tactics," pp. 4–24.

14. The information that follows on the 1982 Lebanon War was collected on the scene by the present author.

15. *Soviet Military Power 1984,* Third Edition (GPO, 1984), pp. 70–72 (strictly factual in this section of the text).

16. For Soviet air-defense weapons and forces see W. Seth Carus, Appendix II, "The Evolution of Soviet Military Power Since 1965" in Edward N. Luttwak, *The Grand Strategy of the Soviet Union, op. cit.,* pp. 180–81; Tables 12 and 13, pp. 187–88; and Tables 26 and 27, pp. 204 and 205; update with *Soviet Military Power,* pp. 36–39, 53–54.

17. For a very interesting comparative analysis see James W. Kehoe, Clark Graham, Kenneth S. Brower, and Herbert A. Meier, "Comparative Naval Architecture Analysis of NATO and Soviet Frigates," *Naval Engineers Journal* (October 1980), pp. 87–89, and *idem* (December 1980), pp. 84–93; also James W. Kehoe, Kenneth S. Brower, and Herbert A. Meier, "U.S. and Soviet Ship Design Practices 1950–1980," U.S. Naval Institute *Proceedings* (May 1982), pp. 118–33.

18. *Ibid.*

19. For a survey of the data see Carus, *op. cit.,* pp. 214–20 and Tables 36–42 and the update in *Soviet Military Power,* pp. 61–69. Neither contains qualitative judgments.

20. Carus, as above.

21. See *Soviet Military Power,* p. 95, and table on p. 99.

22. For outline on Soviet "nonstrategic" submarines, see Carus, *op. cit.,* Tables 34 and 35.

23. Carus, *op. cit.,* Tables 43 and 44.

24. See the discussion in Edward N. Luttwak, *The Grand Strategy of the Soviet Union,* pp. 57–60.

25. *Idem,* pp. 55–57.

26. For an outline, see *Soviet Military Power,* pp. 69–70; there is by now a vast literature on the subject.

27. For detailed numerical data see Carus, *op. cit.,* pp. 206–13, and *Soviet Military Power,* pp. 54–57.

28. Notably Andrew Cockburn, *The Threat: Inside the Soviet Military Machine* (New York, 1983), with much on equipment, and Viktor Suvorov, *Inside the Soviet Army* (New York, 1982), with much on the personnel side.

29. Especially Suvorov, *op. cit.*
30. See the discussion in Edward N. Luttwak, *The Grand Strategy of the Soviet Union, op. cit.*, pp. 4–12.
31. See Stephen Rapawy and Godfrey Baldwin, "Demographic Trends in the Soviet Union: 1950–2000," pp. 265–96.
32. See Murray Feshbach, "Trends in the Soviet Muslim Population," in *Soviet Economy in the 1980's, op. cit.*, Part 2, p. 321.
33. *Idem*, Table 10, p. 292.
34. For a brief summary of the divisional data, see Carus, *op. cit.*, pp. 191–92 and Tables 16 and 17. Update with *Soviet Military Power* (the Madison Avenue prose is carelessly misleading; the data are accurate).
35. Carus, *op. cit.*, Table 28, and *Soviet Military Power*, p. 50 (map) and pp. 54–57.
36. Carus, *op. cit.*, Table 12, and *Soviet Military Power*, pp. 36–39.
37. See the IISS *Military Balance 1983–84* (London, 1983), pp. 16–17.
38. And two-thirds. That number does not include all Soviet divisions (194) but only those "deemed" to be available for use against NATO. See IISS *Military Balance 1983–84, op. cit.*, p. 138 (table).
39. *Ibid.*
40. And without counting the 7 elite airborne divisions. *Ibid.*
41. For the growth in the size of the Soviet divisions, see Carus, *op. cit.*, Table 17, p. 197; and *Military Balance 1983–84*, p. vii.
42. *Idem*, p. 138.
43. *Ibid.*
44. For megatonnage data see *Idem*, pp. 118–20.
45. *Ibid.*
46. *Ibid.*
47. There are no hard data on quality, but see *ibid.* for the numbers.
48. *Ibid.*
49. For the submarine numbers see Carus, *op. cit.*, pp. 178–79, and Table 10, p. 185, updated with *Soviet Military Power*, pp. 24–26.
50. *Idem*, p. 26.
51. *Military Balance 1983–84*, pp. 4, 14–15.
52. See *Soviet Military Power*, pp. 27 (diagram) and 29.
53. *Military Balance 1983–84*, pp. 4–5 and 15.

CHAPTER 5

1. Deborah M. Kyle, "Congress Micromanaging: More than Before?" *Armed Forces Journal* (February 1984), p. 24.
2. Chief of Naval Operations Admiral James D. Watkins, cited in Deborah M. Kyle, "Congress Serious About Defense Reform; 3 Senate Witnesses Endorse Change," *Armed Forces Journal* (February 1982), p. 10.
3. Robert F. Coulam, *Illusions of Choice: The F-111 and the Problem of Weapons Acquisition Reform* (Princeton, 1977).
4. Pierre Sprey, lecture before the American Institute of Astronautics and

Aeronautics Symposium, Dayton, Ohio (December 15, 1978); see also his "The Impact of Avionics on the Effectiveness of Tactical Air," unpublished paper presented at the 21st Military Operations Research Symposium (1968).

5. *Report of the Secretary of Defense to the Congress on the FY 1985 Budget, FY 1986 Authorization Request and FY 1985–89 Defense Programs* (hereinafter *Annual Report*) Washington, D.C. (February 1, 1984), p. 232.

6. Data extracted from *Annual Report for FY 1984*. (Actually, the total was reduced by Congress to $85.9 billion.)

7. *Annual Report* (for FY 1985), p. 120.

8. See Eugene Kozicharow "USAF, Army Agree on Joint Initiatives," *Aviation Week & Space Technology* (May 28, 1984), pp. 22–23.

9. Author's compilation from unpublished sources—e.g., unpublished briefing paper by Richard Polowski; the 1967 *air combat* score was 79/2; in the "war of attrition" June 1967–August 1970 it was 106/3; in the 1970–1973 period it was 13/1; in the October 1973 war 334/6–10; in the 1973–1982 period it was 25/0; and in the 1982 Lebanon war it was 87/0.

10. Polowski, *op. cit.,* "Overall SEA Box Score 1965–1975."

11. That is, for General Richard O'Connor's initial offensive; the overall results in the campaign till February 7, 1941, were much larger, with 130,000 prisoners taken for a total of 500 killed, 1,373 wounded, and 55 missing. See J. F. C. Fuller, *The Second World War* (New York, 1949), p. 98, with numbers cited in William L. Shirer, *The Rise and Fall of the Third Reich* (New York, 1960), p. 818*n*.

12. There is now at last a solid English-language account of *Barbarossa* in John Erickson's *The Road to Stalingrad*, Vol. 1 (London, 1975).

CHAPTER 6

1. For this and all subsequent numbers re officers, see Appendix for the official data reproduced in full.

2. In current dollars, for both cases; Office of the Assistant Secretary of Defense (Comptroller), *National Defense Budget Estimates for FY 1985* (March 1984), Table 6-2, p. 79.

3. See *Defense* (September, 1983), "Almanac" issue, hereinafter cited as *Defense,* p. 27.

4. See e.g., Perry McCoy Smith, *The Air Force Plans for Peace 1943–1945* (Baltimore, 1970), especially pp. 5–14.

5. Major General Avigdor Ben-Gal.

6. See Appendix for these and all subsequent figures.

7. Actually, 10,524 officers in Fiscal Year 1983 (rising to 11,077 by April 1984), as well as 15,000 enlisted men. Source: DCoS Personnel Air Force Systems Command.

8. Jacques S. Gansler, *The Defense Industry* (Cambridge, 1980), p. 280.

9. This and related information was collected by author's interviews with USAF informants. But see *Aviation Week & Space Technology,* July 23,

1979, p. 14; January 21, 1980, pp. 21–22; July 14, 1980, pp. 24–25; September 29, 1980, p. 33, and October 6, 1980, pp. 22–23.

10. See Note 7.
11. The MX ballistic missile, the Maverick AGM, and the Sparrow upgrades, jointly with the Navy.
12. For the 207 figure, see *Annual Report,* pp. 163, 170, 180, 192.
13. *Idem,* p. 163.
14. *Ibid.*
15. *Ibid.*
16. *Annual Report,* p. 162 (prose), 164 (figures).
17. In an article specifically meant to refute the charge that the Air Force overspends on manned aircraft, slighting the munitions that are the payoff, the Air Force was able to cite only a total FY 1985 request of $112.7 million for the engineering development of air-to-ground munitions, versus $494.6 million for tactical-aircraft development. See table in *Armed Forces Journal* (April 1984), p. 26 ($330.4 million minus the $217.7 million for the air-to-air AMRAAM missile); and table in *Idem* (January 1984), p. 34. The total purchase of Maverick IIR missiles in Fiscal Year 1984 was 1,980; see *Annual Report,* p. 164.
18. These are Fiscal Year 1983 figures, Source: NMC release (printed).
19. Source: interview with chief, public affairs, DARCOM.
20. For Army development expenditures on RPVs see *Annual Report,* p. 126. For a comparison of performance, see *Aviation Week & Space Technology* (March 12, 1984), "Inventory and Forecast," tables on pp. 151 and 152, under Israel and Lockheed respectively.
21. Comptroller General Report to the Congress GAO/NSIAD-84-22 (December 23, 1983), "Joint Major System Acquisition by the Military Services: An Elusive Strategy," p. 8, with citations.
22. Eric C. Ludvigsen, "Army Weaponry," *Army* (October 1983), p. 298.
23. *Ibid.*

CHAPTER 7

1. See Appendix A for these and all subsequent officer/enlisted figures, excepted where otherwise stated.
2. *Defense* (September 1983), "Almanac" issue, hereinafter *Defense,* p. 27.
3. *Defense,* p. 35.
4. Office of Air Force History, *Encyclopedia of U.S. Air Force Aircraft and Missile Systems,* Vol. 1: post–World War II Fighters, 1945–1973, pp. 80–81; for production numbers, see pp. 53–79 and specifically p. 79.
5. *Defense,* p. 27.
6. National Security Agency, Defense Intelligence Agency, Defense Logistics Agency, Defense Mapping Agency, Defense Nuclear Agency, Defense Communications Agency, Defense Security Assistance Agency: *Defense,* p. 9.
7. *Defense,* p. 27.

8. *Ibid.*
9. See "Longer Tours for Commanding Officers, " *Marine Corps Gazette* (March 1984), p. 6.
10. General Edward C. Meyer, speech, Luttwak/HME conference, Washington, D.C. (February 15, 1983).
11. *Marine Corps Gazette,* as in Note 9.
12. *Ibid.*
13. *Ibid.*
14. West Point: United States Military Academy *1982–1983 Catalog,* pp. 125–139.
15. A total of 2,746 out of 27,412 commissioned in Fiscal Year 1982: *Defense,* p. 28.
16. For a characteristic *cri de coeur* see Colonel Yasotay (pseudonym of a U.S. Army General on active duty), "Warriors: an Endangered Species," *Armed Forces Journal* (September 1984), pp. 117–19.

CHAPTER 8

1. Deborah M. Kyle, *Armed Forces Journal* (February 1984), p. 26, "Congress Meddled With Over Half of DoD's FY 84 Budget Line Items."
2. Office of the Assistant Secretary of Defense (Comptroller) March 1984, *National Defense Estimates for FY 1985* (hereinafter *Estimates*), Table 4-3, p. 38.
3. Kyle, *op. cit.,* p. 26.
4. All eight multi-year programming requests for Fiscal 1982 were accepted; six of twelve for Fiscal 1983 were approved, and only seven out of the sixteen Fiscal 1984 requests were approved. *Report of the Secretary of Defense to the Congress on the FY 1985 Budget, FY 1986 Authorization Request and FY 1985–89 Defense Programs,* February 1, 1984 (hereinafter *Annual Report*), Chart II.D.1, p. 102.
5. *Annual Report,* Table 1, p. 279.
6. *Ibid.*
7. *Ibid.* and, for 1989, see *Annual Report,* Table II.A.2. p. 71.
8. *Annual Report,* Table 1, p. 279.
9. *Ibid.*
10. *Annual Report,* Chart III. G.6, p. 235.
11. *Annual Report,* Chart III. G.7, p. 235.
12. *Annual Report,* para (3), p. 237.
13. The hair-raising specifics are classified, with excellent reason. The items in short supply include late-model AIM-7 missiles and DU tank ammunition for the 105mm gun.
14. See Note 11.
15. *Annual Report,* p. 159.
16. *Annual Report,* Table 1, p. 279.
17. Korean buildup years from Fiscal 1950 to Fiscal 1952. See *Estimates,* p. 80.
18. *Annual Report,* Table 3, p. 280.

19. *Ibid.*
20. For consolidated data, as in text, see the "Executive Summary" version of the *Annual Report,* p. 32.
21. *Annual Report,* p. 166.
22. *Annual Report,* p. 167.
23. *Ibid.*
24. *Ibid.*
25. These were "class A" accidents (over $500,000 damage or permanent disability); rates for other naval fighters: F-18: 8.49; F-14: 7.99; F-4: 5.97; A-7: 11.51. *Aviation Week & Space Technology* (February 27, 1984), table on p. 65.
26. *Ibid.*
27. For the story, personal information; for the numbers, *Annual Report,* p. 180.
28. Actually $6,545.4 million in Fiscal 1983 after "long-lead" funding of $554.5 million in Fiscal 1982. See *Program Acquisition Cost by Weapon System* (hereinafter *Program*), Department of Defense (January 31, 1983.)
29. See the list in *Annual Report,* p. 162.
30. *Annual Report,* p. 122.
31. DARCOM pamphlet No. 360-1, 1982, p. 7.
32. *Annual Report,* p. 120.
33. *Program,* p. 121.
34. *Program,* p. 149 *(M-16);* p. 134 *(M-60);* p. 133 (9mm).

CHAPTER 9

1. Office of the Assistant Secretary of Defense (Comptroller), March 1984, *National Defense Estimates for FY 1985 (hereinafter Estimates),* Table 6-2, p. 79.
2. *Idem.,* p. 80.
3. Ed. Norman Polmar, *Strategic Air Command: People, Aircraft and Missiles* (Annapolis, 1979), pp. 162–66.
4. *Estimates,* p. 80.
5. Lawrence Freedman, *U.S. Intelligence and the Soviet Strategic Threat* (London 1977). Freedman stresses the influence of the arms advocates, but the same distortion of the Intelligence process was caused by the arms controllers as well when they were predominant, as in the 1964–1968 period.
6. Albert Wohlstetter is the expert on the subject; see, e.g., "Racing Forward or Ambling Back" in *Defending America,* Introduction by James R. Schlesinger (New York, 1977).
7. *Estimates,* Table 6-3, p. 80.
8. *Ibid.*
9. *Ibid.*
10. *Ibid.*
11. *Defense* (September 1983), "Almanac" issue (hereinafter *Defense*), p. 25.

12. Oral communication from CoS U.S. Army, February 15, 1984.
13. *Defense*, p. 25.
14. *Estimates*, Table 6-2, p. 79.
15. *Idem*, Table 6-3, p. 80.
16. *Report of the Secretary of Defense to the Congress on the FY 1985 Budget, FY 1986 Authorization Request and FY 1985–89 Defense Programs*, February 1, 1984 (hereinafter, *Annual Report*) p. 288.
17. *Ibid.*, for both airlift and sealift forces.
18. Navy League of the United States *Almanac 1983*, Table M-5, p. 195.
19. *Estimates*, Table 6-2, p. 79.
20. Selected Reserve 1984 data from *Annual Report*, Table 3, p. 284; Individual Ready Reserve and Inactive National Guard figures for March 31, 1983, from *Defense*, p. 33.
21. *Annual Report*, "Force Tables," pp. 287–88.
22. *Estimates*, Table 6-2, p. 79.
23. *Ibid.*
24. DoD outlays: 1975 civilian, active military, retired pay, and accrual = $46,543 million, versus total nonpay of $38,357 million; 1984, total pay = $91,854 versus total nonpay of $139,146 million. *Estimates*, Table 6-12 cont., p. 115.
25. *Estimates*, Table 6-2, p. 79.
26. In Fiscal 1984, operation and maintenance excluding pay amounted to $45,455 million and procurement came to $85,996 million; the percentage of centralized purchasing was therefore 17.6%; see *Estimates*, Tables 6-12, p. 115, and Table 6-1, p. 78.
27. If twenty-year service had been the rule, the active forces of 1983 (2,123,000) should have required just 106,150 new recruits for replacement, as well as the 13,000 for expansion (assuming that longer-service personnel would offset disablements etc.). For the number of recruits, see *Annual Report*, Table II.B.I, p. 75.
28. *Defense*, p. 25. The sum of personnel in Individual Training (102,500), Students and Trainees (211,100), and Cadets 13,300.

CHAPTER 10

1. Office of the Assistant Secretary of Defense (Comptroller) March 1984, *National Defense Estimates for FY 1985* (hereinafter *Estimates*), Table 6-2, p. 79.
2. *Idem*, Table 6-3, p. 80.
3. *Ibid.*
4. *Ibid.*
5. On the divisional count, compare the IISS *Military Balance 1971–72*, p. 6, with the 1984 edition of *Soviet Military Power*. For the growth in the size of the divisions, compare the table on the "Notes" page of the 1971–72 and 1983–84 editions of the *Military Balance*.
6. See Appendix A and *Estimates*, Table 7-6, pp. 130–31.

7. *Ibid.*
8. *Report of the Secretary of Defense to the Congress on the FY 1985 Budget, FY 1986 Authorization Request and FY 1985–89 Defense Programs,* February 1, 1984 (hereinafter *Annual Report*), p. 287.
9. *Estimates,* Table 7-6, p. 131.
10. *Annual Report,* p. 287.
11. *Estimates,* Table 7-6, p. 131.
12. Considering the insistence with which the "600-ship" slogan is heard, there is a surprising amount of confusion in the mere counting of Navy ships.

    In the *Annual Report,* the "deployable battle force" total for Fiscal 1985 is given as 545 in Table III.B.1, p. 136 (naval forces section); in the end tables of the same document (p. 287) it is given as 546. Both numbers include 43 "strategic" ships, of which 37 are listed as ballistic-missile submarines; the latter source differentiates between active and reserve, listing 14 reserve-forces ships in the "deployable battle forces." The total number in the text (489) was obtained by deduction of the latter as well as the 43 "strategic" ships from the 546 total.

    Samuel L. Morison, editor of *Jane's,* has published ("Tomorrow's Fleet," in U.S. Naval Institute *Proceedings,* Vol. 110/4/974, April 1984, p. 33) a computation that is fuller than the official count because he does not exclude ships in overhaul. The *Annual Report* gives a total of 525 for FY 1984 (pages 136 *and* 287), but Morison calculates 561. For some of the major combat categories the differences are significant:

	Ship Counts: Morison	Fiscal 1984 Annual Report
Aircraft Carriers	14	13
Cruisers and Destroyers	28 87 } 115	98
Frigates	89	103 (classification difference).

13. *Estimates,* Table 7-6, p. 131.
14. *Estimates,* Table 5-10 cont., p. 71.
15. Treating FY 1981 as a baseline, that year's TOA in constant FY 85 dollars ($213,288 million) is multiplied by three and subtracted from the combined FY 82, FY 83, and FY 84 total of $769,886 million to yield a three-year increase over the baseline of $130,202 million. The exercise is repeated for each service: Army FY 81 baseline = $53,001 million; FY 82–84 total = $187,542 million; the net increase was therefore $28.5 billion. Navy FY 81 baseline = $69,871 million; FY 82–84 total = $253,383 million; the next increase was $43.8 billion. The Air Force increase over the baseline was greater at $54,539 million, but that includes large amounts for the strategic forces (B1-B, Stealth and MX) and the mobility forces (C-5; KC-10). (The service totals do not add up to the combined total because there are also the Defense Agency/OSD and Defense-Wide Expenditures.) Data from *Estimates,* Table 6-5, p. 86.
16. *Defense,* p. 27, as compared with *Defense* for September 1982, p. 27.

17. *Defense,* p. 28, as compared with *Defense* for September 1982, p. 28.
18. *Annual Report,* Table III. G.3, p. 229.
19. *Annual Report,* Table III. G.4, p. 232.
20. *Estimates,* Table 6-6 cont., p. 89 (with the addition of separate items under service headings).
21. *Ibid.*
22. *Estimates,* Table 6-7, cont., p. 96, and *idem,* Table 6-3, p. 80.
23. See Note 15.
24. For the repercussions of the navalist emphasis upon the major alliances, see the important study by Robert W. Komer, *Maritime Strategy or Coalition Defense* (Cambridge, Mass., 1984).
25. *Annual Report,* Chart II.D.3, p. 105.

CHAPTER 11

1. From the Introduction to Archie D. Barrett, *Reappraising Defense Organization: An analysis based on the defense organization study of 1977–1980.* National Defense University (Washington, D.C., 1983), p. xxiii.
2. *Ibid.* See the discussion of these issues, especially pp. 27–38; for the numbers, now dated, see p. 24.
3. *Ibid.*
4. *Annual Report,* Budget Tables, p. 279.

INDEX